16ᵛ

THE SIEGE OF LENINGRAD
1941–1944

900 Days of Terror

David M. Glantz

MBI Publishing Company

This edition first published in 2001 by MBI Publishing Company,
729 Prospect Avenue, PO Box 1, Osceola, WI 54020-0001 USA

The information in this book is true and complete to the best of our knowledge. All
recommendations are made without any guarantee on the part of the author or publisher, who
also disclaim any liability incurred in connection with the use of this data or specified details.

We recognize that some words, model names and designations, for example, mentioned
herein are the property of the trademark holder. We use them for identification purposes
only. This is not an official publication.

MBI Publishing Company books are also available at discounts in bulk quantity for
industrial or sales-promotional use. For details write to Special Sales Manager at
Motorbooks International Wholesalers & Distributors, 729 Prospect Avenue, PO Box 1,
Osceola, WI 54020-0001 USA.

Library of Congress Cataloging-in-Publication Data Available.

ISBN 0-7603-0941-8

Printed in Singapore

For Brown Partworks Limited
8 Chapel Place
Rivington Street
London
EC2A 3DQ

Editors: Peter Darman, Anne Cree
Picture research: Susannah Jayes
Design: WDA
Maps: Darren Awuah
Production: Matt Weyland

CONTENTS

KEY TO MAPS

Military units – types

⊠ infantry

▰ armoured

▱ motorized infantry/
panzergrenadier

Military units – size

XXXXX
☐ army group/front

XXXX
☐ army

XXX
☐ corps

XX
☐ division

X
☐ brigade

Military unit colours

▨ Soviet

▨ German

Military movements

➡ Soviet attack

⇢ Soviet retreat

➡ German attack

⇢ German retreat

General military symbols

—— Soviet frontline

⋀⋁ Soviet defensive line

—— German frontline

⋀⋁ German defensive line

Geographical symbols

⊢•⊣ Railway

—— River

● Urban area

⬠ Urban area

PREFACE

No chapter in the Soviet Union's long and gruesome Great Patriotic War is fraught with greater drama, sacrifice and human suffering than the titanic struggle for the city of Leningrad. Born in war, an enduring crucible of revolution, and Russia's window on the West to both tsar and commissar, Tsar Peter the Great's city has long symbolized to Russia's enemies the greatness and often ominous and threatening potential of the Russian Empire and, later, the Bolshevik Soviet Union. It is no coincidence that when Adolf Hitler chose the Soviet Union as one of his priority targets in Germany's drive for *Lebensraum* (living space), Leningrad became a prime target of his ruthless ambition. It could not be otherwise, given the city's momentous symbolic, strategic and ideological significance.

Thousands of books written in Russia and the West alike have recorded the dramatic course of the Battle of Leningrad, relating the feats of the city's heroic military defenders and memorializing the monumental suffering of its population. A few, like Harrison E. Salisbury's *900 Days* and Dmitri Pavlov's *Leningrad 1941: The Blockade* have superbly captured the human anguish and agony associated with the siege's most famous military operations, and the tortured existence of Leningrad's population during their nearly three-year ordeal. Thousands of individual memoirs, some accurate and other apocryphal, embellish Salisbury's account. While the Russian archives have yet to reveal the full extent of the population's suffering in terms of finite human and material cost, and may never do so in full measure, no doubt remains concerning the nature and magnitude of that suffering.

To this day, however, as is the case with military operations in the Soviet Union's Great Patriotic War as a whole, the military dimension of the Battle for Leningrad remains appallingly obscure. While Soviet military historians have produced tens of studies of the Battle for Leningrad and on many of its component military operations, these accounts have ignored as much as 40 percent of the actual combat. A product of political or military embarrassment, vanity, or the Soviet Union's penchant for secrecy in the interest of national security or preserving political and military reputations, these yawning gaps embrace some of the most desperate and heated periods of fighting during the long siege. Nor do histories written from the German perspective adequately fill the gaps. Mesmerized by the imposing and seemingly unbroken mosaic of titanic battles of almost unprecedented proportions that characterized combat on their Eastern Front, German participants and historians scarcely had the desire, time or capacity for detecting and noting the intricacies of the Red Army's military efforts. This applied, in particular, to Red Army operations that failed, the category into which most of the missing 40 percent of the war's forgotten battles fall.

Today, recent Russian archival releases finally permit us to begin correcting the operational record of the Battle for Leningrad and of the war in general. For the first time, we can compare the extensive archival documentation of German army groups, armies and subordinate forces, which has long existed, with the new Russian documentation and, by doing so, begin to fill in the historical record.

By intent, this short volume is primarily a history of military operations. Rather than replicating the already superb accounts written about the unparalleled human suffering engendered by the siege, it simply seeks to establish a sounder and more accurate description of the military operations that provided essential context for all else that occurred at Leningrad. Further, it represents a modest beginning in what will undoubtedly be a long process of restoring to public view what actually occurred during the Leningraders' 900 days of unsurpassed trial under fire. This and more definitive works will finally do justice to the suffering of the 1.6 to two million soldiers and civilians who perished during the battle and siege, the 2.4 million soldiers who became casualties, and the 1.6 million civilians who escaped or survived the siege.

David M. Glantz
Carlisle, Pennsylvania

December 2000

DRAMATIS PERSONAE

SOVIET

Akimov, Lieutenant-General S. D. – Deputy Commander, Northwestern Front (June–August 1941), Acting Commander, V Airborne Corps (June–July 1941), and Commander, Forty-Eighth Army (August–1941).

Antoniuk, Lieutenant-General M. A. – Commander, Forty-Eighth Army (September 1941) and Sixtieth Army (July 1942).

Dukhanov, Lieutenant-General M. P. – Rifle division commander (September–October 1941), Chief of Staff, Neva Operational Group (October 1941), and Deputy Commander and Commander, Neva Operational Group (October 1941–October 1942), Commander, Sixty-Seventh Army (October 1942–December 1943), and Deputy Commander, Eighth Army (March 1944–May 1945).

Fediuninsky, Colonel-General I. I. – Commander, Forty-Second Army (September–October 1941), Leningrad Front (October 1941), Fifty-Fourth Army (October 1941–April 1942), and Fifth Army (April–October 1942). Deputy Commander, Volkhov Front (October 1942–May 1943) and Briansk Front (May–July 1943). Commander, Eleventh Army (July–December 1943) and Second Shock Army (December 1943–May 1945).

Galanin, Major-General I. V. – Commander, Twelfth Army (August–October 1941) and Fifty-Ninth Army (November 1941–April 1942). Deputy Commander, Western Front (May–August 1942) and Voronezh Front (August–September 1942). Commander, Twenty-Fourth Army (October 1942–April 1943), Seventieth Army (April–September 1943), Fourth Guards Army (September 1943–January 1944), Fifty-Third Army (January–February 1944), and Fourth Guards Army (February–November 1944).

Govorov, Marshal of the Soviet Union L. A. – Chief , Dzerzhinsky Artillery Academy (May–July 1941), and Chief of Artillery, the Western Direction and Reserve Front (July–August 1941). Deputy Commander, Mozhaisk Defence Line and Chief of Artillery, Western Front (August–October 1941). Commander, Fifth Army (October 1941–April 1942), Leningrad Group of Forces (April–June 1942), and Leningrad Front (June 1942–May 1945).

Gusev, Colonel-General N. I. – Commander, 25th Cavalry Division (July 1941–January 1942), XIII Cavalry Corps (January–June 1942), Fourth Army (June 1942–November 1943), and Twentieth, Forty-Seventh and Forty-Eighth Armies (November 1943–May 1945).

Iakovlev, Lieutenant-General V. F. – Chief of Rear Services, Southwestern Front and Deputy Chief, Red Army General Staff (June–September 1941). Commander, Fourth Army (September–November 1941) and Fifty-Second Army (January 1942–July 1943). Deputy Commander, Steppe Front (August–October 1943) and Commander, Belorussian and Stavropol Military Districts (1943–46).

Ivanov, Lieutenant-General F. S. – 2nd Deputy Commander, Kiev Special Military District (June 1941). Commander, Eighth Army (June–August 1941), Forty-Second Army (August–September 1941) and Leningrad garrison and internal defence (September–December 1941). Assigned to the Leningrad Front Military Council (15 December) and the NKO's Main Cadre Directorate (18 January 1942). Arrested on 22 January 1942 and imprisoned until 8 January 1946. Freed on 15 January 1946 and retired in 1952.

Khozin, Lieutenant-General M. S. – Chief of Rear Services, Front of Reserve Armies and Deputy Chief, Red Army General Staff (June–September 1941). Chief of Staff, Leningrad Front (September–October 1941). Commander, Fifty-Fourth Army (September–October 1941), Leningrad Front (October 1941–June 1942), Thirty-Third Army (June–December 1942), Twentieth Army (December 1942–February 1943), and Special Group Khozin (February–March 1943). Deputy Commander, Western Front (March 1943–March 1944) and Commander, Volga Military District (March 1944–May 1945).

Klykov, Lieutenant-General N. K. – Commander, Thirty-Second Army (July–August 1941), Fifty-Second Army (August 1941–January 1942), and Second Shock Army (January–April and July–December 1942). Deputy Commander, Volkhov Front (December 1942–June 1943), Moscow Military District (June 1943–June 1944), and North Caucasus Military District (1944–45).

Korovnikov, Lieutenant-General I. T. – Commander, Northwestern Front operational group and Novgorod Army Group of Forces operational group (June 1941–January 1942), Second Shock Army operational group (January–April 1942), and Fifty-Ninth Army (April 1942–May 1945).

Kulik, Marshal of the Soviet Union G. I. – Deputy Peoples' Commissar of Defence and Chief, Red Army Main Artillery Directorate (1939–41). Commander, Fifty-Fourth Army (August–September 1941). Relieved of command and assigned to the NKO (September 1941–April 1943). Commander, Fourth Guards Army (April–September 1943) and Deputy Chief, NKO Directorate for the Formation and Manning of the Soviet Army (January 1944–May 1945).

Kurochkin, Colonel-General P. A. – Commander, Twentieth Army (July–August 1941) and Forty-Third Army (August 1941). *Stavka* representative, Northwestern Front; Commander, Northwestern Front, and Deputy Commander, Northwestern Front (August 1941–October 1942 and June-November 1943). Commander, Eleventh Army (November 1942–March 1943) and Thirty-Fourth Army (March–June 1943). Deputy Commander, First Ukrainian Front (December 1943–February 1944) and Commander, Second Belorussian Front (February–April 1944) and Sixtieth Army (April 1944–May 1945).

Kuznetsov, Lieutenant-General A. A. – 2nd Secretary, Leningrad Communist Party Regional and City Council (1938–45) and Member, Baltic Fleet Military Council (1938–46), Northern Front Military Council (June–August 1941), Leningrad Front Military Council (September 1941–December 1942 and March 1943–May 1945), and Second Shock Army Military Council (December 1942–March 1943).

Kuznetsov, Colonel-General F. I. – Commander, Baltic Special Military District and Northwestern Front (June–October 1941). Commander, Twenty-First Army and Central Front, Chief of Staff, Twenty-Eighth Army, Commander, Fifty-First Army, Deputy Commander, Western Front, and Commander, Sixty-First Army (October 1941–April 1942). Chief, General Staff Academy and Deputy Commander, Volkhov and Karelian Fronts (April 1942–February 1945). Commander, Ural Military District (February 1945–48).

Lazarov, Major-General I. G. – Commander, Fifty-Fifth Army (September–November 1941).

Maslennikov, Colonel-General I. I. – (NKVD officer). Commander, Twenty-Ninth Army (July–December 1941), Thirty-Ninth Army, North Caucasus Front's Northern Group of Forces, and North Caucasus Front (December 1941–May 1943). Deputy Commander, Volkhov, Southwestern and Third Ukrainian Fronts (May–December 1943). Commander, Forty-Second Army (December 1943–March 1944), Deputy Commander, Leningrad Front (March–April 1944), and Commander, Third Baltic Front (April 1944–45).

Mekhlis, L. Z. – Chief, Red Army Main Political Directorate and Deputy Peoples' Commissar of Defence (1941–42), *Stavka* representative, Volkhov Front (January 1942) and Crimean Front (February–May 1942). Member, 6th Army Military Council, Voronezh Front Military Council, Volkhov Front Military Council, Briansk Front Military Council, Second Baltic Front Military Council, Western Front Military Council, Second Belorussian Front Military Council and Fourth Ukrainian Front Military Council (1942–44).

Meretskov, Army General K. A. – Deputy Peoples' Commissar of Defence (January–September 1941) and *Stavka* representative, Northwestern and Karelian Fronts (August–September 1941). Arrested, imprisoned, but exonerated (September–October 1941). Commander, Seventh Separate Army (October–November 1941), Fourth Army (November–December 1941), and Volkhov Front (December 1941–May 1942 and June 1942–February 1944). Commander, Thirty-Third Army (May–June 1942), Karelian Front (February–August 1945), and First Far Eastern Front (August–September 1945).

Piadyshev, Lieutenant-General K. P. – 1st Deputy Commander, Northern Front (June–July 1941) and Commander, Luga Operational Group (6 July–August 1941). Arrested (23 July), sentenced to 10 years' imprisonment, and died in prison in 1943. Rehabilitated posthumously in 1968.

Popov, Lieutenant-General M. M. – Commander, Northern and Leningrad Fronts (June–September 1941) and Sixty-First and Fortieth Armies (November 1941–October 1942). Deputy Commander, Stalingrad and Southwestern Fronts and Commander, Fifth Shock and Fifth Tank Armies (October 1942–January 1943). Commander, Mobile Group Popov (February–March 1943), Reserve Front and Steppe Military District (April–May 1943), Briansk Front (June–October 1943), and Baltic and Second Baltic Fronts (October 1943–April 1944). Chief of Staff, Leningrad and Second Baltic Fronts (April 1944–July 1945).

Roginsky, Lieutenant-General S. V. – Commander, 111th (24th Guards) Rifle Division, and VI and IV Guards Rifle Corps (December 1941–February 1942). Deputy

Commander, Fifty-Ninth, Eighth and Second Shock Armies (February 1942–March 1943). Commander, Fifty-Fourth Army (March 1943–December 1944) and Sixty-Seventh Army (February–May 1945).

Romanovsky, Lieutenant-General V. Z. – Commander, Arkhangel'sk Military District (1941–42). Deputy Commander and Commander, First Shock Army (May–December 1942). Commander, Second Shock Army (December 1942–December 1943) and Deputy Commander, Fourth Ukrainian Front (December 1943–March 1944). Commander, Forty-Second Army (March 1944), Sixty-Seventh Army (March 1944–March 1945) and Nineteenth Army (March–May 1945).

Shcherbakov, Major-General V. I. – Commander, L Rifle Corps (June–September 1941). Commander, Eighth, Forty-Second and Eleventh Armies and Deputy Commander, Twenty-Third Army (September 1941–March 1942). Commander, Fourteenth Army (March 1942–May 1945).

Shevaldin, Lieutenant-General T. I. – Commander, Eighth Army (September–November 1941).

Simoniak, Lieutenant-General N. P. – Commander, 136th (63rd Guards) Rifle Division (June 1941–1942), Commander, XXX Guards Rifle Corps (1942–October 1944), Third Shock Army (October 1944–March 1945), and Sixty-Seventh Army (March–May 1945).

Sobennikov, Lieutenant-General P. P. – Commander, Eighth Army (March–June 1941), Northwestern Front (July–August 1941), and Forty-Third Army (September–October 1941). Deputy Commander, Third Army (1942–May 1945).

Sokolov, Lieutenant-General G. G. – (NKVD officer). Commander, Second Shock Army (December 1941–January 1942).

Stalin, Marshal of the Soviet Union I. V. – First Secretary, Communist Party of the Soviet Union (1941–45), Chairman, State Defence Committee (GKO) (1941–45), Chairman, *Stavka* VGK (1941–45), Peoples' Commissar of Defence (1941–45), Supreme High Commander, Soviet Armed Forces (1941–45), and Generalissimo (1945).

Starikov, Lieutenant-General F. N. – Chief, Luga Operational Group's Eastern Sector (July–August 1941). Commander, Twenty-Third Army and Siniavino Operational Group (December 1941–January 1942). Deputy Commander, Eighth Army and Volkhov Operational Group (January–April 1942) and Commander, Eighth Army (April 1942–May 1945).

Sukhomlin, Lieutenant-General A. V. – Chief of Staff, Northwestern Front and Fifty-Fourth Army (June 1941–January 1942). Commander, Eighth Army (January–April 1942) and Fifty-Fourth Army (April 1942–March 1943). Deputy Commander, Volkhov Front. (March–September 1943) and Commander, Tenth Guards Army (September 1943–February 1944). 1st Deputy Chief, Frunze Academy (February 1944–May 1945).

Sviridov, Lieutenant-General V. P. – Chief of Artillery, Northern Front and Chief of Artillery and Deputy Commander, Leningrad Front (June–November 1941). Commander, Fifty-Fifth Army (November 1941–December 1943), Sixty-Seventh Army (December 1943–March 1944), and Forty-Second Army (March 1944–May 1945).

Timoshenko, Marshal of the Soviet Union S. F. – People's Commissar of Defence (May 1940–June 1941) and Deputy Peoples' Commissar of Defence (July–September 1941). Commander, Western Direction and Western Front (July–September 1941), Southwestern Direction and Southwestern Front (September 1941–June 1942), Stalingrad Front (July–October 1942), and Northwestern Front (October 1942–March 1943). *Stavka* representative, Leningrad and Volkhov Fronts (March–June 1943), North Caucasus Front and Black Sea Fleet (June–November 1943), Second and Third Baltic Fronts (February–June 1944), and Second, Third and Fourth Ukrainian Fronts (August 1944–May 1945).

Tributs, Admiral V. F. – Commander, Baltic Fleet (1939–47).

Vatutin, Army General N. F. – 1st Deputy Chief, Red Army General Staff (1941). Chief of Staff, Northwestern Front (June–August 1941). Deputy Chief, Red Army General Staff (May–July 1942). Commander, Voronezh Front (July–October 1942 and March–October 1943), Southwestern Front (October 1942–March 1943), and First Ukrainian Front (March 1943–March 1944). Killed by partisans in March 1944.

Vlasov, Lieutenant-General A. A. – Commander, 99th Rifle Division and IV Mechanized Corps (June–July 1941), Thirty-Seventh Army (July–October 1941), and Twentieth Army (October 1941–February 1942). Deputy Commander, Volkhov Front (February–April 1942) and Commander, Second Shock Army (April–July 1942). Captured by the Germans in July 1942.

Voronov, Chief Marshal of Artillery – Deputy Peoples' Commissar of Defence (1941) and Chief, Red Army Main Directorate for Air Defence (1941). Chief of Artillery,

Red Army and Deputy Commissar of Defence (July 1941–March 1943). *Stavka* representative, Leningrad Front (October–November 1941) and Commander, Red Army artillery (1943–46).

Voroshilov, Marshal of the Soviet Union K. E. – Member, State Defence Committee (GKO) and *Stavka* (1941–44). Commander, Northwestern Direction Main Command (July–August 1941) and Leningrad Front (September 1941). *Stavka* representative, Volkhov Front (February–March 1942), Leningrad and Volkhov Fronts (December 1942–January 1943), and Separate Coastal Army (December 1943).

Zhdanov, A. A. – Secretary, Communist Party Central Committee and Leningrad Regional and City Party Committees (1934–44). Permanent Advisor, *Stavka* VGK (June 1941). Member, Northwestern Direction Command Military Council (June–August 1941), Leningrad Front Military Council (September 1941–July 1945), and the Red Army's Main Political Directorate's Military-Political Propaganda Council.

Zhukov, Marshal of the Soviet Union G. K. – Chief of Staff, Red Army, and Deputy Peoples' Commissar of Defence (January–June 1941). Member, *Stavka* VGK (1941–45). 1st Deputy Peoples' Commissar of Defence and Supreme High Commander (August 1942–1945). *Stavka* VGK representative, Southwestern Front (June 1941). Commander, Reserve Front (July–September 1941), Leningrad Front (September–October 1941), and Western Front (October 1941–August 1942). Commander, Western Direction Main Command (February–May 1942), *Stavka* VGK representative, Reserve Front (October 1941), Western and Kalinin Fronts (November–December 1942), Leningrad and Volkhov Fronts (January 1943), and Northwestern Front (February–March 1943). *Stavka* VGK representative, Voronezh and Steppe Fronts (April 1943), North Caucasus Front (April–May 1943), Voronezh, Central and Western Fronts (May–June 1943), Southwestern Front (June 1943), Briansk, Central and Western Fronts (June–July 1943), and Steppe and Voronezh Fronts (August–September 1943). *Stavka* VGK representative, Central and Voronezh Fronts (September–December 1943) and First and Second Ukrainian Fronts (January–March 1944). Commander, First Ukrainian Front (March–May 1944). *Stavka* VGK representative, First and Second Belorussian and First Ukrainian Fronts (June–August 1944), Third Ukrainian Front (September 1944) and First and Second Belorussian and First Ukrainian Fronts (September–November 1944). Commander, First Belorussian Front (November 1944–May 1945).

GERMAN

Busch, Colonel-General Ernst – Commander, Sixteenth Army (June 1941–October 1943) and Army Group Centre (October 1943–June 1944).

Halder, Colonel-General Franz – Chief, Army General Staff (OKH) (1941–September 1942).

Hoepner, Colonel-General Erich – Commander, Fourth Panzer Group (June 1941–January 1942).

Keitel, Colonel-General Wilhelm – Chief, German Armed Forces (OKW) (1941–45)

Kuechler, Colonel-General Georg von – Commander, Eighteenth Army (June–January 1942) and Commander, Army Group North (January 1942–February 1944).

Leeb, Field Marshal Ritter von – Commander, Army Group North (June1941–January 1942)

Lindemann, Colonel-General Georg – Commander, L Army Corps (June 1941–January 1942) and Eighteenth Army (January 1942–February 1944).

Manstein, Field Marshal Erich von – Commander, LVI Motorized Corps (March–September 1941), Eleventh Army (September 1941–December 1942), Army Group Don (December 1942–February 1943), Army Group South (February 1943–March 1944).

Model, Field Marshal Walter – Commander, Ninth Army (June 1941–February 1944), Army Group North (February–March 1944), Army Group South and North Ukraine (March–June 1944), Army Group Centre (June–August 1944), Western Theatre (August 1944–April 1945). Killed in action in the Ruhr region in April 1945.

Reinhardt, Colonel-General Hans – Commander, XXXXI Panzer Corps (June–October 1941), Third Panzer Group and Third Panzer Army (October 1941–August 1944), Army Group Centre (August 1944–January 1945).

Schmidt, Colonel-General Rudolf – Commander, XXXIX Motorized Corps (June–November 1941), Second Army and Army Group Schmidt (November 1941–January 1942), and Second Panzer Army (January 1942–July 1943).

Zeitzler, Colonel-General Kurt – Chief of Staff, Army Group D (1941–42) and Chief, Army General Staff (OKH) (September 1942–July 1944).

CHAPTER 1:
THE CITY OF PETER AND LENIN

The city of Leningrad, formerly St. Petersburg, had played an important part in the success of the Bolshevik Revolution in 1917 and the subsequent triumph of the Communists in the Russian Civil War. As a cradle of Bolshevism, it was logical that the German Fascist dictator Adolf Hitler would designate the city a main target in his plans for the invasion and conquest of the Soviet Union.

Adolf Hitler, Nazi dictator of Germany, had good reason for choosing Leningrad as a priority objective for Operation Barbarossa, the codename for his June 1941 invasion of the Soviet Union. From its founding in 1703 as St. Petersburg, the city's history reflected its strategic importance as the northwestern gateway to Russia, an important political, economic and cultural centre, and the symbol of revolution.

Tsar Peter the Great (1672–1725) founded St. Petersburg, Leningrad's imperial ancestor, in 1703 during his Great Northern War with Sweden's King Charles XII. The city was located on primordial Russian land adjacent to the old Varangian trade routes to Byzantium, land which had previously belonged to the feudal principalities of Novgorod and Izhorsk. The land on which Peter built his city

LEFT: After the siege. As life slowly returns to normal, school parties such as this one can resume their ordinary round of visits to places of interest. But although the buildings, roads and pathways are clear, the gardens and windows still bear the scars of 900 days under siege.

had become part of Russia in 1478, along with the remainder of Novgorod.

While struggling to gain supremacy in the Baltic region, on 11 October 1702 Peter's forces stormed the Swedish fort at Noteborg near the old Russian town of Oreshek at the junction of the Neva River and Lake Ladoga, and renamed the fortress *Shlissel'burg* ("key city"). The following year, Peter's armies captured the small Swedish fort at Nyenschantz at the junction of the Neva and Okhta Rivers and renamed it St. Petersburg and, below it, built the Fortress of St. Petersburg (later named Petropavlovsk Fortress) on Zaiachi Island. Peter also built a port, trading facilities and a palace on Lake Berzovyi, Kronshlot (named Kronshtadt after 1723) Fortress on Kotlin Island, and the Admiralty Fortress on the left bank of the Neva River between 1703 and 1704.

Peter built these facilities and the city around them in a strategically vital geographical location at the mouth of the Neva River and on 42 islands in the river's delta.[1] The city's founding, which ended a century-long struggle for access to the Baltic Sea,

LEFT: The grand palace of Catherine the Great, one of the most splendid in the world, was turned into a museum by the Communists. It contrasted sharply with the sprawling slums of Leningrad, most notably the workers' areas of the Petrograd side and the Vyborg quarter.

underscored Peter's intent to seize and maintain access to the Baltic Sea as Russia's "Window on the West". At the same time, however, the city's construction took a terrible toll on its initial population. Tens of thousands of peasants, forcibly recruited from across Russia, perished in epidemics during its construction as they feverishly carved the city out of near-impenetrable marshland.[2]

The conscious decision of Peter and many of his imperial successors to make the city the seat of imperial power, complete with the trappings of a modern Western city, burnished St. Petersburg's strategic value and prestige. A crude backwater before Peter's lifetime, it later became a beautiful shining city under Elizabeth and Catherine the Great. The rule of the two empresses represented the spectacular age of St. Petersburg, the golden age of the nobility, and the legendary age of Russian opulence and glitter. The city developed rapidly according to a distinct plan and served as the Russian Empire's capital from 1712 to 1728 and from 1732 to 1918.[3] By the mid-eighteenth century, Peter and his imperial successors had transformed the city into Russia's most important political, administrative, cultural and military centre and a main outpost on the country's northwestern border. Characterized by its brilliant court, extensive military establishment and bureaucracy, and imposing

shipbuilding and ordnance industries, St. Petersburg became Russia's most important political, administrative, cultural and military centre. Its population grew from 425,000 in 1825 to 1,534,000 in 1905, a reflection of its growing importance.

St. Petersburg developed symbolic significance and a mystique of its own as a bulwark of autocracy, nobility and, later, of the bourgeoisie, for more than 200 years. It also became a centre of Russian science and culture and the focal point of progressive thought and social and revolutionary movements, in part due to its proximity to the West and Western ideas. Understandably, creative tension existed between Peter's fledgling city and Moscow, the capital of the ancient Muscovite State and Tsar Ivan the Terrible's seat of power. While Moscow represented "Old Mother Russia" and Russia's Slavic heartland, St. Petersburg "stood for the tutelary light of the West against the Byzantine dark of Moscow".[4] St. Petersburg's increased stature made it a focal point for both international and internal struggles. As Russia's Baltic military outpost, it served as a base for Russian ground forces and the fledgling Baltic Fleet in the Great Northern War (1700–21) against Sweden. Two centuries later, during the Crimean War (1853–56), Kronshtadt Fortress and the Baltic Fleet prevented an Anglo-French squadron from reaching St. Petersburg.

While appreciating the city's political, economic and cultural significance, Hitler also correctly perceived St. Petersburg as a centre of revolution and the birthplace of the hated Bolshevism. The city was the focal point of revolution on several occasions, in 1820, 1825, 1905–07, in February, August and October of 1918, and in 1921. St. Petersburg's bourgeoisie and, later, its proletariat, indeed formed the vanguard of Russian revolutionary movements from as early as 1802, when the soldiers of the Semenovsky Guards Regiment revolted against the arbitrary policies of Emperor Paul.

After their exposure to Western ideas during the War of Liberation against Napoleon, Russian guards officers founded the "Union of Salvation" and, later, the "Union of Welfare", secret revolutionary political societies in St. Petersburg that sought to promote representative government and also liberate the serfs. The so-called Decembrist Movement, which harboured anti-foreign overtones, led a revolt in the city in December 1825, but was bloodily suppressed. Throughout the ensuing century, democrats and revolutionary leaders were to gravitate towards St. Petersburg.[5] In 1895, V. I. Lenin founded the "Union for the Struggle of the Working Class" in St. Petersburg and began introducing Marxist Socialism to the city's workers' movement. Subsequently, the city was the focal point of revolution in 1904–07,

including the 8 November 1904 Kronshtadt Mutiny and the infamous Bloody Sunday, which occurred on 9 January 1905.

When World War I began in 1914, the Tsarist government renamed the city Petrograd to eradicate its German-associated past. By 1917, however, the rigours of war once again made the city the focal point of revolutionary activity that culminated in the revolutions of February and October 1917 and the Bolsheviks' seizure and consolidation of power. During the ensuing Russian Civil War, the city remained a Bolshevik strongpoint, as Lenin extended his control over the entire country. The Bolsheviks' military arm, the Red Guards, defended the city during the desperate struggle with Germany in 1918 and, after World War I had ended, the new Red Army did the same against counter-revolutionary (White) forces during the Civil War.[6]

After the Bolsheviks transferred the country's capital from Petrograd to Moscow for security reasons, the city became a natural target for White forces. General N. Iudenich's White Northwestern Army attempted to seize Petrograd in the period from May to August and in October and November 1919, in conjunction with White armies advancing from the south and east, but failed on both occasions since the Red Army and Petrograd's workers halted each offensive.[7]

RIGHT: View of the waterfront of the Neva River at Leningrad. During the siege the German Luftwaffe frequently bombed supply barges sent across Lake Ladoga before they reached the city. Loaded with grain and munitions, many foundered in storms on the lake, even before they ran the Luftwaffe gauntlet.

Leningrad's revolutionary traditions continued in Bolshevik times when, in February and March 1921, the sailors of the Kronshtadt Naval Base rose in revolt against the harshness of the new Communist regime. Although Red Army forces brutally suppressed the uprising, it prompted Lenin to introduce his more moderate New Economic Policy in March 1921.[8] After Lenin's death, on 26 January 1924, the 2nd Congress of Soviets of the USSR renamed the city Leningrad at the request of the city's workers.

In the 1930s, Leningrad figured prominently in Stalin's consolidation of power. When S. M. Kirov, the popular Leningrad Party secretary and an advocate of a moderate economic policy, emerged as a potential rival, Stalin orchestrated his murder and used it to justify the subsequent purges.[9] Later, many believed that Stalin's neglect and harsh treatment of the city during and after World War II reflected his hatred for Kirov and fear of the city's great influence.

The Defence of the City

Leningrad's close association with the military continued during the initial period of World War II. In March 1939, in the wake of the infamous Molotov-Ribbentrop Pact between Hitler and Stalin, the Soviet Union provoked war with Finland, mainly to improve the defences along the Soviet Union's northwestern borders. Leningrad served as the command post and base of operations for the Leningrad Military District, which conducted the short war. Ironically, the Red Army's dismal performance in the war encouraged Hitler to launch Operation Barbarossa. The German Führer chose Leningrad as a prime military objective because he believed the city's capture and, if necessary, its obliteration, was necessary to destroy the Soviet state and, with it, the forces of international Bolshevism. Hitler's Wehrmacht (German armed forces) was to inflict this ugly judgement on the city of Peter and Lenin.

Leningrad's long and illustrious military past and its current political, economic, cultural and strategic significance made it an appropriate target for Hitler's wrath. Responsibility for defending the city of 2,544,000 souls and its surrounding region (oblast) rested with the Soviet government's and Party's central, regional and local organs, and the Leningrad Military District. At national level, this meant I. V. Stalin, Chief of State and the Communist Party First Secretary; Marshal of the Soviet Union S. K. Timoshenko, People's Commissar of Defence;

and General G. K. Zhukov, the Chief of the Red Army General Staff. A variety of regional and local organs were directly responsible for the city's and region's defence. Administratively, these included the Leningrad region (oblast), district (raion) and city (gorod) councils (sovety) and mayors. Politically, A. A. Zhdanov, Stalin's close associate, a member of the Politburo and arguably Stalin's heir apparent, served as First Secretary of the Leningrad Communist Party. Zhdanov, together with A. A. Kuznetsov, the Secretary of the Leningrad Regional Party Committee, headed a hierarchy of regional, district and city Party committees, which effectively dominated all matters, both political and military, that took place in or affected Leningrad. As was the case in any totalitarian structure, tight organization, strict centralization of authority and pervasive Party discipline allowed these Party leaders to mobilize virtually all of the city's resources for a given task, in this case defence.

Militarily, the People's Commissariat of Defence (Narodnyi komissarriat oborony – NKO), closely supervised by Stalin and the Communist Party Politburo and Central Committee, formulated all State defence policy and approved general and specific force readiness measures. The Red Army General Staff, headed by General G. K. Zhukov, drafted all mobilization, deployment and war plans, but implemented them only with the NKO's approval and guidance. Finally, the Leningrad Military District was responsible for maintaining the readiness of district forces and fulfilling the General Staff plans, but only when specifically ordered to do so by the NKO. The military district's executive organ was its military council (voennyi sovet), a collective organization consisting of the military district commander, its member of the military council (commissar) and its chief of staff.

The Leningrad Military District

By definition, the Leningrad Military District (LMD) was the "premier operational-strategic territorial formation of the Soviet Union deployed at Leningrad and in the surrounding oblast" on the eve of war. As was the case with other military districts, when war broke out the LMD was to form the Red Army's Northern Front (a Front was roughly equivalent to a German army group), which was responsible for mobilizing and deploying forces and conducting military operations in accordance with the General Staff's plans and directives under strict NKO supervision.

ABOVE: A Finnish machine-gun team during the Winter War. The ill-coordinated Red Army campaign against tiny Finland cost the Soviets nearly 50,000 dead. In Berlin, the ineptitude of the Soviet performance convinced Hitler and his senior commanders that the Soviet Union would rapidly succumb to the Blitzkrieg.

The LMD had a long history as one of the Red Army's premier military districts. Formed on 6 September 1918 as the Petrograd Military District, it being the first military district in the Red Army, it was renamed the LMD on 1 February 1924 when the city itself was renamed. During the ensuing decades, the military district served as the test-bed for many advanced military concepts, such as air and chemical operations, airborne, air assault, and air landing operations, and the twin concepts of deep battle and deep operations. Its distinguished roster of commanders included such future luminaries as M. N. Tukhachevsky, the architect of deep operations, B. M. Shaposhnikov, the father of the Red Army General Staff, S. K. Timoshenko, the Commissar of Defence, and future Front commanders K. A. Meretskov, M. P. Kirponis and M. M. Popov.[10]

The LMD planned, organized and conducted the Soviet-Finnish War of 1939–40, but performed so poorly that it was replaced by the Northwestern Front, which was able to bring the war to a more successful conclusion.[11]

Between the end of the Soviet-Finnish War and the start of the German invasion on 22 June 1941, the LMD was at the forefront of attempts to reform, reorganize and re-equip the Red Army. During this period, the LMD formed new mechanized and aviation formations armed with new types of weaponry. It also created the Northern Air Defence (PVO) Zone and constructed fortifications along the Soviet Union's new borders. When war broke out in June, Lieutenant-General M. M. Popov, who had been assigned command in January, commanded the military district, Corps Commissar N. N. Klement'ev was his commissar (member of the Military Council), and Major-General D. H. Nikishev was his Chief of Staff.

On the eve of war, the LMD encompassed the territory of Leningrad and Murmansk regions and the Karelo-Finnish Republic (SSR). The district's military forces included the Seventh, Fourteenth and Twenty-Third Armies, XIX, XLII and L Rifle Corps, I and V Mechanized Corps, I Fighter Aviation Corps, and II PVO Corps and VII Fighter Aviation Corps PVO (of the Northern PVO Zone) (see *Appendices*). The 15 rifle divisions, one rifle brigade, four tank and two motorized divisions, and eight fortified regions, formed the nucleus of the district's ground forces. The ground forces numbered 404,470 men, supported by 7901 guns and mortars, 1857 tanks (1543 operational) and 1336 combat aircraft (1216 operational).[12]

The Soviet State Defence Plan (DP–1941) ordered the military district to defend the state borders with Finland from the Arctic Sea to the Gulf of Finland, the coast of Estonia, and the naval base on the Hango Peninsula on Finland's southern coast, in cooperation with the Soviet Northern and Baltic Fleets.[13] In the north, the district's Fourteenth Army defended the approach to Murmansk with its XLII Rifle Corps, two separate rifle divisions, one fortified region and I Mechanized Corps' 1st Tank Division. The Seventh Army defended the sector between Lakes Onega and Ladoga in central Karelia with four rifle divisions and one fortified region. Finally, the Twenty-Third Army defended the Karelian Isthmus with the XIX and L Rifle and X Mechanized Corps and two fortified regions. Two rifle divisions, one rifle brigade, four fortified regions and one tank and one motorized division of I Mechanized Corps were directly subordinate to military district headquarters.

On the eve of war, the NKO and the General Staff relied on the Baltic Special Military District, which was to form the Northwestern Front in wartime, to defend the approaches through the Baltic republics towards Leningrad. The LMD was responsible for defending against any Finnish advance along the Karelian Peninsula towards the city. As it turned out, the NKO's assumption that the Northwestern Front could contain any enemy advance along the border or along the Western Dvina River, and certainly well short of Leningrad, proved to be grossly incorrect. This sad reality virtually negated much of the value of the LMD's pre-war military planning.

Air Defence Over the City

However, given its well-defined defensive responsibilities and the NKO's false assumptions, the LMD paid little attention to preparing ground defences along the southern approaches to the city. Only on the morning of 23 June, 24 hours after the German invasion had begun, did General Popov begin worrying about his military district's southern flank.

On that day Popov dispatched his deputy, Lieutenant-General K. P. Piadyshev, to inspect the southern approaches to the city and recommend sites for the erection of new, precautionary defence lines. Even though Piadyshev recommended that the Kingisepp-Luga-Lake Il'men line should be considered as the logical location for a defence line, the absence of resources made it a moot issue, that is, until the worsening situation finally impelled Popov to take action.

The NKO assigned responsibility for providing air defence over the northern Soviet Union, including Leningrad, to the Northern Air Defence (*proti-vo-vozdushnaia oborona* – PVO) Zone. The zone consisted of II PVO Corps and the Vyborg, Murmansk, Pskov, Luga and Petrozavodsk PVO Brigade Regions. On 22 June, II PVO Corps and VII Fighter Aviation Corps were responsible for air defence in the immediate vicinity of Leningrad. II PVO Corps, commanded by Major-General M. M. Protsvetkin, which consisted of the 115th, 169th,

LEFT: Georgi Zhukov, one of the greatest commanders of World War II, was closely involved with the military effort to free Leningrad. The hero of the victory over the Japanese Army at Khalkhin-Gol in August 1939, Stalin appointed him commander at Leningrad in September 1941.

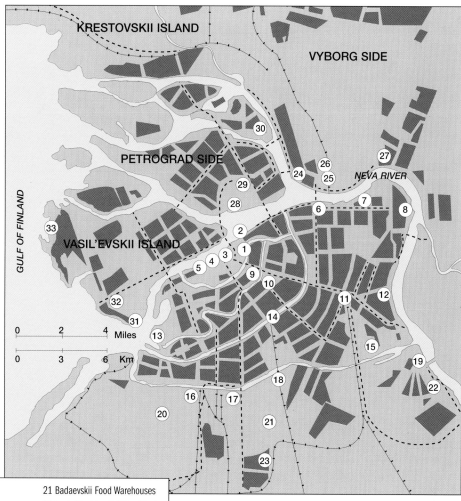

Leningrad

1 Army Headquarters
2 Hermitage
3 Admiralty
4 St. Isaac Cathedral
5 Main Post and Telegraph Office
6 NKVD Headquarters
7 Main water works
8 Smolny Institute
9 Kazan Cathedral
10 Gostinyi Dvor
11 Moscow Railway Station
12 Electric Power Station
13 Marti Shipyards
14 Vitebsk Railroad Station
15 Electric Power Station
16 Baltic Railway Station
17 Warsaw Railway Station
18 Main Gas
19 Kirov Flour Mill
20 Kirov Works

21 Badaevskii Food Warehouses
22 Lenin Machine Building Plant
23 Elektrosila Works

Vyborg Side

24 Liteinyi Bridge
25 Finland Railway Station
26 Military Medical Academy
27 Stalin Works

Petrograd Side

28 Peter and Paul Fortress
29 Zoological Garden
30 Botanical Garden

Vasil'evskii Island

31 Baltic Shipyard
32 Electric Power Station
33 Army Food Storage

ABOVE: The city of Leningrad in 1941, the city that Adolf Hitler wanted to erase from the face of the earth. The Badaevskii Food Warehouses were among the first sites to be destroyed by German bombs, which added to the problems of feeding a city full of refugees and troops.

189th, 192nd, 194th and 351st Anti-aircraft Artillery Regiments, numbered 950 anti-aircraft guns, 230 anti-aircraft machine guns, 300 search-lights, 360 aerial obstacle balloons, 302 VNOS (early warning) posts and eight radio-location sites. The Baltic Fleet's PVO division with 191 guns was also operationally subordinate to II PVO Corps. VII Fighter Aviation Corps, commanded by Colonel S. P. Danilov, consisted of the 3rd and 54th Fighter Aviation Divisions (PVO) and was equipped with 300 fighter aircraft.

II PVO Corps defended the city with a series of defence zones radiating from the city's centre. A system of air observation and early warning posts

(VNOS) was deployed 120–140km (75–87.5 miles) from the city, a zone of aviation cover formed by VII Fighter Aviation Corps defended a belt 20–60km (12.5–37.5 miles) distant from the city, and anti-aircraft artillery defended a zone 35km (21.8 miles) from the city's centre. All of the air defences were centralized under II PVO Corps' control.

Though this defence was imposing on paper, it suffered from several major weaknesses, the most serious of which was a shortage of airfields. Compounding this problem, once war began, the rapid German advance disrupted the VNOS' early warning system, forcing the city's defenders to rely on unreliable radio location and visual observation. The Soviet command tried to solve this problem by mounting eight PVO gun batteries on barges in the Gulf of Finland to increase the depth of the defence. Party organizations also supplemented the PVO effort by forming local air defence (MPVO) forces consisting of 10–12 self-defence groups of 600–800 men and women each, totalling around 300,000 persons, who were responsible for observation, security and defence of city blocks and other important buildings.[14]

ABOVE: Derelict barges stuck fast in ice in pre-war Leningrad, an image that amply conveys the sub-zero temperatures that grip the city during the winter. Death from the cold was common during the first winter of the siege, especially after central heating was cut off in December 1941 due to fuel shortages.

The Red Banner Baltic Fleet, whose long history dated back to its creation by Peter I in 1701, was responsible for defending the Soviet naval bases in the Baltic region and at Leningrad and the Baltic coast against naval, air and ground attack. It was to do so in close cooperation with Red Army forces operating in adjacent land theatres. Vice-Admiral V. F. Tributs, who was promoted to full admiral in May 1943, commanded the fleet throughout the entire war.

On the eve of war, the Baltic Fleet consisted of a surface ship squadron, a light ship detachment, three submarine brigades, two torpedo boat brigades, a wide array of cutters, air forces, coastal defence regions and sectors, and rear service installations and facilities. The fleet's forces were stationed at the Tallin, Hango, Kronshtadt and Libau (near Riga) naval bases. Its 225 combat ships included two battleships, two cruisers, 21 destroyer leaders and destroyers, 68 submarines, two cannon ships, seven destroyer escorts, four armoured cutters, 55 torpedo boats, 34 mine-sweepers, four mine and net layers, 34 submarine hunters, and numerous coastal cutters. The Baltic Fleet's air forces numbered 682 aircraft (595 serviceable), including 184 bombers, 331 fighters and 167 reconnaissance aircraft. The fleet's naval and coastal artillery included 2189 guns and mortars. Its total personnel strength was 119,645 men.

Soviet Naval Forces

While the bulk of the Baltic Fleet supported the Baltic Military District from its bases at Tallin and Libau, the fleet's bases at Kronshtadt and Hango supported the LMD. Although it was not fully activated until October 1941, the Leningrad Military Naval Base at Kronshtadt was responsible for helping to defend the sea approaches to Leningrad and the city itself.[15] The base's primary mission was to conduct counter-battery fire and to serve as a transshipment point for forces between Leningrad and the Oranienbaum bridgehead.

The Soviet Union obtained its naval base at Hango, located on the northern shore of the Gulf of Finland, as a result of the Soviet-Finnish War.[16] The base's primary mission was to defend the sea routes to Leningrad through the Gulf of Finland, and provide a foothold on the southern coast of Finland. On 22 June the 8th Separate Rifle Brigade, border guards, engineer-construction units, coastal and anti-aircraft artillery batteries, an aviation group, and a naval security detachment defended the base. The garrison's overall strength was 25,000 men, equipped with 95 37mm to 305mm guns, 20 aircraft, seven cutter-hunters and 16 auxiliary ships.

North of Leningrad, the Ladoga Naval Flotilla defended Lake Ladoga itself. The flotilla was an "operational-tactical naval formation" which had been created on 25 October 1939, and was subordinate to the Baltic Fleet. Its mission was to defend the shores and waters of Lake Ladoga, primarily with a small force of surface ships. On the eve of war, it consisted of a division of seven training ships, a division of 35 training cutters, and an artillery training battalion with three 102mm and eight 76mm guns. On 25 June 1941, the Commissariat of the Navy (VMF) reorganized the flotilla into a division of cutters, mine-sweepers, security cutters, cutter-mine-sweepers and coastal boats and units.[17] Captain 2nd Rank S. V. Zemlianichenko commanded the flotilla when the war began.

Thus, on the eve of war the LMD, the Baltic Fleet and other organizations which were tasked with the defence of Leningrad were marginally capable of doing so, but only against a Finnish attack through Karelia. Stalin and the General Staff in Moscow believed the powerful Northwestern Front could defend the approaches to Leningrad along the northwestern axis. However, neither the LMD nor the Moscow authorities anticipated how rapid and destructive the German Wehrmacht's advance would be once Operation Barbarossa was under way. They would pay dearly for underestimating the situation. Within just days the deteriorating situation converted their mild concern into near panic.

LEFT: Stalin was determined that Leningrad would not fall to the Germans, but his interference in the organization of the city's defence as the Germans approached during the autumn of 1941 hindered rather than helped those on the ground. He saw plots and treason everywhere, especially when his generals retreated.

CHAPTER 2:
TARGET LENINGRAD

Following the start of Operation Barbarossa, the codename for the German invasion of the Soviet Union, the Red Army suffered a number of crushing defeats along the Soviet frontier region. In the north, Leeb's panzers were soon racing for Leningrad as the military and civilian leaders in the city desperately tried to organize their defences.

Adolf Hitler's plans for Operation Barbarossa, the conquest of the Soviet Union, were contained in Directive No 21 issued on 18 December 1940, which designated Leningrad, Moscow and Kiev as the Wehrmacht's three prime military objectives. Plan Barbarossa required three army groups to attack simultaneously to envelop, trap and annihilate the bulk of the Red Army in the frontier region, to "prevent combat-capable enemy forces from withdrawing into the vast Russian interior". Army Groups North and Centre were to make the main attack along the Leningrad and Moscow axes north of the Pripiat Marshes, while Army Group South was to attack along the Kiev axis south of the Pripiat Marshes. Once Army Group Centre had destroyed enemy forces in Belorussia, it was to assist Army Group North in capturing Leningrad and Kronshtadt. "Only after accomplishing this priority mission," read the directive, "should we initiate operations to seize Moscow."[1]

Field Marshal Ritter von Leeb's Army Group North was to advance along the Leningrad axis,

destroy Soviet forces in the Baltic region and capture Leningrad. Leeb's army group consisted of the Eighteenth and Sixteenth Armies and the Fourth Panzer Group, a total of six army and two motorized corps, backed up by three security divisions and an army corps in army group reserve (see *Appendices* for organization).[2] Colonel-General Erich Hoepner's Fourth Panzer Group, consisting of Colonel-Generals Hans Reinhardt's and Erich von Manstein's XXXXI and LVI Motorized Corps, was to spearhead the army group's advance.[3] Colonel-Generals Georg von Kuechler's and Ernst Busch's Eighteenth and Sixteenth Armies, each with three army corps, were to advance on the flanks and in the wake of the advancing panzers.[4] Leeb retained XXIII Army Corps in army group reserve and could, if need be, call on L Army Corps, deployed in his sector as Army High Command (OKH) reserve. This cast of players would initiate the titanic Battle for Leningrad.

Leeb's strong and experienced force faced Colonel-General F. I. Kuznetsov's Baltic Special Military District, whose Eighth and Eleventh Armies and III and XII Mechanized Corps defended the northwestern strategic axis. Powerful on paper, Kuznetsov's forces suffered from the same debilitating deficiencies that plagued the entire Red Army on the eve of war: they were only partially reorganized, trained and re-equipped.[5] Because Stalin's orders

LEFT: Leningrad as a garrison town was in the forefront of the Red Army's mobilization plans. This infantry unit is boarding a train for the front, men in cattle-cars, their artillery under camouflage on flat cars. The rifle is the standard Red Army Mosin-Nagant Model 1891 – a robust and effective weapon.

LEFT: With their equipment stowed away, these men pose cheerfully for the camera on the steps of the troop train. It would not be long before the front was only a short march from their barracks. It is unlikely that many of these men would have survived the first clashes with the German invaders.

prevented him from mobilizing and defending properly, within weeks, Army Group North had crushed his defences and quickly turned the approaches to Leningrad into a war zone.

Leeb's forces advanced on 22 June, ripped apart partially manned Soviet defences, and plunged deep into Soviet territory, pre-empting Soviet defence plans and generating chaos in the Red Army's ranks. Kuznetsov tried to implement his defence plan, but, given the precipitous and violent German attack, did so in wooden and haphazard fashion. After counterattacking in vain, on 25 June his Eighth and Eleventh Armies withdrew in disorder northwards towards the Northern Dvina River. The newly formed Soviet *Stavka* (High Command) hastily tried to establish new defences to the rear by ordering Kuznetsov to defend along the Western Dvina River with his shattered Eighth and Eleventh Armies and the fresh Twenty-Seventh and Twenty-Second Armies and XXI Mechanized Corps. However, when the Twenty-Seventh Army failed to occupy its defence in time, on 26 June Manstein's LVI Panzer Corps captured a bridgehead over the Western Dvina River. Deprived of his last defensive barrier along the northwestern axis, Kuznetsov withdrew his Eighth Army northwards towards Estonia and the Eleventh and Twenty-Seventh Armies eastwards, leaving the approaches from Pskov and Ostrov to Leningrad unprotected.[6] Faced with the imminent loss of the Dvina River line, on 29 June the *Stavka* ordered Kuznetsov to defend along the former Stalin Line (from Pskov to Ostrov), but Kuznetsov

failed to do so in time. (The Stalin Line was the line of fortifications built along the 1939 Soviet-Polish border. It lost much of its utility after the border moved west as a result of the Soviet invasion of Poland in September 1939. Supposedly, the line was partially dismantled and cannibalized to build new fortifications along the new border. However, the Soviets manned it with fortified regions and, in some sectors – the southwest – the line retained some defensive value.)[7] Reinhardt's XXXXI Panzer Corps seized crossings over the Western Dvina River from the Eighth Army on 30 June, while Manstein's LVI Panzer Corps expanded its bridgehead at Daugavpils.

Faced with looming disaster, on 30 June the *Stavka* shuffled the Front's senior command cadre, replacing Kuznetsov with Lieutenant-General P. P. Sobennikov, the Eighth Army commander, and appointing Lieutenant-General F. S. Ivanov in Sobennikov's stead. At the same time, it sent Lieutenant-General N. F. Vatutin, the Deputy Chief of the General Staff, who had played a vital role in preparing pre-war Soviet defence plans, to serve as Sobennikov's chief of staff, effective from 4 July. Vatutin's instructions were to restore order to the Front at all cost and actively resist the German advance. Meanwhile, the OKH ordered Leeb to advance through Pskov to Leningrad and Lake Ladoga to invest Leningrad. Hoepner's Fourth Panzer Group was to advance northerly or northeastwardly from Pskov, while Kuechler's and Busch's infantry cleared Soviet forces from Estonia and the Baltic coast and protected his right flank against attack from Nevel. Hours later, the OKH added the area between Velikie Luki and Lake Il'men to Hoepner's objectives, but ordered him not to advance further without special authorization.

Army Group North's Advance

Hoepner's panzer group advanced from the Dvina River on 2 July. Reinhardt's XXXXI Motorized Corps captured Ostrov on 4 July and Pskov on 8 July, crushing Soviet defences along the Stalin Line and entering the Leningrad region (*oblast*). To the south, Manstein's LVI Motorized Corps seized Rezekne on 3 July, but then became bogged down for days trying to traverse the nearby swamps, prompting Hoepner to transfer Manstein's 3rd Motorized Division to Reinhardt's corps. At the same time, Kuechler's Eighteenth Army spread into Latvia pushing back Ivanov's severely weakened Eighth Army and supported Reinhardt's panzers to the south, while Busch's Sixteenth Army supported Manstein's armour and protected the army group's right flank. By 6 July the border battles were over. Leeb's army group and Hoepner's panzers had pre-empted *Stavka* mobilization and defence plans, utterly defeated Kuznetsov's Northwestern Front, and advanced northeastwards through the Stalin Line. Leeb's army group now posed a deadly threat to Popov's Northern Front and to the great city of Leningrad itself.

Popov and his military council were acutely aware of the new threat, so much so that on 25 June they accepted General Piadyshev's proposed new defence line along the Luga River and appointed him to command the, as yet, phantom defence. This threat was not Popov's only worry, for enemy forces were threatening his front from Karelia in the north to the Baltic coast, where the Baltic Fleet was withdrawing to Tallin.[8]

Leeb's army group resumed its advance on 9 July. While Kuechler's Eighteenth Army cleared Soviet forces from Courland, Latvia and Estonia, Reinhardt's XXXXI Motorized Corps spread northwards from Pskov and Manstein's LVI Motorized Corps swept northeastwards towards Lake Il'men with Busch's Sixteenth Army protecting its right flank. Since they believed the Red Army was already defeated, Hitler and General Franz Halder, the OKH Chief of Staff, decided to retain the Third Panzer Group in Army Group Centre, only releasing its XXXIX Motorized Corps to Army Group North on 12 August.[9]

The Soviet defences they faced were shaky to say the least. The Northwestern Front's Eighth Army defended southern Estonia and its Eleventh and Twenty-Seventh Armies were withdrawing from what remained of the Stalin Line. Though Sobennikov's mission was to protect the approaches to Leningrad and Tallin, a huge gap existed in his front and most of his surviving divisions numbered less than 2000 men each. On 4 July Zhukov ordered Popov's Northern Front "to immediately occupy a defence line along the Narva-Luga-Staraia Russa-Borovichi front" to shore up the defences south of Leningrad, and, to help beef up his forces, assigned him the Baltic Fleet on 28 June and the Eighth Army on 14 July.[10]

Popov responded to Zhukov's order on 6 July by forming and deploying the Luga Operational Group

BELOW: A feature of Soviet cities was the public address system, which compensated for the lack of privately owned radios. This group, including a sailor of the Baltic Fleet, listens intently to Molotov's speech announcing the German invasion of the Soviet Union in June 1941.

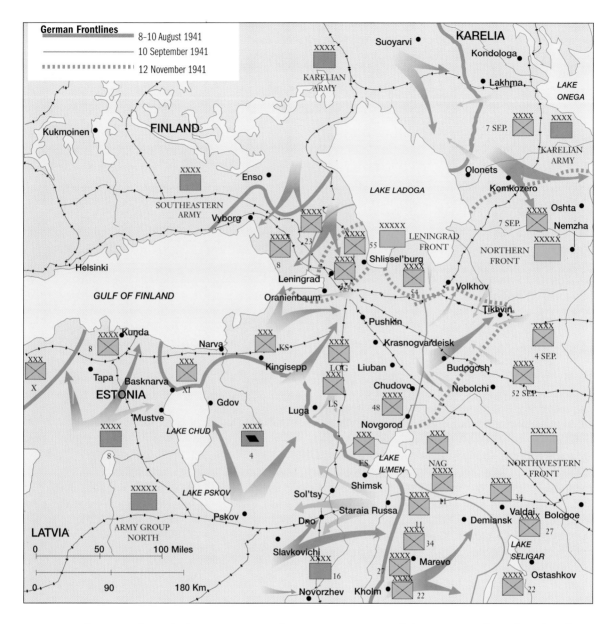

German Frontlines
— 8–10 August 1941
— 10 September 1941
▪▪▪▪▪▪▪▪▪▪▪▪ 12 November 1941

(LOG) with General Piadyshev in command.[11] When its initial forces occupied the line on 9 July, the group consisted of XXXXI Rifle Corps with four rifle divisions, two separate rifle divisions, one mountain rifle brigade, three militia divisions and several training school units.[12] During the next week additional forces filtered into the line and backed up Piadyshev's fragile force with X Mechanized Corps' 21st and 24th Tank Divisions in front reserve. The Northern Front's Rear Line Construction Directorate had begun building the Luga Line on 29 June, after halting all fortification work at Leningrad.[13] The line itself extended from the Gulf of Narva to Lake Il'men with a gap

ABOVE: German and Soviet operations during the Wehrmacht's approach to Leningrad, 10 July to 30 December 1941. Red Army attempts to halt the Germans were heroic but disastrous, as Soviet units were continually outflanked and surrounded by a more organized and mobile enemy.

between Luga and Krasnogvardeisk through which the Northwestern Front's forces could withdraw. Behind the first line and roughly 20–30km (12.5–18.75 miles) from the city itself was a second "outer circle" anchored on the Krasnogvardeisk Fortified Region, extending from Petergof through Krasnogvardeisk to Kolpino. A third line, which formed the city's inner defence, stretched along the railroad line from Avtovo to Rybatskoe on the Neva River. None of these lines, however, was heavily fortified. On 29 June, the *Stavka* approved Popov's request to form people's militia divisions (*diviziia narodnogo opolchanii* – DNO) to generate necessary defence forces. Within days the Northern Front began forming people's militia divisions and immediately dispatched them to the front so they could man the incomplete and fragile defences.

Hold Leningrad "at all Costs"

All of this frenzied activity to shore up Leningrad's defences reflected and was, in turn, effected by Stalin's determined efforts to rationalize Red Army command and control from Moscow. Between 30 June and 10 July, he established the State Defence Committee and, ultimately, the *Stavka* of the High Command to centralize control of operations.[14] Also on 10 July, Stalin ordered the People's Commissariat of Defence (NKO) to organize the Main Command of the Northwestern Direction to coordinate the Northern and Northwestern Fronts' and the Northern and Baltic Fleets' operations. Stalin appointed Marshal of the Soviet Union K. E. Voroshilov as the Main Command's Commander; A. A. Zhdanov, Secretary of the Communist Party's Central Committee and Leningrad Party Chief, as Member of the Military Council (Commissar); and Major-General M. V. Zakharov as Chief of Staff.

Beset by German offensives from north and south, Voroshilov reorganized command and control of the Main Command's forces southwest of Leningrad on 13 July. He transferred the battered Eighth Army and the Eleventh Army's XXXXI Rifle Corps from Northwestern to Northern Front control to help block the German advance on Leningrad, the former to defend Estonia and the latter to reinforce the LOG. The LOG was to defend the southwestern approaches to Leningrad on a 300km (187-mile) front from Narva to Lake Il'men. The Northwestern Front's Eleventh Army, newly formed Thirty-Fourth Army and Twenty-Seventh Army were to defend the Novgorod, Staraia Russa and Velikie Luki axes.[15] Voroshilov stiffened his soldiers' resolve by issuing Order No 3, dated 14 July, which demanded Red Army troops hold Leningrad "at all costs".

Hoepner's Fourth Panzer Group resumed its advance from the Pskov and Ostrov regions on 10 July. Reinhardt's XXXXI Motorized Corps advanced towards Kingisepp with XXXVIII Army Corps of Kuechler's Eighteenth Army in its wake. The corps' 1st and 6th Panzer Divisions pursued the

LOG's forces through Liady towards Luga and captured several small bridgeheads across the Luga River on 13 July. There, the panzer corps' advance stalled for six days in the face of fanatical resistance by the 2nd DNO and two companies of the Leningrad Red Banner Infantry School which Popov had hastily dispatched to that sector to stem the German tide. Reinhardt's panzers were within striking distance – 110km (68.75 miles) – of Leningrad, but could only strike if Manstein's powerful LVI Panzer Corps could provide assistance.

The Front Begins to Crumble

While Reinhardt's forces were marching victoriously towards the Luga River, Manstein's LVI Motorized Corps and the Eighteenth Army's I Army Corps advanced confidently eastwards towards Novgorod and Staraia Russa. The 8th Panzer Division, in LVI Motorized Corps' vanguard, made spectacular initial progress, penetrating 40km (25 miles) and reaching the town of Sol'tsy late on 13 July. There, however, the LOG's 177th Rifle Division and X Mechanized Corps, skillfully exploiting the difficult terrain, struck back at the 8th Panzer Division, isolating it from the 3rd Motorized Division to its left and the SS *Totenkopf* Division still lagging well to its rear. Only days before, an angry Stalin had scathingly criticized Voroshilov's conduct of the defence and ordered Vatutin, the Northwestern Front's new chief of staff, to savage the exposed German panzer force. Vatutin orchestrated a two-pronged assault on Sol'tsy from the north and east by two Northwestern Front shock groups.[16] The surprise Soviet assault forced the 8th Panzer Division to fight a costly battle of encirclement for four days. It also disrupted German offensive plans by forcing Hoepner to divert forces from the Kingisepp and Luga axes to rescue the 8th Panzer Division at Sol'tsy.[17]

Once the crisis at Sol'tsy was over, I Army Corps continued its advance, capturing Shimsk on 30 July.[18] The corps' determined advance forced the Eleventh Army's XXII Rifle Corps and the Twenty-Seventh Army to break contact and withdraw to the Staraia Russa-Kholm line. Busch's Sixteenth Army pursued, capturing Kholm on 2 August and Staraia Russa on 6 August, establishing a continuous front from Lake Il'men to Velikie Luki. Vatutin's counterstroke at Sol'tsy succeeded in delaying the German advance along the Luga Line for about three weeks. While Soviet critiques of the so-called Sol'tsy-Dno counterstroke recognize its impact on the German offensive timetable, they also lamented the attacking forces' poor command, control and coordination that prevented the operation from accomplishing far more.

After the Sol'tsy counterstroke failed, the *Stavka* demanded Voroshilov strengthen his Luga defences. Voroshilov then assembled a new reserve for the Luga Line, consisting of four rifle divisions and the 1st Tank Division sent southwards from northern Karelia. Within days, however, the Finnish advance in Karelia and the Eighteenth Army's attack into Estonia forced him to divert the four rifle divisions, leaving only the 1st Tank Division south of Krasnogvardeisk as a reserve.[19] On 15 July the *Stavka* also ordered Voroshilov to simplify his command structure by forming smaller forces that his commanders could more effectively control.[20] Popov did so on 23 July by relieving Piadyshev and splitting his LOG into the Kingisepp, Luga and Eastern Sectors, each responsible for its own defence.[21] At the same time, having determined that the Luga Line was wholly inadequate for defence, on 29 July Voroshilov ordered construction of the Krasnogvardeisk Fortified Region and subdivided it into the Krasnoe Selo, Central and Slutsk-Kolpino sectors. General Zaitsev, chief of the Northern Front's engineers, was to construct the fortified region with a new military-civilian Special Defence Works Commission, headed by A. A. Kuznetsov, the Leningrad Party chief who was responsible for constructing all defensive works in and around Leningrad. However, even this effort was inadequate, since Voroshilov objected to placing defences

so close to the city and insisted the work be concentrated on the Luga Line. Dissatisfied with the defensive effort, Stalin summoned Voroshilov and Zhdanov to Moscow on 30 July, where he sharply criticized them for "lack of toughness" in conducting operations in the Northwestern Theatre.

Meanwhile, the *Stavka* vigorously strengthened the defences south of Leningrad. On 6 August, it deployed the Thirty-Fourth Army with five rifle and two cavalry divisions, four artillery regiments and two armoured trains to the Northwestern Front, with instructions that it be employed as a single entity rather than be frittered away on peripheral operations.[22] The next day it dispatched the newly formed Forty-Eighth Army with four rifle and one tank division, one rifle brigade and a detachment of ships to operate on Lake Il'men to the Northwestern Front with orders that it protect the Northern Front's left flank north of Lake Il'men.[23]

During the second half of July, Hitler and the OKH formulated their final plans for the assault on Leningrad. Führer Directive No 33 dated 19 July ordered German forces to "prevent the escape of large enemy forces into the depths of the Russian territory and to annihilate them." A supplementary directive issued on 23 July reiterated Hitler's intention to capture Leningrad before marching on Moscow, and assigned the Third Panzer Group to Army Group North for the duration of the operation against Leningrad.[24] Shortly after, an OKW communiqué (*Sondermeldung*) expressed confidence that victory was at hand. Issued on 6 August, it lauded German achievements during the first six

RIGHT: As the threat of German air attacks became a reality, anti-aircraft artillery was positioned to protect the city. The Cruiser *Aurora*, seen here, as a potent symbol of the October Revolution, was a priority target for the Luftwaffe. As a result, its mooring on the Neva was well defended.

weeks of war, noting that Army Group North had cleared almost the entire Baltic States, broken through the Stalin Line, and occupied jumping-off positions along the Lake Il'men-Narva line for the offensive on Leningrad. According to the communiqué, Army Group North had taken or destroyed 35,000 prisoners, 355 tanks, 655 guns and 771 aircraft during this period.

Futile Counterattacks

Given this optimism, on 8 August Hitler declared he would soon reinforce Army Group North with XXXIX Motorized Corps from Army Group Centre and with VIII Air Corps, and ordered Leeb "to initiate the offensive on Leningrad, encircle the city, and link up with the Finnish Army." Leeb was to make his main attack between the Narva River and Lake Il'men on 9 August with XXXXI and LVI Motorized and XXXVII Army Corps, while I and XXVIII Army Corps of Busch's Sixteenth Army were to conduct a supporting attack south of Lake Il'men.[25] Leeb formed three groups to conduct the final offensive towards Leningrad. The Northern Group, with XXXXI Motorized and XXXVIII Army Corps, later reinforced by the 8th Panzer Division, was to attack towards Kingisepp and Leningrad from its Luga River bridgeheads.[26] The Luga Group, consisting of LVI Motorized Corps, with the 8th Panzer Division in reserve, was to attack through Luga towards Leningrad. Finally, the Southern Group, with I and XXVIII Army Corps, was to attack the Soviet Forty-Eighth Army along the Shimsk-Novgorod-Chudovo axis to envelop Leningrad from the east and sever its communications with Moscow.

While the bulk of his forces advanced on Leningrad, Leeb planned major operations on his flanks. On the left, five Eighteenth Army divisions were to advance on Narva, and the Eighteenth Army's XXXXII Army Corps was to clear Soviet forces from the Estonian coast and Tallin. On his right, the Sixteenth Army was to advance eastwards on a broad front south of Lake Il'men, defeat the Soviet Eleventh, Thirty-Fourth, Twenty-Seventh and Twenty-Second Armies, capture Staraia Russa and Velikie Luki and penetrate into the Valdai Hills to sever the vital Moscow-Leningrad railroad line.[27] Leeb and his subordinate armies retained only three security divisions in reserve.

Expecting the renewed German onslaught, on 9 and 10 August the *Stavka* ordered Voroshilov and Vatutin to mount yet another counterstroke. This

ABOVE: The Soviet battleship *Marat* under Luftwaffe attack at Kronshtadt naval base in September 1941. The aged warship, which had shelled German troops as they approached Leningrad on land, was finally sunk on 23 September by Junkers Ju 88 aircraft. Some 200 of her crew were killed or wounded.

time they were to employ the reinforcements provided to them by the *Stavka* in a counterstroke designed to destroy all German forces in the Sol'tsy, Staraia Russa and Dno regions. Planned by Vatutin, the so-called Staraia-Russa-Dno offensive operation required the Northwestern Front's Forty-Eighth, Thirty-Fourth, Eleventh and Twenty-Seventh Armies to conduct concentric attacks on 12 August against the Sixteenth Army's X Army Corps, which occupied an exposed position at Staraia Russa. The pincer attack by the Forty-Eighth Army towards Shimsk and Utorgosh west of Lake Il'men and by the Eleventh, Thirty-Fourth and Twenty-Seventh Armies south of the lake were designed to cut off and destroy the German X Corps and capture Sol'tsy and Dno, thereby disrupting the German advance on Leningrad.

Despite careful preparations, Vatutin's offensive achieved only fleeting success, primarily because the

ABOVE: General Erich Hoepner (centre), commander of the Fourth Panzer Group, watches the progress of his tanks during the opening phase of Barbarossa, the codename for the German attack on the Soviet Union. The officer on the right is General Georg-Hans Reinhardt, commander of XXXXI Panzer Corps.

Sixteenth Army pre-empted and disrupted the Forty-Eighth Army's attack by advancing on Novgorod on 10 August. Worse still for Vatutin, X Army Corps attacked eastwards from Staraia Russa, tying down much of the Eleventh Army's forces. Despite the unanticipated difficulties, the Thirty-Fourth Army, the remainder of Eleventh Army, and the Twenty-Seventh Army attacked early on 12 August. Although the Twenty-Seventh Army's advance faltered against German defences at Kholm, the Thirty-Fourth Army, spearheaded by the 202nd and 163rd Motorized and 25th Cavalry Divisions, thrust westward 40km (25 miles), reaching the Dno-Staraia Russa railroad line early on 14 August. The dramatic advance enveloped X Army Corps in Staraia Russa, separated it from II Army Corps on its right flank, and threatened the rear of the German main panzer force that was advancing on Novgorod.

Despite its auspicious beginning, however, the Soviet counterstroke soon floundered, in part because of the roadless terrain and in part due to the now familiar command and control problems. While the Eleventh Army attacked X Army Corps at Staraia Russa and the Thirty-Fourth Army threatened its communications to the southwest, on 14 August Leeb diverted the SS *Totenkopf* Motorized Division from the Novgorod axis to Dno with

orders to block the Soviet advance. He then transferred LVI Motorized Corps' headquarters and 3rd Motorized Division from the Luga sector, along with VIII Air Corps, to counterattack against the Thirty-Fourth Army late the next day. The counterattack was immediately successful. By 25 August LVI Motorized Corps had driven the Thirty-Fourth and Eleventh Armies back to the Lovat River line, capturing 18,000 Russians and capturing or destroying over 200 tanks, 300 guns and mortars, 36 anti-aircraft guns, 700 other vehicles, and the first Katiusha rocket launchers to fall intact into German hands.

Though Vatutin's counterstroke failed, it did adversely effect the subsequent German advance on Leningrad.[28] First, the increased Soviet resistance prompted the OKH to shift additional forces from Army Group Centre to Army Group North and accelerate transfer of XXXIX Motorized Corps northwards from Smolensk to reinforce the drive on Leningrad. Also, the diversion of LVI Motorized Corps to Staraia Russa seriously weakened and delayed the German advance on Leningrad and the fighting itself took a toll on German strength; by this time, Army Group North's losses stood at a massive 80,000 men.

Slaughter at Kingisepp

In a larger sense, the failed Soviet counterstroke at Staraia Russa also diverted forces from both Army Groups North and Centre away from the vital Leningrad axis by prompting the OKH to eliminate the threat south of Lake Il'men. On 24 August OKH ordered Army Group North's LVI Motorized, II and X Army Corps and Army Group Centre's LVII Motorized Corps to advance through Demiansk towards Valdai against the Soviet Eleventh, Thirty-Fourth and Twenty-Seventh Armies to support the offensive towards Novgorod. After rain delayed the attack for several days, LVII Motorized Corps' 19th Panzer Division finally attacked, capturing Demiansk on 31 August. To the south the corps' 20th Panzer Division and II Army Corps encircled a large Soviet force at Molvotitsy, approached Ostashkov, and closed the gap between Army Groups North and South. The OKW claimed that the operation destroyed the Eleventh, Thirty-Fourth and Twenty-Seventh Armies (18 divisions in all) and captured or destroyed 320 tanks, 659 guns and killed or captured 53,000 men during the month; and 117 tanks, 334 guns and 35,000 men during the operations in the Valdai Hills. After the operation ended, OKH ordered LVI and LVII Motorized Corps to join Army Group Centre's advance on Moscow.

While the Valdai diversion was tying down the better part of two panzer corps, Leeb's army group resumed its advance on Leningrad, achieving immediate success despite its setback at Staraia Russa. Reinhardt's XXXXI Motorized Corps, supported by XXXVIII Army Corps, began the assault along the Kingisepp-Krasnogvardeisk axis on 8 August in driving rain. His objective was the open country south of the Narva-Leningrad railroad, which his shock group, reinforced by the reserve 8th Panzer and 3rd Motorized Divisions, could use as a base to wheel eastwards towards Leningrad. Two days later, Manstein's LVI Motorized Corps and XXVIII Army Corps, attacked along the Luga and Novgorod axes towards the southern and south-eastern approaches to Leningrad.

XXXXI Motorized and XXXVIII Army Corps' 1st and 6th Panzer, 36th Motorized, and 1st Infantry Divisions penetrated the 2nd DNO's and 90th Rifle Divisions' defences along the Luga River at Kingisepp, Ivanovskoe and Bol'shoi Sabsk on 11 August. However, the three days of heavy fighting cost the attackers 1600 casualties.[29] The Germans then committed the 8th Panzer Division (detached from Manstein's corps), which lunged forward and severed the Kingisepp-Krasnogvardeisk railroad line the next day. XXXXI Motorized Corps then wheeled its main force eastwards towards Krasnogvardeisk, while the accompanying infantry launched a supporting attack westwards towards Kingisepp. Voroshilov reinforced the sagging defences in the Kingisepp sector with the 1st Tank Division and the 1st Guards DNO on 9 August, and the 281st Rifle Division on 13 August. At the same time, Popov occupied the Krasnogvardeisk Fortified Region with the 2nd and 3rd Guards DNOs on 17 August and the 291st Rifle Division on 18 August, and formed a Separate Aviation Group to centralize control of his Front's aircraft. The Kingisepp Group launched repeated counterattacks between 13 and 15 August, but they all failed. Beginning on 16 August, XXXXI Panzer Corps' 6th, 1st and 8th Panzer Divisions repeatedly assaulted Soviet positions along the approaches to the Krasnogvardeisk Fortified Region for six days, but failed to crack the Soviet defences. To the west, German infantry occupied Kingisepp on 16 August, forcing the Eighth Army to withdraw its five rifle divisions defending Kingisepp from the Narva region to the eastern bank of the Luga River on 21 August. The Eighth Army reported losing all of its regimental and battalion commanders and their staffs in the vicious fighting around Kingisepp.[30]

Unending Soviet Disasters

However, the German failure to destroy the Soviet forces at Narva and Kingisepp left a worn-down yet still sizeable force threatening the left flank of XXXXI Motorized Corps' forces attacking Krasnogvardeisk.[31] Consequently, Leeb ordered the motorized corps to postpone temporarily its assault on Krasnogvardeisk so that the Eighteenth Army's infantry could eliminate the threat and, at the same time, threaten Kronshtadt and Leningrad from the sea. XXVI and XXVIII Army Corps attacked between 22 and 25 August and, by 1 September, had forced the Eighth Army's forces to withdraw into a tight bridgehead south of Oranienbaum, which Soviet forces would retain until 1944. During the period from 21 August to 9 September, the Eighteenth Army reported it had captured 9774 prisoners and destroyed or captured 60 tanks and 77 guns.[32]

ABOVE: The Communist Party was an integral part of the Red Army at all levels. Here, Major-General A. L. Bondarev (right) confers with Regimental Commissar S. L. Alexandrov. The political officers, plus all Communist Party members, if captured by the Germans, were immediately executed.

While the forces on Leeb's left flank smashed the Northern Front's defences at Kingisepp and assaulted Krasnogvardeisk, Manstein's LVI Motorized Corps' 3rd Motorized Division and L Army Corps' 269th and SS Police Divisions began their assault along the Luga axis on 10 August. Simultaneously, XXVIII and I Army Corps attacked along the Novgorod axis on Manstein's right flank. The three corps tore through the LOG's and Forty-Eighth Army's partially prepared defences forward of Luga and Novgorod. After the 3rd Motorized Division was diverted to deal with the crisis at Staraia Russa, L Army Corps' 269th Infantry Division, reinforced by the 8th Panzer Division, broke into the Luga defence line and outflanked and captured Luga on 24 August after two weeks of very heavy fighting. The bag of captured men and hardware reached a reported 16,000 men, 51 tanks, 171 artillery pieces and 1000 vehicles.

At the same time, XXVIII and I Army Corps smashed the Forty-Eighth Army's defences along the Mshaga River on 10 August and had captured Shimsk by the 12th. After repelling Forty-Eighth Army counterattacks against its left flank between 13 and 15 August, XXVIII Army Corps swung to the northeast, outflanking the hapless Soviet defenders of Luga from the east. I Army Corps captured Novgorod on 16 August and raced northwards to capture Chudovo on 20 August, severing the Moscow-Leningrad railroad line and communications between the Forty-Eighth Army and the remainder of the Northwestern Front, whose offensive at Staraia Russa was by this time faltering. In two weeks of fighting, XXVIII and I Army Corps had taken 16,000 prisoners, destroyed or captured 74 tanks and 300 guns and reached the desolate terrain along the Volkhov River. General Akimov's Forty-Eighth Army was a wreck, with only 6235 men, and 5043 rifles and 31 artillery pieces remaining with which to defend the southeastern approaches to Leningrad.[33]

Faced with these disasters, on 23 August Voroshilov subordinated the Forty-Eighth Army to the Northern Front so that it could better coordinate its actions with other forces defending Leningrad, and ordered Akimov's withered army to defend the Gruzino-Liuban sector protecting the main axis into Leningrad from the southeast. The same day, the *Stavka* split Popov's Northern Front into the Leningrad Front under Popov's command and the Karelian Front under the command of Lieutenant-General V. A. Frolov. The new Leningrad Front assumed control of the Eighth, Twenty-Third and Forty-Eighth Armies, the Kopor, Southern and Slutsk-Kolpino Operational Groups, the Baltic Fleet, and Front air forces. The Karelian Front, which was responsible for operations north of Lake Ladoga, controlled the Seventh and Fourteenth Armies and the Northern Fleet.

The Germans Close In

Voroshilov also attempted to tighten up the Northwestern Command's organization for the defence of Leningrad by setting up a local council to deal with the existing crisis. However, Stalin intervened, forcing him to create the larger and more formal Military Council for the Defence of Leningrad under closer *Stavka* control. The new council's mission was to mobilize all the forces that would be necessary for the city's defences. Its members, by implication, would be held responsible for failing to do so. Council members included Voroshilov, Zhdanov, his commissar, Admiral N. G. Kuznetsov, the Naval Commissar, and others. To ensure stricter *Stavka* control, on 27 August the GKO abolished the Northwestern Direction High Command and merged its remnants into the Leningrad Front, which was still under Popov's command. In doing so, the GKO assumed direct control over the Karelian, Leningrad and Northwestern Fronts' operations. This directive, which was unique in Soviet wartime command and control, effectively ended Voroshilov's and Zhdanov's satrapy over military affairs at Leningrad. Voroshilov, who had displayed his military incompetence on far too many occasions prior to and during the war, would not feel the directive's full effects until almost two weeks later.

By late August German forces were pummelling Soviet defences at Krasnogvardeisk, only 40km (25

miles) southwest of Leningrad, and had reached Chudovo, on the main Leningrad-Moscow railroad line only 100km (62.5 miles) southeast of the city. Worse still, the *Stavka* feared that German forces advancing east of Leningrad might link up with Finnish forces and encircle the city. To protect against that eventuality, on 27 August it began deploying fresh forces along and east of the Volkhov River. These included the newly formed Fifty-Fourth and Fifty-Second Armies and, later, the Fourth Army, which were responsible for protecting the Volkhov axis and preventing German forces from advancing to Tikhvin and the Svir River and linking up with Finnish forces advancing eastwards through the Karelian Isthmus.[34] Finally, on 5 September the GKO appointed Voroshilov to command the Leningrad Front with Popov as his Chief of Staff, ostensibly to foster unity of command.

While the *Stavka* strove desperately to shore up its defences south and east of Leningrad, Leeb prepared to resume his offensive, intending to do so once the crisis at Staraia Russa had passed and after General Rudolf Schmidt's XXXIX Motorized Corps had arrived from Army Group Centre.[35] In the meantime, between 24 and 26 August he concentrated the Sixteenth Army's I and XXVIII Army Corps and XXXIX Motorized Corps in the Chudovo and Novgorod region with orders to penetrate into Leningrad from the southeast along the Leningrad-Moscow road.[36] While Schmidt's motorized corps was encircling Leningrad from the southeast, Hoepner's panzer group and Kuechler's Eighteenth Army were to attack Leningrad from the south and the west. To the south, the remainder of Busch's Sixteenth Army was to defend the army group's right flank along the Valdai Hills and Volkhov River.

A Chaotic Defence

The Leningrad Front's defences opposite the gathering German host were a shambles. The Eighth Army clung to defences west of Leningrad and the LOG attempted to man the Krasnogvardeisk Fortified Region, even though most of its XXXXI Rifle Corps was half encircled between Luga and south of Krasnogvardeisk. To the east, the threadbare Forty-Eighth Army defended the 40km (25–mile) sector from north of Chudovo, while the Northwestern Front's hastily assembled Novgorod Army Group (NAG) screened the Volkhov River north of Novgorod.[37]

XXXIX Motorized Corps, flanked on the left by XXVIII Corps' 121st, 122nd and 96th Infantry

Divisions, smashed through the Forty-Eighth Army's defences and captured Liuban on 25 August. Having uncovered the southeastern approaches to Leningrad, Schmidt's corps fanned out in three directions, the 18th Motorized Division northeastwards towards Kirishi, the 12th Panzer Division westwards towards Kolpino, and the 20th Motorized Division northwestwards towards Volkhov. The next day a frantic *Stavka* allocated the Leningrad Front four days' worth of Leningrad's tank production, four aviation regiments and 10 march battalions with which to reinforce its defences. Popov tried to plug the yawning gap that now existed southeast of Leningrad by reinforcing his Slutsk-Kolpino Group with the 168th Rifle Division, which was transferred from north of Lake Ladoga and the 4th DNO transferred from Krasnogvardeisk. He also ordered the Group and Forty-Eighth Army "to organize a strong defence and conduct counterattacks".

Closing the "Iron Ring"

Despite Popov's bravado, Schmidt's 12th Panzer and 20th Motorized Divisions, followed by the 121st, 96th and 122nd Infantry Divisions, raced forward towards Tosno and Mga Station, while the 18th Motorized Division advanced on Kirishi. The 20th Motorized Division captured Tosno and reached the Neva River at Ivanovskoe on 29 August, threatening to sever the last Leningrad railroad line to the east, and in the process splitting apart Soviet forces defending southeast of Leningrad. With his left flank split asunder, Popov inspected the Krasnogvardeisk Fortified Region and on 31 August requested and received *Stavka* permission to reorganize the region into two armies, the Fifty-Fifth to defend the western portion of the fortified region and the Forty-Second Army to defend its eastern portion.[38]

The reorganization simplified command and control of forces defending the area south of Leningrad, and in so doing significantly influenced the course and outcome of the battle for the city. After piercing the Forty-Eighth Army's defences east of Leningrad, XXVIII Army Corps wheeled westwards towards Leningrad proper. The corps' three infantry divisions, with the 12th Panzer in support, managed to drive the Fifty-Fifth Army back to the Izhora and Neva Rivers, in heavy fighting between 30 August and 8 September. However, three days of fierce fighting at Iam-Izhora forced the Germans to halt their advance on 9 September.

To the east, after seizing Chudovo and Liuban on 25 August, the two motorized divisions of Schmidt's XXXIX Motorized Corps attacked northeastwards towards Mga and the southern shore of Lake Ladoga, and towards Kirishi along the Volkhov River. They pummelled the weakened Forty-Eighth Army, forcing it to withdraw to the Mga-Kirishi line, and captured Mga on 29 August. Meanwhile, Popov ordered the Forty-Eighth Army to recapture Mga and counterattack on 6 September to drive the Germans southwards.[39] He reinforced the army with an NKVD Rifle Division formed from Karelian border guards, which managed to recapture Mga from the 20th Motorized Division on 30 August, and repelled several German assaults on Ivanovskoe and the mouth of the Mga River on 31 August.[40] However, the 20th Motorized Division recaptured Mga on 31 August, and after a week of heavy fighting, during which the 12th Panzer Division reinforced it, on 7 September it finally cracked the Forty-Eighth Army's defences south of Lake Ladoga. The 20th Motorized Division then captured Siniavino after heavy fighting on 7 September and occupied Shlissel'burg the next day. The NKVD Rifle Division withdrew to the Neva River and the 1st Separate Mountain Rifle Brigade to defences east of Siniavino. The OKW announced triumphantly in a communiqué that "the iron ring around Leningrad has been closed", signalling the beginning of the Leningrad blockade.

Fresh Slaughter for no Results

While the loss of Shlissel'burg was disastrous enough for Popov's Front as well as Leningrad's now besieged population, the presence of German forces within striking distance of Volkhov and Leningrad's communications with Moscow and the remainder of the country only served to worsen an already bad situation. Fortunately, Popov could console himself with two positive developments. The arrival of small reinforcements enabled the Neva Operational Group to hold firmly to its defences along the Neva River west of Shlissel'burg. Farther east, Marshal Kulik's new Fifty-Fourth Army, which the *Stavka* had just deployed forward to fill the gap between the Leningrad and Northwestern Fronts, now defended Volkhov and managed to halt the German advance east of Siniavino. However, an even greater Soviet disaster had occurred south of Leningrad.

The German advance on Krasnogvardeisk and the Forty-Eighth Army's loss of Chudovo and Tosno severed the LOG's communications and lines of

ABOVE: As the Germans tightened the noose around Leningrad, senior Wehrmacht officers sometimes made the trip to the frontline to assess the situation for themselves. Here, General Kruger and his adjutant survey the effects of a Luftwaffe air strike on a nearby village.

withdrawal to Leningrad. The Group abandoned Luga on 20 August and attempted to withdraw to Krasnogvardeisk, but was encircled and forced to cut its way out to the north and east in small parties. During their escape, the 8th Panzer, SS Police, 269th and 96th Infantry Divisions hounded the encircled forces unmercifully by constant converging attacks, inflicting estimated losses of roughly 30,000 men, 120 tanks and 400 guns on the beleaguered Soviet force.[41]

The capture of Shlissel'burg on 9 September gave the Germans total control over all of Leningrad's ground communications with the remainder of the country. Henceforth, re-supply of the city was possible only via Lake Ladoga or by air. While these harsh realities convinced the *Stavka* and the Leningrad Front that the fight for Leningrad was fast approaching its climax, most in the German leadership felt the climax had passed and the city was theirs for the taking. On 5 September Halder wrote in his diary: "Leningrad: Our objective has

been achieved. Will now become a subsidiary theatre of operations." Given these strategic perceptions, Hitler decided to prevent unnecessary casualties, avoiding an assault on a city that was already doomed. Enticed by new opportunities in Army Group Centre's sector, he ordered Leeb to encircle and starve out Leningrad rather than seize it by frontal assault. Führer Directive No 35, dated 6 September, ordered Army Group Centre to embark on its Moscow adventure:

"The initial successes in operations against enemy forces located between the adjoining flanks of Army Groups South and Centre, combined with further successes in the encirclement of enemy forces in the Leningrad region, have created prerequisites for the conduct of a decisive operation against Army Group Timoshenko, which is unsuccessfully conducting offensive operations in front of Army Group Centre. It must be destroyed decisively before the onset of winter within the limited time indicated in existing orders."

The Finnish Dimension

Within the context of Operation Typhoon, Leeb's orders were:

"To encircle enemy forces operating in the Leningrad region ... in cooperation with Finnish forces so that a considerable number of the mobile and First Air Fleet formations, particularly VIII Air Corps, can be transferred to Army Group Centre no later than 15 September."[42]

On 4 September, Germans forces began shelling Leningrad daily with 240mm guns from the region north of Tosno, and, four days later, German aircraft began pounding the city with daylight air raids. In response, the *Stavka* ordered the Leningrad Front to form the Ladoga PVO (Air Defence) Brigade Region.

Finnish Army operations on the Karelian Isthmus and to the north further complicated the Soviet defence of Leningrad. Although the Finns were supposed to help capture Leningrad, from 22 June to 10 July they conducted only limited-objective operations, and after 10 July they limited their operations to the sector west of Lakes Onega and Ladoga against the Soviet Seventh Army. Beginning on 31 July, however, Finnish forces attacked the Leningrad Front's Twenty-Third Army defending the Karelian Isthmus, forcing the army to withdraw to new defensive positions astride the isthmus only 30km (18.75 miles) from Leningrad's northern defences. Although the Finns advanced no further, the mere

LEFT: This hastily constructed defence line on the outskirts of Leningrad is manned by infantrymen drawn from the city's garrison. Movement is clearly a risky business, as the men crouching and scampering at the back of the trench demonstrate!

threat of a Finnish attack adversely affected the Leningrad Front's defence in other sectors. For example, at a time when Popov most needed reserves, Finnish operations forced him to transfer the 265th Rifle Division, the Forty-Eighth Army's reserve, and the 291st Rifle Division from the Krasnogvardeisk Fortified Region to bolster the Twenty-Third Army's defence against the Finns.

At the end of the first week of September, the Wehrmacht began operations to isolate and destroy Leningrad. As anti-climactic as it seemed to the Germans, no Russians doubted the battle was at its climax.

Following Hitler's directive, Leeb formulated a plan to encircle Leningrad by sealing off all access routes to it from both east and west. Leeb's original plan called for Hoepner's panzer group to establish a tight inner encirclement line around the city with Reinhardt's and Schmidt's XXXXI and XXXIX Motorized Corps, while Kuechler's Eighteenth Army formed a broader encirclement line extending from Koporskii Bay to Lake Ladoga.[43] However, Hitler's directive ordered Leeb to transfer XXXXI, LVI and LVII Motorized, plus VIII Air Corps, to Army Group Centre, effective 15 September, leaving the field marshal only XXXIX Motorized Corps and, as a later concession, the 8th Panzer Division. Given these realities, Leeb decided to conduct a wider encirclement of the city with XXXIX Motorized Corps, leaving the Eighteenth Army the broad sector south and west of Leningrad. Before it

departed to Army Group Centre, however, XXXXI Motorized Corps would spearhead the advance on Leningrad from the southwest.

On 29 August Leeb ordered his forces to conduct a "wide encirclement of Leningrad" by capturing bridgeheads over the Neva and the towns of Uritsk, Pulkovo, Pushkin (Detskoe Selo), Kolpino and Izhora, and establish a tight ring around the city before the Fourth Panzer Group departed. Leeb organized his attacking forces into two groups: the Krasnogvardeisk and Slutsk-Kolpino Groups. The former consisted of XXXVIII and L Army and XXXXI Motorized Corps, deployed with the 1st and 6th Panzer, and 36th Motorized Divisions in the centre, XXXVIII Army Corps on the left, and the L Army Corps on the right.[44] The 8th Panzer Division, which was refitting after suffering heavy losses the previous month, was in reserve. This group was to capture Krasnogvardeisk, Krasnoe Selo and Uritsk, reach the coast of the Gulf of Finland and isolate Soviet forces west of Leningrad from the city. The Slutsk-Kolpino Group, under Hoepner's command and consisting of XXVIII Army Corps and elements of the 12th Panzer Division, was to penetrate Soviet defences along the Izhora River and capture Slutsk and Kolpino.[45] Farther east, XXXIX Motorized Corps' 20th Motorized Division and the 12th Panzer Division's main force were to widen the corridor to Shlissel'burg and Lake Ladoga, screen the Neva River on its left flank, and drive Soviet forces eastwards from Siniavino.

Voroshilov's Eighth, Forty-Second and Fifty-Fifth Armies defended the southern approaches to Leningrad. Lieutenant-General F. S. Ivanov's Forty-Second Army manned the Krasnogvardeisk Fortified Region from Krasnoe Selo to Pustoshka with two divisions and one fortified region.[46] Major-General of Tank Forces I. G. Lazarov's Fifty-Fifth Army defended the Slutsk-Kolpino Fortified Region from Pustoshka to the Neva River with six divisions, one fortified region and two tank battalions.[47] Finally, Major-General V. I. Shcherbakov's Eighth Army defended the coastal sector west of the city with six weak divisions, four of which were deployed along the main German attack axis.[48] Voroshilov retained the 10th and 16th Rifle Divisions, 5th DNO, the 8th Rifle and 1st Naval Infantry Brigade and the 48th Tank Battalion, and the 500th Rifle Regiment in reserve.[49] On 11 September, the Leningrad Front's strength was 452,000 men, about two-thirds of whom were deployed south of Leningrad facing an equal number of Germans. East of the Shlissel'burg corridor, the 85,000-man Fifty-Fourth Army was assembling at Volkhov, in the rear of the decimated Forty-Eighth Army.[50]

XXXXI Motorized and XXXVIII Army Corps began their assault towards Krasnogvardeisk, Krasnoe Selo and Uritsk early on 9 September. The 36th Motorized Division quickly penetrated the 3rd DNO's defence and advanced 10km (6.25 miles) before being halted by heavy artillery fire late in the day. The day before, the Luftwaffe had begun three days of heavy bombardment against the city to supplement the heavy shelling that had begun on 1 September. The artillery fire's effectiveness, however, was limited since it could not hit the heart of the city. The Luftwaffe dropped 8000 incendiary bombs during the air strikes, causing heavy damage and many fires and destroying the Badaevskii Warehouses where most of Leningrad's foodstuffs were stored.

In response, Voroshilov ordered Ivanov's Forty-Second Army to fire a strong artillery counter-preparation on 10 September and counterattack vigorously with the 3rd DNO. However, XXXXI Motorized Corps committed the 1st Panzer Division to combat late on 10 September, and it punched its way through to the Krasnogvardeisk-Krasnoe Selo road, forcing the 3rd DNO to withdraw northwards. It soon became clear, however, that reinforcements would be necessary to overcome the

BELOW: The Imperial Russian Army had always prided itself on the bravery and efficiency of its artillery arm, and that tradition was maintained in the Red Army. These two howitzers are preparing to fire in support of an armoured attack on the German besiegers.

ABOVE: The conversion of this department store on the Starinevski Prospect into a defensive position demonstrates the architecture and layout of Leningrad: wide, straight avenues, tall, solidly built buildings. These civilian labourers, including women, are working under the supervision of an army engineer section.

Forty-Second Army's well-prepared defences. Since the 6th Panzer Division was engaged in heavy fighting for Krasnoe Selo, Leeb reinforced the 1st Panzer Division with a single tank battalion rather than the entire 8th Panzer Division.[51] At the same time, an increasingly desperate Voroshilov committed his last reserves into battle. Despite the reinforcements, the 1st Panzer Division captured Dudergov on 11 September and Krasnoe Selo on 12 September, but was then halted at Pulkovo after reaching Leningrad's southwestern suburbs.[52] The way was now open for L Army Corps to exploit towards Slutsk and Pushkin and link up with XXVIII Army Corps, which was attacking Pushkin from the east.

The fighting intensified on 12 September when the 1st Panzer and 36th Motorized Divisions outflanked the Forty-Second Army's defences at Krasnogvardeisk, threatening the rear of the Fifty-Fifth Army's forces defending Slutsk and Kolpino. Once again, however, German reinforcements were not available since the 8th Panzer Division was still reorganizing and was unable to exploit the motorized corps' success. Worse still for Leeb, the Fifty-Fifth Army then halted XXVIII Army Corps' advance on Slutsk.[53] As a result, Voroshilov transferred the forces defending Krasnogvardeisk to Fifty-Fifth Army control and ordered Lazarov's

army to defend Pushkin, Krasnogvardeisk and Kolpino at all cost. Leeb now faced a dilemma, in part caused by faulty command and control. The sad fact was that Hoepner could not control Kuechler's corps on the left, or Schmidt's group on the right, nor, as it turned out, his only reserve, the 8th Panzer Division. Furthermore, the attack was not synchronized since L Corps, which was still struggling north of Luga, was not ready in time. Finally, Leeb transferred the 254th Infantry Division, which should have reinforced Reinhardt's panzer corps, to Kuechler. "Such disarray was serious and could have jeopardized the operation if the Russians themselves had not also reached the end of their tether."[54]

Compounding Leeb's dilemma, the OKH's 10 September order transferring Reinhardt's XXXXI Motorized Corps to Army Group Centre "in good condition" finally arrived. At the same time, Schmidt reported that the Soviet Fifty-Fourth Army and a cavalry division threatened his right flank.[55]

Leeb dispatched the 8th Panzer Division to assist Schmidt's corps and the fresh 254th Infantry Division to the Eighteenth Army to fill the gap once Reinhardt's corps had departed.[56] On 13 September XXVIII Army Corps was to advance westwards towards Pushkin, Slutsk and Marino and the 6th Panzer Division was to attack Pushkin from the west. After regrouping to permit the infantry to catch up, the rest of Reinhardt's corps was to spearhead one final attempt to breech Leningrad's defences south of the Pushkin-Petergof road with XXXVIII Army Corps on its left and L Army Corps on its right.

Stalin Reorganizes the Defence

With the German noose around Leningrad tightening, a dissatisfied Stalin made wholesale changes to the Leningrad Front's command structure. On 10 September he appointed Army General G. K. Zhukov to command the Front in place of the hapless Voroshilov, whose incompetence was becoming more evident each day. Stalin was particularly angry over Voroshilov's failure to inform him about the fall of Shlissel'burg, a fact which Stalin first read about in a German communiqué. Stalin also learned of the Leningrad Military Council's decision to demolish Leningrad's military installations in anticipation of the city's fall to the Germans. While meeting with Admiral Kuznetsov, whom he had summoned to Moscow to prepare preliminary instructions for scuttling the Baltic Fleet, Stalin admitted: "It is possible that it (Leningrad) may have to be abandoned." Before Zhukov's departure to Leningrad, Stalin informed him, "It is an almost hopeless situation. By taking Leningrad and joining up with the Finns the Germans can strike Moscow from the northeast and then the situation will become even more critical." Handing Zhukov a slip of paper, Stalin said, "Give this to Voroshilov." The paper read, "Hand over command of the Front to Zhukov and fly back to Moscow immediately."[57]

Stalin also disbanded the Leningrad Front's Forty-Eighth Army, which the advancing Germans had already demolished in any case, and, on 12 September, assigned its forces to Kulik's new Fifty-Fourth Army, then assembling at Volkhov. Stalin ordered Kulik to restore the broken front south of Lake Ladoga, while the Fourth and Fifty-Second Armies defended the Volkhov River line southwards to Lake Il'men. Zhukov, together with Major-Generals I. I. Fediuninsky and M. S. Khozin, trusted lieutenants from his Khalkhin-Gol days, arrived in Leningrad on 13 September and assumed command of the Leningrad Front. He immediately appointed Khozin as his chief of staff, established a new headquarters at the famed Smolny Institute, and suspended the Military Council's plans to demolish Leningrad, even though the *Stavka* reiterated the instructions several days later. The Military Council then ordered its forces "not a step back" under penalty of being shot.[58] The situation was indeed dangerous by the time Zhukov reached Leningrad: German forces had captured Krasnoe Selo, broken into the Krasnogvardeisk Fortified Region and advanced to Uritsk, less than 10km (6.25 miles) from Petergof and Strel'na on the coast. South of the city, they had reached the outskirts of Pulkovo and Pushkin, only 12–18km (7.5–11.25 miles) from the city's outskirts, and to the east they were threatening to capture Volkhov and link up with the Finns. Convinced that the greatest threat existed in the Uritsk and Pulkovo sectors, Zhukov reinforced these areas and ordered relentless counterattacks to blunt the German advance.

Desperate Counterattacks

Leeb resumed his advance on Uritsk and Krasnogvardeisk on 13 September, the same day that Zhukov arrived in Leningrad. XXXXI Motorized and XXXVIII Army Corps' 58th and 1st Infantry, 1st Panzer and 36th Motorized Divisions penetrated the Forty-Second Army's defences north of Krasnoe Selo and approached Uritsk, causing a crisis in the Forty-Second Army. Zhukov reinforced the Forty-Second Army with the 10th and 11th Rifle Divisions, which launched desperate counterattacks.[59] The next day, Zhukov issued new orders designed to regain the initiative. While the Fifty-Fifth Army was stubbornly defending Pushkin, Krasnogvardeisk and Kolpino, the front was to "smother the enemy with artillery and mortar fire and air attacks, allowing no penetration of the defences." At the same time, it was "to form five rifle brigades and two rifle divisions by 18 September and concentrate them in four defence lines for the immediate defence of Leningrad." Most importantly, he ordered Shcherbakov's Eighth Army "to strike the enemy in the flank and rear" and Kulik's Fifty-Fourth Army "to liberate the Mga and Shlissel'burg regions." By this time, XXXXI Motorized and XXXVIII Army Corps' five Eighth and 1st Infantry, 1st Panzer and 36th Motorized Divisions had driven the Forty-Second Army's forces to the outskirts of Uritsk, only 4km (2.5

ABOVE: Adolf Hitler was determined to eradicate Leningrad from the face of the earth. On 8 November 1941, as his forces tightened the noose around the city, he declared: "Leningrad's hands are in the air. It falls sooner or later. No one can free it. No one can break the ring. Leningrad is doomed to die of famine."

miles) from the coast.[60] In desperation, Zhukov backed up Ivanov's army with the newly formed 21st NKVD Rifle Division, the 6th DNO, two naval rifle brigades and PVO troops, which, on 16 September, occupied an army second echelon defence line south of Leningrad from the Gulf of Finland to the Neva River.[61] Zhukov himself forbade commanders from removing forces from this line without his express permission, and Stalin reinforced Zhukov's prohibition by issuing a Draconian order of his own dealing mercilessly with "saboteurs and German sympathizers" who retreated without authorization.

Zhukov sent Fediuninsky to investigate the situation in the Forty-Second Army, but when he arrived at army headquarters he found General Ivanov sitting with his head in his hands, unable to report where his troops were located. Major-General Larionov, Ivanov's chief of staff, reported that the Forty-Second Army was holding "literally by a miracle". Ivanov requested permission to move his headquarters to the rear, but Fediuninsky cate-

gorically refused. Fediuninsky reported to Zhukov that morale in the Forty-Second, as well as the Eighth and Fifty-Fifth Armies, was cracking. Learning also that Ivanov had relocated his headquarters to a safer position further behind the lines in the basement of the Kirov factory, Zhukov ordered Fediuninsky to "Take over the Forty-Second Army – and quickly."[62]

Zhukov's 14 September attack order was based on his perception that the Germans' precipitous advance to Uritsk had exposed their left flank which was pounding the Forty-Second Army, leaving it vulnerable to a flank attack. His intention, therefore, was to catch the German force advancing towards Uritsk between the hammer of the Eighth Army and the anvil of the Forty-Second Army. Shcherbakov's Eighth Army was to attack towards Krasnoe Selo against the German force's left flank with five rifle divisions.[63] When Shcherbakov demurred, claiming that his force was too weak to launch the counterattack, Zhukov relieved him on the spot together with his commissar, I. F. Chukhnov, and appointed Lieutenant-General T. I. Shevaldin to command the army.

Zhukov Slows the Germans

However, the Germans foiled Zhukov's plan by pre-empting the Eighth Army's counterattack. On 16 September their XXXXI Motorized and XXXVIII Army Corps' 58th Infantry and 1st Panzer Divisions, reinforced by the 254th Infantry Division, attacked and defeated the Eighth Army before it had completed its regrouping for its counterattack towards Krasnoe Selo. The three attacking German divisions had captured Uritsk, Petergov and Strel'na by nightfall, reaching the Gulf of Finland and isolating the Eighth Army in the so-called Oranienbaum Pocket, cutting it off from Leningrad proper. However, Fediuninsky's Forty-Second Army was able to stabilize its defences along the Ligovo, Nizhnoe Koirovo and Pulkovo line, even though heavy fighting raged in the sector until 30 September.

Undeterred by the setback and whipped on by Zhukov, Shevaldin, the Eighth Army's new commander, had completed regrouping his forces on 18 September and now attacked towards Krasnoe Selo with four rifle divisions the next day. XXXVIII Army Corps struck back on 20 September, halting the Eighth Army and sending it reeling back to a new defence line where the front stabilized once and for all.[64]

While heavy fighting raged along the Uritsk axis, Leeb began a two-pronged assault on the Soviets' vital Krasnogvardeisk and Pushkin strongpoints. His intention was to destroy the Fifty-Fifth Army's main force in the Krasnogvardeisk, Slutsk and Pushkin region by concentric attacks from east and west and then smash the Forty-Second Army's left flank and open the door to Leningrad. On 12 September, XXXXI Motorized Corps' 6th Panzer Division and L Army Corps' SS Police and 169th Infantry Divisions attacked eastwards towards Krasnogvardeisk and Pushkin. Simultaneously, XXVIII Army Corps' 96th and 121st Infantry Divisions attacked westwards from the Izhora River towards Slutsk and Pushkin.[65] The two attacking German forces captured Krasnogvardeisk on 13 September, but then became bogged down for three days in fierce fighting for possession of the Slutsk-Kolpino Fortified Region. During the fighting, on 14 September soldiers of the SS Police Division reportedly found the dead bodies of General Ivanov, the former Forty-Second Army commander, and his commissar in a bunker (both were actually captured).

The 1st Panzer and SS Police Divisions finally captured Pushkin late on 17 September, and XXVIII Army Corps captured Slutsk the following day, forcing the Fifty-Fifth Army to withdraw to new defences at Pulkovo, Bol'shoe Kuz'mino, Novaia and Putrolovo. In one final desperate lunge, the 1st Panzer Division reached Pulkovo crossroads and Aleksandrovka, the terminus of the Leningrad southwest tram line only 12km (7.5 miles) from the city's centre, but failed to seize Pulkovo Heights. During the fighting, Soviet troops drove into combat tanks that had just left the Kolpino tank factory assembly line. The determined German assault ground to a halt on the bloody southern slopes of the Pulkovo Heights, even though the fighting lasted until 30 September. While the tenacious Soviet defence of Pulkovo Heights convinced Leeb to halt his advance, the scheduled redeployment of XXXXI Motorized Corps, which he dreaded so much, was the most important factor.[66] Although the ground action waned, the Luftwaffe commenced a massive and furious air offensive against the Baltic Fleet and Kronshtadt from 21 to 23 September.

By the end of September, Leeb had indeed hemmed in Zhukov's forces at Leningrad, but not as

BELOW: These warmly clad, apparently well-fed ladies are taking tea in their factory canteen. This picture is typical of those taken to show the Soviet people that, although under blockade, life went on. There even appears to be a "fancy pastry" in the background!

tightly as he and the OKH had wished. Although German forces had dented Soviet defences, Zhukov's defences in the city's southern suburbs and along the Neva River remained intact, and the Finns had yet to attack. Militarily, the "Miracle on the Neva" had occurred, largely due to Zhukov's iron hand, and it was clear to all that Leeb had lost his best opportunity to seize Leningrad. Worse still, from Leeb's perspective, Zhukov did not rest on his defensive laurels. Instead, no sooner had he contained the German assaults than he set about exacting an even greater toll on Leningrad's tormentors, by conducting an offensive of his own. Adding steel to Zhukov's intent, the *Stavka* ordered Marshal Kulik's Fifty-Fourth Army, still operating under its direct control, and Zhukov's Neva Operational Group (NOG) to launch converging attacks towards Siniavino and Mga in an effort to raise the Leningrad blockade.[67]

Kulik's army attacked on 10 September but advanced only 6–10km (3.75–6.25 miles) in 16 days of off-and-on heavy fighting, during which both Zhukov and the *Stavka* repeatedly castigated Kulik for his army's dismal performance.

Ultimately, Schmidt's XXXIX Motorized Corps counterattacked and forced Kulik's forces to withdraw from the Mga-Kirishi railroad line to defensive positions eastwards along the Nasiia River. Both Zhukov and the *Stavka* were angered enough by Kulik's failure to remove him from command and replaced him with another of Zhukov's protégés, General Khozin.[68] While Kulik's ineptly led army faltered, the Neva Operational Group's 115th Rifle Division and 4th Naval Infantry Brigade crossed the Neva River on 20 September and seized a small bridgehead in the Moskovskaia Dubrovka region on the river's left bank, but accomplished little more. Although Zhukov's so-called first Siniavino offensive failed, it did produce some positive results from the Soviets' perspective by forcing the Germans to transfer forces to the Leningrad region and by delaying somewhat the transfer of

BELOW: Troops of Leeb's Army Group North take cover behind a panzer during the advance towards Leningrad. At first, the speed of the Blitzkrieg swept all before it. Some Red Army mechanized units, for example, reported losses of up to 90 percent in manpower and vehicles.

XXXIX Motorized Corps southwards to reinforce Army Group Centre.[69]

After the fighting in the Leningrad region petered out in late September, the front stabilized temporarily. Despite the spectacular gains it had registered since its forces crossed the Western Dvina River in early July, Army Group North had suffered 60,000 losses.[70] However, Leningrad's badly organized, trained and equipped defenders lost far more. The Northern Front reported 55,535 casualties between 10 July and 23 August out of 153,000 men engaged, and the Leningrad Front 116,316 casualties from 23 August to 30 September out of 300,000 engaged. Finally, the Northwestern Front casualty toll between 10 July and 30 September added another 144,788 men out of 272,000 engaged. By any count, the opposing forces were exhausted. Nevertheless, as they licked their wounds and counted their casualties, both sides prepared to resume operations, driven by the knowledge that Army Group North had not achieved the objectives Hitler had assigned it in Plan Barbarossa. Inevitably, this fact alone meant that the struggle would have to continue.

Leeb Runs Out of Momentum

Unfortunately for Leeb, the resources with which he would have to continue the struggle also dwindled. Beginning on 15 September, XXXXI, LVI, LVII Motorized and VIII Air Corps departed for Army Group Centre to take part in Operation Typhoon.[71] Only Schmidt's XXXIX Motorized Corps (the 12th Panzer, and 18th and 20th Motorized Divisions) and, as a later concession, the 8th Panzer Division, remained to provide his army group with armour support.[72] Leeb deployed the 254th Infantry Division from the Oranienbaum bridgehead to shore up the defences on XXXIX Motorized Corps' left flank. Then, on 24 September, he reported candidly to OKH that the situation had "worsened considerably", he could no longer continue offensive operations towards Leningrad, and his forces had no other choice but to go on to the defensive, a declaration that Hitler could not accept.[73]

The Red Army's defence along the southwestern approaches to Leningrad lasted from 10 July to 30 September. Thereafter, the front south of Leningrad stabilized and remained stable until January 1943.[74] During the 50 days of often-desperate and costly defence, the Red Army disrupted Hitler's plan to seize Leningrad by concentric blows from the south and north. Combat steadily intensified as the Red Army increased its resistance and began conducting counterstrokes of its own. As a result, the tempo of the German advance decreased from a rate of advance of 5km (3.1 miles) per day in July, to 2.2km (1.7 miles) per day in August, and 1.4km (.87 miles) per day in September. The Red Army improved its defensive forces and techniques as the offensive developed, largely because it adopted extraordinary and sometimes even Draconian mobilization measures and committed virtually all of its manpower reserves to combat. During July and August, it raised and fielded seven militia rifle divisions and an NKVD Rifle Division and was reinforced by four rifle divisions dispatched by the *Stavka*.

The strength and complexity of the German offensive also increased as the offensive developed. In July, Army Group North and its Finnish Allies attacked simultaneously along the Petrozavodsk, Olonets and Leningrad axes. In mid-August the Germans penetrated Soviet defences along the Novgorod axis, cut off and isolated much of the Eighth Army in Estonia, and attacked simultaneously along the Krasnogvardeisk and Karelian Isthmus axes. In late August and early September, German forces attacked simultaneously along the Mga, Krasnogvardeisk and Karelian axes. During this period, the Red Army experienced major difficulties in mounting large-scale counterstrokes even though it tried to do so at Sol'tsy and Staraia Russa. Intentionally or not, these and other counterstrokes achieved very little other than delaying the German advance. Even though the Red Army managed to halt the German juggernaut on Leningrad's doorstep and forced the Germans to abandon their attempts to capture the city by direct attack, at the end of September the city remained in mortal danger of being encircled and destroyed.

No doubt existed on either side regarding German intentions. A German directive issued on 22 September read:

"The Führer has decided to erase the city of Petersburg from the face of the earth. I have no interest in the further existence of this large city after the defeat of Soviet Russia ... We propose to blockade the city tightly and erase it from the earth by means of artillery fire and continuous bombardment from the air."

Nor did the German artillery and air bombardment that began in late August diminish. And driven by ambition, frustration and sheer hatred, Hitler would force Army Group North to make one last major effort to encircle Leningrad before the onset of winter.

CHAPTER 3:
THE ENCIRCLEMENT STRUGGLE

As Army Group North neared Leningrad, it looked as though the city would fall into German hands. However, though the Red Army's Siniavino Offensive of October 1941 failed to stop the Germans, it did slow their advance. Then, the Tikhvin Counteroffensive of November and December 1941 saved the city from encirclement and brought an exhausted Army Group North to a standstill.

As the heat of summer gave way to the chill of fall in northern Russia, for the first time in the war, German forces in the Leningrad region found themselves playing second fiddle to more momentous developments elsewhere along the Eastern Front. Hitler's Directive No 35 had abruptly shifted the focus of Operation Barbarossa away from Leningrad and towards Moscow, and Leeb's September attempt to encircle the city had failed. Hitler, however, had not abandoned Leningrad as a target of his wrath. Instead, grudgingly admitting that the city's conquest would be far more difficult than originally intended, he turned to Moscow as a far more lucrative and achieveable goal, leaving the task of encircling Leningrad to the bewildered Leeb.

Leeb had to do so in deteriorating weather and without the Fourth Panzer Group, on which he was

LEFT: The PTRD 14.5mm antitank rifle used by the Red Army was of little value when pitted against the medium and heavy tanks of the Wehrmacht. However, in the hands of an expert, when used against soft-skinned vehicles this cumbersome, single-shot weapon could be deadly.

accustomed to rely. By early October, Leeb's army group fielded 53 divisions (including two panzer and two motorized) and seven brigades along the northwestern axis, half of which were deployed with the Eighteenth Army in the Leningrad region. Having already informed Hitler that his forces were in no state to conduct major offensive operations, a debate ensued over what sort of limited offensive Army Group North could conduct before consolidating its positions for the winter. Leeb suggested two options. He could either eliminate the Soviets' bridgehead at Oranienbaum, or he could advance east and northeast from Chudovo or Kirishi to Tikhvin or Volkhov to block the Soviets' remaining access route to Leningrad and, perhaps, link up with the Finns. Leeb chose a lesser variant of the latter, specifically, a limited attack with Schmidt's XXXIX Motorized Corps, reinforced by infantry, northwards from Kirishi to Volkhov to dislodge and perhaps destroy the Soviet Fifty-Fourth Army. He proposed the offensive should begin on 6 October.

Hitler, however, rejected Leeb's proposal on the grounds that his attack would traverse poor terrain unsuited for armoured operations. Instead, he ordered Leeb to advance northeastwards from Chudovo to Tikhvin and then northwestwards along the road and railroad to Volkhov to encircle the Fifty-Fourth Army. This offensive projected German forces twice as far as the operation proposed by Leeb and required greater forces than the field marshal possessed. Leeb reluctantly ordered Schmidt's XXXIX Motorized Corps to conduct the main attack from Chudovo to Tikhvin on 16 October, while infantry conducted a secondary attack northwards from Kirishi towards Volkhov. Ultimately, the two forces were to capture Volkhov and cut the remaining railroad line to Lake Ladoga.

The Red Army Stretched Thin

Stalin was also concerned about the situation on the northern flank, particularly as it related to the Wehrmacht's thrust towards Moscow that began in early October. His intent was to defend Leningrad, attack to raise the blockade of the city, prevent the Germans from transferring forces from Leningrad to the Moscow axis, and block any German attempt to link up with the Finns and completely encircle Leningrad. Days after the Germans began their advance on Moscow, on 5 October Stalin recalled Zhukov to Moscow to take command of the crumbling Western and Reserve Fronts. Zhukov turned temporary command of the Leningrad Front over to his favourite, Fediuninsky, and flew to Moscow the following day. Several days later, Stalin dispatched Colonel-General N. N. Voronov, a Deputy People's Commissar of Defence and Chief of Red Army Air Defence (PVO) to the city as his representative with orders to prepare an operation to raise the blockade of the city. The most important question confronting Stalin, Voronov and Fediuninsky, however, was whether the Leningrad Front, which had just survived the costly defence, was strong enough to mount a successful offensive.

The Leningrad Front's forces were indeed stretched thin. The Twenty-Third Army defended Leningrad's northern and western periphery only 30km (18.75 miles) from the city, and the Eighth Army was isolated in the coastal bridgehead at Oranienbaum.[1] The battle-weary Forty-Second and Fifty-Fifth Armies occupied defences south of the city and the Neva Operational Group was dug in along the Neva River to the east.[2] East of the German corridor to Shlissel'burg, the Fifty-Fourth Army, now under Leningrad Front control, was conducting desultory attacks towards Siniavino.

The Fourth and Fifty-Second Armies, still under *Stavka* control, and the Northwestern Front's Novgorod Army Group defended eastwards to the Volkhov River and southwards along the river's western bank to Lake Il'men.

On 12 October the *Stavka* ordered Fediuninsky to conduct a two-pronged offensive operation beginning on 20 October to crush German forces in the Shlissel'burg corridor and restore communications between Leningrad and the Soviet rear. Lazarov's Fifty-Fifth Army, organized into the so-called Eastern Sector Operational Group, was to conduct the western prong of the attack by assaulting across the Neva River, advancing towards Siniavino, and linking up with the Fifty-Fourth Army advancing from the east. The Neva Operational Group was to conduct a supporting attack on the Fifty-Fifth Army's left flank. Khozin's Fifty-Fourth Army was to attack westwards from the Naziia River, capture Siniavino, and link up with the Fifty-Fifth Army's Operational Group and Neva Operational Group. Once the link-up occurred, the three forces were to destroy German forces in the Shlissel'burg corridor.

The Failed Tikhvin Offensive

The Eastern Sector Operational Group (ESOG), which Fediuninsky formed from the Fifty-Fifth Army and Front reserves, consisted of five rifle divisions, two tank brigades and one separate tank battalion.[3] The group's mission was to assault across the Neva River in the 5km (3.1-mile) sector on the army's right flank, advance towards Siniavino, and help encircle and destroy the German force by the end of the second day of the operation. The Neva Operational Group (NOG) was to defend the northern sector of its Neva River defences with its 1st Rifle Division and 11th Rifle Brigade, and attack eastwards towards Siniavino from its bridgehead across the Neva near Moskovskaia Dubrovka with its 115th Rifle Division and 4th Naval Infantry Brigade. Its assault force was to support the ESOG in destroying German forces in the corridor. The Fifty-Fourth Army was to penetrate German defences between Worker's Settlement No 8 and the Leningrad-Volkhov railroad with a force of three rifle divisions and two tank brigades, capture Siniavino, link up with the ESOG and NOG, and destroy German forces in the corridor.[4]

Fediuninsky's attacking force totalled nine rifle divisions, one rifle brigade, four tank brigades and one separate tank battalion with 70,000 men, 97

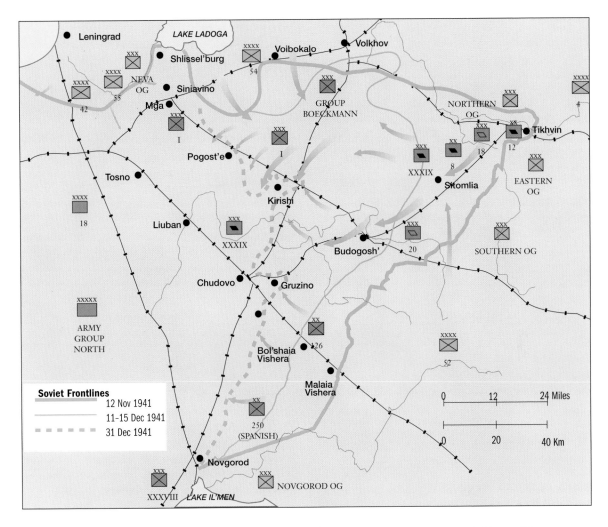

Leningrad
LAKE LADOGA
Shlissel'burg
XXXX — 54
Voibokalo
Volkhov
XXX
XXXX
NEVA OG
55
Siniavino
42
Mga
XXX
GROUP BOECKMANN
NORTHERN OG
XXX
XXXX — 4
XXX
I
XXX
I
Pogost'e
XX
XX
XX
Tikhvin — 12
XXXIX
8
18
XXX
Tosno
Kirishi
Sttomlia
EASTERN OG
XXXX — 18
XXX
Liuban
XXXIX
Budogosh'
XX — 20
SOUTHERN OG
Chudovo
Gruzino
XXXXX
ARMY GROUP NORTH
XX — 126
XXXX — 52
Bol'shaia Vishera
Malaia Vishera

Soviet Frontlines
—— 12 Nov 1941
—— 11-15 Dec 1941
- - - 31 Dec 1941

XX
250 (SPANISH)

0   12   24 Miles
0   20   40 Km

Novgorod
XXX
XXXVIII
LAKE IL'MEN
XXX
NOVGOROD OG

tanks (including 59 heavy KVs), 475 guns, including all available heavy artillery and Katiusha rocket
launchers, and aircraft and artillery from the Baltic
Fleet. The assaulting force faced 54,000 German
soldiers occupying fortified positions in depth
flanked by swampy terrain, supported by 450 guns,
but no tanks.

Despite Fediuninsky's careful preparations, the
Germans pre-empted his offensive by beginning
their thrust towards Tikhvin on 16 October.
Nevertheless, the *Stavka* insisted the Leningrad
Front's shock groups attack as planned on 20
October. Although the attacking forces achieved
only meagre gains in three days of fighting, Stalin
repeatedly ordered Fediuninsky to complete the
operation successfully regardless of the deteriorating situation along the Volkhov River. The only
redeeming feature of the failed offensive was that it
tied five German divisions down in the Siniavino
salient. On 23 October, the *Stavka*'s nerve finally

**ABOVE: Red Army operations around Tikhvin and Siniavino
between October and December 1941. Although the Soviet
offensives were not successful in themselves, they did bring
Army Group North's advance to a halt, and thereby were
instrumental in saving Leningrad.**

cracked, and it ordered Khozin to dispatch two rifle
divisions to Tikhvin. Three days later, it assigned
Fediuninsky command of the Fifty-Fourth Army
and appointed Khozin as Leningrad Front commander, ostensibly because the latter outranked the former, but more likely because Fediuninsky had developed a well-deserved reputation as a fighter – and a
fighter was what was most needed along the
Tikhvin axis. On 28 October, the *Stavka* finally
ordered Fediuninsky's Fifty-Fourth Army to cease
its offensive at Siniavino and, instead, divert forces
to defend Volkhov.[5] By then, the *Stavka*'s optimism
over prospects for raising the blockade of Leningrad
had faded, replaced by a deep foreboding over the

prospects of the total isolation of the city. That would certainly occur if the Germans were able to capture Tikhvin and Volkhov.

The *Stavka*'s concerns were very real indeed. Leeb's mission was to exploit apparent Soviet weakness along the Volkhov River and Tikhvin axis and complete operations around Leningrad as quickly as possible to free up forces to strengthen the offensive towards Moscow. He was to attack through Tikhvin to Lake Ladoga to sever Leningrad's last rail links to Moscow and completely encircle the city. If successful, it was remotely possible that German forces could link up with the elusive Finns along the Svir River. In either case, Leningrad's fate would then be sealed.

Leeb concentrated his XXXIX Motorized and most of I Army Corps at Kirishi, Liuban and southwards along the Volkhov River. Schmidt's motorized corps was to conduct the main attack from Chudovo through Gruzino, Budogosh and Tikhvin, to Lodeinoe Pol'e on the Svir River with the 12th Panzer, 20th Motorized and 21st and 126th Infantry Divisions. On its left flank, the 11th Infantry Division was to advance from Kirishi towards Volkhov. To the south, the 8th Panzer and 18th Motorized Divisions were to attack towards Malaia Vishera and Bologoe to link up with forces operating

ABOVE: This artillery crew manhandles its 76.2mm field gun into a newly finished position. Although this model 1902 weapon was obsolete by 1941, many were pressed into service during the early months of the siege. The upper part of the shield has been lowered for ease of placement.

on Army Group Centre's left flank, which were to attack northwest along the Moscow-Leningrad railroad from Kalinin through Vyshii Volochek to Bologoe. Even if the offensive failed to reach the Svir River, it would likely encircle and destroy the Fifty-Fourth Army operating west of the Volkhov River.

In mid-October the Leningrad Front's Fifty-Fourth Army, the Fourth and Fifty-Second Armies under *Stavka* control, and the Northwestern Front's Novgorod Army Group (NAG), defended the 200km (125-mile) front from Lipka on Lake Ladoga to Kirishi and southwards along the eastern bank of the Volkhov River to Lake Il'men. Khozin's Fifty-Fourth Army defended the 35km (21.8-mile) sector from Lipka halfway to Kirishi and was preparing to attack towards Siniavino. Lieutenant-General V. F. Iakovlev's Fourth Army occupied shallow defences along the 50km (31.25-mile) front west of Kirishi and southwards along the Volkhov River. His army consisted of three rifle divisions, one cavalry division, one separate tank battalion, one corps artillery regiment, and one pontoon bridge battalion, all of which were understrength.[6] Lieutenant-General N. K. Klykov's Fifty-Second Army defended the 80km (50-mile) sector along the Volkhov River to 25km (15.6 miles) north of Novgorod with two understrength rifle divisions, four corps artillery regiments, and one anti-tank artillery regiment, but with no reserve.[7] Finally, the NAG defended the 30km (18.75-mile) sector along the Volkhov north of Lake Il'men with two rifle and one tank division, which had no tanks.[8] Since the bulk of the Fifty-Fourth Army was concentrated for the attack on Siniavino, only five rifle divisions, one cavalry division, one tank battalion, five artillery regiments, and one anti-tank regiment defended the 130km (81.25-mile) sector opposite the German main attack. This force was wholly inadequate to deal with the German offensive.

Early on 16 October, German infantry of the 21st and 126th Infantry Divisions stormed across the Volkhov River, followed later in the day by the 12th Panzer and 20th Motorized Divisions. The assaulting forces penetrated the Fourth Army's fragile defences in four days of heavy fighting in roadless terrain covered by 3–4in (76–102mm) of snow. The assault forced the Fourth Army's 288th and 267th Rifle Divisions to withdraw, creating an immense gap between the Fourth and Fifty-Second Armies which the defenders were unable to close. From 21 to 23 October the attacking force fanned out, the 12th Panzer and 20th Motorized Divisions advancing towards Budogosh and Tikhvin, the 21st Infantry Division towards Kirishi, and the 126th Infantry Division towards Bol'shaia and Malaia Vishera. The advance, however, was tediously slow because the few roads were often impassible and periodic thaws turned the adjacent terrain into a thick gluey mass that severely inhibited movement and re-supply of the advancing force. Despite the problems, on 23 October the 12th Panzer and 20th Motorized Divisions captured Budogosh on the Fourth Army's left flank, but the 285th and 311th Rifle Divisions on the Fourth Army's right flank halted the 11th Infantry Division's attacks north of Kirishi the following day. To the south, the 18th Motorized and 126th Infantry Divisions forced the Fifty-Second Army to abandon Bol'shaia Vishera and withdraw southeast.

BELOW: The terrain around Leningrad was not ideal country for armoured operations, as this pair of BT-7 Soviet Medium tanks demonstrates. Caught in the open, advancing along a narrow track, the Russians fell victim to a heavy German artillery barrage. The BT series was the forerunner of the legendary T-34.

ABOVE: As in London during the "Blitz", so in Leningrad barrage balloons were to form an important part of the air defences of the city. These "aerostats" are being guided into position by their handlers outside the Drama Theatre on the Nevsky Prospect.

Given the obvious threat to Tikhvin, the *Stavka* reinforced the Fourth and Fifty-Second Armies with six rifle divisions and one tank division, four of which it deployed along the approaches to Tikhvin, and ordered the armies to halt the German advance, counterattack, and restore the Volkhov River defences.[9] At the same time, it ordered the Fifty-Fourth Army to continue its attacks at Siniavino to tie down German forces. Once reinforced, Iakovlev's Fourth Army should have been capable of driving German forces back to the Volkhov River. However, his defences continued to collapse because he committed his reserves in piecemeal fashion and without adequate preparation or command and control. For example, on 27 October the 191st Rifle Division and elements of the 4th Guards Rifle and 60th Tank Divisions attacked the 12th Panzer Division's vanguard near Sitomlia on the road to Tikhvin. The counterattack failed because it was poorly coordinated, although it did force the 12th Panzer Division

to halt its advance and regroup. By this time, Schmidt's corps reported capturing 12,500 prisoners and seizing or destroying 66 Russian guns.

Further south, the Fifty-Second Army, now three divisions strong, delayed the German 8th Panzer and 18th Motorized Divisions' advance long enough to occupy new defences at Malaia Vishera.[10] So strenuous was the defence that, by 27 October, the German advance in this sector ground to a halt. At this juncture, increasing Soviet resistance west of Tikhvin forced Schmidt to regroup the 8th Panzer and 18th Motorized Divisions from Malaia Vishera to Sitomlia to reinforce his main attack. The following day he reinforced the 11th Infantry Division, whose attack north of Kirishi had failed, with part of the 21st Infantry, renamed the force Group von Boeckmann, and ordered the new group to attack northwards towards Volkhov to protect his main force's left flank.

With the pace of his offensive slowing, on 26 October Leeb visited Hitler at his Wolf's Lair (*Wolfsschance*) headquarters and requested that Army Group Centre support his offensive by attacking from Kalinin through Vyshii Volochek to Bologoe with its Third Panzer Group and part of the Ninth Army. Although Leeb's request seemed reasonable at the time, violent Soviet counterattacks at Kalinin soon made it impossible.[11] In any case, Hitler, whose attention was fixed on Moscow, refused Leeb's request. However, he did agree to cancel plans for an attack to eliminate the Oranienbaum bridgehead, in so doing saving three of Leeb's divisions. Before leaving Hitler's headquarters, Leeb expressed doubts to Hitler that his forces could take Tikhvin. Hitler, however, insisted that the offensive continue.

The Cold Begins to Bite

In late October, the *Stavka* began planning and orchestrating a series of counterstrokes it hoped would defeat the German offensive. On 30 October it ordered the Fourth Army to concentrate two shock groups, each of roughly two divisions, southwest of Tikhvin with orders to attack towards Budogosh and Gruzino on 1 November, destroy the German force advancing on Tikhvin, and restore Soviet defences along the Volkhov River.[12] The counterattack began on 2 November but failed after four days of heavy fighting.[13] Undeterred by the counterattack and taking advantage of a fresh blast of cold weather on 6 November that began freezing rivers and streams in the region, Schmidt's corps resumed its advance towards Tikhvin on 5 November. The 12th Panzer Division, now reinforced by the 8th Panzer and 18th Motorized Divisions, brushed aside the 191st Rifle Division and captured Tikhvin during a snowstorm on 8 November, severing the last railroad line from Moscow to Lake Ladoga. In the process, the corps reported capturing 20,000 prisoners and seizing or destroying 96 tanks, 179 guns, and an armoured train since the beginning of the operation.[14]

Despite this success, it was also increasingly clear that Schmidt's forces had already "shot their bolt". The prolonged advance had seriously weakened his forces, the ravages of winter were taking their toll of German armoured vehicles, and Soviet resistance was stiffening both north of Tikhvin and at Malaia Vishera. Even before the Germans captured Tikhvin, the temperature had fallen to as low as -40 degrees Fahrenheit and many soldiers were frostbitten or had simply frozen to death. The 12th Panzer and 18th Motorized Divisions were hemmed in by menacing Russian troop concentrations around Tikhvin and were not able to attack northwards. The 8th Panzer, 20th Motorized, and 126th Infantry Divisions manned defences scattered through the 100km (62.5-mile) gap between

Tikhvin and Malaia Vishera, and Russian forces were counterattacking against the 126th Infantry Division at Malaia Vishera. To the west, Group von Boeckmann continued its advance along the Volkhov axis, but at a much slower pace, reaching within 14km (8.75 miles) of Volkhov before its attack became totally bogged down. Leeb's entire offensive ground to a halt on 8 November as if locked in place by the extreme cold weather. His forces had neither eliminated the Soviet Fifty-Fourth Army nor reached the Finns, and although they had taken Tikhvin and cut the Moscow-Ladoga railroad line, his force was now overextended and threatened from every direction. With the temperature falling to -20 degrees Fahrenheit and the terrain covered by deep snow, the bitter cold caused more casualties than Russian bullets.

Hitler, however, permitted Leeb no respite. Goaded on by the Führer, he stoically reinforced Group von Boeckmann with the 254th Infantry Division and dispatched the 61st Infantry Division to Tikhvin to reinforce Schmidt's corps. He then altered his plan by shifting his emphasis from Tikhvin to Volkhov. His revised plan called for Group von Boeckmann to capture Volkhov with its vital aluminum plant and power station and then Novaia Ladoga on the southern shore of Lake Ladoga to cut off transportation of supplies to Leningrad via Lake Ladoga and encircle and destroy the Fifty-Fourth Army. Boeckmann's force, reinforced by the 254th Infantry Division, had been attacking along the Kirishi-Volkhov axis since 28 October, slowly driving the Fourth Army's four defending divisions northwards towards Volkhov.[15] Boeckmann's group approached the southern outskirts of Volkhov on 8 November, driving a deep wedge between the Soviet Fifty-Fourth and Fourth Armies. At this point Leeb dispatched a task force from the 8th Panzer Division to support Boeckmann's advance. However, a counterattack by the 310th Rifle Division thwarted the 8th Panzer Division's attempt to outflank Soviet defences east of the town.[16]

The Panzers Grind to a Halt

The appearance of 8th Panzer Division forces at Volkhov, which threatened both Volkhov and the Fifty-Fourth Army's rear, forced the *Stavka* to react. On 9 November it appointed Army General K. A. Meretskov, just released from NKVD imprisonment, to command the Fourth Army.[17] At the same time, it ordered the Leningrad Front to halt the Fifty-Fourth Army's offensive against Siniavino and employ the

LEFT: Red Army troops under artillery fire as they probe German positions on the Leningrad frontline. These troops are wearing the typical Russian greatcoat made of dark grey cloth, which was double-breasted with a fall collar and fly front. As can be seen, much of the terrain around the city was marshy, which hindered large-scale operations.

bulk of Fediuninsky's army to destroy German forces in the Volkhov region. Fediuninsky, in turn, requested the *Stavka* assign the four rifle divisions and one naval rifle brigade operating on the Fourth Army's right flank to his army.[18] The *Stavka* approved his request on 12 November, and ordered Fediuninsky to form a new shock group to defeat Boeckmann group's advance towards Volkhov. Fediuninsky's task became more challenging when, on 18 November, Leeb reinforced Boeckmann's group with a combat group from the 12th Panzer Division.

Fediuninsky moved his army auxiliary command post to the Volkhov region, began assembling a shock group southwest of Volkhov, and ordered the group to attack Boeckmann's forces on 25 November. While Fediuninsky was preparing his counterstroke, however, Boeckmann's 254th Infantry Division attacked northwest towards Voibokalo Station in the Fifty-Fourth Army's rear along the shortest route to Lake Ladoga. Fediuninsky's 285th Rifle Division and 122nd Tank Brigades managed to halt the thrust in late November just short of Voibokalo Station. This set the stage for Fediuninsky's army to participate in the general Soviet Tikhvin counteroffensive, which was already beginning to ripple across the entire front in the Volkhov and Tikhvin regions.

Leeb's offensive along the Tikhvin and Volkhov axes had become bogged down by mid-November in the face of intensified Soviet resistance, debilitating weather, and Leeb's forces' heavy losses. Over the course of 30 days of heavy fighting, his front east of the Volkhov River had expanded from 70 to 350km (43.75 to 218.75 miles), his forces were exhausted, woefully overextended, and at the end of their logistical tether, and Schmidt's main force was half encircled in Tikhvin. Leeb's only consolation, that his forces held the Moscow-Ladoga and Tikhvin-Volkhov railroad lines in a stranglehold and, by doing so, posed a mortal threat to Leningrad was, however, illusory. The reckless advance deep into the Soviet rear area in the dead of winter created favourable conditions for a concerted Soviet counteroffensive, a circumstance that the watchful *Stavka* decided to exploit to full advantage. Despite the heavy fighting underway along the Moscow axis, the correlation of forces east of Leningrad had shifted significantly in the Red Army's favour. Finally, Army Group Centre's 15 November assault on Moscow made it essential that the Red Army go on the offensive in the Leningrad region. It did so after mid-November, by unleashing a series of counterattacks and counterstrokes that grew inevitably into a fully fledged counteroffensive.

Stavka's Objectives

When the *Stavka* began orchestrating its counterattacks and counterstrokes northeast of Leningrad, it focused on several priority objectives. First and foremost, it sought to save Leningrad by destroying German forces at Tikhvin and Volkhov and restoring communications between Leningrad and Moscow via the Tikhvin-Volkhov railroad. Second, it tried to tie down as many German forces as possible along the northwestern axis in the interests of its Moscow defence.

In late November, the Leningrad Front's Fifty-Fourth Army and the Fourth and Fifty-Second Armies under *Stavka* control faced a German force of 10 infantry, two motorized and two panzer divisions deployed between Lakes Ladoga and Il'men. The German force, whose divisions were at about 60 percent strength, numbered roughly 120,000 men, 100 tanks and assault guns, and 1000 guns and mortars. The *Stavka* was able to concentrate 17 rifle and two tank divisions, one cavalry division, three rifle and two tank brigades, and three tank and two ski battalions, organized into three armies and fielding 192,950 men, against the Germans. However, while the Soviets enjoyed a considerable

superiority in manpower and guns, they were slightly inferior in armour.

Soviet Deployments

The *Stavka* ordered the Fifty-Fourth, Fourth, and Fifty-Second Armies to defeat the opposing German forces, drive them back to the Volkhov River, and establish a bridgehead on its western bank by conducting concentric attacks towards Kirishi and Gruzino. Meretskov's Fourth Army, conducting the main attack, was to encircle German forces at Tikhvin, exploit through Budogosh to the Volkhov River, link up with the Fifty-Fourth Army at Kirishi and the Fifty-Second Army at Gruzino, and capture bridgeheads over the river. His army faced the 12th Panzer, 18th and 20th Motorized, and 61st Infantry Divisions, and one third of the 8th Panzer Division.

Meretskov divided his army, which consisted of five rifle, one tank, and one cavalry division, one rifle and one tank brigade, and three separate tank battalions, into Northern, Southern and Eastern Shock Groups, each with a specific mission.[19] The Northern Group was to attack German forces at Tikhvin from the north with one rifle division and one tank brigade, while the Eastern Group attacked Tikhvin from the east with two cavalry divisions, and a composite infantry and tank force.[20] The Southern Group was to assault the Germans' communications routes southwest of Tikhvin with two reinforced rifle divisions.[21] Once it captured Tikhvin, the Northern Group was to advance northwestwards to assist the Fifty-Fourth Army's attack on Boeckmann's forces south of Volkhov, while Meretskov's main force advanced towards Gruzino to link up with the Fifty-Fourth Army's main force and envelop Boeckmann's forces from the south.

Fediuninsky's Fifty-Fourth Army, which consisted of eight rifle divisions, one tank division without tanks, two rifle and two tank brigades, and two ski battalions, was to launch its main attack west of Volkhov and at Voibokalo, link up with Fourth Army near Kirishi, and encircle and destroy Boeckmann's forces. His remaining forces were to defend the army's right flank towards Siniavino and Lake Ladoga.[22] If successful, the Fifty-Fourth and Fourth Armies' converging attacks would also sever German withdrawal routes westward from Tikhvin. To the south, the four divisions of Klykov's Fifty-Second Army and two divisions of the Northwestern Front's NAG were to destroy German forces in the Malaia Vishera region, advance to the Volkhov River, capture bridgeheads over the river, and help cut German withdrawal routes from Tikhvin.[23]

Since the chaotic operational situation and a shortage of forces prevented the *Stavka* from initiating operations simultaneously in every sector, it began the attacks piecemeal, building it to the crescendo of a full counteroffensive as the month progressed. The Fifty-Second Army initiated the process, attacking along the Malaia Vishera axis on 12 November, the Fourth Army unleashed its attacks around Tikhvin on 19 November, and the Fifty-Fourth Army attacked west of Volkhov on 3 December.

Schmidt's Corps Buckles

As the Soviet attacks began rippling across the front, Schmidt's motorized corps was ill-deployed to deal effectively with the expanding torrent of attacks. While his 12th Panzer and 18th Motorized Divisions were bottled up in Tikhvin proper, his 8th Panzer, 20th Motorized, and newly arrived Spanish 250th "Blue" Infantry Division clung precariously to a string of strongpoints along the corps' long right flank from Tikhvin southwest to Malaia Vishera. Throughout this period Leeb steadily withdrew his armour from Tikhvin, reinforcing Group Boeckmann south of Volkhov with parts of the 8th Panzer Division and shoring up the vulnerable defences on his right flank. On 3 December Leeb subordinated Boeckmann's three divisions to I Army Corps headquarters, which he transferred from Leningrad, and reinforced the army corps with additional 8th Panzer Division forces. By now, the infantry forces of Kuechler's Eighteenth Army were strung out far to the west, manning an extended front from the Gulf of Finland to Shlissel'burg on Lake Ladoga and eastwards to the Volkhov-Tikhvin railroad. Busch's Sixteenth Army, also vastly overextended, defended the long front from Lake Il'men southwards to the Valdai Hills. Nor did the weather cooperate with Leeb's defence. As the temperatures dropped another 10 degrees, his men were soon fighting in desperation as machine guns and artillery pieces jammed, and horses collapsed, freezing solid in a matter of minutes.

The Fifty-Second Army attacked early on 12 November, while Meretskov's forces were still struggling to contain German forces in Tikhvin. The army's four rifle divisions repeatedly assaulted the 126th Infantry Division's defence on a broad front north and south of Malaia Vishera for four days, but made no appreciable progress. Failing to concentrate his forces, instead Klykov employed fruitless frontal

attacks with inadequate artillery support against poorly reconnoitered German strongpoints.[24] The OKH responded to the attacks by transferring the 61st and 223rd Infantry Divisions from Army Group Centre's reserve and France to reinforce Malaia Vishera's defences and protect the right flank of its forces at Tikhvin. The NAG's initial assault also failed for the same reasons.

Urged on by the *Stavka*, Klykov regrouped his forces on 16 and 17 November and resumed his attack overnight on 17–18 November. This time he infiltrated two detachments from the 259th and 111th Rifle Divisions into the Germans' rear, and the two divisions successfully stormed and captured the village the next morning, forcing the defending 126th Infantry Division to withdraw. Although Klykov's forces pursued the retreating Germans towards Bol'shaia Vishera, the pursuit was too slow to prevent Leeb from reinforcing his forces at Tikhvin, then under assault by the Fourth Army's forces, with the 61st Infantry Division. Within days, Leeb also reinforced the 126th Infantry Division with the 215th Infantry Division transferred from France.

A Slow Advance

The three shock groups of Meretskov's Fourth Army attacked German forces defending the Tikhvin region on 19 November. Advancing through deep snow at an agonizingly slow pace against determined German resistance, Meretskov's northern group finally fought its way to the outskirts of Tikhvin on 7 December. By this time, his eastern shock group had stalled, locked in heavy combat west of the Tikhvinka River and along the Tikhvin-Tal'tsy road with the 20th Motorized and 61st Infantry Divisions (the latter had just arrived from Malaia Vishera). Schmidt's 12th Panzer and 18th Motorized Divisions in Tikhvin were now enveloped from three sides and suffering heavy casualties fighting in the deep snow and bitter cold. The 18th Motorized Division alone lost 9000 men in the fierce fighting, leaving it with a combat strength of 741 men. The 3rd Battalion of its 30th Panzergrenadier Regiment had already lost 250 men, most of whom had frozen to death, during the advance from Chudovo to Tikhvin. Worse still, Meretskov's southern group had penetrated the 18th Motorized Division's defences to the south and now threatened the Tikhvin group's communications with the rear.

After withdrawing more troops from Schmidt's beleaguered forces at Tikhvin to defend their vital communications lines to the rear, Leeb requested permission from the OKH to withdraw Schmidt's forces back to the Volkhov River. Shortly after midnight on 7 December, Halder informed Leeb that Hitler still insisted the original plan be fulfilled. The next day, Leeb informed Hitler that his forces at Tikhvin were outnumbered by more than two to one, adding that, if he did not agree to a withdrawal, they might be destroyed. By this time, the Red Army had already begun its massive Moscow counteroffensive. Bowing to the inevitable, at 02:00 hours on 8 December, exactly one month after the 12th Panzer Division captured Tikhvin, Hitler consented to Leeb's request (hours before a distraught Leeb had already issued the evacuation order).

On 9 December, the 12th Panzer and 18th Motorized Divisions began their painful withdrawal westwards from Tikhvin towards the Volkhov River over roads clogged with deep snow. Leeb raced reinforcements to Sitomlia, Gruzino and Volkhov to support the withdrawal, which Schmidt was supposed to complete by 22 December. By this time, Schmidt's two panzer divisions numbered only 30 tanks apiece (full strength 160 tanks each). As they withdrew, Meretskov's northern and eastern groups assaulted German rearguards and captured Tikhvin late in the day. While the three German divisions withdrew in orderly fashion, the 61st Infantry Division's 151st Regiment, supported by the 11th and 12th Companies of the 18th Motorized Division's 51st Panzergrenadier Regiment, attempted to block the pursuing Russians. During the heavy fighting, the regiment suffered heavy losses and the panzergrenadier companies were wiped out to the last man. On 10 December, Meretskov's forces began their pursuit, also hindered by the heavy snow. To the south, Krykov's Fifty-Second Army captured Bol'shaia Vishera on 16 December and pushed the two defending German divisions westwards to their new defences along the Volkhov River.[25]

While one act of the *Stavka*'s drama was playing out around Tikhvin, another was developing in the Volkhov sector to the west. Fediuninsky's Fifty-Fourth Army had halted I Army Corps' attacks south of Volkhov and at Voibokalo Station by 25 November. The next day Fediuninsky's initial shock group, made up of three divisions and a rifle brigade, attacked I Army Corps' 21st Infantry

BELOW: A Red Army tank-hunting unit marches out of the city towards the front. The long-barrelled weapons are Degtaryev 14.5mm PTRD antitank rifles. A large and cumbersome weapon, it weighed 16kg (35.2lb) and could penetrate 35mm (1.38in) of armour up to a range of 100m (328ft).

ABOVE: Soviet troops on the Leningrad Front move through the rubble of a destroyed village. They are armed with the standard rifle of the Red Army during World War II: the 7.62mm Moisin Nagant Model 1891/30 bolt-action model. Somewhat archaic, it was preferred to the unreliable automatic Tokarev SVT-40.

Division south of Volkhov, driving it back several kilometres south of the town by 29 November.[26] Several days later, Khozin reinforced Fediuninsky's forces with the 80th Rifle Division and ordered him to form another shock group at Voibokalo Station by 1 December and strike I Army Corps' left flank. The new shock group, consisting of four rifle divisions, one rifle brigade and one tank brigade, attacked on 3 December and drove the German I Army Corps' left flank southwards, successively encircling and destroying several companies of the 254th Infantry Division.[27] The 115th and 198th Rifle Divisions, transferred from Leningrad, joined the army's assault on 15 December and drove the Germans back to Olomny on 17 December, enveloping I Army Corps' left flank on the western bank of the Volkhov River.

At the same time, the northern group of Meretskov's Fourth Army penetrated German defences along the Tikhvin-Volkhov railroad, and reached the Lynka River southeast of Volkhov, enveloping I Army Corps' right flank and forcing the beleaguered corps to withdraw southwards towards Kirishi. During its withdrawal, the Fifty-Fourth Army's 1st and 2nd Ski Battalions constantly harassed the Germans' flanks and rear. Although I Army Corps attempted to hold on to the critical Mga-Kirishi railroad line, the Fifty-Fourth Army's 311th, 80th and 285th Rifle Divisions penetrated across the railroad, forming a shallow salient in the German defences west of Kirishi. The remainder of the Fifty-Fourth Army struggled to expel German forces from Kirishi and the surrounding villages until 28 December, but failed to dislodge the defenders and suffered massive losses. During the fighting, Leeb reinforced the Kirishi strongpoint with the 291st and 269th Infantry Divisions transferred from Leningrad, transforming it into the vital apex of the German defences along the Volkhov River.

While its Tikhvin counteroffensive was reaching its climax, the *Stavka* reorganized its forces in the Volkhov region to facilitate future operations. Two days after Tikhvin fell, Stalin summoned Meretskov, his chief of staff General Stelmakh, Khozin and

Zhdanov to Moscow to discuss how the offensive could best be expanded. The first order of business was to reorganize Red Army forces in the region into a proper Front structure capable of controlling multiple armies in a major new offensive push. When the conference ended on 11 December, the *Stavka* formed the new Volkhov Front effective on 17 December with Meretskov as its commander and Stelmakh as its chief of staff. In addition to Meretskov's Fourth and Krykov's Fifty-Second Armies, the *Stavka* assigned the new Front Lieutenant-General G. G. Sokolov's Twenty-Sixth Army (designated the Second Shock in late December) and Major-General I. V. Galanin's Fifty-Ninth Army, both of which had been formed in the *Stavka* reserve.

The Moscow meeting also produced an ambitious new plan for an expanded offensive to accomplish nothing less than the complete lifting of the Leningrad blockade. The 17 December *Stavka* directive stated:

"The Volkhov Front, consisting of the Fourth, Fifty-Ninth, Second Shock and Fifty-Second Armies, will launch a general offensive to smash the enemy defending along the western bank of the Volkhov River, and reach the Liuban and Cholovo Station front with your armies' main forces by the end of ...... Subsequently, while attacking to the northwest, encircle the enemy defending around Leningrad, destroy and capture him in cooperation with the Leningrad Front, and if the enemy resists capture, destroy him....

"The *Stavka* of the Supreme High Command I. Stalin, B. Shaposhnikov"

A companion directive sent to Khozin the same day ordered the Leningrad Front, "to help the Volkhov Front destroy the enemy defending around Leningrad and raise the Leningrad blockade by active operations with the Forty-Second, Fifty-Fifth, Eighth and Fifty-Fourth Armies, and the Coastal Operational Group." In addition, the *Stavka* ordered the Northwestern Front to conduct a major offensive to capture Demiansk, Novgorod and Dno. The twin offensives were to begin soon

BELOW: The youthfulness of this Red Army soldier of the Leningrad Front is obvious. The young man is being welcomed back to his unit, having been wounded and treated by the staff at the aid post in the background. The men are all wearing the 1940 model winter fur hat.

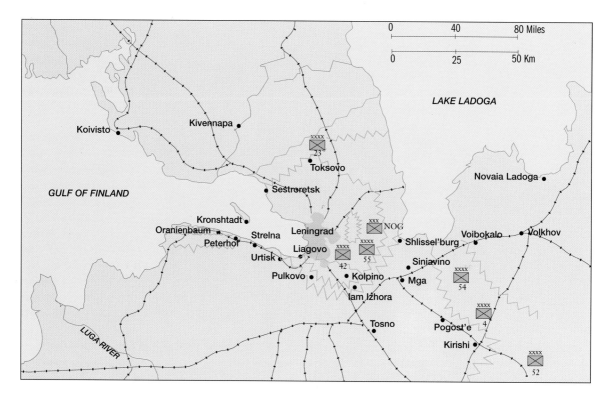

after Meretskov's forces reached the Volkhov River. The perilous situation at Leningrad, which was being subjected to near-constant artillery fire and was facing famine, and Stalin's desire to maintain the initiative, prompted him to demand that Meretskov begin his offensive with the forces he had at hand.

The seamless expansion of the Tikhvin counteroffensive into the expanded Volkhov-Leningrad offensive depended entirely on Meretskov's armies reaching and establishing adequate bridgeheads across the Volkhov River. To Stalin's obvious disgust, Meretskov's armies, in particular, Fediuninsky's Fifty-Fourth, were too slow. After Stalin sent them numerous, increasingly caustic, messages ordering them to accelerate their advance, the Fourth and Fifty-Second Armies finally reached the river near Kirishi, Gruzino and north of Novgorod on 27 December, seized bridgeheads, and began expanding the bridgeheads against determined German resistance. However, despite Stalin's exhortation, Fediuninsky failed to capture Kirishi and Iakovlev could not seize Tigoda Station. By 30 December Meretskov's three armies had driven the two German corps back to positions from which they had begun their Tikhvin offensive on 16 October. Utterly exhausted and at the end of their supply lines, Meretskov's forces had no choice but to dig in, fortify their positions and go over to the

ABOVE: Leningrad's defences on 31 December 1941. Strenuous efforts had been made by the Red Army and the city's population to stiffen the defences as the Germans got nearer. Unfortunately, the city was still within range of German siege artillery, which started to inflict damage and losses.

defence. The grand new offensive would have to await the New Year.

The Red Army's Tikhvin defence and counteroffensive were component parts of a far greater strategic duel, which was occurring along the entire Soviet-German front, but particularly along the Moscow axis. Army Group North's bold lunge towards Tikhvin symbolized the optimism that gripped Hitler and the OKH when they launched Operation Typhoon in October 1941. The ensuing defeats at both Tikhvin and Moscow were sober reminders that this optimism was misplaced. In reality, the Red Army's victory at Tikhvin represented the culmination of a process begun at Sol'tsy in July and continued at Staraia Russa and Luga in August and at Leningrad in September. Although costly in terms of lives, the *Stavka*'s insistence on an active defence and merciless counterattacks and counterstrokes finally caught up with an exhausted Wehrmacht in November and December. At the same time, the Wehrmacht learned, to its everlasting consternation, that warfare in Russia was far from the sport it had been in the West.

The Tikhvin counteroffensive was the Red Army's first large-scale military success in the Great Patriotic War. In addition to ending Hitler's dream of encircling Leningrad in 1941, the counteroffensive assisted in the defeat of German forces at Moscow and drove home to German leaders the realization that this war would not be easily won. The victory, however, was difficult to achieve and proved costly. The Red Army employed about 280,000 troops in the Tikhvin defence, the Tikhvin counteroffensive, and the associated Siniavino offensive. When the fighting ended, it had suffered more than 140,000 casualties, including 62,878 dead, captured or missing.[28]

The Germans also suffered heavy losses. Leeb committed more than 100,000 troops in the advance to Tikhvin and Volkhov and another 60,000 to the defence at Siniavino, and suffered roughly 40,000 casualties. Despite his defeat, Leeb issued a proclamation to his forces on Christmas Day proclaiming his army group's victories:

"In the battles on and to the east of the Volkhov – as well as in the withdrawal of the front into a secure winter position behind the Volkhov – you have again met the highest requirements of defensive power and of physical resiliency in fulfilling the mission. The enemy arrives at the Volkhov empty handed.

"Since 22 June and up to 20 December, Army Group North has taken 438,950 prisoners and captured or destroyed 3847 tanks and 4590 guns.

"We reverently bow our heads to those who have given their lives. The Homeland thanks us for having protected it and counts on us in the future.

"We shall justify this trust. The New Year will find us ready to repel all enemy breakthrough efforts, until the Führer calls on us again to resume the attack."[29]

Leeb's inspirational message belied the grim reality that German forces had failed to achieve the missions that Hitler had assigned to them. Less than two weeks later, Leeb's tired forces would have to respond to their commander's bold summons when, on 7 January, the Red Army assaulted their defences along the Volkhov River with renewed determination. Leeb's Christmas message was also his swan song. As the new Soviet offensive began, he submitted his resignation to Hitler. After five days of indecision, on 18 January Adolf Hitler replaced von Leeb with Kuechler.

BELOW: One of the most famous images of the siege of Leningrad: a Red Army soldier stares at the victims of a German artillery barrage. Once Hitler had decided against a direct assault against the city, the main German weapons used against the defenders were bombs and artillery shells – and starvation.

CHAPTER 4:
WINTER AGONY 1941–42

The iron grip that the Communist Party maintained over the population of Leningrad ensured that the city did not fall into the Germans' hands in late 1941. Party functionaries organized civil defence teams, and the city's factories continued to produce war material. However, shortages, air attacks and shelling combined to make life hell for the inhabitants as the winter began.

The German invasion struck like a thunderbolt, as it did with the Soviet Union as a whole, catching government and population alike by surprise. The devastating effects of the Wehrmacht's rapid advance disrupted defence and mobilization plans and quickly transformed Leningrad into an active war zone. As the front collapsed, the first order of business was defence and mobilization. At 05:00 hours on 22 June, Major-General D. N. Nikishev, the Leningrad Military District Chief of Staff, summoned his army commanders and implemented the district's mobilization plans, which by then seemed utterly irrelevant to the situation. From this point forth, mobilization and preparation of the city's defence was largely an *ad hoc* and increasingly frantic affair.

The Leningrad Party organization, under Party chief A. A. Zhdanov, now began mobilization in

LEFT: Two civil defence officials patrol the streets. Essential workers such as these sometimes received an extra ration allowance, as did the maintenance gangs on the "Road of Life". The armband denotes the woman's status.

accordance with the 29 June directives of the USSR's Council of People's Commissars and the Communist Party.[1] These directives required the Party to supervise preparation of the city's defences, mobilize industry, raise People's Militia forces, and form and field partisan forces in close cooperation with the Northern Front's Military Council, the Leningrad city Party Committee, and city's workers' council. The most urgent task was to organize Leningrad's military defences: first, the distant approaches to the city and, later, around the city itself. To do so, the authorities mobilized the city's population. On 27 June 1941 the Leningrad City Council's Executive Committee (*Ispolkom*) ordered all able males between the ages of 16 and 50 years and women between 16 and 45 to participate in the defensive work being carried out.[2]

Those civilians formed work details that began constructing defences on Leningrad's southern outskirts and within the city itself in late July.[3] Subsequently, an average of 125,000 Leningraders per day expended a total of 8,757,600 man-days working on defensive belts and fortified regions on

ABOVE: The residential Narva district near the Gulf of Finland was directly in the path of the German assault. The cobbles from the road have been used to build the barricade. The poster shows Lenin in defiant mode and proclaims: "Death for death, blood for blood".

the approaches to the city during July, August and the first 10 days of September. Organized as factory teams and working under military supervision, the population built a staggering number of defensive works ranging from simple slit trenches to 1.96-tonne (two-ton) reinforced concrete artillery positions and anti-tank obstacles.[4] Despite accomplishing a prodigious amount of work, however, the effort was fraught with problems, particularly in July and August, when the rapidly changing military situation prevented sound planning and pre-empted much of the work done. Worse still, the work was poorly organized and there was a chronic shortage of qualified supervisors and labour to perform the tasks. Since most weaponry and explosives were required at the front, the defences were deficient in anti-tank and anti-personnel mines and other explosive obstacles. The defensive construction effort went on after the front reached Leningrad, with an average of 45,000 people per day spending 6,596,000 man-days preparing the defences between 1 August and 31 December.

Defensive work within the city itself began in late August and accelerated on 2 September when German forces reached the city's southern outskirts. The Leningrad Front organized a "sector defence"

within the city, whose outer forward edge extended along the city's ring railroad, and subdivided the defence into six sectors corresponding to the city's six districts (raion).[5] Each sector consisted of several defensive positions 1.2–2km (0.75–1.25 miles) apart, and each defensive position consisted of separate but mutually supporting battalion defensive regions. The six sectors encompassed a total of 99 battalion regions. A defence staff formed from the Secretary of the district Party organization, the chairman of the district executive committee and representatives of local NKVD and workers' organizations commanded each sector. Local NKVD and fire security forces, city militia and workers' formations manned the defensive regions, but only as the combat situation required.

An elaborate system of barricades and anti-tank defences formed the backbone of each sector's defence. The defenders erected barricades up to 2.5m

(7.2ft) high and 3.5m (11.5ft) deep between blocks of houses and individual buildings on the periphery and within each sector. For example, the Kirov sector built 17.2km (10.75 miles) of barricades protected by anti-tank ditches around its circumference. Since anti-tank defences were particularly vital given the Germans' reliance on armour, construction forces attempted to erect continuous anti-tank defences echeloned in depth along all dangerous tank approaches. For example, by 1 November the Forty-Second Army, whose sector included the most dangerous tank axis, built 41 mutually supporting anti-tank regions in addition to those already created on the edge of the city.[6] The anti-tank defence also included extensive networks of anti-tank obstacles and barriers that exploited unique terrain features such as rivers, ravines, streams and forested regions, and covered these features with over-watching fire. Where no such natural obstacles existed, engineers filled in the gaps with dragon's teeth obstacles, escarpments and anti-tank ditches.

Leningrad's defenders also had to counter the ability of the Luftwaffe potentially to pound the city into submission with air attacks. Although initially weak, Leningrad's air defences (PVO) improved markedly during the fall. Initially, four organizations were

responsible for air defence of the Leningrad region. II PVO and VII Fighter Aviation Corps defended Leningrad proper, the Ladoga Brigade PVO Region defended water routes across the lake, and the Svir Brigade PVO Region defended the railroad line from the depths of the country to Lake Ladoga. In an effort to improve air defence by centralizing it, in November 1941 the State Defence Committee (GKO) reorganized the Soviet Union's National Air Defence (PVO *Strany*), converting II PVO Corps into the Leningrad Corps' PVO Region. While not affecting the Svir and Ladoga Brigade PVO Regions' organization, it subordinated the three regions to the Leningrad Front rather than the commander of PVO *Strany*. This facilitated concentration of air defence resources and fostered better fire coordination between PVO and air units, which was especially critical for successful city defence. Subsequently, air defence forces operated independently only when protecting specific objectives within their own zones of fire.

BELOW: Dressed for the cold weather in their padded jackets, these civilians labour to complete a machine-gun position in a wooded area on the approaches to Leningrad. Such civilian workers were a vital part of the city's defences, enabling soldiers to concentrate on the fighting.

PVO fighter aviation concentrated on repelling German air attacks on the city as far forward as possible, and associated searchlight batteries supported the aircraft at night. Anti-aircraft artillery regiments subordinate to the Leningrad Front's armies established anti-aircraft artillery fire zones on the city's outskirts and in the city itself, concentrated primarily along the western and southwestern approaches to the city. PVO also mounted anti-aircraft batteries on ships in the Gulf of Finland to strengthen and add depth to the western defence sector, and protected the approaches to the city itself with aerostatic (barrage) balloons.

The city's defenders also had to counter the threat of artillery fire, once German forces advanced to within artillery range of the city, by initiating extensive counter-battery programmes to halt or impede the destructive fire delivered against the city's population, factories and buildings. In late September, the Leningrad Front developed a common artillery and air fire plan to deal with this threat. The plan allocated specific targets to the artillery and aircraft, the most distant obviously to aircraft. In October, the front also formed counter-battery artillery groups, each consisting of two to three anti-aircraft artillery battalions. These groups, which included the Forty-Second and Fifty-Fifth Armies' anti-aircraft artillery

and all coastal and naval guns, were subordinate to the front's chief of artillery. When the threat became especially critical in the fall, the *Stavka* sent Colonel-General of Artillery N. N. Voronov to Leningrad to advise on the counter-battery struggle.

During the winter, when the surface of the Gulf of Finland and lakes and rivers in the Leningrad region froze, permitting possible German or Finnish attacks across their surfaces, coastal defence became a major concern. The Leningrad Front addressed this threat by forming the Internal Defence of the City (VOG), formed around the nucleus of a rifle brigade.[7] This unit's mission was to organize continuous defences in Leningrad's western sector, prevent the enemy reaching the city from the Finnish Gulf, and ensure normal communications between Leningrad and forces isolated in the Oranienbaum bridgehead. During the same period, the *Stavka* transferred the bulk of the Baltic Fleet's ships from Kronshtadt to Leningrad, strengthening Leningrad's defences but also necessitating the reinforcement of Kronshtadt's ground defences with army troops. The task of countering possible German air assaults against the city fell to the ground commanders of each defensive sector and special anti-*desant* detachments. Headed by a special three-man committee (*troika*) formed from representatives from militia, fire and *Komsomol* elements, these detachments included forces from each element.

Leningrad was in the greatest danger in September, when German forces approached the city's suburbs and Zhukov commanded the Leningrad Front. During this period, the *Stavka* directed Khozin, Zhukov's Chief of Staff, to prepare the city's bridges and factories for demolition and the city's defences for final German assault by 17 September. However, the failure of the German assault and Hitler's decision to encircle the city, ended the immediate crisis.

In response to GKO instructions to exploit "local resources for its defence", from July through September military and Party authorities instituted an ambitious and extensive mobilization programme to generate military manpower, whose centrepiece was the formation of People's Militia (*narodnoe opolchanie*) forces, primarily in divisional configuration, and armed workers' detachments. The Party began forming the Leningrad People's Militia Army (*Leningradskoi armii narodnogo opolchaniia* — LANO) on 30 June 1941, and the Front appointed General A. I. Subbotin as its commander. Originally,

Subbotin's army was to consist of 15 divisions of the "best workers, students and teachers" in Leningrad. The collapse of the Northwestern Front's defences in early July, however, forced acceleration of the process, and LANO sent the first three divisions to man the Luga Line by 7 July.

LANO fielded its subordinate forces in three stages. From 4 to 18 July, the army formed three divisions of people's militia divisions (*divizii narodnogo opolchaniia* — DNO), designated the 1st, 2nd and 3rd DNOs, with strengths of 12,102, 8721 and 10,094 men, respectively.[8] During the same period, it formed 16 machine gun–artillery battalions and six destroyer regiments with a total of 16,800 men and 5000 men, respectively. Since the first levy was clearly inadequate, on 16 July the Northwestern Direction Command ordered five new divisions be formed between 18 July and 20 August. The 4th DNO was a light division formed from three destroyer regiments, and the 1st, 2nd, 3rd and 4th Guards DNOs (GDNOs) were made up of men from former workers'

BELOW: This local Party official, Comrade Pristavko, is addressing a group of civilians in the "Red Corner" of the area management office. Everyone looks healthy and well-fed. It would seem that blackout regulations have been relaxed for the occasion!

volunteer detachments. The four Guards DNOs, which numbered 10,538, 11,489, 10,334 and 8924 men each, were at or above required establishment strength.[9] Finally, the Northwestern Direction Command ordered the 6th and 7th DNOs be formed between 1 and 15 September, also on the basis of existing workers' battalions. Since the two divisions numbered 8189 and 8454 men, respectively, each was roughly 2500 men below strength. Thus, by 15 September the Northwestern Direction Command had fielded 10 DNO divisions and 16 separate machine gun–artillery battalions with a total strength of 135,000 men.[10]

Raw Courage Not Enough

Each DNO resembled a normal rifle division and was manned primarily by reservists and other volunteers.[11] However, the divisions' senior command cadre of roughly 20 officers per division were inexperienced, poorly trained and unfamiliar with the employment of modern military equipment, while the divisions' mid- and low-level cadre were former sergeants or from the ranks. The DNOs were woefully short of light and heavy machine guns and anti-tank and anti-aircraft artillery. To compensate for these grave shortages, the divisions formed anti-tank destroyer groups of men armed with anti-tank grenades or anti-tank mines.

The Northwestern Direction Command sent the DNOs to the Luga front from 10 to 20 July, immediately after their formation and without providing the officers or soldiers with any refresher training. The results were predictable. Despite the enthusiasm and ardour of officers and soldiers, the divisions had no staying power and their troops died like flies. Since all of its divisions had been dispatched to the front, the Direction Command disbanded the Militia Army at the end of September. Those DNOs that survived ultimately provided the backbone of the Forty-Second and Fifty-Fifth Armies and the Neva Operational Group. In late September the General Staff renumbered the seven surviving DNOs as regular Red Army rifle divisions and disbanded the 1st DNO and the 2nd and 4th GDNOs, which had been annihilated in combat.[12]

While the People's Militia was forming, the Party and industrial enterprises created armed workers' detachments and instituted military training for workers. Large factories such as the Kirov and Lenin Factories formed workers' detachments headed by *troikas*, made up of the factory director, the local Party secretary and the trade union chairman. About

107,000 workers received military training during July and August, while on the job, and then formed armed detachments on the basis of one company per factory shop or section. In this fashion, the Party organized 123 workers' detachments totalling 15,460 worker-soldiers by 1 November. Since most of these detachments were ineffective, on 9 October the authorities reorganized some of the detachments into rifle battalions, companies and platoons and, later, five workers' brigades, and assigned to them responsibilities in the city's internal defence. These workers' battalions served as reservoirs for the formation of DNOs and later to replenish the Leningrad Front's line forces.[13]

Women on the Frontline

When the Germans intensified their air offensive against the city in early 1942 and manpower shortages became critical, military authorities began employing many women, particularly *Komsomol* members, in combat assignments in addition to their more traditional roles. Based on GKO instructions, the Leningrad Front Military Council initially accepted 1000 women into the PVO.[14] The Leningrad *Komsomol* regional committee raised the female volunteers through special committees established in each district and also accepted volunteers from among non-union youth. The PVO commands assigned women primarily to PVO anti-aircraft artillery batteries, projector (searchlight) stations, balloon-obstacle sub-units, telephone and radio stations, and aerial reconnaissance and radio location points and installations. An additional 1000 women had joined the ranks of the Leningrad PVO by May 1942 alone.

One of the most ubiquitous tasks performed by Leningrad's population was local air defence (*mestnaia protivo-vozdushnaia oborona* — MPVO) supervised by local authorities. Soon after the war began, the Party assigned the Leningrad Council (*Sovet*) of Workers' Deputies responsibility for organizing MPVO. In turn, on 27 June the Council's Executive Committee (*Gorispolkom*) ordered workers in all factories, installations, schools and universities, social organizations and housing authorities to organize round-the-clock MPVO sentry duty. Sentries were to issue air raid warnings to the population, organize fire fighting and enforce blackouts (light discipline) to protect against enemy air attack.[15] MPVO personnel also prepared specially equipped collective air-raid shelters and field air-raid shelters throughout the city, and manned and provided permanent cadres

ABOVE: Soldiers and civilians queue at a newspaper kiosk on the Leittiny Prospect. The faces of the civilians are beginning to show signs of the strain and deprivation that was to become more common as the first winter drew on.

to maintain them and control their use.[16] Later, the MPVO formed brigades to fight fires in factories and other installations, and self-defence groups and fire teams to perform the same functions in homes and apartment blocks. More than 3500 of these groups were operating by early September manned by 270,000 men and women – 16,000 women were serving in the Frunze district alone. Finally, on 27 July the Council's Executive Committee ordered the entire able-bodied population in the city to receive MPVO training.

All of these measures paid off, particularly when the Luftwaffe began its intense bombing campaign on the night of 6 September and continued the bombing through 27 September.[17] During this period, the Luftwaffe conducted 11 day and 12 night air raids, 480 of the total 2712 German aircraft successfully penetrated the city's air defences. In addition, Soviet aircraft and anti-aircraft artillery shot down 272 of the aircraft, forcing the Luftwaffe to bomb from ever-increasing heights and more often at night. The

Luftwaffe conducted 108 air raids during the rest of the year and 1499 of its aircraft (79 percent) penetrated the city's defences. The 3295 high-explosive and 67,078 incendiary bombs these aircraft dropped caused 88 percent of the casualties Leningrad's population suffered from air attack throughout the war.

The German air bombardment decreased sharply between January and March 1942, when the attacks dwindled to individual sorties by single aircraft. For example, 572 aircraft attacked the city in April and only 95 made it through the city's anti-aircraft defences. The Germans ceased their air attacks entirely in May and did not resume them until October. Thereafter, German air activity was light for the remainder of the year. The marked decrease in German air activity, the German air blockade's collapse, and associated decreases in civilian losses due to air attack resulted largely from the growing strength and resilience of Leningrad's PVO and the efforts of the MPVO.

Before the war began, Leningrad was one of the most important centres for weapons production in the Soviet Union. It remained so after the war began as the State and Party tasked the city's factories with supplying the Red Army with weapons, ammunition and other supplies and equipment, under the slogan

"Everything for the front". Immediately after war began, the government ordered the city's industries to shift to production of military products only, a process that took two to three months to complete. Factories such as Kirov, Frunze and *Bol'shevik* accelerated their production after 22 June, enlisting large numbers of women in their workforces.

While the factories' workload increased, working conditions deteriorated sharply as the front neared the city. German artillery pounded Leningrad and its factories 272 times from 4 September to 31 December, firing more than 13,000 shells into the city, exacerbating the devastation produced by the more than 70,000 aerial bombs already dropped there. Shelling sometimes lasted for more than 18 hours in a single day, reaching a crescendo on 15 September when it lasted 18 hours and 32 minutes and on 17 September, which endured one minute more. Another 21,000 artillery shells and more than 950 bombs struck the city in 1942. This prolonged enemy bombardment killed 5723 civilians and wounded 20,507 from September 1941 to the end of 1943.

Soviet heavy industry was the primary target for German artillery and aerial bombardment. Artillery fire struck the *Elektrosila* Factory, located along the southern ring railroad, nine times from September through November 1941 and 73 of the 333 shells fired struck the factory's buildings. Artillery hit the Kronshtadt Factory 114 times from 22 September 1941 to 25 January 1942 and the 1420 shells killed 26 persons and wounded another 58. The artillery raids finally tapered off after July 1942 as a consequence of successful Red Army ground operations. Thereafter, a total of 15,462 artillery shells hit the city during the first half of 1943 and 5535 during the last six months of the year. Despite the appalling working conditions, factory production remained substantial through 31 December 1941 and included 491 tanks (from the Kirov Factory), many of which rolled off the assembly line directly into the front-lines.[18] In addition to supplying the Northern and Leningrad Fronts' needs, the factories produced 1000 guns and mortars and millions of shells for the defence of Moscow.

After the Germans captured Shlissel'burg in early September and began their ground blockade of the city, on 4 October the GKO ordered Zhdanov and Kuznetsov to evacuate key industries and technical personnel from Leningrad to the Volga and Ural regions. The evacuation of heavy tank and armoured vehicle factories and many other plants with their qualified workers, which had already begun in August, accelerated in October when German forces began operations to cut off the remaining communications routes east of the city and began bombarding these routes. The evacuation routes extended by rail to Lake Ladoga, by barge across the lake, and by rail though Volkhov and Tikhvin to Vologda and the depths of the country. By 31 August, 282 trains had left Leningrad, but the German capture of Mga complicated movement plans, forcing Lieutenant-General of Technical Services V. A. Golovko, who was in charge, to rely more heavily on barges to ferry the equipment across Lake Ladoga from Shlissel'burg. The subsequent German capture of Shlissel'burg closed the evacuation routes, leaving tons of industrial equipment stranded on rail sidings and roads from Leningrad to the lake. Ultimately the Kirov and Izhora tank factories relocated to Cheliabinsk and Sverdlovsk in the Ural region. At the same time, aircraft evacuated 10,500 of the most qualified technical personnel. These factories and

technicians soon resumed their production work in the new locations.

Despite severe shortages in personnel and supplies and constant enemy bombardment, the factories continued producing during the evacuation by using locally available resources. Beside the Germans' intense September bombardment, the most trying period for factories was from November 1941 to early 1942, when fuel and electricity shortages and personnel losses due to famine forced many factories to cease production altogether. At the height of the famine, 50 to 60 percent of factory workers were absent from work at any given time. This had a devastating impact on the availability of ammunition at the front. Even during this period, though, Leningrad's factories continued supplying Red Army forces in other critical regions, particularly the Moscow sector. On GKO instructions, in October and November, Leningrad transported vital weapons and ammunition to Moscow via Lake Ladoga and by air. The Special Northern

BELOW: A grisly photomontage of the Nevsky Prospect under fire. Civilians can be seen running along the pavement on the left away from the explosion farther down the road. The corpses on the right, although clearly out of scale, are certainly real.

Aviation Group, which flew key Kirov and Izhora Factory technicians to the Urals, participated in the airlift of critical supplies to Moscow.

Factory production improved significantly in the spring of 1942, when supplies transported across Lake Ladoga on the ice road permitted the resumption of some factory production and city transport. However, since shortages of trained managers and workers still limited full production, the Party and city government established technical schools and training programmes. Understandably, the authorities focused on restoring weapons and munitions production, and the number of functioning weapons factories rose from 50 in April to 57 in May and 75 in June, although most remained quite small. Arms production rose modestly from 1 January through 30 September 1942, particularly of light weaponry and munitions.[19] Thus, although arms production decreased drastically during the first 18 months of war, Leningrad's factories were able to satisfy the city's basic defence needs despite experiencing the harshest rigours of war, the blockade and famine.

The German blockade of Leningrad trapped more than three million souls in the city. With win-ter approaching, the food and fuel supplies cut off, and inadequate reserves dwindling, the city's inhabitants faced a frozen hell of starvation and disease while they fought for survival under enemy fire. It was indeed fortunate that the Wehrmacht failed to draw the noose tight around Leningrad by severing all of the city's communications lines east of Lake Ladoga. This reality came back to haunt the Germans and, in the end, saved the city and its population from utter starvation and destruction. Nor did the Germans get close enough to the city to destroy it by artillery fire. In addition, in early September Richtofen's VIII Air Corps (360 aircraft), which was scheduled for transfer to Army Group Centre in mid-September, attacked the Baltic Fleet, damaging the battleships *Marat* and *Oktiabrskaia Revolutsiia* and the cruisers *Kirov* and *Maksin Gorki*. However, these attacks failed to achieve their goal of destroying the fleet before Richtofen's departure.

BELOW: Small workshops such as this sprang up all over the city. This worker is repairing a PPSh submachine gun. The simple construction and robustness of many Soviet weapons made such work relatively straightforward for the least skilled workers.

With the bulk of Leningrad's male population at or on their way to the front, the first crisis faced by the Leningrad Defence Council was to look after the soldiers' families. To do so, the Council established special departments in regional, city and district executive councils, which were responsible for the support and welfare of soldiers' families. These departments distributed benefits and pensions and determined and attempted to satisfy the families' legal benefits and material needs, a process that became quite difficult during the winter famine.[20] Despite this special assistance, the soldiers' families shared many of the blockade's hardships with the population as a whole.

Leningrad's population suffered immensely during the German blockade, particularly during the first winter when shortages, famine and disease ravaged the city. The blockade's most immediate impact was to reduce drastically the supply of food, ammunition, fuel, fat and other materials necessary to sustain human life. Even though the GKO, the Party and city government were preoccupied with the desperate situation at the front, they mobilized all of the city's resources to save it and its population. When the Germans first disrupted Leningrad's supply lines in early September, the city's reserves were insufficient to meet the population's needs. Since bread and flour reserves totalled 34,381 tonnes (35,000 tons) on 26 September and daily requirements were at least 1081 tonnes (1101 tons) of flour, the city had just over one month's supply of this staple remaining. Reserves of other foodstuffs were just as low. Thus the authorities' first priority was to ensure that some essential supplies reached the city.

The only routes by which supplies could reach the city were by water across Lake Ladoga and by air. The Lake Ladoga route relied on flimsy and slow barges and cutters to cross the lake around the clock, in stormy weather, and under constant German air attack. From 1 October to 30 November these ships transported 44,204 tonnes (45,000 tons) of food,

6098 tonnes (6208 tons) of ammunition, 6520 tonnes (6638 tons) of fuel and lubricants, and 2321 tonnes (2363 tons) of other cargo across the lake. This totalled 58,939 tonnes (60,000 tons) of supplies or 1791 wagonloads at a rate of 30 wagons per day. Aerial re-supply by 30 to 50 aircraft per day during the period 14–28 November managed to transport 1179 tonnes (1200 tons) of high-calorie foods to the city. However, these deliveries fell far short of the city's requirements.

The establishment of the blockade on 8 September and the destruction of the city's Badaevskii food warehouses by German aerial bombardment on 12 September, created a food supply crisis in the city. Consequently, Stalin sent D. V. Pavlov, a representative of A. Mikoian's Food Commissariat, to Leningrad with orders to institute food rationing and conservation systems. Pavlov established and managed the food and fuel rationing system for two years in close cooperation with the city administration and Party. Pavlov's rationing system established strict norms based on the military function or work status of each soldier

ABOVE: On 20 August 1942, tragedy struck the Amelkin family – their apartment was heavily damaged by enemy fire. The thickness of the wall must have absorbed much of the explosion as the furniture and the family samovar are almost undisturbed.

and inhabitant in the city. For example, bread norms that had been established even before his arrival, were to decrease five times between 2 September and 20 November.[21] The 20 November daily bread ration was a bare minimum of 375 grams (13.2 ounces) for workers in priority shops, 250 grams (8.8 ounces) for engineer and technical workers, and 125 grams (4.4 ounces) for employees, dependents and children. Compared with 22 June 1941, this represented a 60 percent decrease in the workers' bread ration norm and a more than 80 percent decrease in the employees' norm. The 20 November norm endured until 31 December. During the same period, the bread norm for soldiers decreased three times, on 2 October, and on 7 and 20 November. This represented a decrease of 44.5 percent for frontline soldiers who received 500 grams (17.6 ounces) each after 20 November, and a

62.5 percent decrease for troops in rear service units and installations. On 20 November, the city required 501 tonnes (510 tons) of bread each day to support the population of 2.5 million souls.

To help make up for the bread shortage, the city's bakeries increased the bread's baked weight compared with the amount of flour used by shifting from hearth baking to form baking, which increased the bread's baked weight by 68 percent. In addition, on 23 September the Leningrad Front ceased beer production and ordered all malt, barley, soybeans and

bran reserves be sent to the bread factories to economize on the use of flour. However, the measures only eased rather than solved the shortages. Therefore, on 24 September the Front ordered bakeries to adulterate the bread further (40 percent of the bread already consisted of such additives as malt, oatmeal and husks). Finally, as bread supplies continued to dwindle, in late November bakeries began adding edible cellulose to the bread, which, depending on the day, constituted between 20 and 50 percent of each loaf. This use of additives and decreasing norms extended

RIGHT: These three victims of the German bombing are starkly recorded by the Soviet caption as: "S. A. Gorshkov, nine years old, a pupil at the Leninsky District School No 122; Zoya Khulikova, factory worker, and construction worker Alexandra Illyina." All died in their hospital beds.

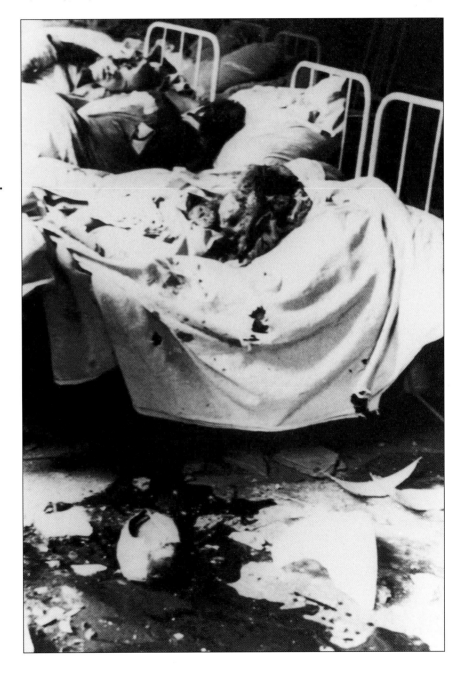

the bread supply more than one and a half months. But it was still inadequate.

The early onset of an abnormally severe winter sharply curtailed navigation on Lake Ladoga in late November 1941, and significantly worsened the supply situation in the city and at the front. More than 982 tonnes (1000 tons) of cargo daily was required just to sustain the city's population and the ice road, which was just beginning to operate in mid-January, could not satisfy these supply requirements. This forced the city authorities to search for new ways to increase the volume of cargo crossing Lake Ladoga and mobilize Leningrad's internal resources.

First, in late December the front released to the population 294 tonnes (300 tons) of food reserves stored at Kronshtadt and on other islands. At the same time, soldiers assigned to the fleet, forts and the Fifty-Fourth Army reduced their rations voluntarily for the sake of the population. All the while, search parties scoured all buildings formerly used for food and bread storage for food remnants.

As supplies dwindled and the Germans intensified their bombardment of supply depots and the ice road, the city's population began suffering from hunger and famine, casualties rose, and normal work became difficult and then impossible. As hunger spread, fuel supplies also ran out in January 1942, electricity became unavailable, the city's

ABOVE: Throughout the early years of the siege, a vast array of small ships and barges was constantly employed ferrying in munitions and foodstuffs. The return journeys often saw them conveying non-essential workers, the old and the young to places of greater safety elsewhere in the Soviet Union.

trams ceased operating, water supply was interrupted, ferry and boat transport ended, and all business activity ceased. The city's inhabitants had to obtain water from the icy Neva River, walk to work from one end of the city to the other or live in the factories, and operate machine tools by hand or by generator. Since the population had no choice but to use wood stoves to cook their food or heat their lodgings, numerous fires broke out, which were no less dangerous than the German bombardment and were difficult to fight because of the lack of water. The government established numerous fire commands to advise the population on the dangers and fight fires.

Lyudmila Anopova, born in 1931, lived through the siege of Leningrad. Her father, Akindin Kadykov, was a writer who had completed a novel about Cossack life. The manuscript was lost during the blockade of the city, and Kadykov himself died shortly after escaping from the besieged city. Lyudmila's story is but one of thousands of experiences from the city of Leningrad during this terrible time:

"The grown-ups told me they did not know when the war would begin, but I could feel the sense of anticipation in every bone of my body. The radio was never turned off. The whole world was at war. My father moved little flags around a map of Spain. There was fighting in nearby Finland. But then, one summer's day, the black, bent receiver of our street radio announced that the war had spilled over our borders. At first they tried to save the children.

"They knitted me a little shoulder bag. I had to leave alone, without my parents, with a troop of other children carrying the same little shoulder bags. We assembled at the factory where my mother worked – and then we all returned home. The city was surrounded. The evacuation had been cancelled. The siege had begun.

"Try getting dressed in a hurry when they wake you up every few hours of the night. You're only nine years old and you could easily sleep through any bomb raid or artillery barrage. Your mother is rushing you – 'Quickly! Quickly!' But your boots have so many eyelets, it takes an interminable time to lace them up – no, that's not right, that's the wrong hole. But it's good enough. You pull on the second boot without bothering. You grab your bundle – that's it, off you go.

"The air-raid shelter is in the neighbouring house. The road is dark. You know it well, but it's pockmarked with shell holes and your right foot gets caught in something, makes you stumble. You search for the light – there it is! The shelter is well-lit inside. There's still room to sit down. There are benches in the centre, at the entrances.

"We waste no time in taking our places and piling up our bundles. There is already a rumbling sound in the far distance. They are firing, the bombs are already dropping. But it's not them I'm afraid of. I am hiding my right foot from the other people. I've just noticed that I'm wearing my grandmother's boot, laced up by one eyelet. Has no-one seen it yet? I am so clumsy. It's five sizes too big. How could I not have seen that – even half-asleep? How careless, what a muddlehead I am! I can't stand it. I hate everyone

BELOW: Traditional celebrations still carried on despite the situation. Here, a young girl considers which decoration to choose from those on offer at this toy counter. Despite being indoors, both customer and assistant are dressed to keep warm as heating was carefully controlled to save fuel.

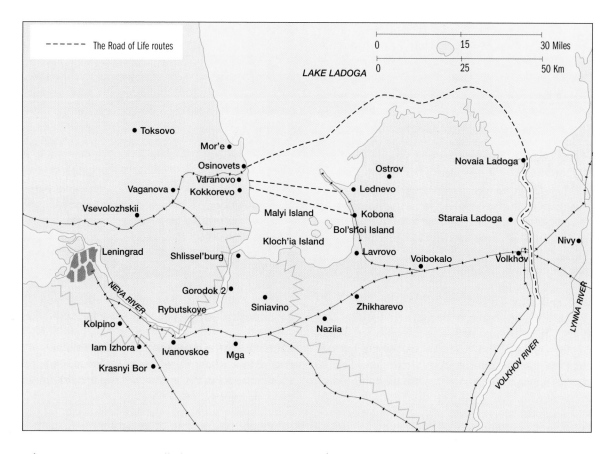

who's sitting near me – all those people throwing such apparently indifferent glances in my direction. The all-clear sounds. Safe at last. The dark road with its potholes. Autumn. Stars. Just like in the woods. My grandmother's boots slip and slide. There is a smell of burning in the air.

"During the days and nights that followed, all the provisions in the town were burned – and with them all traces of the old life. Famine descended upon Leningrad. And once again there was an evacuation – this time troops from the frontline and the outskirts were retreating to the centre of the city under heavy fire.

"That was the beginning of the worst winter in living memory. The father of my best friend was the first of my close acquaintances to die. His coffin stood in their best room and the dead man lay inside, dressed in his best clothes, washed and carefully combed, ready for the last journey. And it was terrible indeed. But it wasn't long before we ceased to be afraid of death.

"They cut off the water supply. The Neva was close by, only 500 meters away. But how could we reach it? We lowered sledges, saucepans and milk churns from the fourth floor. We made our way slow-

ABOVE: The "Road of Life" across Lake Ladoga saved Leningrad during the first winter of the siege, and thereafter continued to be an important winter supply route for the city. Like Leningrad itself it was under constant Luftwaffe threat, and so anti-aircraft positions were set up along its various routes.

ly to the Neva, across the snowdrifts, and scooped up freezing water from the ice holes. On both sides lay the abandoned corpses of the dead. Some were clothed, others were covered in shrouds.

"The windows are boarded up with plywood. It's dark everywhere. The only warmth is in the kitchen by the iron stove, and a tiny wick is burning on the table. It's just a twisted piece of cloth dipped in oil. We already take no notice of the shells exploding around us. We no longer go down to the air-raid shelters. We just sit together in the gloomy kitchen.

"I read to myself all day. And such wonderful books! About Suvorov! About the young princess who became Catherine II. I draw pictures of little houses, trees, a wood. But I'm hungry every moment of the day. Provisions are sold on ration books. We have to stand in a long queue at the shop on Kirovsky Prospect. For our six ration books we get a little millet, some dry onion, now and again a piece of frozen meat. We stand there for hours. We are frozen but we wait and suffer in silence."

"Dying Was Painful But Not So Terrible"

"In the morning, we do not have the strength to get up, but my mother forces us to climb out of our beds and then to make them up. I do this on my knees. I have no need to dress. We sleep in our overcoats. My parents have already decided to leave the city, even though my father has work. Once an engineer, he now works as a van driver at the bakery and unloads the bread in a wheelbarrow at the bread shop. My mother pushes the wheelbarrow from behind and guards it at the same time, fearing that they will be robbed. But one day I found myself pushing the barrow instead of my mother. It was the day my family had decided to leave – to the south, to the Don.

"They baked the bread in enormous ovens. The crusts curled over and fell off in crumbs. The workers treated me to the crusts. I ate and ate and ate. I didn't save a single crumb that the bakery chief gave me. I don't remember how many crusts I ate in that day – probably a whole loaf of them. By evening I was full. That night I thought I was dying but my father didn't notice.

"He didn't look after me. I knew that I'd never have such a day again. Dying was painful but not so terrible. By morning, it had all passed – the pain, the feeling of satiety. But the smell of the bread crusts has remained with me forever.

"On maps of the Leningrad *oblast*, the Road of Life across Lake Ladoga is clearly marked. On April 4, 1942, we made our way along that road – just the four of us and a few meagre possessions. We went by car, then by train to the Borisovaya Ridge, to the banks of the lake strewn with people and their luggage. The lorries came up and the drivers gave preference to those who had vodka on them – that eternal hard currency. We had nothing but eau de cologne. We were the last to go. The wind was cruel and piercing. There were people and their possessions bundled together in the back of the lorry.

"The driver had not slept for three days. Just as we were approaching the other bank, he fell asleep on the wheel, crashed into a pine tree and threw the passengers across the ice. My father fell out of the lorry. He died two months later. My sister and I became orphans."

Spreading disease was a natural outgrowth of the famine. The percentage of the population ill with scurvy and malnutrition (dystrophia) increased drastically and the death toll rose catastrophically. The same number of people perished in December 1941 that had died in all of 1940, and in January 1942 3500–4000 succumbed to disease and famine daily. After the famine began in November, the monthly death toll rose from 10,000 in November to more than 50,000 in December and more than 120,000 in January. During the winter of 1941 and 1942, the worst period of the siege when scurvy became rampant, the authorities began producing Vitamin C from pine needles, manufacturing 162,010 gallons (738,500 litres) of pine extract in the first half of 1942. In addition, the population of Leningrad region provided food to the Leningraders through the porous blockade.[22] The city's fuel supplies also remained critically short, largely due to the Front's and fleet's requirements. Despite strict rationing and conservation, all fuel supplies had been exhausted by

BELOW: This female traffic officer is guarding the entrance to the Leningrad Front and the beginning of the "Road of Life". The Gaz lorry is typical of thousands of such vehicles that made the dangerous journey across the ice day after day.

ABOVE: An essential feature of the "Road of Life" was the thickness of the ice. The Red Army's meteorological branch performed a vital, if unsung, service from isolated stations such as this ice-block hut dotted across Lake Ladoga.

1 January 1942. The authorities then collected firewood and peat from neighbouring districts, particularly from the city's suburbs and the northeast, where more than 3.5 million cubic meters of firewood were gathered in 1942.

Leningrad's sole ground supply route during the first harsh winter was the so-called Ladoga ice road (*Ladozhskaia ledovaia trassa*), which crossed the surface of Lake Ladoga. This legendary road earned the well-deserved name, the "Road of Life" (*Doroga zhizni*), because it was critical to Leningrad's survival. The *Stavka* ordered construction of a supply route across the lake in early November even before the lake froze, when it became obvious that the Leningrad Front could not raise the blockade. On 19 November the Leningrad Front ordered that a military vehicular road (*voenno-avtomobil'naia doroga* – BAD), designated the 101st BAD, be built from Kobona on the eastern bank of Lake Ladoga across the ice of Shlissel'burg Bay to Vaganovo on the lake's western bank. However, the German capture of

Tikhvin on 8 November forced construction of a far longer road, the 102nd BAD, which bypassed Tikhvin from the north.[23] The ice road itself followed the shortest possible route – 28–32km (17.5–20 miles) – across the lake and was constructed in extremely difficult conditions. Units constructing the road had to contend with almost constant German artillery fire and air bombardment, which required extensive use of camouflage and anti-aircraft defence. The builders also had to contend with ever-changing ice conditions on the lake, frequent and numerous cracks and fissures in the ice, periodic thaws that effected the ice's thickness, and recurring storms.

Road exploitation parties reconnoitred and marked routes across the lake in mid-November and, after testing the routes' viability, the first cargo reached Leningrad on 23 November.[24] Subsequently, harsh and ever-changing weather conditions continually battered the routes and limited their carrying capacity, requiring Front engineers to work constantly to repair, improve and expand them. Between 18 and 28 November, the engineers managed to build a second route extending 27km (16.8 miles) across the lake from Kokkorevo via Kloch'ia Island to Kobona. As the ice thickened, the engineers also created multiple new routes to the north. By the end of December the ice had thickened to 1m (3.2ft) and was covered by 300mm (11.8in) of snow cover, permitting almost unlimited use. Thereafter, the routes were able to sustain the weight of almost any type of military vehicle up to and including heavy KV tanks. The engineers configured the ice roads to accommodate around-the-clock, two-way traffic in any weather. When construction was completed, the roads extended a total of 1770km (1106 miles), 1650 of which had to be repeatedly cleared of snow.[25] The Front also had to create and deploy an elaborate network of road guides, communications points, road service commandant posts, medical and rescue service points, feeding points, and combat security posts along the routes to ensure the routes functioned reliably.[26]

Initially, however, the new ice road fell far short of satisfying Leningrad's needs and the Leningrad Front's plan for supplying 1965 tonnes (2000 tons) of supplies to the city per day.[27] Worse still, a thaw that began on 30 November limited vehicular movement and reduced the shipment that day to only 61 tonnes (62 tons). Even after the ice thickened, the supply effort was plagued by congenitally poor and ineffective organization, which reduced food, ammunition and fuel reserves to catastrophically low levels and threatened the survival of soldier and civilian alike in

the city. Therefore, Party leaders Zhdanov and Kuznetsov took personal charge of the supply effort, after which the situation slowly improved. Daily supply shipments rose to 687 tonnes (700 tons) on 22 December and 786 tonnes (800 tons) on 23 December, for the first time exceeding Leningrad's daily consumption rate. Since the city and its defending front and the fleet were being fed "on wheels", the effort could not diminish, since even the slightest disruption in the flow of supplies had immediate adverse consequences for the population and the troops.

On 25 December the flow of supplies had improved enough that the Front could increase the daily bread ration by 100 grams (3.5 ounces) for workers and engineer and technical personnel and 75 grams (1.8 ounces) for employees, dependents and children. However, the increased bread ration alone did not satisfy the exhausted population's food needs, and they continued to endure incredible deprivation well into January 1942. In early

BELOW: The reflected light from the ice makes it difficult to identify the aircraft, but judging by the calm manner of the troops on the ice it is unlikely that they are German. The loads carried by the lorries was determined by the thickness of the ice; their speed was often only the equivalent of walking pace.

January Leningrad's food reserves shrank to two days' supply and fuel reserves to 213,163 tonnes (217,000 tons), well short of the required 1700 wagonloads per day.[28]

Given the catastrophic shortages, the Front accelerated work on the ice road, expanding its capacity and usage to two or three convoys per day along multiple routes and increasing the speed of convoy movement. As a result, deliveries doubled and by 18 January 1942 road traffic finally fulfilled the Front's norms, permitting it to increase daily rations and begin building up reserves.[29] The improved supply transport prompted the front to double the population's and soldiers' daily bread rations on 24 January.[30] All categories of rations increased once again on 10 February, with frontline soldiers receiving 800 grams (28.2 ounces) of bread daily and rear service troops 600 grams (21.1 ounces). The effort to increase the quantity of ice routes and their capacity continued unabated until the road was no longer needed. This required tremendous exertions. "Two convoys per driver per day" became a slogan that 261 drivers achieved in January and another 627 in March. During March, 355 drivers completed three trips and 100 completed five. The supply flow across the lake increased

ABOVE: With weapons shortages it was essential to collect and repair as many arms as possible. This squad has just taken delivery of refurbished Moisin Nagant rifles. The face of the civilian passer-by shows a distinct preoccupation with matters other than guns – rations, maybe?

further in the second half of January 1942, with foodstuffs making up 75 percent of the cargo. At the same time, convoys began evacuating women, children, the sick and wounded, as well as valuable cargoes from the city.

However, the ice road's usefulness began decreasing rapidly after the spring thaw set in. On 25 March the thickness of the ice began eroding, pools of water and numerous cracks began appearing on and in the ice, and transport had to be curtailed. Buses could not use the road after 15 April and tanker trucks after 19 April. The Front ordered all movement across the ice halted, effective 12:00 hours on 21 April. Despite the order, a 64-tonne (65-ton) shipment of spring onions made it to Leningrad on 23–24 April. That, however, was the end, and all vehicular traffic stopped the next day.

The ice road contributed enormously to the city's defence and its population's survival before the spring thaw ended its usefulness. By February, Leningrad's civilians received daily food rations comparable to those received by workers elsewhere in the country, and bread adulteration fell to less than two percent during the first quarter of 1942. During the final three weeks the road was functioning, it transported four and a half times as many supplies as it had in November and December 1941, including special high-calorie products.[31] Furthermore, the reserves amassed during its operations were sufficient to feed the population from the time the ice road melted and lake water transport resumed.

Beside vital ammunition, food and fuel supplies, the ice road served as a means for evacuating civilians, key personnel and factories. As soon as the ice road opened, the Leningrad Front began a massive evacuation of those who were not capable of working, in particular, women, children and the disabled. The number evacuated rose from 11, 296 persons in January to 117,434 in February, 221,947 in March, and 163,392 in April. By April the total number of evacuees reached 514,069, an average rate of 5000–6000 persons per day. Industrial evacuation also began in December. From December 1941 to April 1942, the Leningrad Front sent 3677 railroad cars loaded with dismantled factory machine equipment, valuable cultural items and cargo destined for the "mainland", from Leningrad to Lake Ladoga's eastern shore. About 20 percent of these transfers occurred along the ice road.

The Defence of the Ice Road

Since the ice road operated under almost constant German air attack, road security and defence were immensely important. The Leningrad Front deployed rifle units and naval infantry brigades along the lake's coast to defend against German or Finnish diversionary attacks, and aircraft and anti-aircraft units to defend against air attacks. These forces defended the road's many routes, roads and railroads adjacent to the lake, and bases and warehouses on the lake proper or on its approaches. PVO fielded 200 mid-calibre anti-aircraft guns, 50 small-calibre guns, 100 anti-aircraft machine guns, and 100 searchlights to defend against enemy aircraft. Forces from the Fifty-Fourth Army defended the lake's southern shore, and the 10th Rifle Division, 4th Naval Infantry Brigade and

BELOW: When ships of the Baltic Fleet were in dock their weaponry would be used to supplement the main anti-aircraft defences. Sailors were also used in the frontline fighting alongside the Red Army. These sailors are wearing the navy issue black naval winter hat.

Twenty-Third Army units, reinforced by armoured cutters and coastal artillery of the Baltic Fleet, defended the western shore. These forces organized observation points, patrols, outposts and local security along the ice road and mined and deployed ski patrols along the approaches to the lake and ice road. German air attacks on the road and associated installations intensified throughout March 1942, and, on some days, German aircraft attacked the road repeatedly around the clock. The Leningrad Front PVO countered with all means at its disposal, including the entire 13th Fighter Aviation Regiment.

The Leningrad Front's Road-Commandant Service maintained and regulated traffic along the ice road. Initially, it established 20 traffic control posts, 3–400m (984–1312ft) apart, to control traffic, but ultimately increased the number of posts to 75 by 1 January 1942. At that time, 350 traffic regulators controlled vehicle intervals, movement and dispersion, verified the thickness and condition of the ice, and deployed 150–200 blackout lanterns along the routes to light the way. Later, when the weather became more settled and when high snow walls flanked the roads, traffic control became easier, the number of regulators decreased, and posts were deployed 1–2km (.62–1.25 miles) apart. The regulators contributed significantly to the ice road's success, doing so while stoically withstanding the extreme cold and German air attacks.

Hand in hand with the military defence of the city itself, the Party and military leadership worked to establish a partisan movement in the German rear area, which it hoped could disrupt German operations and logistics, and gather intelligence on enemy troop movements and intentions. Initially, the suddenness of the German offensive and Army Group North's rapid advance towards the city paralyzed the Soviet authorities, leaving them little time to ponder partisan operations. However, the Germans' subsequently harsh treatment of the population and the large number of Soviet soldiers bypassed in the German rear created partisan forces spontaneously. In time, the *Stavka* and the Front moved decisively to create and expand a partisan movement, first, by exploiting underground Party organizations in the German rear area and, later, by sending specially trained teams and detachments into the German rear to organize partisan forces.

The Partisan Effort

Initially, from mid- to late July the Northwestern Direction Command and Leningrad Party Committee met with provisional partisan command and political cadres, formed initial partisan detach-

ments, and assigned missions to partisan forces through the Northern and Northwestern Fronts' headquarters.[32] By September 1941, Party and *Komsomol* regional and district committees formed 227 partisan detachments and smaller diversionary groups composed of carefully selected volunteers totalling roughly 9000 men. During August and September the two Fronts inserted 67 detachments of these (totalling 2886 men) into the German rear area and disbanded the remaining detachments, using their personnel to man newly formed destroyer detachments and guards DNO divisions. The Leningrad Regional Party Committee established a *troika* headed by G. Kh. Bumagin, a regional Party secretary, to direct partisan operations, and on 2 August the Leningrad Front appointed Lieutenant-Colonel E. N. Artoshchenko to head an Operational Group to direct the Front's partisan detachments. Finally, on 27 September the Leningrad Front and Party established a partisan headquarters headed by M. N. Nikitin, the secretary of the Regional Party Committee, to control partisan actions and coordinate them with front operations.

Initially, Party members formed the nucleus of these partisan detachments and diversionary groups, and Party secretaries at each level directed both the partisan units and Party underground groups operating in territories under their jurisdiction.[33] By 22 October 1941, this increasingly elaborate partisan effort encompassed 38 district Party and 38 district *Komsomol* organizations composed of 125 Party and 100 *Komsomol* groups and 84 partisan detachments numbering more than 3000 men operating in the regions west and southwest of Leningrad. Although scarcely operational and lacking even rudimentary command and control, these early partisan detachments initiated a series of low-level sabotage and diversionary actions in June and July.[34]

The 2nd Partisan Brigade

The most significant partisan action during this period took place in the southern portion of the Leningrad region. There, the 2nd Partisan Brigade, headed by N. G. Vasilev, seized and held most of the Belebelkovskii, Ashevskii and Dedovichi regions, which became one of the first so-called "Partisan *krai*".[35] The area under the 2nd Brigade's control extended 120km (75 miles) from north to south and 90km (56.2 miles) from east to west, encompassing the area bounded by Dno, Staraia Russa, Bezhanits and Kholm. Throughout July and early August, the partisans successfully parried German attempts to penetrate and occupy this region, and, during October and November, the Party re-established village councils, many collective farms, 53 schools and numerous medical points within the region. Although Army Group North organized several punitive expeditions against the Partisan *krai* in August and September, its use of SS units only inflamed partisan activity and German forces were not able to re-establish control over the region.

In the final analysis, however, at best, partisan activities during the first few months of the war were crude, poorly organized, sporadic and, hence, only marginally effective. Nevertheless, their limited actions and the Germans' often arrogant and brutal response towards the inhabitants paved the way for the emergence of an even more effective partisan movement in the future.[36]

While fierce debates still rage over the numbers of civilians who perished from famine or enemy fire during the first year of the Battle for Leningrad, no one can question the horrors of the first terrible winter under the blockade. The gruesome toll rose from at least 10,000 dead in November, to 50,000 in December, to in excess of 120,000 in January. Dmitriy Pavlov, who fed the Leningraders during the blockade, states that 199,187 persons were officially reported to have perished during the winter. Although the Funeral Trust, which was responsible for individual and mass burials, maintained no records for January and February, it recorded 89,968 bodies buried in March 1942, 102,497 in April, and 53,562 in May. The average of 4000–5000 bodies buried through autumn 1942 brought the total from February 1941 to February 1942 to 460,000 persons. In addition, individual work teams of civilians and soldiers estimated they transported 228,263 more bodies from morgues to cemeteries from December 1941 to December 1942.

When the winter evacuations via the Ladoga ice road ended in April 1942, Leningrad's population had fallen from about 2,280,000 million in December 1941 to an estimated 1,100,000, a decline of 1,180,000. Considering the 440,000 persons who were evacuated during the winter and the 120,000 soldiers sent to the front or evacuated in May and June, the city's civilian population suffered at least 620,000 dead by 1 July 1942, not counting the many who perished in the city's suburbs.

As far as military casualties were concerned, official figures indicate that the Red Army and Baltic Fleet lost 344,926 personnel during the Leningrad strategic defensive operation from 10 July to 30 September 1941. This included 214,078 dead and 130,848 wounded or sick. The Fifty-Fourth Separate Army lost

ABOVE: Another corpse is hauled away for disposal. Of the first winter of the siege, when starvation killed many, one survivor wrote: "In the worst period of the siege Leningrad was in the power of the cannibals. God alone knows what terrible things went on behind the walls of apartments."

54,979, including 22,211 dead and 32,768 wounded or sick in the Siniavino offensive (10 September–28 October). Total losses during the Tikhvin defence and offensive (16 October–30 December) were 89,490 including 40,667 dead and 48,823 wounded or sick. The Liuban offensive and subsequent encirclement (7 January–10 July 1942) cost the Red Army 403,118 casualties, including 149,838 dead and 253,280 wounded and sick. This grim toll in major operations amounted to 825,513 casualties, including 426,794 dead and 465,719 wounded and sick. Losses during other periods were likely to have raised the military death toll during the first year of the Battle for Leningrad to in excess of 500,000 soldiers and the overall military and civilian death toll to more than 1.1 million persons. Regardless of the death toll, these figures accord the Battle for Leningrad and its associated winter blockade the dubious honour of being the most terrible and costly siege in recorded history.

CHAPTER 5:
FALSE DAWN

As the Wehrmacht ground to a halt on the Eastern Front in December 1941, the *Stavka* and Stalin thought that determined counterattacks could inflict a severe defeat on the Germans. In the Leningrad area the Red Army launched its Liuban Offensive, but the German troops proved tenacious and the Soviets had too few resources to achieve victory. The threat to Leningrad continued.

The Red Army's victories at Moscow, Rostov and Tikhvin in December 1941 made it possible for the *Stavka* to expand its ongoing operations in these regions into a general winter offensive encompassing the entire Soviet-German front. Khozin's Leningrad Front defended Leningrad and the Neva River line just east of the city, and Meretskov's Volkhov Front manned continuous defences from the southern shores of Lake Ladoga to Kirishi and southwards along the Volkhov River to Lake Il'men. Meretskov's forces were attempting to expand their bridgeheads west of the Volkhov River, but gave up the effort on 3 January because of stiff German resistance.

To the south, the Northwestern Front defended between Lakes Il'men and Selizharevo and was preparing to attack westwards along the Staraia Russa and Velikie Luki axes. Along the vital western axis, the Kalinin and Western Fronts were pressing German Army Group Centre westwards from Moscow, threatening to envelop the army group's flanks. In southern Russia, the bulk of the Briansk, Southwestern, Southern and Caucasus Fronts were on the defensive, tying down substantial German forces and defending Sevastopol and the Kerch peninsula.

LEFT: Although obviously a posed shot, these Red Army soldiers are properly equipped for the rigors of winter warfare in their camouflage dress. The leading man is holding a grenade with a metal handle, dangerous in sub-zero temperatures (bare flesh could stick to it), and the popular PPSh "burp gun".

The *Stavka* had begun planning for a fully fledged Winter Campaign in mid-December, during the midst of its Tikhvin, Moscow and Rostov counteroffensives. On 10 January 1942 it ordered the Red Army to commence a general offensive to exploit its December successes. The *Stavka*'s aim was to:

"Deny the German-Fascist forces a breathing spell, drive them to the west without a halt, and force them to expend their reserves before spring when we will have large, fresh reserves and the Germans will not have greater reserves, thus paving the way for the complete destruction of Hitlerite forces in 1942."

The primary objective of the *Stavka* was to capture Smolensk and destroy German Army Group Centre. Simultaneously, it hoped to liberate the Donbas region and create prerequisites for liberating the Crimea, and defeat German Army Group North and raise the Leningrad blockade. While these objectives reflected Stalin's political aims, they did not accord with the Red Army's real military capabilities. Worse still, as they mounted their expanded offensives, Stalin and the *Stavka* failed to concentrate their forces decisively along any single axis by dispersing their forces and attacking along every conceivable point.

On 17 December, the *Stavka* ordered the Leningrad and Volkhov Fronts and the Northwestern Front's right wing to conduct the Leningrad-Novgorod offensive by launching concentric attacks on Army Group North, to defeat the

ABOVE: Marshal of the Soviet Union K.A. Meretskov commanded the Volkhov Front at the beginning of 1942. Ordered by Stalin to launch an offensive to destroy the German Eighteenth Army, his forces suffered a series of defeats, culminating in the destruction of the Second Shock Army.

army group and raise the Leningrad blockade. Within the context of the larger offensive, the Leningrad and Volkhov Fronts were to conduct the Leningrad-Volkhov offensive to cut off and destroy German forces in the Mga, Tosno and Liuban region, and, by extension, in the Shlissel'burg salient by attacking southeastwards from Leningrad and northwestwards from the Volkhov River. To the south, the Northwestern Front was to attack to capture Demiansk and Staraia Russa, exploit towards Sol'tsy and Dno, and cut off German withdrawal routes from Novgorod and Luga in cooperation with the Volkhov Front. Since Meretskov's Volkhov Front was to play the primary role in raising the Leningrad blockade, the *Stavka* provided him with significant reinforcements.

In early January the Wehrmacht was already facing increasingly powerful and violent Red Army assaults across the breadth of its Eastern Front,

some of which jeopardized large groups of its forces. Therefore, Hitler and the OKH ordered the Wehrmacht to hold on to its positions, rest and replenish its forces, form new strategic and operational reserves, and prepare to resume decisive offensive operations in the spring and summer of 1942. Along the northwestern axis, Army Group North and the Finnish Southeastern Army were to blockade Leningrad, firmly defend the Volkhov River line, refit their forces, and prepare a new offensive to capture Leningrad in the summer. Axis forces along the northwestern axis numbered 26 infantry, two panzer, two motorized, three security divisions and two brigades, concentrated primarily south and east of Leningrad, in the Kirishi strongpoint, and also along the Demiansk and Staraia Russa axis.

Kuechler's Eighteenth Army with 17 divisions, including the 8th and 12th Panzer and 20th Motorized Divisions, was deployed along the front extending from south of Oranienbaum and Leningrad proper to the Shlissel'burg salient south of Lake Ladoga and southeastwards to the Volkhov River at Kirishi. XXVI and L Army Corps contained the Soviets' Oranienbaum bridgehead and defended south of Leningrad, the XXVIII Army Corps occupied the vital Shlissel'burg salient and the sector to the southeast, and I Army and XXIX Motorized Corps defended the Kirishi region. Busch's Sixteenth Army, with 11 divisions, including the 18th Motorized, protected the 350km (219-mile) front south along the Volkhov River from the Kirishi region to Lake Il'men and eastwards through the Valdai Hills to Ostashkov. The army's XXXVIII Army Corps defended the Volkhov River line, X Army Corps, backed up by the 18th Motorized Division, covered from Staraia Russa to Demiansk, and II Army Corps the region from Demiansk to Ostashkov.

Stavka's Winter Plans

The two German armies occupied strong and deep defences anchored on numerous strongpoints along the front and to the rear. The most formidable strongpoints were at at Ropsha, Krasnoe Selo, Iam-Izhora, Mga, Siniavino, Liuban, Spasskaia Polist, Staraia Russa, Demiansk and Vatolino. The German positions skillfully integrated their defences with many terrain obstacles in the region, especially the multitude of rivers, lakes and swamps. While the hard freeze of winter reduced the obstacle value of these terrain features, it also created terrible fighting conditions for the troops of both sides.

The Leningrad and Volkhov Fronts' Leningrad-Volkhov offensive was only one part of the centre-piece of the *Stavka*'s Winter Campaign along the northwestern axis. But, at the same time, it was only part of a larger effort to liberate the entire region from Leningrad southwards to Staraia Russa, an effort that involved the Northwestern Front as well.

Plans for the Offensive

The *Stavka* assigned the leading role in the offensive to Meretskov's Volkhov Front. His fresh Second Shock and Fifty-Ninth Armies were to conduct his main attack westwards from the Volkhov River to sever the Leningrad-Dno and Leningrad-Novgorod railroads, and destroy German forces in the Liuban and Chudovo region in cooperation with the Leningrad Front's Fifty-Fourth Army attacking from the north. Subsequently, the three armies were to advance northwestwards to raise the Leningrad blockade in cooperation with the Leningrad Front's other armies. The Fifty-Second Army, on Meretskov's left flank, was to attack north of Novgorod and help the Northwestern Front's Eleventh Army destroy the German Sixteenth Army's forces in the Novgorod, Sol'tsy and Dno regions. Meretskov's Fourth Army, east of the Shlissel'burg salient, was to support the main and secondary attacks and protect their flanks, while the front's 52 aircraft were to provide air support.[1]

Khozin's Leningrad Front was to penetrate German defences west of Kirishi and southeast of Leningrad with its Fifty-Fourth and Fifty-Fifth Armies, capture Tosno, encircle and destroy German forces at Mga and in the Shlissel'burg salient, and raise the Leningrad blockade. His Forty-Second Army and the Coastal and Neva Operational Groups, which were blockaded in Oranienbaum and Leningrad, were to support the offensive, and, subsequently, attack to the south as soon as the Fifty-Fourth, Second Shock and Fifty-Ninth Armies reached the Leningrad-Dno railroad. The 345 aircraft assigned to the Leningrad Front, the Baltic Fleet and PVO were to protect Leningrad, Kronshtadt, the Tikhvin-Leningrad sector and communications routes into Leningrad, and support the ground offensive.[2] When the operation began, Khozin's and Meretskov's Fronts committed 325,700 troops to combat and reinforced them with upwards of 100,000 more during the offensive.

Kurochkin's Northwestern Front was to attack German forces at Staraia Russa, Demiansk and Toropets simultaneously with two shock groups. The first shock group, the Eleventh Army deployed on the front's right wing, was to advance through Staraia Russa to Dno, link up with the Volkhov Front's Fifty-Second Army, and destroy German forces in the Novgorod region.

The second shock group, the Third and Fourth Shock Armies (formerly the Sixtieth and Twenty-Seventh Armies) on the Front's left wing, was to advance through Toropets to Rudnia and destroy German forces in the Rzhev and Viaz'ma regions in cooperation with the Kalinin and Western Fronts. The Thirty-Fourth Army, deployed in the Front's centre, was to encircle and destroy German forces in Demiansk. A total of 89 aircraft, many in disrepair, were to provide the Front with air support. Initially, Kurochkin committed 105,700 men to the

RIGHT: This artillery officer is wearing the Red Army's standard winter camouflage gear of hood, smock and overalls. The entrance to the battery office has been reinforced with generous layers of ice blocks, which improved the insulation and strengthened the building against counter-battery fire.

offensive, but reinforced the operations with another 200,000 during its course.

The *Stavka* ordered the forces participating in the offensive to seize jumping-off positions and complete the concentration of their forces by 26 December. However, neither the Germans nor the weather cooperated, forcing the *Stavka* to delay the main operation until 6 January. Meanwhile the Fifty-Fourth Army was to begin its assault west of Kirishi. Because of the innumerable delays, the *Stavka* decided to launch its main offensive in staggered fashion, with the Fifty-Ninth, Fourth and Fifty-Second Armies attacking on 6 January and the Second Shock joining the effort on 7 January. Even so, the attacking forces completed few of their offensive preparations on time. Meretskov did not complete the concentration of his infantry and armour until 7 and 8 January, his artillery until 12 January, and his rear services until well after the operation began. Despite these delays and the incomplete attack preparations, Stalin insisted Meretskov begin his assault on 6 January as planned, before his forces were fully concentrated

ABOVE: Following the German failure to take Moscow at the end of 1941, Stalin was convinced he could defeat the Wehrmacht all along the front. But his armies lacked training, equipment and sound leadership, and soon ground to a halt despite the demands he made upon their commanders.

and without necessary artillery and logistical support. The results were predictable.

From its very beginning, the overly ambitious offensive encountered recurring and insurmountable difficulties. Inevitably, the attacking forces suffered from acute and persistent ammunition and fuel shortages, the unavailability of reserves necessary to exploit successes, and congenitally poor command and control and coordination of forces. Worse still, as the offensive developed, the three Fronts' axes of advance diverged sharply in three directions and combat developed in three sectors, separated from one another in both space and time. The Volkhov Front's Second Shock and Fifty-Ninth Armies advanced into the frozen swampy wastelands south of Liuban, where they fought in relative isolation between January and June. During the same period, the Northwestern Front's armies bypassed and encircled German forces in Demiansk and reached the eastern outskirts of Staraia Russa, becoming engaged in prolonged and fruitless operations in both regions. The Leningrad Front's Fifty-Fourth Army became locked in a fruitless struggle west of Kirishi, and the Front's armies south and west of Leningrad made no progress whatsoever, in part because conditions within Leningrad made them too weak to do so.

Fediuninsky's Fifty-Fourth Army, which initiated the offensive by attacking German defences near Pogost'e west of Kirishi on 4 and 5 January, advanced only 4–5km (2.5–3.1 miles) before German counterattacks threw the army's troops back to their jumping-off positions. Although the Fifty-Fourth Army's failure seemed insignificant, it set the pattern for what was to come and, worse still, prevented the army from supporting the Volkhov Front once it began its offensive. Meretskov's and Khozin's forces attacked on 6 and 7 January as Stalin demanded, but their initial assault was aborted almost immediately after they had achieved only meagre gains. Galanin's Fifty-Ninth Army began Meretskov's main attack early on 6 January, when its lead divisions attempted to seize and expand the Front's bridgeheads west of the Volkhov River so that Sokolov's Second Shock Army could exploit westwards the next day. While a portion of Galanin's forces struggled west of the river, Meretskov completed concentrating the remainder of the Fifty-Ninth and the Second Shock Armies on the river's eastern bank. By the day's end Galanin's initial assault expired amid the Germans' strong defences. Undeterred, Meretskov committed the remainder of the Fifty-Ninth Army and Sokolov's Second Shock Army to combat early on 7 January, but only in piecemeal and uncoordinated fashion. Reinforcing failure, the hapless forces immediately got bogged down with heavy losses, the Second Shock Army alone losing more than 3000 men in the first three minutes of its ill-fated assault. Driven on by Stalin's incessant orders, exhortations and threats, the two armies struggled for two more days before the attacks ended in utter exhaustion and confusion.[3]

Stalin's Frustration
Nonplussed by these failures, Stalin ordered Meretskov to regroup his armies and resume the offensive in more coordinated fashion on 13 January, this time leading the assault with the full

Second Shock Army. To ensure his orders were carried out to the letter, Stalin dispatched L. Z. Mekhlis, Chief of the Red Army's Main Political Directorate and his special emissary and personal hatchet man, to supervise Meretskov's attack preparations. Uncharacteristically, Mekhlis' first action, the appointment of General Klykov, the experienced Fifty-Second Army commander, to replace the incompetent Sokolov as Second Shock Army commander, was a positive step.[4] However, the arrival of Mekhlis did not bode well for the operation's success. His legendary vile temperament and military incompetence was only exceeded by his ruthless treatment of commanders and soldiers alike. Here along the Volkhov, the dreaded Mekhlis would begin earning his well-deserved reputation as a harbinger of military disaster.

Red Army Failure
After regrouping and refreshing their forces for several days, Meretskov's Second Shock, Fifty-Ninth, Fourth and Fifty-Second Armies and Khozin's Fifty-Fourth Army resumed the offensive early on 13 September, this time almost simultaneously and preceded by proper artillery preparations. Even so, ammunition was still woefully inadequate to sustain the fresh attacks. In the Second Shock Army's sector, the 90-minute artillery preparation and subsequent ground assault shattered German defences at the junction of XXXVIII Army Corps' 126th and 215th Infantry Divisions, producing panic in the former, which had only recently arrived from the West. In heavy fighting from 13 to 16 January, the army's forces managed to carve small wedges in the Germans' defences west of the Volkhov and Tigoda Rivers. They were not able, however, to capture key German strongpoints on the rivers' western banks and penetrate deep into the Germans' defences, largely because Meretskov and his army commanders once again failed to concentrate their attacking forces. On the Second Shock Army's flanks, the Fourth and Fifty-Second Armies also failed to record any progress and went over to the defence on 14 and 15 January.

Fediuninsky's Fifty-Fourth Army also attacked early on 13 January with full kit, but immediately encountered determined resistance by XXVIII Army Corps' 269th, Infantry Division, reinforced by elements of the 223rd and 291st Infantry and 12th Panzer Divisions. Although Fediuninsky's forces captured Pogost'e on 17 January, they failed to penetrate the German defences, reportedly

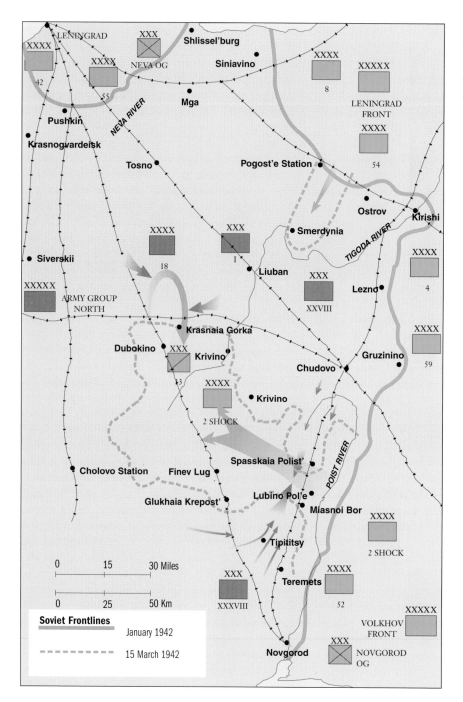

LEFT: The Soviet Liuban offensive operation and the encirclement and destruction of the Soviet Second Shock Army, January–June 1942.

because, despite repeated *Stavka* instructions to do so, Fediuninsky also failed to concentrate his forces and, instead, attacked in dispersed fashion across a 30km (18.75-mile) front. The failure, which the General Staff also attributed to poor command and control, prompted Stalin to subdivide Fediuninsky's army into the Fifty-Fourth and Eighth Armies in late January to tighten command and control. The new Eighth Army, commanded by

Major-General A. V. Sukhomlin, manned what had formerly been the Fifty-Fourth Army's right flank south of the Ladoga. Sukhomlin's army, together with the Fifty-Fourth Army on its left flank, was to smash German defences in the Lodva region, east of Siniavino, and advance westwards to Tosno, where it was to link up with the Fifty-Fifth Army, whose forces were to attack Tosno from the north-west. The *Stavka* left Fediuninsky's mission unchanged. His Fifty-Fourth Army was to advance southwestwards from Pogost'e, link up with the Second Shock Army at Liuban, and destroy German forces at Liuban, Chudovo and Kirishi. However, neither army was to achieve any success.

On 17 January, the same day that Fediuninsky's forces captured Pogost'e, Klykov's Second Shock Army resumed its attack. Supported by more than 1500 aircraft sorties, the army finally penetrated the Germans' first defensive position on the left bank of the Volkhov River, advanced 5–10km (3.12–6.25 miles), and created conditions that Meretskov deemed favourable for developing success. However, once again the attacking forces failed to capture key German strongpoints, the weather deteriorated, and the offensive faltered with heavy losses.[5] On 21 January, after a four-day halt to regroup and receive reinforcements, the Second Shock Army resumed its struggle, this time focusing on capturing the German strongpoints of Spasskaia Polist, Mostki, Zemtitsy and Miasnoi Bor at the base of the shallow penetration.

On the night of 23/24 January, Meretskov finally convinced himself that Klykov's forces had blasted a large enough hole through German defences to commit his exploitation force. The next morning Major-General N. I. Gusev's XIII Cavalry Corps, consisting of the 25th and 87th Cavalry Divisions and an attached rifle division from the Fifty-Ninth Army, lunged through the narrow gap into the German rear. However, once Gusev's cavalry and Klykov's infantry made it through the gap, the German XXXIX Motorized and XXXVIII Army Corps hurriedly assembled forces to hold the flanks of the penetration and contain the exploiting Soviet forces in the forested swamps south of Liuban. The Fifty-Ninth and Fifty-Second Armies frantically struggled to widen the narrow gap at the base of Second Shock Army's penetration, but were unable to capture the German strongpoints along the flanks of the gap.

An Enticing Target

Meretskov's offensive once again stalled in late January, this time with about 30,000 Soviet troops lodged precariously in the Germans' rear area. From Meretskov's perspective, this force was in an ideal position to perform its vital mission, but only if he could reinforce it and secure its supply lines. From the German perspective, although the large Soviet force threatened the viability of the whole German defence south of Leningrad, it also represented an

enticing target for destruction, but only if they could contain it and sever its logistical umbilical cord.

On 27 January, Meretskov regrouped his forces and ordered them to capture the key German strongpoints on the flanks of the gap and widen the penetration. Within the penetration "sack", the Second Shock Army was to attack the German strongpoints and capture Liuban in cooperation with an attack from the north by Fediuninsky's Fifty-Fourth Army. Klykov formed three operational groups in the Second Shock Army to conduct the attacks. The first two, commanded by Major-General I. T. Korovnikov and Colonel Zhil'tsov, were to seize the German strongpoints at Spasskaia Polist and Zemtitsy, and then fan out westwards into the German rear with the third operational group. Simultaneously, Gusev's cavalry corps was to capture Liuban, while Meretskov's other armies attacked elsewhere along the front.

Agonizingly Slow Advance

However, once again, the Second Shock Army's assaults on Spasskaia Polist and Zemtitsy failed.[6] Nevertheless, the remainder of Klykov's force penetrated between the two strongpoints, advanced 75km (46.8 miles), and joined Gusev's cavalry. More than 100,000 Soviet troops were now in the German rear area, poised to advance on Liuban and threatening the very survival of German forces in the Liuban, Chudovo and Kirishi regions. However, the army's failure to seize Spasskaia Polist and the difficulties it experienced in moving across terrain that was covered with frozen swamps and peat bogs, seriously hindered the Soviet advance and permitted German forces to contain the thrust.

Kuechler did so by assigning Busch's Sixteenth Army the responsibility for the southern flank of the penetration and Lindemann's Eighteenth Army the responsibility for the northern flank.[7] The former's XXXVIII Army Corps erected strong defences south of Miasnoi Bor and at Zamosh'e, and the latter's I Army Corps did the same at Spasskaia Polist, Miasnoi Bor and south of Liuban. In early February, I Army Corps cordoned off the salient's northern face with its 225th, 212th, 254th, 61st and 215th Infantry and SS Police Divisions, and XXXVIII Army Corps the southern face with the 285th and 126th Infantry and 20th Motorized Divisions.

In early February, the *Stavka* dispatched A. V. Krulev, the Deputy People's Commissar of Defence for Logistics, to the Volkhov Front to help

ABOVE: A Soviet patrol cautiously approaches a wooded area during the January offensive. Only the soldier at the back has attempted to camouflage himself by whitening his helmet; the others stand out quite clearly in their greatcoats. They have advanced past the remains of a German bomber.

Meretskov solve his persistent logistical problems. Meretskov then prepared a special assault group under the command of Colonel S. V. Roginsky, consisting of the 11th Rifle Division and 22nd Tank Brigade, and ordered the group to attack the German strongpoints at Liubino Pole and Mostki, south of Spasskaia Polist. Roginsky's assault group captured the two strongpoints on 12 February, widening the mouth of the penetration to 14km (8.75 miles), and Meretskov threw fresh forces into the penetration with orders to reinforce the advance on Liuban. On 19 February, the Second Shock Army's 327th, 46th Rifle and 80th Cavalry Divisions, and 39th and 42nd Ski Battalions attacked northwards towards Liuban, enveloping and capturing Krasnaia Gorka at the junction of the German 291st and 254th Infantry Divisions' defences. Klykov then ordered the two divisions to capture Liuban, which was less than 10km (6.25 miles) distant, and his cavalry and ski forces to cut the Leningrad-Liuban railroad at Riabovo, 10km (6.25 miles) northwest of Liuban.

The Second Shock Army's advance towards Liuban posed a serious danger to German defences by threatening to separate I Army Corps from the rest of the Eighteenth Army, destroy it, and open

the road to Leningrad. However, I Army Corps' 291st Infantry Division and Group Haenicke attacked the flanks of the small penetration, recaptured Krasnaia Gorka on 27 February, and encircled the Soviet 327th Rifle and 80th Cavalry Divisions in Riabovo.[8] Although most of the encircled Soviet forces escaped, the Germans claimed 6000 Russian prisoners by 15 March.

By late February, Meretskov's forces had utterly failed in their multiple attempts to destroy German forces in the Kirishi, Liuban and Chudovo regions and to raise the Leningrad blockade. They failed because they attacked the complex network of German points frontally and in dispersed and uncoordinated fashion without adequate fire or logistical support. Because of the Front's repeated failures, Stalin dispatched Marshal Voroshilov and GKO member G. Malenkov to Meretskov's headquarters in mid-February to oversee planning for a renewed offensive. With them was Lieutenant-General A. A.

offensive. With them was Lieutenant-General A. A. Vlasov, who had recently distinguished himself as Twentieth Army commander in the fighting west of Moscow and who the *Stavka* appointed as Meretskov's deputy. On 28 February, the *Stavka* ordered Voroshilov, Meretskov and Khozin to draft a new plan to liquidate German forces in the Liuban and Chudovo regions.

Once completed, Voroshilov's plan required the Second Shock Army to attack northwest towards Liuban with a shock group of five rifle divisions, one cavalry division, and four rifle brigades, reinforced with tanks and artillery. The shock group was to cut the Leningrad-Liuban railroad line, link up with the Fifty-Fourth Army, and encircle and destroy German forces in the Liuban and Chudovo region. Fediuninsky's Fifty-Fourth Army, reinforced by the fresh IV Guards Rifle Corps, and Sukhomlin's Eighth Army were to attack Liuban from the north and west.

At the same time, the Fifty-Ninth Army, now commanded by Major-General I. T. Korovnikov, was to attack and destroy German forces defending Chudovo. The bulk of the Leningrad Front's aircraft were to strike German defences and their rear area installations prior to the attack, which was to commence simultaneously in all sectors on 4 March. The combined force attacked as ordered early on 4 March, but once again achieved only limited gains against strong German resistance. After several days of intense fighting, Fediuninsky's army finally managed to penetrate the German 269th Infantry Division's defences near Pogost'e on 15 March and advanced 22km (13.75 miles) southwards to within 10km (6.25 miles) of Liuban. However, quick reaction by the German 5th, 93rd, 217th and 21st Infantry Divisions successfully contained Fediuninsky's army on 31 March. The other Soviet assaults also failed utterly.

While Meretskov and Voroshilov were conducting their March offensive, Army Group North was preparing a counterstroke of its own. During a meeting between Hitler and Kuechler on 2 March, Hitler ordered his army group commander to mount an operation between 7 and 12 March to close the penetration gap and encircle the Soviet's Liuban force in conjunction with a counterstroke

BELOW: As a counter to the siege artillery deployed by the Wehrmacht, the Red Army employed units of heavy artillery such as this 203mm howitzer, which has just been towed into place. To the left of the picture is the crane for lifting the round.

The objectives of Kuechler's attack were the two narrow snow-packed Soviet supply lines, nicknamed Erika and Dora, that ran through the 10km- (6.25-mile-) wide corridor between the Second Shock Army and the Soviet frontlines along the Volkhov River. Hitler gave Kuechler 5–10 days to plan the counterstroke, which the OKH codenamed Operation Beast of Prey (*Raubtier*). If successful, it would thwart the Second Shock Army's attack on Liuban and totally encircle and destroy Klykov's isolated army. Although his Army Group North was ready to begin the operation on 9 March, Kuechler had to delay the operation for one day since the Luftwaffe was tied down in dealing with Soviet attacks on Kholm.10

Operations Grind to a Halt

The Eighteenth Army began its counterstroke at 07:30 hours on 15 March, when two shock groups totalling five divisions with strong air support attacked from Spasskaia Polist and Zemtitsy, at the base of the Second Shock Army's penetration, towards Liubino Pole. The northern shock group, consisting of I Army Corps' SS Police, 61st and 121st Infantry Divisions, advanced 3km (1.8 miles) on the first day of the attack; the southern shock group, made up of XXXVIII Army Corps' 58th and 126th Infantry Divisions, advanced 1km (0.62 miles). After two days of agonizingly slow movement through boggy terrain against heavy resistance, the northern shock group severed route Erika on 18 March and the southern group route, Dora, the following day. The two groups linked up on 20 March, trapping the Second Shock Army in the half-frozen wasteland south of Liuban. Even though it successfully slammed the door shut on the Second Shock Army, on 23 March the Eighteenth Army reported to OKH that it was becoming impossible for the army to keep the Russians from taking Liuban since it lacked sufficient manpower to do so. Worse still for the Eighteenth Army, the Soviets positioned their tanks so that they could rake route Erika with constant fire, preventing the Germans from capturing it and turning it into a bloody no man's land.

Meretskov answered the German counterstroke by counterattacking towards Liubino Pole with all of his reserves. By 27 March, the desperate and costly assaults managed to carve out a narrow but tenuous corridor to the Second Shock Army near the village of Miasnoi Bor. Meanwhile, Kuechler relieved XXXVIII Army Corps' commander for

failing to seize route Erika, and, over Kuechler's objections, Hitler demanded that the 58th Infantry Division commander also be relieved. Within days, the Second Shock Army also recaptured route Dora and built a new supply road. However, in early April the rainy period (*rasputitsa*) set in, the road became impassable for all but foot traffic, and German fire paralyzed all movement along the 3–4km- (1.8–2.5-mile-) wide corridor. Within days, both routes Erika and Dora were under water, the Second Shock Army ran short of ammunition, fuel and food supplies, and command, control and communications within the army became impossible. These appalling conditions paralyzed all operations and left the Leningrad and Volkhov Fronts no choice but to halt their offensive in late April, dig in, and await more favourable conditions to resume the offensive or to rescue the Second Shock Army.

Reorganization

Khozin then asked Stalin to centralize control of all forces operating in the region under his Leningrad Front. Stalin agreed despite Shaposhnikov's objections, and on 23 April the *Stavka* ordered the Leningrad and Volkhov Fronts be combined into a larger Leningrad Front consisting of a Leningrad Group of Forces and a Volkhov Group of Forces. The *Stavka* appointed Lieutenant-General L. A. Govorov, the former Fifth Army commander, to command the Leningrad Group of Forces, which consisted of the Twenty-Third, Forty-Second and Fifty-Fifth Armies and the Coastal and Neva Operational Groups. Khozin retained command of the Leningrad Front and also commanded the Volkhov Group of Forces, which consisted of the Eighth, Fifty-Fourth, Fourth, Second Shock, Fifty-Ninth and Fifty-Second Armies and IV and VI Guards Rifle and XIII Cavalry Corps. Meretskov became deputy commander of Zhukov's Western Direction Command.

Although designed to streamline command and control of forces in the Leningrad and Liuban regions, the new force configuration only confused matters more. Only days before, on 20 April with Stalin's permission, Meretskov sent General Vlasov, his deputy, into the pocket to assume command of the Second Shock Army from the ailing General Klykov. Vlasov's mission was either to reinvigorate the Second Shock Army's offensive or extricate his army from its perilous position.

In four months of intense fighting in heavy terrain and generally terrible weather conditions, the

LEFT: The failure of the series of Red Army offensives in the Leningrad area in early 1942 doomed the city's population to further privations. Enemy bombing and shelling, combined with power failures, often resulted in the breakdown of essential services. Leningraders had to manage as best they could, which included queuing for water, as here.

Volkhov Front managed to penetrate German defences, insert a full army into the German rear area, and threaten the German I Army Corps with encirclement. However, skillful and resolute German resistance and numerous problems with command and control, fire support and logistics prevented Soviet forces from exploiting the opportunity and also jeopardized more than 100,000 Second Shock Army troops in the swamp west of Miasnoi Bor.

While the Leningrad-Volkhov offensive failed to meet *Stavka* expectations, the Northwestern Front accomplished considerably more in its portion of the Leningrad-Novgorod offensive. Even so, Kurochkin's Front fell well short of achieving the ambitious mission the *Stavka* assigned to it.

Lieutenant-General V. I. Morozov's Eleventh Army began its advance on 7 January along the Staraia Russa axis on the Front's right flank. Morozov's army penetrated German defences and advanced almost 60km (37.5 miles) in two days of fighting, reaching the eastern outskirts of Staraia Russa. Army ski battalions bypassed German strongpoints, crossed frozen Lake Il'men north of the city, and cut off the road leading from Staraia Russa to Shimsk, while other army forces dug in all along the Lovat River to the south. Thereafter, however, the army's attack faltered badly against heavy German resistance.

Major-General N. E. Berzarin's Thirty-Fourth Army attacked along the Demiansk axis on 7 January, then penetrated German defences, and

ABOVE: General Simoniak, a hero of the siege, points towards German trenches during a tour of the front. Popular among his men, Simoniak once argued with Zhukov for refusing to send an attack through a swamp, which would have resulted in slaughter. Zhukov was incensed, but Simoniak refused to back down.

advanced very slowly through heavy snow in tandem with the Kalinin Front's Third Shock Army positioned on his left flank. The Thirty-Fourth and Third Shock Armies then reached the Vatolino and Molvotisty region south of Demiansk, enveloping the German II Army Corps in the town from the south. Halted by heavy German resistance south of Demiansk, Kurochkin ordered his forces to bypass German strongpoints and sever their communications.

By late January, Kurochkin's armies had almost completely encircled II Army Corps in Demiansk, leaving only the narrow Ramushevo corridor connecting the beleaguered corps with the German Sixteenth Army's main force at Staraia Russa. By this time Red Army forces had utterly demolished the Sixteenth Army's front from Staraia Russa to Ostashkov, and all that stood between the Red Army and Smolensk was a series of unconnected strongpoints northwest of the city. Kurochkin's forces threatened Demiansk and Staraia Russia and the Kalinin Front's Third Shock Army encircled German forces in Kholm.

However, the *Stavka* realized that the fate of its Leningrad-Novgorod offensive depended on its ability to capture Demiansk and Staraia Russa.

Accordingly, on 26 January it reinforced the Northwestern Front with the First Shock Army and I and II Guards Rifle Corps and ordered Kurochkin to seize both cities. His Thirty-Fourth Army and the two reinforcing rifle corps were to complete encirclement of the German forces in Demiansk, and the First Shock and Eleventh Armies were to advance towards Sol'tsy and Shimsk to cut the communications lines of the German forces defending Novgorod and Staraia Russa. On 29 January, I and II Guards Rifle Corps attacked the Ramushevo corridor from the north and the Thirty-Fourth and Third Shock Armies from the south. After almost a month of complex and bloody fighting, the two forces linked up near Zaluch'e on 26 February, encircling 70,000 German troops in the Demiansk Pocket.[11]

With Demiansk encircled, the *Stavka* ordered Kurochkin to crush the encircled German force as quickly as possible and advance northwest to help the Leningrad and Volkhov Fronts raise the Leningrad blockade. This meant that Kurochkin had to destroy II Army Corps before it fortified its defences around Demiansk and before the *rasputitsa* began. To assist Kurochkin, the *Stavka* combined all forces taking part in the reduction of Demiansk, including the Kalinin Front's Third Shock Army, the Thirty-Fourth Army and I Guards Rifle Corps, under his control.[12] Kurochkin's offensive, during which he employed élite airborne forces in a joint air-ground role, lasted from 6 March until 9 April and ended in failure.

The Germans resisted skillfully and re-supplied their encircled forces by air.[13] Worse still, on 16 March Army Group North assembled a force of five divisions under Group Seydlitz with orders to advance east from Staraia Russa and relieve the encircled II Army Corps. Group Seydlitz attacked on 20 March, linked up with the Demiansk force on 21 April after weeks of prolonged fighting in quagmire conditions, and established a 4km (2.5-mile) corridor through Ramushevo, linking II Army Corps with the Sixteenth Army's main forces. Urged on by the *Stavka*, Kurochkin's forces attacked incessantly from 3 to 20 May, attempting to close the corridor, but all of the attacks failed with heavy losses. The front in the Northwestern Front's sector finally stabilized along the Lovat River at the end of May.[14]

Grand Strategy

Although the Leningrad-Novgorod offensive failed spectacularly, it provided a model for future *Stavka* offensives in the region, in particular Zhukov's Operation Polar Star the next winter.

As had been the case in the summer and the fall of 1941, Red Army military operations along the northwestern axes were closely related to those along other more critical axes. In fact, the Leningrad-Novgorod offensive was but one segment of a far grander *Stavka* scheme to defeat all three German army groups, raise the blockade of Leningrad, and recapture many lost cities, including Smolensk, Briansk, Orel, Kursk, Khar'kov and Dnepropetrovsk.

Ultimately, the *Stavka*'s aim was to drive German forces back to the Narva, Pskov, Vitebsk and Gomel line and southwards along the Dnepr River to the Black Sea. However, as the course of operations indicated, this aim clearly exceeded the Red Army's capabilities. During the Winter Campaign, Stalin and his *Stavka* displayed a congenital over-optimism that would characterize their

strategic planning well into the future of the war. Unrealistic military objectives, unwarranted rashness, and frustration from not being able to achieve them, generated much of the ensuing carnage and damaged the Soviet war effort by squandering precious human and material resources that more patient leaders could have put to better use.

As usual, the losses suffered by Soviet forces were massive. The Volkhov and Leningrad Fronts suffered 308,367 casualties during the ill-fated operation, including 95,064 men killed, captured or missing. The Northwestern Front lost 245,511 more casualties, including 88,908 killed, captured or missing. None of the Fronts had accomplished its mission and the operation ended with the Second Shock Army isolated in the frozen swamps southeast of Leningrad. The only saving graces were that the offensive inflicted modest damage on German Army Group North and forced the OKH to reinforce the Leningrad and Demiansk regions at the expense of other sectors on the Eastern Front. Finally, the scope, intensity, duration and cost of these operations clearly indicated that Stalin wished to raise the Leningrad blockade and was making every attempt to do so.

Defective Command and Control

The course and outcome of the offensive vividly revealed the gross errors that Khozin, Meretskov and their subordinate commanders made when planning and conducting the offensive. Lacking experience in conducting major offensive operations, they neglected to exploit their numerical superiority by concentrating their forces at decisive points, although the orders they received somewhat mitigated their guilt. In this regard, Stalin ordered them to do on a smaller scale precisely what he was doing on a larger scale. As a result, the armies often attacked one after the other in separate sectors, often regrouping for new attacks in sectors where previous attacks had already failed. Throughout the offensive, command, control and communications often collapsed and the forces had wholly inadequate fire and logistical support.

All in all it was a depressing beginning to the New Year, which, in turn, promised ill-consequences for the coming summer months. Most tragically of all, the offensive's failure condemned Leningrad's civilians and defenders to the spectre of unrequited famine, misery and death during the winter and the spring that was to follow.

CHAPTER 6:
FRUSTRATED HOPES

The *Stavka* and Stalin were determined that Leningrad would be relieved, and in May–August 1942 launched fresh offensives to achieve this. But the Red Army discovered that enthusiasm and numbers could not compensate for poor planning and deficiencies in command, control and equipment. The Germans held, defeated the Red Army and then launched their own counterattack.

In late April 1942, the Red Army's winter offensive collapsed in utter exhaustion before it was able to fulfil the ambitious objectives that had been assigned to it by the *Stavka*. Nevertheless, the massive offensive had saved Moscow, denied Hitler his Barbarossa objectives, and inflicted an unprecedented defeat on the Wehrmacht. The Red Army's multiple offensives left the Soviet-German front a crazy patchwork quilt of interlocking and often overlapping forces arrayed from the Leningrad region to the Black Sea.[1] The configuration of the front itself, disfigured by numerous salients and large Soviet forces lodged deep in the German rear area, illustrated the unfinished nature of the first six months of operations. Understandably, neither Hitler nor Stalin could accept the winter decision as final, each viewing it as an aberration that could be corrected in the summer. In short, both sides planned to seize the strategic initiative and complete the missions left unfulfilled during the first six months of war.

LEFT: A Red Army Guardsman of the Leningrad Front poses with a 50mm mortar. The designation "Guards" was a collective title awarded to Soviet land, air and naval units that had distinguished themselves in action. The Guards honorific was established in late 1941.

After considerable deliberation, the *Stavka* decided to conduct a strategic defence along the vital western axis in the summer against an anticipated new German offensive towards Moscow, while conducting spoiling offensives of their own in southern Russia during the spring. At the same time, Hitler ordered the Wehrmacht to conduct Operation *Blau*, a major offensive by Army Group South to conquer the Stalingrad and oil-rich Caucasus regions. Führer Directive No 41, issued on 5 April 1942, set the parameters of the offensive, which was to begin in late June:

"Initially, it is necessary to concentrate all existing forces for the conduct of a main operation in the southern sector of the front to destroy enemy forces west of the Don River and, subsequently, capture the Caucasus oil regions and the passes across the Caucasus Mountains."

The directive also provided context and rationale for Army Group North's summer operations:

"We will refrain from the final encirclement of Leningrad and the capture of Ingermannland [Oranienbaum] until such time as the situation in the enveloped areas or the availability of otherwise sufficient forces permits."

Accordingly, Army Group North's initial mission was to improve its position around Leningrad by

ABOVE: These Guards infantry pictured in 1942 are manning a DT tank machine gun with a bipod attached. This weapon had a small drum magazine that made for ease of reloading in the cramped conditions of the trenches. The stock was collapsible.

liquidating Red Army bridgeheads on the western bank of the Volkhov River. Subsequently, after the Wehrmacht's offensive in southern Russia began successfully, the OKH planned to reinforce Army Group North so that it could launch its summer offensive. Kuechler's army group was to capture Leningrad, establish contact with the Finnish Army on the Karelian Isthmus, and seize Oranienbaum in accordance with Plan *Nordlicht*, which Army Group North had already prepared early the previous winter. After seizing Leningrad and establishing contact with the Finns, Army Group North's Eighteenth Army was to sever Soviet rail communications between Moscow and Murmansk. Simultaneously, the army group's Sixteenth Army was to attack southeastwards from Demiansk in tandem with an attack by Army Group Centre's Ninth Army northwards from Rzhev. The twin assaults were to encircle and destroy Soviet forces occupying the large salient in the Ostashkov, Kholm

and Toropets regions, which threatened Smolensk and Army Group Centre's rear area.

In accordance with Stalin's strategy, the *Stavka* conducted its Khar'kov and Crimean offensives operations in May. However, both offensives ended catastrophically with the complete defeat and destruction of both attacking forces. German forces then captured Sevastopol and the Kerch peninsula, advanced eastwards across the Northern Donets River, and initiated Operation *Blau* on 28 June, shattering Red Army defences in southern Russia. The German victories at Kharkov, in the Crimea, and across southern Russia between May and July enabled the OKH to dispatch substantial reserves to the Leningrad region with which to mount Operation *Nordlicht*. However, at the same time, Soviet operations around Leningrad and Demiansk between January and May ended German hopes of enveloping the city by an advance northeastwards from Demiansk. Conversely, the failure of the Soviet Leningrad-Novgorod offensive and the successful German relief of Demiansk worsened the Soviet situation along the northwestern axis and encouraged Army Group North to mount serious new operations in the region.

With combat raging in southern Russia, in May the *Stavka* ordered the Leningrad Front to strengthen Leningrad's defences, conduct local operations to weaken German forces besieging the city, and liberate the Second Shock Army from the German trap south of Liuban. On 19 May, Khozin, the Leningrad Front commander, proposed to the *Stavka* that his Front attack and destroy German forces in the Mga-Siniavino salient to raise the Leningrad blockade. The *Stavka* approved Khozin's plan and sent him substantial reserves with which to mount his offensive.[2]

While planning his new offensive at Leningrad, Khozin also planned to free Vlasov's Second Shock Army from its near encirclement. However, before doing so he agreed with a *Stavka* request to dispatch the fresh VI Guards Rifle Corps, which Meretskov had intended to employ in the relief of the Second Shock Army, to reinforce the Northwestern Front's operations at Demiansk. By this time, Vlasov's beleaguered army had decreased 70 percent in strength and lacked tanks, artillery, ammunition and food. Nevertheless, the *Stavka* approved Khozin's plan for the Second Shock Army's breakout on 20 May. Vlasov's army attempted to break out several times over the next few days, but the Eighteenth Army

reinforced its cordon of troops around it and foiled all of the attempts. The Second Shock Army and relief forces from outside the encirclement tried repeatedly to break out but failed in heavy fighting that lasted throughout early July.

In the midst of these battles, on 24 May Kuechler ordered Lindemann's Eighteenth Army to orchestrate an offensive to trap Vlasov's army completely, a task Lindemann assigned to XXXVIII and I Army Corps. After a delay due to heavy rains, the two corps began their joint offensive against the base of the Second Shock Army's pocket on 30 May. Despite suffering heavy losses, XXXVIII Corps continued its assault into the night, linking up with I Army Corps' forces at 01:30 hours on 31 May, and severing the vital route Erika.[3] The two corps established a continuous front facing east at 12:00 hours on 31 May, and a front facing west later in the day. Finding themselves totally trapped, the remnants of Vlasov's once proud army desperately attempted to escape by

BELOW: The classic image of the Red Army. The army did not generally use a knapsack or other specialized equipment, simply the rolled greatcoat and bread bag. The Maxim model 1910 machine gun, seen here with troops in the Leningrad area, is being carried to avoid damaging the metal wheels on the rocks.

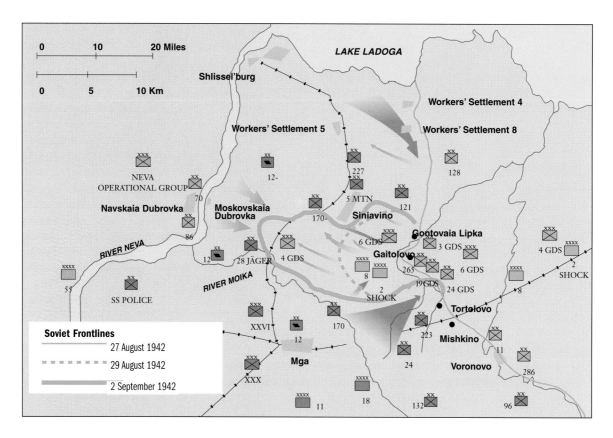

attacking eastwards on 4 June. The Germans repelled the attacks, which according to Wehrmacht reports, were made by troops who were all "drunk". The next day German forces also beat off a major attack from the east.

After several telephone conversations with his senior commanders, including Meretskov, on 8 June Stalin re-established the Volkhov Front under Meretskov's command, ordered the latter to rescue the Second Shock Army, and sent Vasilevsky from the General Staff to assist him.[4] Stalin then assigned Lieutenant-General L. A. Govorov to replace Khozin as Leningrad Front commander and transferred the latter to the Western Front to command the Thirty-Third Army. Thereafter, in mid-June Meretskov made several attempts to free the Second Shock Army, but all failed. German forces subsequently destroyed the encircled army, capturing a reported 15,000 Soviet troops at the corridor's eastern end in mid-June and another 33,000 by 28 June. On 12 July, Vlasov himself fell into German hands. Official Soviet figures recorded 94,751 casualties from 13 May to 10 July, including 54,774 killed, căptured or missing, most suffered by Vlasov's army.

With Operation *Blau* well underway and apparently successful, the Germans began planning a new

ABOVE: This map illustrates the Soviet Siniavino offensive operation between 19 August and 9 September 1942, and the German counterstroke at Siniavino between 20 September and 15 October 1942. The latter ended Soviet hopes of relieving Leningrad in 1942.

offensive in the Leningrad region. On 30 June Kuechler briefed Hitler at the Führer headquarters, detailing offensive options other than *Nordlicht* that his army group was capable of undertaking. These operations included two in the Leningrad region.[5] The first, codenamed Operation *Moorbrand* (Moor Fire), involved either capturing the Pogost'e salient, west of Kirishi, which was still held by the Soviet Fifty-Fourth Army, or totally destroying the entire Soviet force west of the Volkhov River. The second, codenamed Operation *Bettelstab* (Beggar's Staff), called for the elimination of the Soviet bridgehead south of Oranienbaum. Kuechler added details to these proposed operations when he returned to his headquarters on 1 July, and ordered his staff to begin work on *Moorbrand* first and then *Bettelstab*. In the meantime, the OKH ordered its siege artillery batteries, named *Dora, Gamma* and *Karl,* regrouped from Sevastopol to Leningrad between 2 and 23 July so they could assist in the reduction of the Kronshtadt fortress.

On 23 July, Hitler issued revised guidance for Wehrmacht offensive operations to be executed in late summer in his Führer Directive No 45.[6] The directive added yet another offensive option for Army Group North, Operation *Feuerzauber* (Fire Magic), which required Kuechler's army group to capture Leningrad by early September. To do so, Hitler transferred General Erich von Manstein's Eleventh Army headquarters with five infantry divisions northwards from the Crimea to reinforce the Eighteenth Army and the heavy artillery already sent to the region. One week later, the OKH renamed Operation *Feuerzauber* Operation *Nordlicht*.[7] Hitler ordered Kuechler to conduct operations *Moorbrand* and *Bettelstab* in "short order" before embarking on *Nordlicht* and to complete them all by early September.

Since conducting all of these operations was clearly beyond the army group's capability, Kuechler convinced Hitler and the OKH to delay Operation *Bettelstab* until after the successful completion of Operation *Nordlicht*.[8] On 23 August he assigned Manstein responsibility for conducting *Nordlicht* and ordered him to execute it in any way feasible with his fresh Eleventh Army as long as he linked up with the Finns and "levelled Leningrad to the ground". To ensure that his orders were carried out, Hitler subordinated Manstein's forces directly to the OKH rather than Army Group North. The Finnish Army on the Karelian Isthmus was to assist the operation with artillery support and by conducting a feint north of Leningrad.

Red Army Local Offensives

After the Germans destroyed the Second Shock Army in late June, the *Stavka* and Leningrad Front anticipated renewed German offensive operations in the Leningrad region some time during mid-summer. In early July, Soviet intelligence reported a build-up of German forces in the Siniavino and Chudovo regions, possibly in preparation for a major advance on Volkhov. To forestall the German offensive and pave the way for a larger offensive of its own, Govorov's Front mounted several "local" offensives in late July and early August against German forces south of Leningrad. The Forty-Second Army attacked in the Staro-Panovo sector on 20 July and the Fifty-Fifth Army attacked in the Putrolovo and Iam-Izhora sectors three days later. Although the fighting was costly and inconclusive, Govorov did not halt the Fifty-Fifth Army's operation until 4 August and the Forty-Second Army's until 26 August. Although the twin offensives achieved very little, they did force the German Eighteenth Army to shift substantial forces to the threatened sectors.[9]

German Defences at Siniavino

The growing fear of impending German offensive operations against Leningrad prompted the *Stavka* to demand that Govorov's and Meretskov's Fronts conduct a larger-scale offensive to pre-empt the possible German offensive and, if possible, raise the German blockade. The *Stavka* and two Fronts chose the German Shlissel'burg-Siniavino-Mga salient south of Lake Ladoga as their target. The offensive plan required the Leningrad and Volkhov Fronts, supported by the Baltic Fleet and Ladoga Flotilla, to conduct concentric attacks to defeat and destroy German forces in the salient and restore ground communications with Leningrad. By doing so successfully, the *Stavka* hoped it could forestall any German offensive farther east and draw German reserves away from the Stalingrad region.

The task confronting Govorov and Meretskov was not an easy one, since Lindemann's Eighteenth Army had erected strong and deep defences in and around its Siniavino "bottleneck". The bulk of the army's forces were concentrated south of Leningrad and in the Mga-Siniavino salient.[10] XXVI Army Corps' 227th and 223rd Infantry Divisions defended the eastern flank of the salient opposite the Volkhov Front's Eighth Army. It was flanked on the left by L Army Corps' SS Police Division deployed along the Neva River opposite the Neva Operational Group, and on the right by I Army Corps' 96th Infantry Division. A second German defence line was anchored on the Siniavino strongpoint and a third line was located forward of the Mga River with elements of the 12th Panzer and 5th Mountain Divisions positioned nearby.

The German defence consisted of a dense network of strongpoints and centres of resistance protected by extensive obstacles, interconnected by trenches, and protected by interlocking artillery and mortar fields of fire. The most important German strongpoints were at Workers Settlements Nos 7, 8 and 4 and at the villages of Tortolovo and Porech'e. Worse still for the Soviets, on the eve of their offensive OKH alerted Kuechler to increased Soviet attack preparations and ordered him to move the 170th Infantry Division, one of the Eleventh Army's divisions preparing for Operation *Nordlicht*, northwards from Mga into the bottleneck. It also gave

Kuechler several new Tiger tanks that had been en route by train from Pskov.

Although at first sight the Soviet offensive plan seemed simple and direct, Govorov and Meretskov tried to eliminate the glaring deficiencies so evident in their early offensives. In the Leningrad Front's sector, Major-General V. P. Sviridov's Fifty-Fifth Army and the Neva Operational Group were to attack towards Tosno and Siniavino to link up with the Volkhov Front's forces and destroy German forces in the salient. Farther west, Lieutenant-General I. F. Nikolaev's Forty-Second Army and other Fifty-Fifth Army forces were to attack towards Uritsk and Staro-Panovo to tie down German forces.[11] Meretskov's Eighth Army, commanded by Major-General F. N. Starikov, was to penetrate German defences west of Gaitolovo at the base of the salient, destroy German forces at Siniavino, exploit towards Mga, and link up with Govorov's Fifty-Fifth Army.[12] General Klykov's Second Shock Army, just re-established after its predecessor's destruction at Liuban, was in second echelon behind Starikov's Eighth Army.[13] Klykov's army was to destroy German forces at Mga, link up with Leningrad Front forces near Krasnyi Bor, and then exploit the offensive southwards towards Tosno. In addition, Meretskov

ABOVE: A Red Army battery outside the city of Leningrad prepares to launch a barrage against the enemy. Red Army doctrine laid great stress on the use of mass barrages, which used up vast quantities of ammunition.

established a strong reserve of five rifle divisions and one rifle brigade and positioned it in the Volkhov region in Starikov's deep rear.[14] Meretskov was to begin his offensive on 28 August. However, Govorov was to attack to secure bridgeheads over the Neva River on 19 August and conduct his main offensive on 28 August.

Unlike the case in previous offensives, Meretskov provided Starikov's army with significant armour and artillery support so that, at least in theory, it could penetrate the entire depth of the German defence and capture Siniavino.[15] During the assault, the Eighth Army was to deploy strong screening forces along its flanks to protect the shock group's advance.[16] Meretskov's remaining armies deployed from Kirishi to Lake Il'men were to conduct diversionary attacks to tie down German forces.

Although Govorov and Meretskov spent roughly 30 days regrouping and preparing their forces for the offensive, five rifle divisions, four tank brigades, and many specialized forces failed to complete their movements by the appointed time.[17] Since only two rifle divisions and one rifle brigade had reached Meretskov's reserve in Volkhov when the offensive began, both his first and second echelons had to defend their own flanks as they conducted the breakthrough and exploitation. Nevertheless, when preparations were complete, the Soviet forces outnumbered the German forces by more than four to one.[18] However, for the offensive to succeed it had to develop quickly, since the Germans had six to seven divisions in operational reserve which they could use to reinforce the threatened sector by the eighth or ninth day of the operation.

Heavy Losses for No Gains

The Fifty-Fifth Army attacked across the Neva River on 19 August and seized a bridgehead near Ivanovskoe, but the SS Police Division contained the Soviet attack. Although Govorov reinforced the bridgehead with portions of three more divisions, the advance still stalled.[19] With his preliminary operations to cross the Neva River proving unsuccessful, Govorov postponed any further operations until Meretskov's forces had penetrated German defences east of Siniavino.

To the east, in the Volkhov Front's sector, Starikov's Eighth Army attacked at 02:10 hours on 27 August, striking at the junction of the German 227th and 223rd Infantry Divisions. The army's main shock group, consisting of the four divisions of Major-General Biakov's VI Guard Rifle Corps, supported by one division on the right flank and two on the left, penetrated between the 227th and 223rd Infantry Divisions, and captured Tortolovo, driving a 3km (1.8–mile) wedge into the German defences on the first day of the operation. The attack caught the Germans by surprise since Soviet operations along the Neva had just failed. Shortly before 12:00 hours, Lindemann reported to Kuechler that attacks were underway along the entire front north of the railroad, that 20 enemy tanks had achieved a small penetration, but no discernable enemy main attack was apparent. At this point, Kuechler's primary concern was the fate of Operation *Nordlicht*, which a prolonged Soviet offensive might disrupt.

Starikov's shock group advanced slowly and painfully towards Siniavino from 28 to 30 August against strong German counterattacks, finally reaching the southern approaches to Siniavino in the centre of his attack sector on 31 August. At this point the banks of the Neva River were only 7km (4.3 miles) to his front. While the shock group gnawed its

way through the German defence, its flanking divisions tried in vain to expand the flanks of the penetration.[20] The German defence of its strongpoints on the shock group's flanks tied down Soviet forces and weakened the strength of the main effort towards Siniavino and Mga.

Fearing that the attacking Soviets were heading for the Neva River by way of Siniavino, on 28 August Kuechler ordered his 5th Mountain and 28th *Jäger* Divisions to move from their staging areas for Operation *Nordlicht* to Mga. Later in the day, Hitler diverted the 3rd Mountain Division, which was en route by sea from Norway to Finland, to Reval, Estonia, and Kuechler brought up the 12th Panzer Division to protect the Neva River front and accelerated the 170th Infantry Division's movement to Siniavino. These forces and part of the 96th Infantry Division assembled near Siniavino between 27 and 30 August. Finally, Kuechler committed his four Tiger tanks to combat south of Siniavino Heights on

BELOW: The order "man the guns" takes on a new meaning as the all-female crew of this anti-aircraft gun at Leningrad hurry to take their positions! From the early days of the siege, women had taken over many jobs to enable the men to join combat units. The gun is an 85mm model dating from 1939.

29 August, but two of the new tanks broke down almost immediately. The redeployment and commitment of these forces succeeded in slowing down the Volkhov Front's offensive, prompting Lindemann to report that the crisis had passed and the penetration had been contained.

By this time, Meretskov had already begun frittering away his second echelon forces and reserves to sustain the Eighth Army's advance. He began committing his second echelon IV Guards Rifle Corps in support of VI Guards Rifle Corps prior to 30 August.[21] The 259th Rifle Division and a tank brigade went into action on 29 August and the additional rifle brigades in piecemeal fashion beginning on 30 August, although it was too late, since the shock group had already been severely weakened. The Eighth Army's shock group continued struggling for Siniavino and the surrounding German strongpoints on 31 August. Although reinforced, its main attack finally faltered south of Siniavino on 1 and 2 September in the face of counterattacks by the 28th *Jäger* Division and part of the 170th Infantry Division. On its right flank, the 128th Rifle Division surrounded and then captured Worker's Settlement No 8 in some brutal hand-to-

ABOVE: Infantry and a pair of T-34/76 tanks advance. More modern versions of the T-34, such as the T-34/85 (armed with an 85mm gun) were supplied to other areas of the front, where tank-to-tank combat was a more decisive factor on the battlefield. The T-34/76 was adequate for the Leningrad Front, where the scope for armoured action was limited by the terrain.

hand fighting, but was halted on 3 September after advancing only 2–3km (1.25–1.8 miles). On its left, the 11th Rifle Division captured Mishino, but the 286th Rifle Division failed to seize Voronovo, which was defended by the 223rd Infantry Division and a task force from the 12th Panzer Division. Thus, despite three days of heavy fighting against heavy resistance, on 3 September the Volkhov Front's secondary attacks faltered with heavy losses only 2–3km (1.25–1.8 miles) into the German defence. By this time, Starikov's shock group, now reinforced by all of IV Guards Rifle Corps, was lodged in the woods southwest of Siniavino Heights almost 10km (6.25 miles) deep into the German defences and only 5km (3.12 miles) from the Neva River. An increasingly frustrated Meretskov reinforced Starikov's shock group with the Second Shock Army's 191st Rifle Division.

With Meretskov's assault faltering, Govorov's Fifty-Fifth Army and the Neva Operational Group joined the assault on 3 September, attacking across the Neva River or from bridgeheads on its eastern bank. The Fifty-Fifth Army attacked in the Iam-Izhora sector with two divisions, but its attack failed. At the same time, part of the Fifty-Fifth Army and the Neva Operational Group attacked north and south of Moskovskaia Dubrovka in an attempt to advance to Siniavino from the west and link up with Meretskov's shock group. Two rifle divisions managed to force the Neva River in the Annenskoe and 1st Village sector, and smashed into the German SS Police Division's defence. Once again, however, the attack bogged down and the *Stavka* ordered the forces to withdraw to their jumping-off positions on 12 September.[22]

Hitler was "exasperated" by the fact that the Soviet assault had tied up four of the divisions earmarked for Operation *Nordlicht* in the Mga-Siniavino bottleneck without any appreciable effect on the Soviet offensive. Noting these "atrocious developments", he ordered Manstein and his Eleventh Army to take command in the bottleneck to "restore the situation offensively" to "report immediately failures on the part of any commanders". An increasingly desperate Meretskov then committed the remainder of his Second Shock Army into combat on 5 September. However, the army was unable to make any further progress, and the German XXVI Army Corps' 121st Infantry, 5th Mountain, 28th *Jäger* and 223rd Infantry Divisions contained the Soviet attacks in heavy fighting on 8 and 9 September. Having halted the Soviet advance on Siniavino, Manstein ordered his 24th and 170th Infantry and 12th Panzer Divisions to attack the Soviet penetration from the southeast on 10 September. This attack immediately collapsed when his infantry ran into heavy artillery and mortar fire and his tanks stumbled into Soviet minefields. Manstein cancelled the attacks the next day, ordered his army to neutralize the Soviet artillery and to prepare another attack from both north and south. Meanwhile, from 4 to 20 September, counterattacks by the 121st Infantry and 5th Mountain Divisions

BELOW: The almost static condition of the Leningrad Front made for an ideal sniping environment. The sergeant and corporal pictured here are both armed with the Moisin Nagant Model 1891/30 with the PU sniper sight. Experts such as these would remain in situ for several days, waiting for the right target to present itself.

from the north, the 28th *Jäger* from the west, and the 170th Infantry from the south, compressed the attacking Soviet forces back into a tight salient southeast of Siniavino.

After heavy rains forced a three-day delay, on 21 September Manstein began a more carefully planned counterstroke involving pincer attacks towards Gaitolovo at the base of the Soviet's penetration from north and south. XXVII Army Corps' 121st Infantry Division formed the northern prong of the pincer and XXX Army Corps' 24th, 132nd and 170th Infantry Divisions the southern prong, while the 3rd Mountain and 28th *Jäger* Divisions contained Soviet forces in the penetration. Overcoming desperate Soviet resistance, the counterattacking forces linked up near Gaitolovo on 25 September, encircling the bulk of Meretskov's Eighth and Second Shock Armies. However, before Manstein could begin mopping-up operations, Govorov's forces attacked once again across the Neva River.

With Meretskov's shock group imperiled west of Gaitolovo, the *Stavka* immediately ordered Govorov to mount a relief operation. At 03:00 hours on 26 September, the Fifty-Fifth Army and the Neva Operational Group assaulted across the Neva River

ABOVE: This patrol of sailors is guarding the Haanko peninsula. All the men are wearing the standard Red Navy uniform with the distinctive long cap bands. On the left is the petty officer commanding the group, who is wearing a peaked cap.

against the 12th Panzer Division's defences at Annenskoe and the 1st Village. The Neva Group's 70th and 86th Rifle Divisions and 11th Separate Rifle Brigade managed to capture bridgeheads at Arbuzovo, Annenskoe and Moskovskaia Dubrovka, into which they moved 28 guns, 281 mortars and 12 tanks. These forces continued assaulting German defences until the end of September, but failed to expand the bridgeheads despite suffering heavy losses. Adding insult to injury, 12th Panzer Division forces recaptured Arbuzovo and Annenskoe in counterattacks on 29 September. After a further week of futile fighting, on 7 October Govorov ordered the Fifty-Fifth Army to abandon its bridgehead and withdraw back across the Neva. Although the 28th *Jäger* Division recaptured most of the Neva Operational Group's bridgehead at Moskovskaia Dubrovka, a single company of the 70th Rifle Division, later reinforced by the 46th Rifle Division, retained a small foothold over the river until January 1943.

Govorov's assault delayed the German destruction of Meretskov's shock group in the Gaitolovo Pocket, but accomplished little more.[23] In heavy fighting from 30 September to 15 October, Manstein's forces systematically reduced the encirclement, recaptured all previously lost strongpoints, and restored the front. The German success, however, was costly since Wehrmacht forces suffered 26,000 casualties.[24] Worse still, the counterstroke totally "burned out" several divisions earmarked for participation in Operation *Nordlicht*.

Belatedly, on 29 September, the *Stavka* ordered Meretskov to withdraw his forces from the Siniavino Pocket. Within days after the remnants of his two armies escaped from encirclement, on 1 October an undaunted Meretskov noted the continued German threat to Volkhov and requested permission to mount a new offensive to reduce the threat. The *Stavka* refused categorically on 3 October, instead ordering him to establish new defences along the Chernaia River and forbidding him from undertaking any new operations until he gave his forces the rest they obviously required. Although the Siniavino offensive utterly destroyed any German hopes of conducting Operation *Nordlicht* and capturing Leningrad, the offensive took a heavy toll on Red Army forces. In addition to losing the Second Shock Army for the second time in less than a year, the two Fronts lost 113,674 men, including 40,085 dead, captured and missing, out of a total of 190,000 committed to combat.[25] Combined with the almost 400,000 casualties the two Fronts suffered earlier in the year, both urgently needed a respite.[26]

Wehrmacht Reorganization

On 14 October, the OKH ordered Army Group North to go on the defence during the forthcoming winter but left Operation *Nordlicht* as a future option.[27] Given the state of Manstein's Eleventh Army, however, soon after Hitler postponed the operation, instead ordering Manstein to smash Soviet defences at Leningrad by artillery fire. Manstein remained custodian of a dormant front until 20 November, when he was summoned south to deal with the growing crisis in the Stalingrad region.

As in previous periods, the Red Army's operations around Leningrad had a significant impact on operations elsewhere along the front in the summer of 1942. The most important impact was the transfer of the Eleventh Army to the region, which deprived the Wehrmacht of critically important reserves in southern Russia at a time when they most needed

them. After the Eleventh Army failed to capture Leningrad, the OKH transferred its divisions to the south, but they arrived too late to help prevent the disaster that beset German forces in that region.

Reflections on the Offensive

Although most Soviet accounts ignore the 1942 Siniavino offensive or mention it only briefly in passing, the operation had far greater significance than simply providing command cadre and staff with valuable experience in conducting offensive operations. More importantly, the operation underscored Stalin's preoccupation with the offense, even at a time when the Red Army faced a major crisis in southern Russia. It also vividly illustrated Stalin's continued determination to raise the Leningrad blockade regardless of cost.

Finally, operations in the summer and fall of 1942 brutally revealed how much more the Red Army command cadre and forces would have to learn if they ever hoped to defeat German forces and raise the Leningrad blockade. During this period the two Fronts repeated many of the mistakes they had made in previous operations with the same adverse effect. The catalogue of deficiencies was long and too familiar. First and foremost, Govorov and Meretskov failed to synchronize their offensives, allowing the Germans to shift forces between threatened sectors and defeat the attacks in detail. Ineffective preliminary reconnaissance did not "reveal" the true nature of German defences, and thus largely negated the effectiveness of artillery preparations. During the offensive, artillery was too decentralized to provide effective, concentrated and flexible artillery support. Commanders failed to concentrate their forces properly before the offensive, to control and coordinate infantry, tank and artillery forces effectively before and during the offensive, and to manoeuvre their forces properly during the operations. Often, they committed their forces to battle piecemeal and without adequate flank protection, failed to anticipate German counterattacks, and belatedly shifted forces from secondary to main attack sectors. Poor logistical support throughout the offensives made it difficult if not impossible to sustain operations, and equally poor movement and engineer support led to excessive losses of tanks to enemy mines.

The two Fronts would have to address and solve these and other glaring problems before they could achieve any success in future offensives. They did not have long to do so, for in October 1942 Stalin was already planning for even larger-scale offensives in the Leningrad region.

CHAPTER 7:

A CITY BESIEGED 1942–43

Having survived the terrible winter of 1941–42, the Leningrad authorities continued to strengthen the city's defensive network, while supply routes across Lake Ladoga became more organized, and tenuous ground communications were even established with the Soviet rear area. Throughout, German bombs and artillery shells continued to pound the city.

While the Red Army fought to raise the blockade of Leningrad in 1942 and 1943, the *Stavka* exploited its experiences in other front sectors and progressively strengthened and deepened the city's defences.[1] Ultimately, the defences consisted of distinct defensive belts, echeloned in depth and equipped with numerous anti-tank obstacles, integrated artillery positions, and a mature system of interlocking anti-aircraft positions and arcs of fire. The backbone of the defence during the first half of 1942 was a continuous trench system, which connected separate battalion defensive regions, fortified strongpoints, and other lesser defensive lines into a single mutually supporting defence network. The battalion defensive regions, which consisted of rifle battalions, supporting weapons and a well-developed

LEFT: T-34 tanks rumble down a Leningrad street on their journey to the front following manufacture in the city. Leningrad was an essential industrial centre, producing 10 percent of the entire Soviet industrial production during World War II. Its environs, for example, contained over 500 factories.

system of trenches and communications trenches, formed the tactical foundation of each separate defensive belt.

Throughout the rest of 1942, the Leningrad Front improved the defence's strength and resilience, largely because it organized the defensive work more effectively. Under its supervision, the city's civilian population constructed additional defensive works along Leningrad's southern, south-eastern and northern approaches, which formed both main and second defensive belts, and a series of cut-off positions and fortified regions in the Twenty-Third, Forty-Second and Fifty-Fifth Armies' and the Neva Operational Group's defensive sectors.[2]

The Leningrad Front finally completed the entire system of continuous defensive belts around the city during the second half of 1942. The heart of the system were three defensive belts around the city proper and a series of intermediate lines and cut-off positions linking the three belts, which were themselves equipped with extensive engineer works and fortifications. By this time, the Front's forces

ABOVE: Preparing one of the city's artillery pieces for a barrage against the Germans. The weapon appears to be a 152mm Model 1937 gun-howitzer. Having a range of 17.2km (10.75 miles), it had a rate of fire of up to four rounds per minute. Many of these guns had been lost to the enemy in 1941.

were able to occupy all three belts in depth.[3] Forces from the defending armies' first and second echelons and fortified regions occupied the first and second defensive belts, the Front and army reserves occupied the third defensive belt and intermediate and cut-off positions, and NKVD troops manned positions in the city itself. This complete defence system permitted the armies to manoeuvre their forces and weaponry laterally and in the depths, improved the ammunition re-supply, and provided better protection against German artillery and air attack. By the end of the year, the Front had sufficient resources to organize the entire defence on the basis of field fortified regions (FFRs), whose attached transport made them more mobile than earlier wartime fortified regions.

The artillery of the Leningrad Front, Baltic Fleet and the Ladoga Flotilla materially assisted the city's defence by being able to conduct better-organized

counter-battery fire against German artillery. This fire forced the Germans to move their artillery 10–15km (6.25–9.3 miles) back from the front and curtailed the frequent fire raids on the city. The Baltic Fleet and Ladoga Flotilla concentrated their fire against German forces, communications and supply routes, and the fleet had established complete superiority over the Gulf of Finland by the end of 1942. The Ladoga Flotilla protected the supply routes across the lake to facilitate the build-up of supplies necessary for the city's survival during the winter.

Leningrad's armed workers' forces also increased in strength in 1942, as the number of workers' battalions rose to 52 by the year's end, manned by 26,897 personnel, including more than 10,000 women. In early 1943, the commander of the Internal Defence of the City (VOG) recommended that the Leningrad Front improve the city's internal defence forces by forming 12 workers' battalions modelled on the existing machine gun-artillery units, and another 40 resembling Red Army automatic weapons battalions. Govorov approved of and implemented the proposal. After the Red Army penetrated the German blockade in

January 1943 and established the narrow land corridor connecting Leningrad with the country as a whole, on 3 April the *Stavka* ordered the Leningrad and Volkhov Fronts to dig in to defend the corridor and strengthen the city's defences.

The Leningrad Front responded by converting the Forty-Second Army's final defence line into a reinforced concrete defensive belt occupied by VOG forces. This measure converted a defence line that had consisted of anti-tank obstacles and

armoured and wooden fortifications into a series of permanent fortified regions. Govorov also erected new fortifications and cut-off positions along the eastern bank of the Neva River north of Gorodok Nos 1 and 2. To the east, the Volkhov Fronts also established continuous and deeply echeloned defences anchored on numerous strongpoints and obstacles, which extended to a depth of 80km (50 miles) on its right wing and 35–50km (21.8–31.2 miles) on its left. This eliminated any possibility of

RIGHT: A beautifully composed image, more *son et lumière* than war. Silhouetted against the night sky is the dome of St. Isaac's cathedral in Leningrad. The weapon is the 4M, a special mounting of 7.62mm Maxim machine guns, which was the most common air defence piece in the Leningrad area.

German forces threatening either the corridor north of Siniavino or the city of Volkhov.

After weathering the terrible famine of winter 1941–42, the city's civilian and military leadership worked frantically to eliminate the famine's effects and restore as much normality to Leningrad as a city under siege could expect. At the same time, however, they had to prepare to defend the city against an expected German summer offensive. This meant that they had to balance carefully the city's defensive requirements, particularly the soldiers' needs, against the needs of the city's shrunken surviving population.

The most serious problem facing Leningrad other than the food supply was the spectre of epidemic produced by the city's poor living conditions and the spring thaw. The thaw, which released bodies, garbage and debris from the grip of the winter's ice, produced immense numbers of rodents and other vermin. The city managed to avoid major outbreaks of disease throughout 1942 because the authorities implemented a series of stringent hygienic measures to prevent it. Between 27 March and 15 April 1942, the city government and Party and factory cadres organized a public effort to remove all vermin and garbage from streets, basements, homes, buildings and waterways. During the massive clean-up operation, more than 300,000 people cleaned 16,000 buildings, three million square meters (9.84 million square feet) of streets, squares and alleys, and removed about 982,318 tonnes (one million tons) of refuse and garbage.

During the spring of 1942 the city's transport system once again began to operate, its population returned to work, and the authorities and public worked frantically to improve the city's still scarce food supplies. The trams, water supply, canals and many factories began working on 15 April, and the city government ordered the population to plant gardens wherever possible. It exploited every park and vacant area in the city to assign plots of land to the population on which to grow vegetables. Ultimately, more than 200,000 Leningraders planted an area encompassing 2000 hectares.

BELOW: German artillerymen prepare one of their pieces to fire at Leningrad in July 1943 (note mosquito nets draped over their headgear). As well as shells, the Germans dropped booby traps disguised as children's toys on the city in an effort to break the morale of the population.

Factories also began production, albeit slowly, particularly those producing weaponry, to which the government assigned priority in the allocation of critical resources. Weapons factories increased their production from five machine guns, 649 sub-machine guns and about 70,000 shells and mines in April 1942 to 150 machine guns, 2875 subma-chine guns and more than 145,000 shells and mines in May. Since coal and other fuels were still in short supply, the factories and other enterprises burnt only wood and peat. Once again, the city mobilized the entire population and they gathered one million cubic meters (9.84 million cubic feet) of fuel during the summer. Since this amount was still totally insufficient, the authorities ordered all buildings not suited for occupancy to be torn down for fuel.

Food and Fuel Supplies

In the fall of 1942, as the second winter under siege approached, the city's entire population, together with soldiers and sailors, helped prepare the city for the coming winter. Every able-bodied man and woman repaired buildings and gathered foodstuffs, including 74,656 tonnes (76,000 tons) of vegeta-bles, considerably lightening transport require-ments across Lake Ladoga in the summer and early fall. To help solve the fuel shortage, on 25 April 1942 the GKO ordered Red Army engineers to lay a welded fuel pipeline across Lake Ladoga. When it went into operation on 18 June, the 35km- (21.8-mile-) long and 12m- (39.3-feet-) deep pipeline car-ried 295 tonnes (300 tons) of fuel per day to Leningrad. Finally, in September 1942, the city began receiving electrical power from the power station at Volkhov, transmitted across the lake by underwater cable.

While the population and military struggled to make Leningrad as safe and self-sufficient as possi-ble, the Leningrad Front and Ladoga Flotilla worked with equal determination during the sum-mer to expand transport capacity into the city. On 9 April 1942, the GKO approved a new transport plan that established daily targets for shipment of food, ammunition, military equipment and fuel and lubricants into the city, and of evacuees and some cargoes out of the city.[4] The Ladoga Military Flotilla was responsible for organizing and manag-ing this transport effort. The flotilla and Baltic Fleet repaired ships during the winter, and Leningrad's shipbuilders built barges and both towed and self-propelled boats for use on the lake,

ABOVE: The desperation to survive during the blockade led many people to thieve and, particularly following a heavy air raid or period of shelling, loot. To prevent these situations getting out of hand, young members of the Party, as above, were armed and given the power to arrest suspected looters.

and the flotilla requisitioned other boats from local fishermen.[5] Similar work went on at docking facil-ities, which were greatly expanded.

Navigation across the lake began on 22 May when the steamer *Gidrotekhnik* towed a string of barges from Kobona to Osinovets. Soon after, other ships began travelling the 150km (93.75 miles) from Novaia Ladoga to Osinovets, and the 29km (18 miles) from Kobona to Osinovets. The first full convoy left Novaia Ladoga on 28 May. From May to 31 December 1942, more than 200 ships trans-ported a total of 765,801 tonnes (779,586 tons) of cargo across the lake, half of which constituted foodstuffs and the remainder coal, lubricants and military equipment.[6] The foodstuffs primarily included flour, grain, macaroni, butter, fat, meat, sugar, preserves and chocolate. Once the Ladoga routes were operational, the evacuation of factory equipment and critical technical personnel

increased dramatically as, during the summer, the flotilla evacuated 539,597 personnel and 287,721 tonnes (292,900 tons) of factory equipment across the lake. On its return trip it transported 310,000 combat replacements to the Leningrad Front, turning the city into an immense military encampment. These shipments materially improved the city's food supply, avoided new famine in the winter of 1942 and 1943, and permitted industry to resume its operations.

Since Leningrad remained in the grip of a tight siege throughout 1942, the defence of the supply lines remained a critical requirement, particularly

LEFT: Leningrad was an important centre for heavy industry. Here, lathes are being loaded onto lorries for evacuation. The machinery is from the Stankilov Facility, which was targeted by the Germans during the period 1941–43 due to the vital nature of its work.

BELOW: Straight from the paint shop to the frontline. A column of SU-122 self-propelled howitzers, produced by the Kirovsky factory in Leningrad, rolls past a triumphal arch evoking memories of past Russian victories. Such symbolism became more politically acceptable as the war continued.

against German air attack. During the summer, the Germans, in conjunction with their anticipated Operation *Nordlicht* against the city, tried to interdict the flow of supplies into the city by bombing its port facilities and vital supply routes across Lake Ladoga and the Gulf of Finland between Leningrad and Oranienbaum.

The Germans began their air campaign on 4 April when they conducted heavy attacks against Baltic Fleet and Ladoga Flotilla ships. They repeated the attacks on 24, 25 and 27 April in conjunction with a heavy artillery bombardment of the city's port facilities.[7] The heaviest German air attacks, however, occurred in the early fall of 1942, when Hitler ordered Manstein to pound the city into submission. In September alone German aircraft dropped 120 bombs in several raids on the Kobona region. Throughout the fall, the Germans conducted a total of 122 daylight and 15 night raids involving between 80 and 130 aircraft each, and dropped a total of 6400 bombs on the city. However, PVO anti-aircraft gunners and aircraft inflicted increasingly heavy aircraft losses on the Luftwaffe, forcing it to reduce sharply the size and number of its raids. In the end, these raids had only a negligible effect on transport and re-supply,

ABOVE: This soldier is buying a ticket for Shostakovich's 7th Symphony. Such cultural events were very popular with the population, military and civilian alike, throughout the 900 days of the siege, acting as a reminder of more peaceful times.

reducing cargo shipments by only 0.4 percent – but at a cost of 160 aircraft lost by the Germans.

Lake Ladoga Defences

Ground defence of Lake Ladoga's southern shore and the approaches east and west of the lake remained vital to the defence of the water routes throughout mid-January 1943, since the Germans' frontlines still clung to the lake's southern shore, perilously close to the city. Throughout 1942, the Ladoga Flotilla manned the "*Oreshek*" Fortress opposite Shlissel'burg to defend the southwestern shore of the lake and maintained a naval garrison on Sukho Island to protect the lake's southeast shore. The Leningrad and Volkhov Fronts protected the ground approaches to these routes, especially the critical road and rail network between Novaia Ladoga and Volkhov. Largely due to this effective defence, the Ladoga water routes managed to function normally throughout 1942 despite nearly constant navigational difficulties caused by

storms, rough water and the German air and artillery action.

Frustrated by their inability to halt or slow the steady flow of vital supplies across the lake, on several occasions the Germans attempted direct action to close the routes. For example, in April and May 1942 they convinced the Finns to deploy a small naval and amphibious force on the lake.[8] Soviet intelligence detected the presence of these ships and a landing force of 3000 men at and around the ports of Sortavala, Lakhdenpokh'ia and Impilakhti the following month. In addition, the Germans deployed a detachment of landing barges to Keksholm in August, and began conducting reconnaissance and diversionary actions on the lake in late September, laying magnetic mines on the sea routes on 27 September and also cutting communications west of Sukho Island. Govorov responded by deploying a naval detachment of 100 men and three 100mm guns to occupy defences on Sukho Island. Thereafter, the Finns made two attempts in October to land forces on Sukho Island but both of these failed.[9]

When winter began in late 1942, German forces defending the Mga-Siniavino salient east of the city still held all land routes into the city in a stranglehold. Once again it seemed as if the Leningraders would have to rely on the ice road, the "Road of

ABOVE: **Marines of the Baltic Fleet on patrol. The task of the fleet was to support Leningrad with its shipborne guns and the guns sited in land batteries. Its vessels were also tasked with guarding against a possible enemy amphibious landing from the Gulf of Finland.**

Life", as their lifeline during the coming winter. Since few Leningraders had forgotten the horrors of the previous winter's famine, they and the city authorities redoubled their efforts to avoid repeating the catastrophe that had befallen them the previous year. However, four, and ultimately five, factors combined to alleviate the situation.

First, and tragically, because of the previous year's death toll and the summer evacuations, the size of Leningrad's population was far smaller in November 1942 than it had been in November 1941. Leningrad now had only 700,000 civilian and about 420,000 soldiers to feed. Second, the Leningraders amassed far greater food reserves in 1942 than had existed in 1941. Third, the winter of 1942–43 was far less severe than the winter of 1941–42. The freeze arrived later in 1942 and, as a result, navigation and transport on the lake continued until 27 November and, in some instances, until 7 January 1943 farther north on the lake where the ice formed later. Fourth, despite the later freeze, the authorities were far more experienced with the exploitation of the ice road. Fifth, the Red Army finally cracked the blockade in mid-January 1943.

When the lake finally did freeze, the Leningrad Front and Ladoga Flotilla exploited their experiences of the previous winter to improve the road and also began constructing railroad lines to supplement the existing road routes, whose use precluded painstaking and time-consuming transfer of cargoes from railcars to boats. Red Army engineers began building the railroad line simultaneously from east and west, and by mid-January had laid 15km (9.3 miles) of operational track across the western extremity of the lake. However, after Red Army forces opened the land corridor to Leningrad in January 1943, the engineers halted construction of the lake route and instead moved the railroad to a land route through the corridor, even though the land corridor remained quite narrow and was subject to constant German artillery fire.[10] Although the engineers abandoned the lake railroad, they continued to improve and expand the ice roads across the lake.

The Ice Road

Despite the late freeze and the frequent thaws, the ice road finally opened for traffic on 19 December.

The first convoy passed over it on 20 December, but the 160 trucks carried only 300kg (660lb) of cargo each. Subsequently, larger columns of several hundred trucks travelled the route on 27 December and 8 January, but thereafter the convoys ended due to weak ice.[11] The traffic resumed on 12 January, but ended again on 30 March when the Leningrad Front closed the road because of another thaw. Over the course of the winter, the ice road was serviceable for only 101 days between 20 December and 30 March, and suitable for massive truck movement on only 97 days. During this period, trucks transported 210,745 tonnes (214,539 tons) of cargo, predominantly food and ammunition, and more than 200,000 personnel and evacuees over the ice road.[12] Even after the railroad line through the Shlissel'burg corridor became operational, the ice road still functioned as a reliable communication route for the Leningrad Front. The Germans continued their air attacks on the ice road

BELOW: Holding the sniper's rifle is Captain Grigoriev, who has been awarded the Order of the Patriotic War (Second Class). Grigoriev and his men are being visited by Party members from the Oktobersky district on a morale-boosting tour. The shoulder boards were reintroduced into the Red Army in 1943.

LEFT: Shelling and bombing continued to cause hardship for the population, and added to the general terror. The apartments over this boarded-up food shop have taken a direct hit. The wagons drawn up outside 119, 25th October Prospect, have removed much of the debris.

throughout the winter, even after the Red Army had recaptured the narrow land link into the city, but failed to hinder movement over the ice road.[13] To the relief of the road's defenders, German artillery fire ended after the Red Army seized the land corridor to the city in January.

After Operation Spark in January 1943, the Leningrad Front worked feverishly to restore reliable ground communications between Leningrad and the Soviet rear area. On 21 January, railroad and construction troops began building a railroad line along the southern shore of Lake Ladoga from Shlissel'burg to Poliana. The railroad bed, which ran through rough terrain only 6–8km (3.75–5 miles) from the frontlines near Siniavino, was constructed under constant artillery fire and air attack in severe winter conditions. Despite the difficulties, the 33km (20.6–mile) route opened on 6 February. Thereafter, the railroad and lake water routes supplied Leningrad's military and civilian needs. In terms of its capacity, the rail line was far more important than the water routes across Lake Ladoga. Construction forces continued to improve the rail passage as spring approached, opening a new railroad bridge across the Neva River on 18 March, which permitted through traffic along the entire rail line.[14] However, the incessant German artillery fire caused heavy casualties and constantly forced the constructors to repair and restore the line. Construction troops built a second railroad line parallel to the first in May 1943. This 18km (11.2-mile) railroad line, which was closer to the

lake, improved the efficiency, capacity and safety of rail transport through the Shlissel'burg corridor.[15]

The Germans did everything in their power to disrupt or halt rail movement by conducting artillery fire and air strikes on the roadway, bridges and other rail installations. Since the Germans believed that they could cut off supplies both to Leningrad and the Volkhov Front by destroying bridges across the Volkhov River, in May and June they mounted heavy air raids against these bridges, but failed to hinder significantly the re-supply effort.[16] Subsequently, the railroad lines through

LEFT: Visibly shaken but still alive, Mrs Korobova, shown here, stands beside her wrecked apartment following a German artillery barrage. Incredibly, given the damage to floors and walls, the furniture seems to have survived intact and in place.

the corridor played an immense role supplying Leningrad's population and defenders. During the period from 6 February 1943 to 6 March 1944, for example, 5334 cargo trains with 225,859 railroad cars traversed the land route to Leningrad.

With the new land route into Leningrad functioning effectively, re-supply of the city and defence of the supply lines became a far easier process during the spring and summer of 1943. In addition, the nature of transported cargo also changed considerably as the Leningrad Front used the lake routes to transport primarily wood and wood products.[17] The supply routes across Lake Ladoga gradually lost their military importance after September 1943, when the Leningrad Front transferred all berths, ports and cargo means on the lake's eastern and western shores to civilian control.[18] Throughout the entire Leningrad blockade, the water routes across Lake Ladoga transported 2,234,477 tonnes (2,275,000 tons) of cargo, including 1,836,935 tonnes (1,870,000 tons) of cargo sent to the city.

Although the partisan movement in the Leningrad region grew significantly in 1942 and

ABOVE: Always a feature of life in Russia, the clearing of snow from the main roads had to be carried out siege or no siege. Leningraders of all ages were enlisted to carry out this necessary work.

1943, its military importance remained limited. On 1 January 1942, an estimated 1994 partisans were operating in the northwestern, western and southern parts of the Leningrad region, most actively in the Partisan *krai*. While these forces were loosely organized into the Leningrad, Valdai and Volkhov Operational Groups, each consisting of separate detachments, the latter were weak and poorly organized, and the heavy snow and extreme cold severely hindered their operations.[19] Therefore, the partisan headquarters spent the winter attempting to improve the organization, command and control, and firepower of partisan detachments.[20] During the winter, partisan operations were weak and episodic and only loosely coordinated with Front operations.[21] At the same time, however, partisans operating in and around the Partisan *krai* gathered and sent foodstuffs to Leningrad, the first delivery reaching the city by circuitous route on 25 February. Partisan detachments also sent representatives and delegations to and from the city to receive instructions and coordinate their actions with the Leningrad Front. Despite its relative inactivity, the partisan movement and associated Party underground structure grew throughout the winter. By April 1942, 50 new partisan detachments had formed and began operating in the Leningrad region, and the Party formed and fielded numerous partisan cells throughout the region to establish an underground infrastructure, communications and liaison with partisan detachments.[22]

The Partisans

Partisan organization and operational effectiveness improved in the summer and fall of 1942, primarily because the Party, GKO and Red Army exercised more effective centralized control over partisan organizations and operations. On 30 May 1942, the Party and GKO formed the Central Staff of the Partisan Movement to centralize State control over all partisan organizations and detachments. The new headquarters established an elaborate hierarchy of command and control organs extending from Moscow through the Fronts to individual partisan headquarters in the German rear, and dispatched Red Army and NKVD officers to create new partisan forces and control all partisan operations. At Leningrad, Govorov established the Leningrad Headquarters of the Partisan Movement in July 1942, which he tasked with centralizing all planning for and control over partisan warfare in the region. The plan created new partisan forces and diversionary groups, ordered these forces to sabotage and destroy German garrisons, installations and communications, and to attack German headquarters, supply depots, airfields and communications centres, and also established priority intelligence collection requirements in support of Red Army ground combat operations.

The strength and dynamism of partisan forces in the Leningrad region increased sharply in the summer of 1942. Throughout the year the number of partisan brigades and the strength of partisan forces operating in the German rear grew from two partisan brigades and 30 weak detachments with 2000 fighters, to four brigades and numerous separate detachments with more than 3000 personnel.[23] Although these forces engaged primarily in sabotage and diversionary operations, their actions were bothersome enough to provoke an organized

German response in the form of formal anti-partisan operations. In Führer Directive No 46 issued on 18 August 1942, Hitler declared: "The bandit monstrosity in the East has assumed a no longer tolerable scope and threatens to become a serious danger to front supply and exploitation of the land." Hitler assigned Heinrich Himmler, head of the SS, the responsibility for rooting out partisan activity, charged the Chief of Staff of OKH with conducting anti-partisan warfare, and ordered the Replacement Army (each formation in the German Army had its own replacement unit) to be employed as anti-partisan forces when they completed their training. Subsequently, the Germans mounted numerous operations against partisans, but particularly against the Partisan *krai*. In about 30 days of anti-partisan operations, 6000 German troops turned the *krai* into a virtual desert.[24]

The German punitive operation inflicted significant casualties on the partisans and forced the Partisan Movement to move its forces to safer locales out of harm's way.[25] However, the fury of the German operation produced a backlash by prompting virtually all of the region's inhabitants to join the partisan movement. Despite destroying the Partisan *krai*, German losses to partisan activities continued to mount in a vicious circle that ultimately ignited revolt throughout the entire German rear area. Worse still for the Germans, the near constant heavy fighting in and around Leningrad and to the south around Demiansk forced Army Group North to reduce the size and number of its rear area security installations, which significantly improved partisan morale.

Increasing Guerrilla Activity

The partisan movement in the Leningrad region increased from 2993 enrolled fighters on 1 January 1943 to 14,358 on 1 November. The scope of diversionary, reconnaissance and underground activities also widened. By 1 January 1943, the Leningrad Party Regional Committee had established 11 inter-regional underground Party centres in major cities and towns throughout the region.[26] Headed by a first secretary and full staff, each centre coordinated the activities of all partisan groups, detachments and underground organizations operating in each region and consolidated these forces into larger and more effective formations. By 1 August 1943, five partisan brigades, a separate partisan regiment, and tens of detachments and groups operated throughout the Leningrad region.[27] Before

ABOVE: The ice on Lake Ladoga had to be at least 200mm (7.87in) thick to support a loaded truck – a thickness of 100mm (3.93in) was sufficient to support the weight of an unladen horse. Driving across the lake was always dangerous: many trucks and their drivers fell through the ice.

RIGHT: These cheerful Leningrad youngsters have managed to keep their spirits up. All have a malnourished look while the boy on the right, although well-provided with skis, does not seem particularly well-dressed for the weather. The smoker in the middle seems very pleased with his appetite suppressant!

the year's end, the number of brigades grew to 10 with an eleventh formed in early January 1944.[28] By 1 December these forces encompassed 35,000 active fighters and thousands of auxiliaries. This expanded partisan and underground structure organized local government organs and conducted a propaganda war by publishing underground newspapers and pamphlets. All the while, it intensified its reconnaissance and diversionary operations in support of Red Army military operations.

In mid-1943, partisan brigades and detachments began conducting coordinated large-scale raids and attacks on German lines of communications and military installations. For example, on 1 August

ABOVE: Although communications with the outside world had been established by the end of 1943, the "Road of Life" was not immediately redundant. With their transport parked carefully on thicker ice, this section of Red Army engineers gingerly inspects a weak point. Groups such as this worked around the clock and in all conditions to maintain ice routes.

1943 partisan forces began Operation Railroad War (*Relsovaia voina*), concerted attacks on German rail communications across the entire Soviet-German front controlled by the Central Staff of the Partisan Movement and the *Stavka*.[29] So successful were these operations and so confident were the Leningrad partisans of imminent victory, that, in September, the partisan movement began speaking openly about the Red Army's forthcoming liberation of the region and accelerated its activities against German rear area installations. Partisan attacks then intensified and, by October, the concerted attacks ignited a full-scale popular uprising in the entire region. The ferocity and scope of this partisan revolt had a singularly adverse effect on German control of the region, and hastened Hitler's decision to permit the whole of Army Group North first to construct and then to withdraw to the Panther Line.

Although the Germans had initially treated the partisans' actions with contempt, comparing their impact to mere discomfort produced by "Red lice under the German's hide", ultimately partisan warfare had an adverse impact on their military operations. While the Germans could and did dismiss the hundreds of partisan pinprick attacks as inconsequential, the cumulative effect was debilitating: they tied down an ever-increasing number of German security troops at a time when manpower was becoming critical at the front. They also gave the lie to the Germans' stated intent regarding the future political, economic and social organization of captured territories, and rendered German propaganda utterly useless.

However, the less tangible aspects of partisan warfare had a more telling effect on the Germans. As partisan operations expanded in scope from mere harassment to concerted attacks that produced real pain, they undermined the Germans' will for victory. By early 1944, as the Red Army mounted its major assaults that liberated the Leningrad region, the partisan movement assumed proportions that accurately reflected the immense suffering of their countrymen who had been confined for three years in the hellish prison that was the city of Leningrad.

CHAPTER 8:

CRACKING THE BLOCKADE

The *Stavka* was determined to raise the Leningrad blockade in 1943, and thus launched a number of offensives between January and September. The Third, Fourth and Fifth Siniavino Offensives, and Operation Polar Star, were bloody affairs, but by the end of 1943 the Wehrmacht threat to Leningrad had been removed forever – Army Group North began its retreat west.

After its successful counteroffensive in the Stalingrad region in November and December 1942, the *Stavka* exploited the Axis defeats by expanding its offensive operations to encompass virtually the entire Soviet-German front. Understandably, the *Stavka* included the Leningrad region in its offensive plans since the city's defenders faced a second harsh winter in blockade and a continued, if reduced, threat of German attack. Therefore, the *Stavka* decided to conduct a major offensive in the Leningrad region timed to correspond with the expanded Red Army offensive in southern Russia. Although its initial aim was to raise the Leningrad blockade, by February 1943 the *Stavka* also hoped to defeat Army Group North decisively and drive its forces from the entire Leningrad region. By this time, the Leningrad offensive was part of a grander scheme aimed at defeating all three German army groups in the East and driving them back to Narva, Vitebsk, Kiev and the Dnepr River line, the same objectives the Red Army had failed to achieve in the winter of 1941–42.

LEFT: A German Tiger heavy tank in wooded terrain on the Leningrad Front in the summer of 1943. The mighty Tiger, armed with an 88mm gun, was not a decisive factor in the fighting in the trees and marshes of northern Russia. It was to have more impact on the open steppes in the south.

On 1 January 1943, the Red Army's strategic situation in the Leningrad region was serious but no longer grave. Although the threat of a major offensive against the city had lessened, German forces still encircled the city from three sides and Finnish forces threatened it from the north.[1] Govorov's Leningrad Front defended the isolated Oranienbaum bridgehead west of the city and the city's southern, southeastern and eastern approaches. The city was still cut off from the rest of the Soviet Union, the Baltic Fleet was bottled up in the eastern Gulf of Finland, and German artillery continued to pound Leningrad. To the east, Meretskov's Volkhov Front defended vital communications lines to Lake Ladoga's eastern shore and the wide sector between Lakes Ladoga and Il'men.

The Leningrad Front's Twenty-Third Army defended the northwestern approaches to the city along the Karelian Isthmus against possible Finnish attack, and the Coastal Operation Group (COG – formerly the Eighth Army) defended the isolated Oranienbaum bridgehead west of the city.[2] The COG's bridgehead protected the approaches to Kronshtadt with long-range artillery and threatened the left flank of German forces south of Leningrad. The Internal Defences of the City (VOG) and the Baltic Fleet's Kronshtadt Naval Defensive Region protected the sea approaches to Leningrad, and the

ABOVE: Finnish officers (in fur caps) during a visit to German military installations south of Lake Ladoga in 1943. Finland's participation in the siege of Leningrad was a great disappointment to the Germans, who expected their allies to display the same ideological convictions as themselves.

Kronshtadt Naval Defensive Region defended islands in the Gulf of Finland and maintained communications between these islands by the use of aircraft and aerosleighs.

Colonel-General I. I. Maslennikov's Forty-Second and Lieutenant-General V. P. Sviridov's Fifty-Fifth Armies defended the southern and southeastern approaches to the city along a front extending from Uritsk on the Gulf of Finland through Pushkin and Kolpino to the Neva River.[3] Major-General M. P. Dukhanov's Sixty-Seventh Army, which had been formed in October 1942 from the Neva Operational Group, occupied a 55km (34.3-mile) sector northwards along the Neva River to Shlissel'burg on the Front's left flank. It also defended Lake Ladoga's western shore north of the Neva River's mouth.[4] Govorov retained two rifle divisions, two rifle and two tank brigades, one ski brigade and one fortified region in

the Front reserve near Leningrad for employment on the Karelian Isthmus.[5]

The Leningrad Front's air forces consisted of the Thirteenth Air Army and Baltic Fleet aviation, which protected the Leningrad Front and naval base. The Thirteenth Air Army, which had been formed in November 1942, consisted of three aviation divisions, five separate aviation regiments and one mixed aviation regiment, which was still forming.[6] It had 150 combat aircraft at its disposal, augmented by the 235 aircraft from the Baltic Fleet's three aviation brigades. The Leningrad PVO Army and the Ladoga Division PVO Region defended Leningrad and its environs against air attack. The Leningrad PVO Army's VII Fighter Aviation Corps and anti-aircraft artillery and machine-gun regiments fielded 550 anti-aircraft guns and 150 heavy anti-aircraft machine guns, supplemented by a further 180 anti-aircraft guns and 60 heavy anti-aircraft machine guns assigned to the Ladoga Division PVO Region.[7] The Baltic Fleet, still subordinate to the Leningrad Front, consisted of the Kronshtadt Naval Base and adjacent forts, the Izhorsk and Ostrov Fortified Sectors, the Leningrad Naval Base, which repaired fleet ships, squadron ships and submarines based at

Kronshtadt and Leningrad, the Ladoga Military Flotilla, coastal defences, and aviation units. The Baltic Fleet protected the sea approaches to Leningrad and the vital Lake Ladoga supply routes.[8]

Meretskov's Volkhov Front defended the 300km (187.5-mile) sector from Lake Ladoga to Lake Il'men. Starikov's Eighth Army defended the 50km (31.25-mile) sector on the Front's right flank from the Novo Ladoga Canal to the Kirov railroad and was backed up by Lieutenant-General V. Z. Romanovsky's Second Shock Army, which was in second echelon preparing for offensive operations. [9] The Fifty-Fourth, Fourth, Fifty-Ninth and Fifty-Second Armies, commanded respectively by Lieutenant-General A. V. Sukhomlin, Major-General N. I. Gusev, Lieutenant-General I. T. Korovnikov and Lieutenant-General V. F. Iakovlev, were deployed from the Kirov railroad south to Lake Il'men.[10] Meretskov retained one rifle division and two ski brigades in his reserve.[11] The Fourteenth Air Army, formed in July 1942, provided air support to the Volkhov Front with more than 200 aircraft organized into three aviation divisions and seven separate aviation regiments.

After the Wehrmacht's defeats in southern Russia, the OKH deferred further action in the Leningrad region until the situation stabilized in the south. In the meantime, it ordered Kuechler's army group to go on the defence, and weakened it considerably by transferring the Eleventh Army to Army Group Centre in October. In addition, it transferred nine divisions from the Eighteenth Army to other front sectors during October and November 1942. On 1 December, Lindemann's army consisted of 26 divisions deployed on a 450km (281-mile) front from the Baltic Sea to Lake Il'men opposite the Red Army's Leningrad and Volkhov Fronts. Severe force shortages caused Lindemann to deploy virtually all of his divisions in a single line, with each division defending roughly a 17km (10.6-mile) front. Lindemann retained portions of two divisions in reserve at Mga and west of Krasnoe Selo.[12] The OKH tried to compensate for the shortages by sending Lindemann the 10th Luftwaffe Field Division, which, on 1 December, was en route from Kingisepp to Krasnogvardeisk. The Luftwaffe's First Air Fleet provided Lindemann's army with air support by conducting a limited number of reconnaissance and bombing sorties against Leningrad.[13]

German Dispositions

The Eighteenth Army's L Army Corps defended the sector south of Leningrad from the western edge of the Oranienbaum bridgehead to Pushkin with four divisions, and, farther east, LIV Army Corps deployed three divisions in the sector from Pushkin to Annenskoe on the Neva River.[14] Three XXVI Army Corps divisions manned fortifications from Annenskoe to south of Voronovo in the critical Mga-Siniavino salient south of Shlissel'burg, and six I Army Corps divisions defended from the south of Voronovo to the Volkhov River south of Kirishi.[15] Finally, XXVIII Army Corps and XXXVIII Army Corps defended the front southwards along the

RIGHT: German artillery in action in January 1943. The gun is a 105mm leFH18 standard field howitzer, which was equivalent to the British 25-pounder. It was a versatile weapon, capable of firing all types of projectile and even knocking out tanks at short ranges.

THE SIEGE OF LENINGRAD 1941–1944

Volkhov River to Lake Il'men with three divisions each, and the 285th Security Division protected the army group's rear area as a whole.[16]

The German defences were strongest in the Shlissel'burg-Siniavino bottleneck, where five experienced German divisions with 10,000–12,000 men each, manned strongly fortified defences in the region's forested and swampy terrain.[17] The depth and width of the Neva River, which was partially frozen during the winter, and the nearly impassable forested and swampy terrain in the Mga-Siniavino salient, which was laced with many fortified stone villages, facilitated German defence and maintenance of the blockade as a whole. Even in early 1943, Hitler considered the salient as a vital launching pad for future attacks against the ice road and Leningrad from the east, and a vital link in the blockade, since it blocked communications between the Leningrad and Volkhov Fronts. Therefore, the Germans established three strong defence lines within the salient, each consisting of three trench lines, and formed defensive regions and larger centres of resistance anchored on numerous fortified villages.[18] These strong defences in the salient represented the "nut" that Soviet forces had to crack if they were to raise the blockade of Leningrad.

Govorov and Meretskov began planning the offensive to raise the Leningrad blockade in late November and early December 1942 under the watchful eye of Stavka representative Voroshilov, just as the Red Army was beginning to exploit its Stalingrad victory by conducting a major winter offensive in southern Russia. Originally, Govorov proposed two separate offensives, the first named the Uritsk Operation, to penetrate the blockade and restore communications south of Lake Ladoga, and the second, the Shlissel'burg Operation, to re-establish communications between the Coastal Operational Group and the Forty-Second Army. In the Uritsk offensive, the Leningrad Front's Coastal Operational Group and Forty-Second Army were to smash German defences and restore a continuous front west of the city.[19] In the Shlissel'burg offensive, the Leningrad Front's Sixty-Seventh Army and the Volkhov Front's Second Shock and Eighth Armies were to penetrate German defences east of the city and raise the Leningrad blockade.[20] These Red Army operations were to be conducted successively – the Shlissel'burg operation in the second half of December and the Uritsk operation in February 1943.[21]

Soviet Attack Plans

Govorov recommended that both Fronts attack simultaneously with powerful shock groups to avoid any repetition of the problems experienced in August 1942. He requested also that the Stavka reinforce his Front with three to four rifle divisions and bring the Thirteenth Air Army up to full strength.[22] The Stavka approved Govorov's plan on 2 December with only minor amendments, ordered Govorov and Meretskov to complete their planning by 1 December, and assigned a codename, Spark, (Iskra) to the offensive. It designated Romanovsky's

LEFT: The Luftwaffe did not have things all its own way in the skies over Leningrad. This Tupolev SB-2 medium bomber has just returned from a night raid. The SB-2 was reaching the end of its useful life by the mid-war years, but air operations against the Germans were very good for the city's morale.

RIGHT: Well-dressed for the bitter conditions, this Soviet Maxim gun crew prepares to fight off a German counter-attack on the Volkhov Front. The Maxim, although dating from 1910, provided valuable service throughout the war and served with other Soviet-sponsored armies during the second half of the twentieth century.

Second Shock Army as the Volkhov Front's shock group and Dukhanov's Sixty-Seventh Army as the Leningrad Front's shock group and ordered Fediuninsky, the deputy Front commander, to supervise Romanovsky's operations and Govorov himself to direct Dukhanov's operations. Finally, the *Stavka* ordered Marshal Voroshilov to coordinate the offensive as a whole as its representative, assigned the two Fronts specific missions on 8 December, and dispatched significant reinforcements during the remainder of the month.[23] Although the two Fronts managed to complete their offensive preparations by 1 January, ice conditions on the Neva forced the *Stavka* to agree with Govorov and postpone the offensive until 10–12 January.

According to the final offensive plan, the two shock groups were to destroy German forces defending the Shlissel'burg-Siniavino salient and raise the Leningrad blockade. Thereafter, in early February they were to attack southwards, destroy German forces in the Mga region, and establish a broad land corridor to Leningrad to restore reliable ground communications to the city.[24] Govorov's shock group, Dukhanov's Sixty-Seventh Army, was to penetrate German defences in the 13km (8.1-mile) sector between Moskovskaia Dubrovka and Shlissel'burg, defeat German forces in the western portion of the salient, and link up with the Volkhov Front's shock group to restore ground communications with Leningrad.[25] Subsequently, its forces were to wheel southwards and occupy new defences along the Moika River north of Mga. Dukhanov's

army consisted of eight rifle divisions, five rifle, two ski and three tank brigades, one fortified region, and an imposing array of supporting forces deployed in two echelons to strengthen the force of its attack.[26] The shock group was to attack early on 12 January and operate round-the-clock so as to penetrate the blockade in three to four days.

Meretskov's shock group, Romanovsky's Second Shock Army, was to smash German defences in the 12km (7.5-mile) sector from Lipka to Gaitolovo, destroy German forces in the eastern part of the salient, and link up with the Leningrad Front, while defending across the remainder of its front.[27] Subsequently, its forces were to dig in, protect the Shlissel'burg axis and its left flank, and link up with the Leningrad Front's Sixty-Seventh Army. Romanovsky's army consisted of 11 rifle divisions, and one rifle, two ski and four tank brigades deployed in two echelons with specific forces assigned to capture specific objectives.[28] Starikov's Eighth Army, on Romanovsky's left flank, was to penetrate German defences from Gaitolovo south to the railroad, advance westwards and southwestwards, and establish new defences in tandem with the Sixty-Seventh Army northwest of the town of Mga. Meretskov was also to begin his offensive on 12 January.

On 27 December Voroshilov approved Govorov's and Meretskov's plan for cooperation, which required the Fronts' two shock groups to link up along a line passing through Workers' Settlements Nos 2 and 6.[29] Dukhanov and Romanovsky did most of their planning based on Front warning orders, even before receiving the Front directives, and had submitted their plans to Govorov and Meretskov by 1 January. Dukhanov ordered his shock group to cross the Neva River's ice and penetrate enemy defences between Moskovskaia Dubrovka and Shlissel'burg. It would then attack towards Siniavino, destroy German forces in Shlissel'burg and Siniavino, and capture the Arbuzovo, Marker 22.4, Workers' Settlement No 6, Siniavino, Workers' Settlement No 1, and Shlissel'burg strongpoints. Subsequently, his shock group was to link up with the Volkhov Front's shock group, restore a continuous front south of Lake Ladoga, and attack southeast to capture the Moika River line. Other Sixty-Seventh Army forces defended the Neva River and the ice road across Lake Ladoga, and the Baltic Fleet provided the army with additional fire support.[30]

Romanovsky ordered his shock group to penetrate German defences between Lipka and Gaitolovo, destroy German forces in the Lipka, Workers' Settlement No 8, "*Kruglaia*" Grove and Gaitolovo regions, and capture Workers' Settlement Nos 1 and 5 and Siniavino. Subsequently, while protecting its left and right flank, the shock group was to reach the Neva River and link up with the Leningrad Front's shock group.[31] On Romanovsky's left flank, Starikov ordered his Eighth Army to penetrate German defences in the Gaitolovo and Mishino sector with two rifle divisions and one rifle brigade, and advance towards Mga to protect Romanovsky's left flank.

To conduct so complex an offensive against enemy forces occupying strong defences in very difficult terrain and poor weather conditions necessitated careful and effective command and control and massive but thoroughly integrated and coordinated artillery, air, armour, engineer and logistical support.[32] This was particularly true since previous offensives had often illustrated what not to do. Both Govorov and Meretskov planned to provide massive artillery support to their shock groups both before and during the offensive. Govorov concentrated 1873 guns and mortars in the Sixty-Seventh Army's sector alone, formed numerous special-purpose artillery groups, and planned a 150-minute artillery preparation before the assault.[33] Meretskov concentrated 2885 guns and mortars in his offensive sector, employed the same types of artillery groups as Govorov, and planned an 80-minute preparation in the Second Shock

Army's sector and a 100minute preparation in the Eighth Army's sector.[34]

Major-General S. D. Rybal'chenko's Thirteenth Air Army, reinforced by Baltic Fleet aircraft, the Leningrad PVO Army's VII Fighter Aviation Corps, and four mixed aviation divisions assigned to the armies, supported Govorov's offensive with 414 aircraft, predominantly fighters.[35] Rybal'chenko concentrated his air sorties during the preparation against targets in the forward edge and, later, against enemy reserves and artillery positions, while small groups of aircraft supported the advancing troops on an on-call basis.[36] Major-General I. P. Zhuravlev's Fourteenth Air Army, reinforced by II Fighter Aviation Corps, the 232nd Assault Aviation Division, and three mixed aviation regiments assigned to subordinate armies, supported Meretskov's offensive with 395 aircraft, most of which were ground-attack types and fighters.[37] The greater proportion of assault aircraft permitted Zhuravlev's air army to provide more effective ground support while striking enemy strongpoints.

Engineer Support for the Assault

Large tank forces could not operate in the broken, forested and swampy terrain around Leningrad, particularly in winter, and the short distances to the shock groups' objectives denied tank forces adequate room to manoeuvre. Therefore, both Fronts assigned their shock groups tank brigades, regiments and battalions simply as infantry support units. Govorov assigned the Sixty-Seventh Army three tank brigades and two separate tank battalions totalling 222 tanks and 37 armoured cars, distributed equally between the first and second echelons, with light tanks deployed forward to negotiate the Neva River's icy surface.[38] Meretskov attached four tank brigades, one tank regiment and four separate tank battalions – a total of 217 tanks – to the Second Shock Army, and one regiment and two battalions with 92 tanks to the Eighth Army.[39] In addition, the 32nd and 44th Aerosleigh Battalions, equipped with lightly armoured machine-gun aerosleighs, conducted reconnaissance and raids in the German rear.

Given the strong German defences and difficult terrain, extensive engineer support was vital for the operation's success, particularly for the Sixty-Seventh Army, which had to assault across the frozen surface of the Neva River.[40] Govorov supported the Sixty-Seventh Army with 15 engineer-sapper, pontoon and other battalions, seven river-crossing parks, and

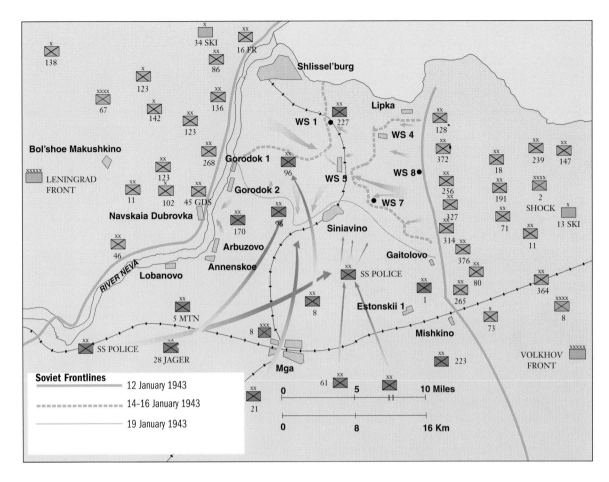

camouflage (*maskirovka*) and hydro-technical companies. Meretskov allocated two complete engineer-sapper brigades, one separate mine-sapper battalion, and one motorized engineer battalion to the Second Shock Army, and an engineer-miner brigade and separate motorized engineer battalion to support the Eighth Army. Finally, for the first time in the war the two Fronts were able to provide their forces with adequate logistical support, even though the blockade still adversely affected the Leningrad Front and the Volkhov Front's supply lines were overextended.[41] When the offensive began, for example, the Leningrad Front's Sixty-Seventh Army had 22 days' supply of food and forage and three refills of fuel. The Volkhov Front's Second Shock Army had 20 days' supply of food, 58 days' supply of forage and two to three refills of fuel per fighting vehicle.

Throughout the preparatory period, both Fronts observed strict security requirements, limiting the number of written planning documents, restricting daytime movement, and concealing all attack preparations. At the same time, they conducted specialized training in combat techniques unique to the operation, such as the assault across the Neva River's ice, and practice attacks against specific objectives, which encompassed numerous rehearsals and exercises in the rear area conducted on detailed mock-ups of each objective. Just prior to the attack, they simulated attack preparations in other front sectors to prevent the Germans from determining the exact time and location of the offensive. On the eve of the offensive, the artillery had occupied its forward firing positions by 5 January, rifle divisions had moved into their jumping-off positions by 11 January, and first echelon tanks had moved into their advanced positions on 12 January.

The Leningrad and Volkhov Fronts' third Siniavino offensive took place within the context of the Red Army's expanding winter campaign in southern Russia. Shortly before the offensive began

LEFT: Another posed shot of Red Army infantry undergoing training, the objective is the ruined building. Advancing through knee-deep snow and supported by submachine gunners, the lightly equipped troops move cautiously forward in preparation for the real thing later in the year.

the *Stavka* sent Zhukov to Leningrad to coordinate the operation. Less than a month before, Zhukov had coordinated Operation Mars, the Western and Kalinin Front's unsuccessful attempt to smash Army Group Centre's Rzhev salient.[42] Zhukov remained in Leningrad between 12 and 24 January, and, in February, after the operation was complete, he developed the plan for the even more ambitious Operation Polar Star. Thus while Operation Spark was underway, the Red Army was conducting or preparing to conduct major offensive operations along the entire front.[43]

The Leningrad and Volkhov Fronts' forces attacked simultaneously early on 12 January after extensive air and artillery preparations. Govorov began his artillery preparation at 09:30 hours on 12 January, taking care to protect the ice on the Neva River's surface. At 11:45 hours, five minutes before the artillery preparation ended with a Katiusha barrage, the massed Soviet infantry of Dukhanov's Sixty-Seventh Army assaulted across the Neva River with remarkably light casualties. The day was clear and the temperature at dawn was -23 degrees Centigrade (-9 degrees Fahrenheit).

Led by special assault groups, the 86th, 136th and 268th Rifle Divisions crossed the river and pierced German defences between Mar'ino and Gorodok No 1, as the protective artillery fire slowly shifted into the depths.[44] Major-General N. P. Simoniak's 136th Rifle Division advanced due east and Colonel S. N. Borshchev's 268th Rifle Division began enveloping German defences at Gorodok Nos

1 and 2 from the northeast. By the day's end the two divisions had carved out a 5km- (3.1-mile-) wide and 3km- (1.8-mile-) deep bridgehead between Shlissel'burg and Gorodok No 2 at the boundary of the defending 170th and 227th Infantry Divisions. At 18:00 hours, sappers built bridges over the Neva River north and south of Mar'ino for the passage of the second echelon's heavy tanks. However, the divisions attacking on the shock group's flanks achieved far less success. On the right flank, the 45th Guards Rifle Division, which was attacking through the 46th Rifle Division's forces already in the Moskovskaia Dubrovka bridgehead, captured the first trench line but was halted by German counterattacks. On the left, the attack by Colonel V. A. Trubachev's 86th Rifle Division faltered, forcing it to regroup in the 136th Rifle Division's sector later in the day.

General Karl Hilpert, XXVI Army Corps commander, whose forces were defending the Shlissel'burg bottleneck, reacted quickly to the Soviet assault. He immediately reinforced his beleaguered 170th Infantry Division at Gorodok No 2 with part of the 96th Infantry Division from Mga, and dispatched a combat group from the neighbouring 5th Mountain Infantry Division to reinforce his defences south of Moskovskaia Dubrovka. At the same time, the shaken 170th and 227th Infantry Divisions consolidated their defences west of Gorodok No 1 and south of Workers' Settlements Nos 2 and 3, leaving a sizeable gap in between which Hilpert tried to fill by sending another 96th Infantry Division combat group to Workers' Settlement No 1.

After regrouping and replenishing its forces overnight, Dukhanov's forces resumed their offensive along the entire front on 13 January after another short artillery preparation. Simoniak's 136th Rifle Division, supported by tanks from the 61st Light Tank Brigade, enveloped the 96th Infantry Division's right flank, advanced 4km (2.5 miles) eastwards, and within 1.5km (.93 miles) of Worker's Settlement No 5, forming a deep wedge only 4–5km (2.5–3.1 miles) west of the advancing Second Shock Army. Simultaneously, Trubachev's 86th Rifle Division, following after the 136th, approached Workers' Settlement No 3 and Preobrazhenskoe Hill, the main German strongpoint protecting the southern approaches to Shlissel'burg, where heavy resistance by the 227th Infantry Division halted its advance. However, on Dukhanov's right flank, Borshchev's 268th Rifle Division failed to dislodge the German defenders of Gorodok Nos 1 and 2 and, worse still, at 16:15 hours the 96th Infantry Division, supported by 15 tanks, counterattacked, forcing Borshchev's division to withdraw 2km (1.25 miles) in near panic. On Borshchev's right flank near Moskovskaia Dubrovka, the 5th Mountain Division also counter-attacked, forcing the 45th Guards Rifle Division to withdraw several hundred meters. At nightfall, Dukhanov ordered his second echelon to go into action the next morning.

To the east, Meretskov began his artillery and air preparation at 09:30 hours on 12 January, while special groups of snipers picked off German officers and soldiers and sappers cut lanes through the German minefields. A captured sergeant from the 227th Infantry Division's 366th Infantry Regiment, described the scene:

"It was a nightmare. In the morning, the Russians opened fire from guns of all calibre. The shells impacted precisely where the bunkers were located. Even before the Russians attacked many were killed and wounded. In the 10th Company Lieutenant Dehl, the company commander, and his senior sergeant and sergeant were killed. The soldiers were

BELOW: The real thing! Moving through the smoking remains of a recently liberated village, these Red Army infantrymen look as if they have seen hard fighting. The somewhat bulbous figures they cut are accounted for by the layers of clothing worn beneath their camouflage smocks, including steel helmets, padded jackets and trousers.

overcome by panic. The Russians had hardly approached when those located in the trenches greeted them with raised hands."

Romanovsky's first-echelon rifle divisions assaulted at 11:15 hours across the entire sector from Lipka to Gaitolovo, and the assault groups on the right flank of Starikov's Eighth Army joined the attack at 11:35 hours. Against heavy resistance, the assaulting infantry and infantry support tanks penetrated the forward edge of the 227th Infantry Division's defences and attacked the German strongpoints at Lipka, Workers' Settlement No 8 and "*Kruglaia*" Grove. On the right flank, Major-General F. M. Parkhomenko's 128th Rifle Division penetrated German defences but was halted south of Lipka by heavy fire from snow-covered German bunkers in a hilltop cemetery on the division's right flank.[45] In the centre, Colonel P. I. Radygin's 372nd and Colonel A. P. Baraboshkin's 256th Rifle Divisions penetrated up to 2km (1.25 miles) north and south of Workers' Settlement No 8, but were halted by heavy German flanking fire from the settlement and from "*Kruglaia*" Grove. With his attack faltering, Romanovsky received permission to commit Major-General M. N. Ovchinnikov's second echelon 18th Rifle Division and 98th Tank Brigade to combat early on 13 January to outflank Worker's Settlement No 8, and link up with the Sixty-Seventh Army.[46] However, heavy snow and strong winds caused the attack to abort.

On the left flank, Colonel N. A. Poliakov's 327th Rifle Division, supported by the 32nd Heavy Tank Regiment and 507th Tank Battalion, assaulted and captured "*Kruglaia*" Grove on 12 January in heavy hand-to-hand fighting. However, farther to the left, the attack by the Second Shock Army's 376th Rifle Division and the Eighth Army's 80th and 265th Rifle Divisions and 73nd Rifle Brigade aborted after only minimal gains. The defending 1st Infantry Division repelled repeated attacks all day on 12 January and on the morning of the 13 January. Meanwhile, Hilpert launched heavy counterattacks to recapture "*Kruglaia*" Grove and strongpoints protecting the Siniavino-Gaitolovo road. Meretskov countered, reinforcing the 376th Rifle Division's advance on Siniavino with Major-General N. M. Zamarovsky's 71st Rifle Division. As the battle raged on, deteriorating weather and the heavy forests hindered supporting artillery fire and severely curtailed air support.[47]

By day's end on 13 January, Romanovsky's Second Shock Army had penetrated German defences in two sectors along the 10km (6.25-mile) front between Lipka and Gaitolovo. Two of his divisions had driven a 3km- (1.8-mile-) deep wedge into the 227th Infantry Division's defences southeast of Workers' Settlement No 5, and two others formed a smaller penetration south of Lipka. The attackers had almost encircled Lipka and Workers' Settlement No 8, captured most of "*Kruglaia*" Grove, and had almost reached Workers' Settlements Nos 4 and 5,

BELOW: Soldiers of the Volkhov and Leningrad Fronts meet near Workers' Settlement No. 5 on 18 January 1943. Though Leningrad was far from free, the linking up of the two fronts made the fall of the city a remote possibility, and brought ultimate Soviet victory a step closer.

where the 227th and 1st Infantry Divisions struggled to avoid encirclement. Faced with this determined and clearly better-organized Soviet offensive,
Kuechler desperately sought to defend the
Shlissel'burg bottleneck and prevent the two attacking fronts from linking up. He ordered the 61st
Infantry Division at Kirishi to reinforce German
defences at Workers' Settlement No 6 and Gorodok
Nos 1 and 2, and elements of the 5th Mountain and
SS Police Divisions to reinforce German defences at
in and around Siniavino.

Early the next day, Golikov ordered the Sixty-
Seventh Army to commit its second echelon, link up
with the Volkhov Front and capture Gorodok Nos 1
and 2. Dukhanov committed one rifle division and a
rifle and tank brigade to support the 136th Rifle
Division's attack in his army's centre, and one rifle
division and two rifle brigades to reinforce the assault
on Gorodok Nos 1 and 2.[48] In addition, Govorov
committed a ski brigade from his reserve to support
the 86th Rifle Division's assault on Shlissel'burg.[49]
However, this piecemeal commitment of the second
echelon across so broad a front to reinforce already
exhausted forces was a mistake that actually slowed
the Sixty-Seventh Army's advance. Subsequently,
beginning on 14 January, Dukhanov's forces gnawed

their way through German defences, suffering heavy
losses as they did so.

In four days of bitter fighting Simoniak's 136th
Rifle Division, supported by the 61st Tank Brigade,
advanced up to 2.5km (1.56 miles), reaching the western outskirts of Workers' Settlement No 5 late on 17
January. To the south, Dukhanov's forces captured
Workers' Settlement No 3 on 17 January, but were
unable to capture Workers' Settlement Nos 1 and 2,
despite improved air support.[50] On Dukhanov's left
flank, Trubachev's 86th Rifle Division finally stormed
Preobrazhenskoe Hill at 15:00 hours on 15 January,
and in heavy fighting fought its way into the southern
portion of Shlissel'burg proper at 12:00 hours the
next day. For the next two days, the 86th Rifle
Division fought intense street battles with rearguard
forces of the 227th Infantry Division, which had just
received orders to withdraw.

Meanwhile, to the east Romanovsky's forces
were advancing at a snail's pace in intense fighting,

largely because both he and Meretskov replicated Govorov's mistake of committing their second-echelon and reserve forces in piecemeal fashion.[51] Despite this, Baraboshkin's 256th Rifle Division captured Podgornyi Station on 14 January and, wheeling its front to the southwest, attacked German defences at Siniavino. The next morning Radygin's 372nd Rifle Division captured Workers' Settlement No 8, and the German defenders escaped west with heavy casualties. Radygin's forces pursued, reaching Workers' Settlement No 1 late on 17 January at the same time as the 18th Rifle Division fought its way into the outskirts of Workers' Settlement No 5. By this time, Govorov's and Meretskov's forces were only 2km (1.25 miles) apart, threatening to encircle German forces in the Shlissel'burg Pocket.

Both Kuechler at army group and Lindemann at Eighteenth Army understood the perilous situation they faced late on 17 January. Clearly, one more determined Soviet thrust would cut off and destroy German forces in the Shlissel'burg region. Therefore, with Kuechler's approval, Lindemann ordered these forces, now organized into Group Huhner, to break out southwards through the narrow forested corridor north of Siniavino in con-

ABOVE: Bearing pictures of Stalin and Molotov and decorated with congratulatory words extolling the valour of the people of Leningrad in the struggle against the German Fascists, the first train pulls into the Finland Station in Leningrad following the breaking of the blockade.

junction with an attack by the SS Police Division against the Sixty-Seventh Army's right flank at Workers' Settlement No 5.[52] However, before the Germans could act, at 09:30 hours on 18 January lead elements of the Sixty-Seventh Army's 123rd Rifle Division and the Second Shock Army's 372nd Rifle Division linked up just east of Workers' Settlement No 1. Less than an hour later Simoniak's 136th Rifle Division captured Workers' Settlement No 5, and soon after made contact with the Second Shock Army's 18th Rifle Division.[53]

The struggle reached a crescendo as victorious Soviet forces tried to destroy German forces desperately trying to escape from Shlissel'burg and Lipka. Trubachev's 86th Rifle Division captured Shlissel'burg at 14:00 hours on 18 January after intense street fighting, and then set about liquidating German forces scattered in the forests south of Lake Ladoga. At the same time, Romanovsky's 128th and 372nd Rifle Divisions captured Lipka and cleared German forces from the forests northeast of Workers' Settlement No 1. Finding itself trapped between Dukhanov's and Romanovsky's forces, Group Huhner ran the gauntlet southwards past Workers' Settlement No 5 and Podgornyi Station, reaching the relative safety of Siniavino on 19 and 20 January.

After linking up, Dukhanov and Romanovsky wheeled their armies southwards to capture Gorodok Nos 1 and 2 and Siniavino. In turn, Lindemann reinforced his Siniavino defences with the SS Police and 21st Infantry Divisions and, soon after, with the 11th Infantry Division and his defences at Gorodok Nos 1 and 2 with the 28th *Jäger* Division. Spurred on by an impatient Zhukov, beginning on 20 January the Sixty-Seventh and Second Shock Armies delivered attack after attack against the German defences across a broad front from Gorodok Nos 1 and 2 through Siniavino to Gontovaia Lipka. Dukhanov's army attacked east of Gorodok Nos 1and 2 in an attempt to capture Mustolovo, cut the road and railroad from Siniavino to Mga, and outflank Siniavino from the west, while other army forces attacked Gorodok No 1 and Siniavino.[54]

Although the advance on Mustolovo failed, Dukhanov's forces attacking Siniavino managed to advance 2km (1.25 miles) against heavy resistance, severing the railroad line southeast of Gorodok No 1 and capturing Workers' Settlement No 6 west of Siniavino. At the same time, Romanovsky's forces drove a wedge into German defences south of Workers' Settlement No 7, but were also unable to achieve a clean breakthrough. Govorov's and Meretskov's offensive collapsed from utter exhaustion on 31 January, and the front finally stabilized north of Siniavino.

Victory Tinged with Disappointment

Operation Spark was a clear Red Army victory. During the operation Soviet forces penetrated German defences to a depth of 15km (9.3 miles) in a period of seven days, captured numerous German strongpoints, and opened an 8–10km (5–6.25-mile) corridor between Leningrad and the rest of the country.[55] The successful offensive also vastly improved the Soviets' strategic situation along the northwestern strategic axis by eliminating the possibility of a German-Finnish link-up and improving cooperation between the Leningrad and Volkhov Fronts. Most important to Leningraders themselves, the victory opened supply links between Russia, the city and the city's defenders.[56] However, to

Zhukov's consternation, the elusive target of Siniavino and the adjacent Siniavino Heights remained in German hands.

Red Army Losses

If the third Siniavino offensive was a victory, it was a costly one. The attacking Soviet forces suffered 115,082 casualties, including 33,940 killed, captured or missing and 81,142 wounded, out of 302,800 troops engaged. Several senior Soviet officers were among the casualties, including Meretskov's deputy, Fediuninsky, who was seriously wounded by mortar fire on 20 January, and Major-General N. A. Bolotnikov, Meretskov's Chief of Armoured and Mechanized Forces, who was killed by a German air strike on 26 January. The Germans also suffered greatly, admitting to 12,000 dead and many wounded, losses the Eighteenth Army could ill-afford.[57]

General Zhukov, whom Stalin promoted to Marshal of the Soviet Union on 1 January, the same day that Govorov's forces captured Shlissel'burg, conducted the operation in characteristically brutal fashion and suffered characteristically heavy losses. An exchange between Zhukov and General Simoniak, the commander of the Sixty-Seventh Army's 136th Rifle Division, vividly describes Zhukov's command style:

"Rows broke out among the Soviet generals. Marshal of the Soviet Union Georgi Zhukov, hero of the Battle of Moscow, hero of Stalingrad, had been sent in to 'coordinate' between the Volkhov Front and Moscow. He got on the VC high-security line to General Simoniak of the 136th Division. Why didn't Simoniak attack the Siniavino Heights? The Nazi positions there were holding up the Second Shock Army.

"For the same reason the Second Army doesn't attack them,' Simoniak replied. 'The approach is through a marsh. The losses would be great and the results small.'

'Trotskyite! Passive resister!' shouted Zhukov. 'Who are those cowards of yours? Who doesn't want to fight? Who needs to be ousted?'

Simoniak angrily replied that there were no cowards in the Sixty-Seventh Army.

'Wise guy,' snapped Zhukov. 'I order you to take the heights.'

'Comrade Marshal,' Simoniak rejoined. 'My army is under the command of the Leningrad Front commander, General Govorov. I take orders from him.'

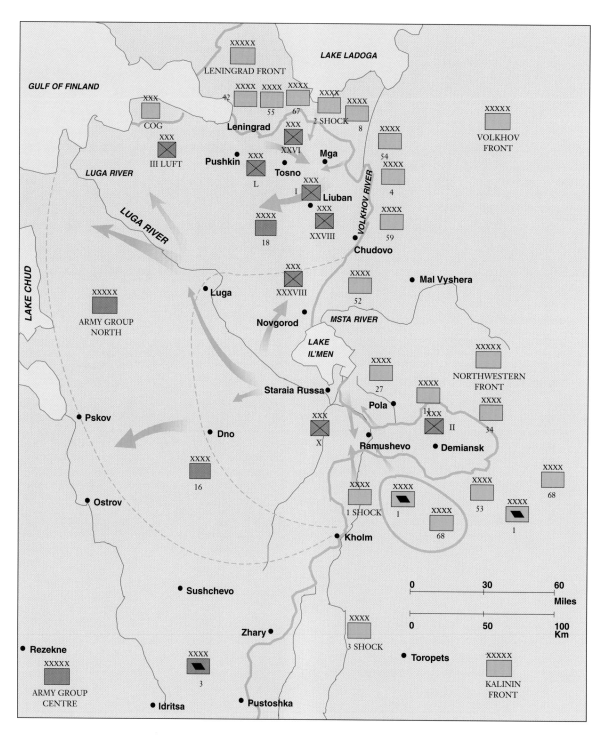

ABOVE: Marshal Zhukov's plan for Operation Polar Star, which aimed at the complete destruction of Army Group North and the liberation of the entire Leningrad region. Massive in scale and scope, Zhukov intended to involve no less than seven fronts. However, like previous offensives, the results were disappointing and Army Group North still existed, but it had been severely depleted in the fighting.

Zhukov hung up. Simoniak got no orders to attack the Siniavino Heights."[58]

Despite the high cost of victory, the offensive did crack the Leningrad blockade, but only barely. The Soviets were able to restore ground communications with the city, but those communications lines remained tenuous at best and subject to German artillery interdiction. During the ensuing days the Soviets built the Shlissel'burg-Poliany railroad, and on 6 February opened regular rail communications between Leningrad and the rest of the Soviet Union. Despite the construction of the new railroad line, the corridor was only 10km (6.25 miles) wide, it was subject to constant German artillery fire, and the German interdiction meant that its carrying capacity remained low. Mga Station, the most important point on the old main rail line from Leningrad to Volkhov, remained in enemy hands and heavy German troop concentrations still posed a threat to the tenuous corridor.

Expanding the Offensive

Although the third Siniavino offensive was a relatively small-scale component of the much vaster Soviet winter campaign, the operation had more than just symbolic significance. It marked the first time in the modern era when major offensives from within and without raised the siege of a large city and port. What made it more impressive was the fact that the attacking forces had to assault well-prepared enemy defences on the far bank of an ice-covered river 500–600m (1640–1968ft) wide.

The third Siniavino offensive served only as a prelude for an even more ambitious Red Army offensive in the Leningrad region. By early February 1943, the Red Army had smashed German Army Groups B and Don west and south of the Don River, and Army Group A was in full retreat from the Caucasus region. The *Stavka* was already planning to expand its winter offensive to include the region from Rzhev in the north to Khar'kov in the south during February and March 1943 and, soon, would plan an advance to the Vitebsk region and the Dnepr River from Gomel to the Black Sea. It was only reasonable that the *Stavka* would include the Leningrad region in its plans.

At Leningrad, the Siniavino offensive created conditions that the *Stavka* considered conducive to the conduct of an even larger offensive. The fighting around Siniavino had forced the German Eighteenth Army to concentrate its forces in that region and had weakened its forces elsewhere.[59] Worse still, the army was overextended, it had had only two security divisions in reserve, and since its strongest forces faced the Sixty-Seventh and Second Shock Armies, the flanks of the Siniavino corridor appeared vulnerable.

After Govorov and Meretskov proposed an offensive to cut off, encircle and destroy German forces in the Mga and Siniavino region, Zhukov recommend-

ABOVE: Northwestern Front commander Marshal Timoshenko. A cavalryman in the Tsarist army, he joined the Red Army in 1917. A strict disciplinarian, he was the only one of the prewar marshals to retain his standing throughout the war – no doubt due to his insistence on iron discipline, which endeared him to Stalin.

ed that *Stavka* broaden the offensive to destroy Army Group North completely and liberate the entire Leningrad region.[60] The *Stavka* accepted Zhukov's proposal and designated the offensive, Operation Polar Star. According to the operational plan, the Northwestern Front was to attack from the Demiansk region through Dno and Luga to Pskov and Narva on the Gulf of Finland. Simultaneously, the Leningrad and Volkhov Fronts were to attack the Eighteenth Army around Leningrad and, ultimately, link up with the Northwestern Front's forces to encircle almost all of Army Group North south of Leningrad. The *Stavka* timed the operation to coincide with a major offensive by the Kalinin, Western, Briansk and Central Fronts towards Smolensk, and by the Voronezh, Southwestern and Southern Fronts to the Dnepr River line.

Operation Polar Star

The Northwestern Front, now commanded by Marshal of the Soviet Union S. K. Timoshenko, was to play the major role in Polar Star by destroying

THE SIEGE OF LENINGRAD 1941–1944

the German II Army Corps at Demiansk and advancing through Staraia Russa and Dno to Pskov and Narva. The Northwestern Front's left wing, consisting of the Twenty-Seventh, Eleventh, Thirty-Fourth, First Shock and Fifty-Third Armies, was to make Timoshenko's main attack through Staraia Russa towards Luga and Dno and destroy German forces at Demiansk. Subsequently, a Special Operational Group made up of the First Tank and Sixty-Eighth Armies under Colonel-General M. S. Khozin's command, was to advance northwest, capture Pskov and Narva, and cut off and destroy the German Eighteenth Army in cooperation with the Leningrad and Volkhov Fronts.[61] The Northwestern Front was to begin its offensive on 15 February.

In the Leningrad region, the Leningrad Front's Fifty-Fifth Army was to attack southeastwards towards Tosno, wheel eastwards across the Tosno River, and link up with the Volkhov Front's Fifty-Fourth Army, advancing on Tosno from the northeast. The twin pincers would encircle all German forces in the Mga-Siniavino region, widen the narrow corridor to Leningrad, and, subsequently, serve as a hammer to smash the bulk of Army Group North against an anvil formed by the Northwestern Front advancing in the south.[62] While the Fifty-Fifth and Fifty-Fourth Armies were conducting their pincer manoeuvre towards Tosno, the Leningrad Front's Sixty-Seventh and Volkhov Front's Second Shock Armies were to attack Gorodok Nos 1 and 2 and Siniavino and capture Mga and the Leningrad-Volkhov railroad.

Before the operation began, the *Stavka* transferred the Second Shock Army and its sector north of Siniavino to the Volkhov Front to provide for a more unified command and control structure. The Leningrad and Volkhov Fronts were to begin their offensive on 8 February, one week before the Northwestern Front, to draw Army Group North's reserves northwards to Leningrad and away from the Northwestern Front's main attack sector. The fact that the *Stavka* assigned Zhukov, Timoshenko, Katukov and Tolbukhin to plan or participate in Operation Polar Star was indicative of the importance the *Stavka* attached to the offensive.

Major-General V. P. Sviridov's Fifty-Fifth Army, which formed the Leningrad Front's arm of the pincer, consisted of eight rifle divisions, two rifle and two ski brigades, and one tank regiment.[63] Sviridov planned to lead the assault with three rifle divisions and one ski brigade in the first echelon supported by a tank regiment, a force numbering 33,000 men and

30 tanks.[64] Once his first echelon smashed German defences at Krasnyi Bor, a mobile group consisting of a ski and tank brigade was to advance along the Oktiabr railroad, capture Ul'ianovka Station, and lead the advance on Tosno.[65] Sviridov's forces faced L Army Corps' 250th "Spanish Blue" Infantry Division and the 4th SS Police Division deployed in the 32km- (20-mile-) wide sector from Krasnyi Bor to the Neva River east of Kolpino. General Esteban-Infantes' Spanish division had a reinforced regiment and three infantry battalions – 4500 men but no tanks – facing the Fifty-Fifth Army's main attack.

Depleted Armies

The Volkhov Front's arm of the pincer, Major-General A. V. Sukhomlin's Fifty-Fourth Army, consisted of 10 rifle divisions, three rifle brigades and two tank brigades with a strength of more than 70,000 men and 60 tanks.[66] Sukhomlin's forces were to assault a sector defended by XXVIII Army Corps' 96th Infantry Division, which was flanked on the left by the 69th Infantry Division and on the right by the 132nd Infantry Division. General Noeldechen's 96th Infantry Division had been assigned this "quiet" sector after being decimated in the earlier fighting at Siniavino.

Although imposing on paper, the Sixty-Seventh and Second Shock Armies designated to attack at Gorodok Nos 1 and 2 and at Siniavino, were still woefully understrength after the January fighting. Romanovsky's Second Shock Army consisted of 12 understrength rifle divisions, one rifle, one ski and two tank brigades, one tank regiment and four separate tank battalions – roughly 60,000 men and 50 tanks. Dukhanov's Sixty-Seventh Army consisted of six rifle divisions, eight rifle, two ski and four tank brigades, two tank regiments, two separate tank battalions, and one fortified region – about 40,000 men and 30 tanks in all.[67] The German XXVI Army Corps (Group Hilpert) defended the Gorodok Nos 1 and 2 salient with its 28th *Jäger* and 21st Infantry Divisions and the Siniavino region with the 11th and 61st Infantry Divisions, giving a combined strength of roughly 35,000 men.

Sviridov's Fifty-Fifth Army attacked early on 10 February after a two-hour artillery preparation. Catching the defenders by surprise, the 63rd Guards Rifle Division captured Krasnyi Bor at 12:00 hours, and the 45th Guards Rifle Division captured Mishkino later in the day. Satisfied by the 5km (3.1-mile) advance, Sviridov then committed his mobile group into action to exploit the 45th Guards Rifle

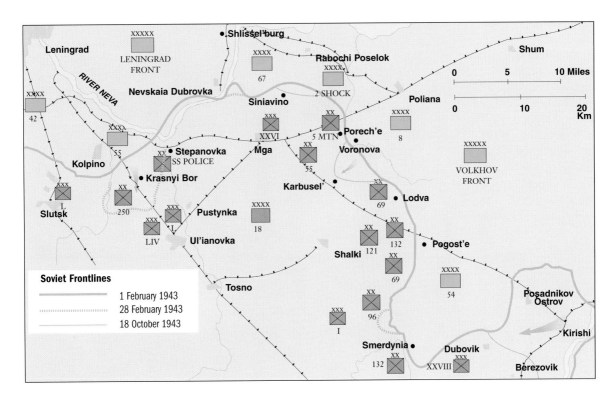

ABOVE: Soviet offensive operations in the Leningrad area between February and December 1943. As ever, German units fought with skill and tenacity and often frustrated Red Army attempts at deep penetration and encirclement. In addition, Soviet tactics continued to be crude and unimaginative.

Division's success. However, heavy resistance and an unexpected thaw, which prevented the ski brigades from operating off the road, halted the mobile group attack short of its objective. Sviridov's tanks and infantry got bogged down in hand-to-hand fighting with Spanish defenders along the Izhora River and the narrow roads south of Krasnyi Bor. During the later stages of the operation, the Germans reinforced the Spaniards' defences with regimental combat groups from the 212th and 215th Infantry Divisions transferred from Chudovo and Uritsk.

The forces on Sviridov's left flank fared little better. The 43rd Rifle Division and 34th Ski Brigade advanced 4km (2.5 miles) in two days of heavy fighting, driving the SS Police Division's forces back towards the Tosno River. Once again, however, the Germans quickly reinforced their defences and stopped the Soviet advance far short of its objectives.[68] Sviridov's forces had advanced 5km (3.1 miles) on a front of 14km (8.7 miles) by 13 February, but could advance no more since his army had lost

an estimated 10,000 casualties and most of his tanks in the heavy fighting. The Spanish 250th Infantry Division's gallant defence cost it 3200 casualties.[69]

While Sviridov's forces were conducting their futile offensive at Krasnyi Bor, the Fifty-Fourth Army went into action early on 10 February in the sector north of Smerdynia and the Tigoda River, aiming its thrust at the railroad line south of Tosno. Sukhomlin ultimately attacked the 96th Infantry Division's defences with four rifle divisions, three rifle brigades and one tank brigade.[70] Despite employing this overwhelming force, in three days of heavy fighting his shock group penetrated only 4km (2.5 miles) into the German defence along a front of some 5km (3.1 miles). The Germans halted the assault by reinforcing the 96th Infantry Division with regimental combat groups drawn from the 61st Infantry Division at Siniavino, the 121st Infantry and 217th Infantry Divisions, transferred from the Volkhov River Front, and from the adjacent 132nd Infantry Division.

The Sixty-Seventh and Second Shock Armies joined the offensive early on 12 February, capitalizing on the fact that the Eighteenth Army had transferred forces from the Siniavino region to reinforce the sectors already under assault. Dukhanov's shock group assaulted German defences at Gorodok Nos 1 and 2 at the same time as Romanovsky's shock

RIGHT: An infantry section probes cautiously forward. By 1943 the myth of German invincibility had been shattered by the defeats at Stalingrad and Kursk. As the Red Army prepared to break the siege, patrols such as this gained valuable intelligence about the German dispositions.

group struck German defences east and west of Siniavino. In six days of heavy fighting, Dukhanov's forces managed to capture Gorodok Nos 1 and 2 and advanced several kilometres southwards to the outskirts of Arbuzovo. Although they pinched off the small German salient pointing menacingly towards Shlissel'burg, the forces were too exhausted to accomplish more. To the east, however, Romanovsky's assault on Siniavino faltered immediately with heavy losses. The Soviet fourth Siniavino offensive ended with the Siniavino strongpoint still firmly in German hands.

The Leningrad and Volkhov Fronts' Tosno offensive failed for a variety of all too familiar reasons.[71] In a directive the *Stavka* issued on 27 February, it noted: "The basic shortcoming was the fact that the Sixty-Seventh and Second Shock Army operated separately … They dispersed their forces … and suffered unjustifiable casualties." In reality, Govorov's and Meretskov's forces were so exhausted by previous fighting that they lacked the strength and endurance necessary to fulfil the *Stavka*'s overly ambitious missions.

Despite the obvious failure of the secondary attacks to the north, Zhukov decided to capitalize on their diversionary effect and unleash the Northwestern Front's main attack. Meanwhile Timoshenko's armies were completing their final

offensive preparations. However, deteriorating weather prevented his armies from concentrating in time, forcing Zhukov to delay the operation. No sooner had he authorized the delay than Soviet intelligence detected German preparations to abandon the Demiansk salient. Therefore, Zhukov ordered Timoshenko to begin his offensive prematurely with the forces he had at hand. The offensive thus developed in piecemeal fashion, with predictable results.

The Eleventh and Fifty-Third Armies assaulted the flanks of the Ramushevo corridor on 15 February, while the Thirty-Fourth Army began a series of harassing attacks on German positions northeast of Demiansk. When the initial assault failed, on 23 February Zhukov threw the Twenty-Seventh and First Shock Armies into combat, the former just south of Staraia Russa and the latter at the base of the corridor. However, both armies' attacks faltered against the strong defences German forces had erected to protect their withdrawal from the Demiansk salient.[72] Urged on by Zhukov, the two armies tried to resume their offensives on 27 February but once again failed with heavy losses. Upset over the heavy casualties and limited gains, Stalin halted the attacks on 27 February and ordered Zhukov to orchestrate a new offensive in March. The defeat cost Zhukov's and Timoshenko's forces 33,663 casualties, including 10,016 dead, captured or missing.

Neither Zhukov nor the *Stavka*, however, were ready to abandon the offensive entirely. On Zhukov's recommendation, the *Stavka* ordered the Northwestern, Leningrad and Volkhov Fronts to conduct a truncated version of Operation Polar Star against the same objectives as in the original operation.[73] This time, the offensive was to begin in staggered fashion with the Northwestern Front attacking on 4 March and the Leningrad and Volkhov Fronts on 14 March. Zhukov subordinated the Thirty-Fourth, Fifty-Third, Sixty-Eighth Armies and First Tank Army under Khozin's control, and ordered the Twenty-Seventh and First Shock Armies to capture Staraia Russa. If the latter two armies captured the town, Khozin's entire force was to exploit towards Pskov and Narva. The *Stavka* ordered the Leningrad and Volkhov Fronts to conduct a supporting attack in the Leningrad region, this time a shallower envelopment of German forces located north of Mga without a frontal assault on Siniavino itself.[74]

Plans for the Attack

In the Leningrad region, the Leningrad Front's Fifty-Fifth Army and the Volkhov Front's Eighth Army were to destroy German forces at Siniavino and Mga in conjunction with Zhukov's assault near Staraia Russa, while the Fifty-Second Army was to conduct a diversionary attack near Novgorod. Sviridov's Fifty-Fifth Army was to attack from its Krasnyi Bor salient with eight rifle divisions and three rifle brigades, capture Ul'ianovka, sever the Ul'ianovka-Mga railroad, and link up with the Eighth Army. Starikov's Eighth Army was to attack in the Voronovo-Lodva sector east of Mga with 10 rifle divisions and four rifle brigades, capture Mga, and link up with the Fifty-Fifth Army at Voitolovo. This time, the totally exhausted Sixty-Seventh and Second Shock Armies, which remained on the defensive opposite Siniavino, were to join the attack only if it succeeded.[75]

The second attempt to conduct Operation Polar Star faltered from the very start and, thereafter, developed piecemeal as a frustrated *Stavka* and Zhukov strained to milk some success from the effort. The Northwestern Front's Twenty-Seventh and First Shock Armies attacked on 5 March (after a one-day delay) but achieved virtually nothing. Then, in reaction to a successful German counteroffensive in the Khar'kov region, on 7 March the

Stavka ordered Zhukov and Timoshenko to transfer the First Tank Army southwards to Kursk and limit Operation Polar Star to the capture of Staraia Russa and the elimination of the Mga salient.[76] Timoshenko's armies assaulted German defences east of Staraia Russa and south of Ramushevo on 14 March, but advanced several kilometres only while suffering heavy losses.[77] After further intense but futile fighting, on 17 March the *Stavka* ordered Zhukov to end the offensive and fly to Kursk to restore some order to the Red Army's deteriorating situation in that region. Many of the Northwestern Front's best forces soon followed Zhukov south. While the dramatic events were playing out in the Northwestern Front's sector, Govorov and Meretskov began their Mga offensive.

Frustration All Along the Line

Lieutenant-General V. F. Iakovlev's Fifty-Second Army began diversionary operations in the Novgorod region early on 14 March, when his small army attacked across the Volkhov River south of Novgorod against XXXVIII Army Corps' 1st Luftwaffe Field Division.[78] The fighting, which lasted until 27 March, achieved its ends since Lindemann reinforced the Novgorod sector with the 217th and 58th Infantry Divisions from the Kirishi region and Demiansk. Sviridov's Fifty-Fifth Army began its attack south of Krasnyi Bor on 19 March after a two-day delay to complete its offensive preparations. His first echelon 268th Rifle Division and 55th Rifle Brigade penetrated the SS Police Infantry Division's defences and had advanced 3km (1.8 miles) by the day's end.[79] However, the Flanders Legion and the 502nd Heavy Tank Battalion counterattacked and drove Sviridov's forces back to their jumping-off positions.[80] Sviridov tried in vain for eight days to rekindle his offensive, but failed. The bitter but fruitless fighting lasted until 2 April, when the *Stavka* ordered Govorov's Front to abandon further offensive operations. By this time, both sides had suffered very heavy losses.[81]

Starikov's Eighth Army began its assault south of Voronovo on 19 March after an artillery preparation. His army, which consisted of nine rifle divisions, two rifle and two separate tank brigades, and four separate tank regiments, was opposed by the 1st, 223rd and 69th Infantry Divisions of the Eighteenth Army's XXVI Army Corps, which occupied defences from Gontovaia Lipka, north of the Mga railroad, to Pogost'e.[82] During the first three

LEFT: Red Army marines in a forward trench in the Leningrad region. The man in the foreground is armed with the weapon that was most associated with the Red Army in World War II – the PPSh submachine gun. The soldier next to him is armed with a Tokarev SVT-40 automatic rifle.

days of intense fighting, the army's first echelon divisions penetrated 4km (2.5 miles) along a 7km (4.3-mile) front at the junction of the defending 1st and 223rd Infantry Divisions. Advancing in heavy rain, Starikov's small mobile group reached the Mga-Kirishi railroad before being halted by reinforcing German forces.[83] Lindemann reinforced the 69th Infantry Division combat groups from the 21st, 61st and 121st Infantry Divisions. Although the reinforcements halted the Eighth Army's advance, Zhukov insisted that Starikov continue his attacks throughout the remainder of March. On 1 April, Zhukov ordered him to commit his reserve 14th Rifle Division and 1st Separate Rifle Brigade in support of yet another assault by the 64th Guards Rifle Division on Karbusel, just east of the Mga-Kirishi railroad. The German 121st Infantry Division repelled the assault, inflicting heavy losses on the attackers. Finally, on 2 April the *Stavka* permitted the Eighth Army to halt its attacks and go over to the defence.

In part, the *Stavka* ordered the two Fronts to end their Mga offensive because their forces failed to dent German defences south of Leningrad and in part because the spring *rasputitsa* had begun. Actually, however, the *Stavka* halted the operation because Operation Polar Star, which gave meaning and context to the offensive at Leningrad, had failed. Further, even the *Stavka* could no longer permit the immense waste of manpower in continued futile offensives in the region. However, despite its failure, the offensive contributed significantly to the *Stavka*'s overall efforts by ending, once and for

all, any German thoughts about capturing Leningrad. In addition, it pinned down 30 German divisions, some of which could have helped the OKH stabilize the situation along the western and southwestern axes.[84]

After the Red Army failed to achieve the objectives the *Stavka* assigned to it in February and March, a period of relative calm descended over the Soviet-German front, with the spring *rasputitsa* halting all operations in its watery grip. During the three-month lull, both Hitler and Stalin planned feverishly to regain the strategic initiative in the summer. Ultimately, Hitler decided to conduct yet another summer offensive, this time more limited in scope and aim. He chose as his objective the Kursk "bulge", a large salient jutting westwards between German Army Groups Centre and South, which, to the Soviets, symbolized the success their forces had achieved the previous winter and, to the Germans, represented an inviting target. By striking the Kursk "bulge" and destroying the large Red Army forces inside it, Hitler hoped to undo some of the damage done to the Wehrmacht during the past winter and restore German fortunes in the East.

In the Soviet camp, Stalin sought to exploit the Red Army's winter victories by conducting a series of massive new offensives in the summer to achieve the objectives the Red Army had failed to gain the previous winter. Based on earlier experience, Stalin decided to blunt the Wehrmacht's summer offensive before unleashing the Red Army on a major summer offensive of its own.[85] The *Stavka* decided to begin with a premeditated defence of the Kursk salient. During its initial defence at Kursk and its counteroffensives thereafter, Soviet forces in the Leningrad region would remain on the defence, conducting only limited offensives to support the far larger Red Army operations to the south. Thus, prior to the Battle for Kursk, the *Stavka* secretly transferred sizeable forces, including the Northwestern Front's Eleventh, Twenty-Seventh, Fifty-Third and Sixty-Eighth Armies, southwards to the Kursk region. Deprived of much of their strength, the three Soviet Fronts operating along the northwestern axis temporarily deferred any offensive operations and, in a sharp departure from previous practice, rested and refitted their forces throughout the spring and summer.[86]

After Red Army forces had defeated the Germans at Kursk in early July 1943, the *Stavka* ordered offensive operations to resume along the northwestern axis. This time, however, its aims were limited to attracting German attention and forces away from more critical front sectors. By early July, Soviet intelligence indicated that the Leningrad Front outnumbered German forces by a factor of two to one and the Volkhov Front by a factor of 1.3 to one, and German estimates confirmed this Soviet superiority.[87] In the *Stavka*'s judgement this was sufficient force with which to conduct a new offensive.

Immediately after the Battle of Kursk, the *Stavka* ordered Govorov and Meretskov to conduct a new offensive to pin down and, if possible, crush the Eighteenth Army by an offensive against German forces in the Mga and Siniavino region. They were to do so by attacking the Mga salient from three sides with their Fifty-Fifth, Sixty-Seventh and Eighth Armies. Sviridov's Fifty-Fifth Army was to attack across the Neva River towards Mga in tandem with an assault by Dukhanov's Sixty-Seventh Army between the Neva and Siniavino, and an offensive by Starikov's Eighth Army from the Gaitolovo-Lodva sector towards Mga. If successful, the offensive would capture Mga and Siniavino, destroy the German XXVI Army Corps, and set up the Eighteenth Army for subsequent destruction.

Dukhanov's Sixty-Seventh Army was to conduct Govorov's main attack east of the Neva River with the newly formed XXX Guards Rifle Corps, under the command of General Simoniak, the former 136th Rifle Division's commander.[88] Simoniak's

BELOW: Tired German troops of Army Group North return from an engagement with enemy troops. The soldier in the centre of the photograph is carrying a captured Soviet 7.62mm Degtaryev DP machine gun, nicknamed the "record player" on account of its large drum magazine.

four rifle divisions, two tank brigades and two tank regiments were to capture Arbuzovo and advance on Mga from the north. To the east, four divisions of Dukhanov's army were to attack in the Siniavino-Gontovaia Lipka sector to tie down German forces defending Siniavino.[89] XXVI Army Corps' 121st, 23rd, 11th and 290th Infantry Divisions manned defences between Arbuzovo and Gontovaia Lipka. This force of roughly 35,000 men faced a Soviet force in excess of 75,000 men and 120 tanks. Sviridov's Fifty-Fifth Army was to support Dukhanov's advance with a smaller attack of its own south of the Neva River, but only if Dukhanov's assault succeeded.

Dukhanov's Plans

East of Mga, Starikov's Eighth Army was to conduct its main attack in the Voronovo region to link up near Mga with the Sixty-Seventh and Fifty-Fifth Armies attacking from the north and west, and a supporting attack north of Pogost'e to protect the main shock group's left flank.[90] To penetrate the strong German defences, Starikov organized two shock groups, each consisting of four rifle divisions and supporting armour, to attack north and south of the Mga railroad.[91] He ordered two rifle divisions and two rifle brigades to conduct the supporting attack, while he defended his right flank with one rifle division and retained a rifle division and rifle brigade in reserve.[92] Starikov's northern shock group faced the bulk of the German 5th Mountain Division deployed astride the Mga-Volkhov railroad line, and his southern group faced the remainder of the 5th Mountain Division and the 69th Infantry Division's left flank. The 132nd Infantry Division faced his supporting attack north of Pogost'e. Starikov's reinforced army, which fielded about 80,000 men supported by more than 250 tanks, had a two- to five-fold superiority over the defending Germans.[93] Victory seemed certain.

Dukhanov's forces began their assault early on 22 July after a 90-minute artillery preparation. Simoniak's 63rd and 45th Guards Rifle Divisions spearheaded the assault on German defences at Arbuzovo, while the 43rd Rifle Division attacked west of Siniavino.[94] Although the 63rd Guards Division achieved its first day's objectives, XXVI Army Corps quickly reinforced its defences across the entire Siniavino front, converting the struggle into what a Soviet participant called "an offensive on our bellies."[95] Dukhanov's assault soon degener-

ated into a slugfest with advances measured in only tens of meters. The fierce fighting, which lasted until 22 August and ended with Siniavino still in German hands, caused heavy Soviet casualties and only minimal gains. Dukhanov's failure also prompted Govorov to cancel Sviridov's supporting attack.

MGA Still an Elusive Goal

Starikov's two Eighth Army shock groups launched their assault against German defences along the Mga-Volkhov railroad north and south of Voronovo at 06:35 hours on 22 July. Despite six days of preliminary artillery bombardment, his assaulting troops captured the forward German trenches, but then ran into stiff resistance and heavy air strikes that slowed their forward progress to a snail's pace.[96] With his offensive at a standstill, in late July Starikov reinforced his shock groups with two fresh divisions and withdrew two others for refitting.[97] However, the reinforcements did not improve the situation. By this time, Lindemann had replaced the 132nd Infantry Division, which had repelled all Soviet attacks in its sector, with the 121st Infantry Division from the Arbuzovo sector, and sent the 132nd Infantry Division to reinforce the beleaguered 5th Mountain Division.

As it turned out, the reinforcements arrived just in time. On 9 August, Starikov's assault groups detected what they thought was a weak spot in the 5th Mountain Division's defences around a small bridgehead on the eastern bank of the Naziia River. Two days later, Starikov reinforced the four divisions already attacking the seriously weakened 5th Mountain Division's bridgehead with two fresh rifle divisions and two tank regiments.[98] Although his reinforced shock group almost enveloped the defending Germans and the 256th Rifle Division captured Porech'e, the attack once again stalled in the face of heavy German fire as the 132nd Division joined the fight. A frustrated Meretskov then threw his last reserves, a rifle division and separate tank battalion, into the bloody mêlée in one final desperate attempt to crack the German defences.[99] After repeated attacks that decimated both the attacking and defending forces, Starikov's offensive collapsed in utter exhaustion. His army had captured the Porech'e bridgehead, which the Germans evacuated on the night of 14/15 August, but it was still far from Mga.

Early on 16 August the fresh 1st and 254th Infantry Divisions relieved the battered 132nd,

which, in the words of one division member, was "reduced by casualties and exhausted to the point of incoherence." A German participant captured the ferocity of the battle:

"During the course of this battle, the enemy had thrust these divisions and armoured units into the battle: 364th Rifle Division, with parts of three regiments; 374th Rifle Division, with two regiments; 165th Rifle Division, with two regiments; 378th Rifle Division, with two regiments; 311th Rifle Division, with one regiment; 256th Rifle Division, with one regiment; 503rd Armoured Battalion, with 14 tanks; 35th Armoured Regiment, with 15 tanks; 50th Armoured Regiment, with 15 tanks; and 77th Independent Engineer Battalion.

"Twelve to fourteen enemy battalions were reported as decimated. Twenty-four tanks were destroyed, 10 of which were knocked out in close combat with light weapons. The Russians suffered extremely high casualties during the intensive attempts to break the defence line. With the withdrawal of our division, the battle south of Lake Ladoga came to an end."

The Leningrad and Volkhov Fronts' fifth offensive at Siniavino certainly burnished Siniavino's reputation as a graveyard for Red Army soldiers. Of the 253,300 soldiers the two Fronts committed to

ABOVE: The growing strength and confidence of the Red Army during 1943 is evident here. This training shot has T-34 tanks armed with 76mm guns transporting and giving fire support to an infantry squad behind the lines of the Volkhov Front.

battle, 79,937 became casualties, including 20,890 dead, captured and missing. With losses that high one might have assumed the *Stavka* would desist from further offensives, at least for a time. This was not to be the case.

As if drawn to the Siniavino strongpoint by some perverse force, the carnage repeated itself in mid-September, when Govorov once again tried to expel German forces from Siniavino. On 15 September Dukhanov's Sixty-Seventh Army resumed its assaults on German defences east and west of Siniavino.[100] This time, the three divisions of General Simoniak's XXX Rifle Corps pummelled German defences at and west of Siniavino, supported by three divisions attacking on their left flank, and first one and then two divisions attacking towards Arbuzovo on their right flank.[101] Although this offensive also failed, the assaulting forces captured Siniavino village and about half the adjacent heights, but at a cost of heavy losses as the Germans once again shuffled reserves to stem the tide. The short but violent assaults cost the attackers another 10,000 casualties.

LEFT: These wounded Luftwaffe aircrew are shown shortly after their aircraft was shot down over Leningrad during a bombing mission. The pilot has suffered burns to his hands and is being supported by an infantry NCO.

At this point, mercifully, a period of relative calm descended over the front south of Leningrad. Kuechler used the respite to prepare for what he was certain would be yet another Soviet onslaught. His most serious problem was his total lack of reserves necessary to counter any new Soviet thrust. Therefore, in late September, he and Lindemann requested and received Hitler's permission to abandon the Kirishi salient to free up four divisions for employment elsewhere.[102] The four divisions began withdrawing from the salient on 3 October back through successive defence lines. Although Meretskov's Fourth Army attempted to trap the German forces, the latter were able to escape unharmed and then erect new defences along the Tigoda River.[103]

The course and outcome of the *Stavka*'s summer and fall campaign in the Leningrad region was indeed frustrating. While its operations made Leningrad more secure and ended any possibility of a future German offensive in the region, the repeated offensives failed spectacularly and did not appreciably widen the Siniavino corridor. However, while the Soviet casualty toll mounted to well over 150,000 men, German strength was also seriously eroding. While Army Group North's strength fell from 760,000 in mid-July to 601,000 men on 14 October 1943, during the same period Soviet strength increased from 734,000 men with 491,000 in reserve, to 893,000 with 66,000 in reserve. Worse still for Kuechler, beginning in early October the situation to the south deteriorated, forcing him to transfer sizeable forces from the Eighteenth Army at Leningrad to the Sixteenth Army in the Nevel region.[104] So perilous was Army Group North's situation that, in early September, the OKH ordered a new defence line, the so-called Panther Line, be constructed from Narva to Ostrov deep in Army Group North's rear. In addition, Kuechler's army group began building an elaborate system of intermediate positions forward of the Panther Line in case it needed to withdraw from the Leningrad region.

The Panther Line

The Germans began constructing the Panther Line, which extended from Narva through Pskov and Ostrov to the south of Nevel, on 8 September.[105] In addition, Army Group North constructed a series of intermediate lines forward of the Panther Line at varying distances from the front, whose phased occupation would make for an orderly withdrawal westwards. The most important of the lines (*stellung*) were the Rollbahn *stellung*, parallel to and just east of the Leningrad-Moscow railroad, and the Luga *stellung*, along the Luga River and southeastwards to Novgorod.[106] These lines were anchored on fortified city strongpoints, such as Narva, Krasnogvardeisk and Luga, and most were fairly well developed by late 1943.[107]

Army Group North began planning for a withdrawal to the Panther Line in September under the codename Operation *Blau*. When implemented, the plan required forces to withdraw successively through the series of intermediate lines. The most serious dilemma faced by the army group concerned the fate of the approximately 900,000 civilians living in the area, who the Red Army would undoubtedly conscript when it reached the region. Attempts to move the population back to Germany in early October produced "so much confusion, misery, and hostility that Kuechler ordered the rear area commands to adopt less onerous methods." Thereafter, German forces forcibly moved the male population (some 250,000) back into Lithuania and Latvia until accommodations were no longer available. Initially, Army Group North planned to complete the withdrawal in stages from mid-January through the spring of 1944. On 22 December, however, Halder informed army commanders that Hitler would not implement Operation *Blau* unless a new Soviet offensive forced him to do so. Hitler believed the Red Army had lost so many men in the Ukraine that it could ill-afford a major offensive elsewhere.

The Red Army's victory in Operation Spark was more significant than the modest territorial gains indicated. Not since December 1941, when the Leningrad Front blunted the Germans' bold attempt to encircle Leningrad, did the *Stavka* have as much to celebrate. The Red Army's wresting of the narrow land corridor from the Wehrmacht's grasp in January ended more than 12 months of repeated, embarrassing and often staggering defeats. Spark, however, was also frustratingly incomplete because the vital Siniavino strongpoint was still in German hands and the *Stavka* knew that as long as it was, neither Leningrad's defences nor its supply lines would be entirely secure. This alone turned the January struggle for Siniavino into a prelude rather than a postscript. Pride as well as strategic imperatives compelled the *Stavka* to order its forces to seize Siniavino as soon as possible and at any costs.

It was, therefore, inevitable that Operation Polar Star would follow closely after Operation Spark.

Given the *Stavka*'s ambitious strategic aims in the winter of 1942–43, Operation Polar Star represented a logical culmination to the series of Red Army offensives that spread from south to north across the entire Soviet-German front. Given the Red Army's capabilities, however, Polar Star failed like the other offensives. It did so because the Red Army was not yet capable of winning such victories, certainly not in the difficult terrain of the Leningrad region, where large tank forces could not be brought to bear. Thereafter a more sober and realistic *Stavka* chose when and where to fight more carefully, attacking only if victory seemed achievable. Despite this greater prudence, Siniavino remained its nemesis and, even in the summer, the *Stavka* could not resist its enticement.

A High Price in Blood

Like previous operations, Operations Spark, Polar Star and Fifth Siniavino proved costly to many hundreds of thousands of Red Army soldiers who fought in them. The Leningrad, Volkhov and Northwestern Fronts suffered more than one million casualties during 1943, including 255,447 killed, captured or missing.[108] German sources indicate that the Red Army lost 270,000 men in the fighting for Siniavino alone. German forces also suffered grievously in the hard-fought battles, although far less so than the Red Army. Army Group North's strength fell from 760,000 men in July 1943 to 601,000 in October, in part due to casualties. The fighting in 1943 severely weakened virtually every division in Army Group North because, like the French Army at Verdun in 1916, every division was blooded at or around Siniavino.

After January 1943 Army Group North had no operational reserves, and, as a result, had to rely on the swift manoeuvre of regimental- and battalion-sized combat groups to contain Red Army offensives.[109] With strength decreasing and replacements dwindling, it was only a matter of time before Army Group North could no longer stem the tide.

Finally, Operations Spark and Polar Star clearly demonstrated the *Stavka*'s intent to achieve victory at Leningrad, a concern many histories of the war have ignored. At the same time, the two operations indicated how difficult this task would be. Armed with this awareness, when it formulated its strategic priorities for 1944, the *Stavka* would place the liberation of Leningrad at the top of its list.

CHAPTER 9:
1944 – LIBERATION

In January 1944, the Red Army launched its Leningrad-Novgorod Offensive. Vast in scale, its end result was finally to liberate Leningrad. But the successful ending of the siege was bought for a heavy price in terms of blood, for Army Group North still had a lot of fight left and its units, though outnumbered, conducted a skilful defence as they withdrew to the Baltic states.

By the end of 1943, the Red Army had seized the strategic initiative on the Soviet-German front. It had won the Battle of Kursk, and its forces had driven the Wehrmacht back to the Sozh and Dnepr Rivers in central and southern Russia, and were beginning operations into Belorussia and the Ukraine. By this time, Red Army forces had penetrated the Panther Line, the vaunted German Eastern Wall, at several locations in the central and southern sectors of the front. Worse still for the Germans, the Red Army Air Force had complete air superiority over the battlefield, the partisan movement was growing in the Wehrmacht's rear, and Soviet industry was producing and equipping its forces with immense quantities of new tanks, artillery and aircraft of all types.

As the year ended, the *Stavka* planned to conduct a series of major strategic offensives aimed at clearing enemy forces from all Soviet territory and beginning the liberation of Nazi-occupied Europe. These offensives, which had already begun in the mid-fall against German forces in Belorussia and Ukraine,

LEFT: Red Army soldiers examine a captured trench of the German Panther Line. This defensive zone skirted the River Narva, the banks of Lake Chud, Lake Pskov, and the towns of Pskov and Ostrov. The Germans grandly titled it an impregnable "Northern Wall".

would grow to embrace all three strategic axes. The Soviets' two-fold military superiority over Axis forces seemed to guarantee success.[1] At the least, Soviet superiority forced the Germans to go over to the strategic defence in virtually every sector.

Along the northwestern axis, by 1 January 1944, the Leningrad and Volkhov Fronts had restored communications to Leningrad, removed any chance of a German offensive against the city, and created conditions suitable for the utter defeat of German Army Group North. Kuechler's army group still occupied defences close to the city, and was able to strike at it and its communications lines with artillery and air strikes. However, the deteriorating situation elsewhere along its Eastern Front precluded the OKH from providing Kuechler with any reinforcements. Thus, the *Stavka* decided to liberate the city and all of the Leningrad region as its first order of business in 1944.

On 1 January, the Leningrad and Volkhov Fronts, supported by the Baltic Fleet, faced Finnish forces north of Leningrad and German forces south of the city. Govorov's Twenty-Third Army defended against Finnish forces north of Leningrad, the Second Shock Army occupied the Oranienbaum bridgehead, and the Forty-Second and Sixty-Seventh Armies defended the southern and southeastern approaches to Leningrad from the Gulf of Finland to

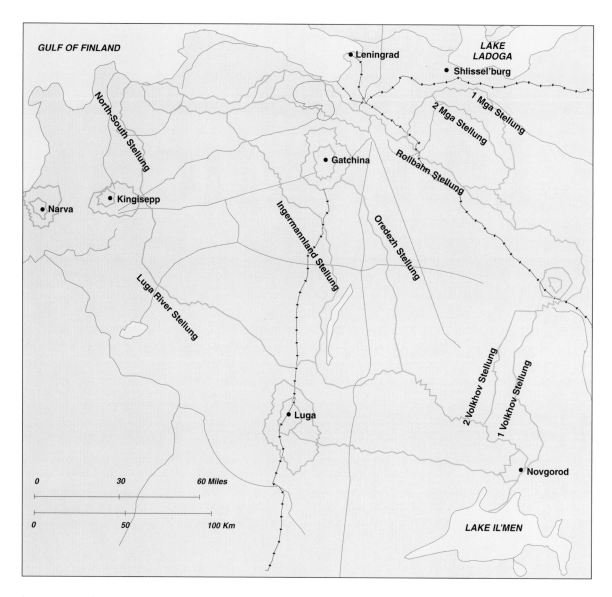

ABOVE: The position of German defensive lines and strongpoints in the Leningrad area in January 1944. Though Army Group North had made strenuous efforts to turn the area into an impregnable fortress, it had neither the manpower nor the equipment to withstand the Soviet offensive when it came.

east of Siniavino against the German Eighteenth Army's left wing.[2] Meretskov's Eighth, Fifty-Fourth and Fifty-Ninth Armies faced the German Eighteenth Army's right wing from east of Siniavino to Lake Il'men, and occupied an 8km (5-mile) bridgehead on the western bank of the Volkhov River 50km (31.2 miles) north of Novgorod.[3] To the south, Army General M. M. Popov's Second Baltic Front defended the sector from Lake Il'men southwards to just north of Nevel with its Twenty-Second,

First and Third Shock, Sixth Guards and Fifteenth Air Armies opposite Army Group North's Sixteenth Army.[4] The Sixth Guards and Third Shock Armies on Popov's left flank were pursuing German forces who were withdrawing northwards from Nevel to new defences west of Novosokol'niki. The three Fronts fielded 822,000 troops, supported by roughly 35,000 partisans operating in the German rear.[5]

Army Group North's Eighteenth and Sixteenth Armies defended the front from the Gulf of Finland southwards to the Nevel region with 44 infantry divisions (including one panzergrenadier) totalling roughly 500,000 men.[6] By concentrating its forces, the Red Army could improve its strategic superiority of less than two to one to a more than four-fold superiority operationally and more than eight-fold tactically. Worse still for Kuechler, his army group had few reserves.[7] The Germans compensated for their numerical weakness by constructing strong defences organized in great depth back to the Panther Line. The weakest German defences were in the sector opposite the Oranienbaum bridgehead, and the strongest were south and east of Leningrad.[8] The Germans fortified virtually every town and village around the front and in the shallow depths, and formed multiple strongpoints into larger centres of resistance.[9] Weather conditions in the winter of 1944, which were mild and subject to frequent thaws, favoured defence. The ice cover on rivers and lakes could support trucks and regimental artillery, but not heavy weaponry or tanks, and the swamps were only partially frozen and difficult to traverse.

New Offensives

Based on intelligence reports, Kuechler concluded that any Red Army offensive in early 1944 would be no larger than previous operations, and Lindemann declared his Eighteenth Army could successfully fend off any Soviet attack.[10] Based on this assessment, Hitler ordered Army Group North to hold firmly to its positions at all costs. Despite this order, Kuechler secretly prepared plans to withdraw in December and established new supply bases in Estonia. In the meantime, his forces in the Leningrad area dug in, convinced they could hold on. On 10 January, the Eighteenth Army commander, Lindemann, assessed the Soviet build-ups in the Oranienbaum Pocket and east of Novgorod as modest, particularly in reserves. Without reserves, he claimed, the attacks could not go deep and any assaults from Oranienbaum and at Novgorod would "very likely" be staggered.

While the German command exuded confidence, on 9 September Govorov had already proposed a massive new offensive to the *Stavka* that would utilise his and Meretskov's fronts. His plan required the Leningrad and Volkhov Fronts to conduct two successive operations to capture Luga and encircle and destroy the Eighteenth Army. In the first offensive, his Forty-Second Army and Coastal Operational Group (COG) would attack southwards towards Krasnoe Selo, link up, and organize a continuous front south of Leningrad. After capturing Krasnoe Selo, the Sixty-Seventh Army would join the offensive and capture Krasnogvardeisk, and the Forty-Second Army and COG would attack towards Kingisepp. Taken together, the two offensives were designed to expel German forces from the Leningrad region and cut off the Eighteenth Army's withdrawal routes to the west. In turn, on 14 September, Meretskov recommended that his Volkhov Front attack from the region north of Novgorod towards Luga to encircle and destroy the Eighteenth Army's main force and prevent it from withdrawing westwards to the Luga or Panther Line.

Driven on by fears that German forces would escape destruction by conducting a pre-emptive withdrawal, the *Stavka* approved Govorov's and Meretskov's proposals on 12 October with a tentative attack date in early January, and modestly reinforced their Fronts.[11] It ordered the Leningrad Front to transfer its Second Shock Army to the Oranienbaum bridgehead, and prepare to conduct two strong concentric assaults from Leningrad and the Oranienbaum bridgehead to encircle German forces in the Petergof and Strel'na regions. The revised *Stavka* objective required the two fronts to

RIGHT: A German Pak anti-tank gun crew frantically prepare their weapon to meet enemy tanks. In general, the Germans in the north were able to withdraw in order in the face of Russian offensives, as Soviet tactics were often crude and unimaginative. The Wehrmacht retreat never became a rout.

destroy the Eighteenth Army south of Leningrad, raise the city's blockade, and liberate the entire Leningrad region. Initially, they were to smash the Eighteenth Army's flanks by simultaneous attacks southwest of Leningrad and in the Novgorod region, and then destroy the entire army and reach the Luga River from Kingisepp to Luga. Subsequently, they were to advance towards Narva and Pskov to clear German forces from the Leningrad region, and then begin liberating the Baltic region. Simultaneously, the Second Baltic Front was to attack the Sixteenth Army's right flank north of Nevel to tie down the army's forces and prevent it from reinforcing German forces in the Leningrad region.

Operation Neva

Govorov began planning his initial offensive, code-named Operation Neva, on 6 October.[12] His final concept required that the Second Shock and Forty-Second Armies penetrate German defences in the eastern flank of the Oranienbaum bridgehead and southwest of Leningrad Pulkovo, link up at Ropsha, and encircle and destroy German forces in the Krasnoe Selo, Ropsha and Strel'na regions. The Sixty-Seventh Army was to tie down German forces south and east of the city to prevent them from reinforcing the Second Shock and Forty-Second Army sectors. Subsequently, the Second Shock and Forty-Second Armies were to attack southwest towards Kingisepp and south towards Krasnogvardeisk, while the Sixty-Seventh Army attacked through Mga and Ul'ianovka towards Krasnogvardeisk from the northeast. Govorov assigned missions to the three armies participating in the Ropsha offensive between 6 November and 23 December. To confuse the Germans, the Second Shock Army was to attack a day before the Forty-Second Army.[13]

Govorov's first shock group was the Second Shock Army, now commanded by the experienced Colonel-General I. I. Fediuninsky, which consisted of two rifle corps, seven rifle divisions, one rifle, two naval infantry and one tank brigade, one fortified region, and three tank regiments. Fediuninsky was to attack eastwards from the Oranienbaum bridgehead with his XXXXIII and CXXII Rifle Corps, capture Ropsha, link up with the Forty-Second Army, and help destroy German forces in the Krasnoe Selo and Ropsha regions.[14] Before doing so, however, Govorov faced the daunting task of transferring the entire Second Shock Army into the Oranienbaum bridgehead. He accomplished this complex task between 5 November and 21 January 1944.[15]

Govorov's second shock force, the Forty-Second Army, commanded by the equally experienced Colonel-General I. I. Maslennikov, consisted of three rifle corps, 10 rifle divisions, one fortified region, two tank brigades and five tank regiments. His army's XXX Guards, CIX and CX Rifle Corps were to penetrate German defences and capture Krasnoe Selo. Attacking from second echelon, the army's CXXIII Rifle Corps was to link up with the Second Shock Army at Ropsha, and help destroy German forces in the region. An army mobile group consisting of the 1st and 220th Tank Brigades and two self-propelled artillery regiments was to envelop Krasnoe Selo from the south and spearhead his advance on the town of Ropsha.[16]

Meretskov ordered his Fifty-Ninth Army to conduct two attacks: a main attack from its bridgehead on the western bank of the Volkhov River, and a secondary attack across Lake Il'men south of Novgorod. The attacks were to converge west of Novgorod, encircle and destroy the German XXXVIII Army Corps, and capture the city. Subsequently, the Fifty-Ninth Army was to exploit westwards and southwestwards, capture Luga, and cut off the withdrawal of German forces in the Tosno and Chudovo regions. Simultaneously, the Eighth and Fifty-Fourth Armies were to attack towards Tosno, Liuban and Chudovo to prevent the Germans from transferring forces to Novgorod, and to encircle and destroy German forces in the Tosno and Chudovo regions.[17]

The Fifty-Ninth Army

Meretskov's largest army, Lieutenant-General I. T. Korovnikov's Fifty-Ninth Army, consisted of three rifle corps, nine rifle divisions, one rifle brigade, three tank brigades and four tank regiments. His VI and XIV Rifle Corps were to penetrate XXXVIII Army Corps' defences 50km (31.2 miles) north of Novgorod and sever German communications routes into Novgorod from the west. South of the city, his Southern Operational Group, consisting of a reinforced rifle brigade, was to cross Lake Il'men (on the ice), link up with the main shock group west of Novgorod, and help capture Novgorod and destroy German forces in the city.[18] Subsequently, Korovnikov's army was to advance westwards to Luga to assist in the total destruction of the Eighteenth Army.[19]

Finally, both Govorov and Meretskov employed stringent operational security measures and deception plans to confuse the Germans regarding the

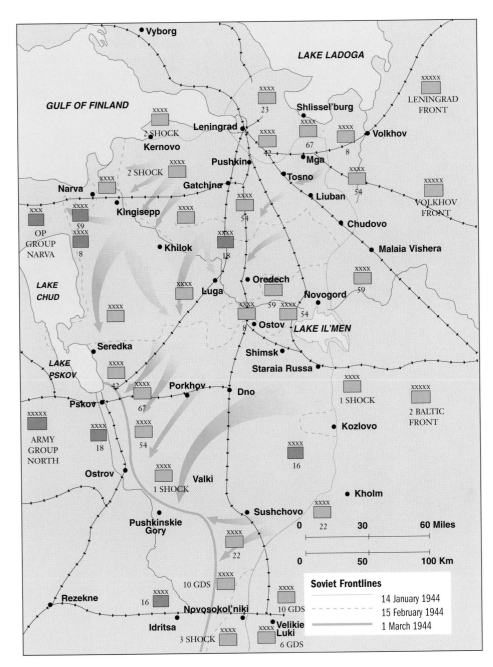

ABOVE: The Soviet Leningrad-Novgorod strategic offensive operation of January–March 1944. Vast in scale and intensity, it finally freed the city of Leningrad and signalled the beginning of the Red Army's liberation of the Baltic States. The 900-day ordeal of Leningrad was over.

timing and location of the offensive: Govorov by posturing to mount an offensive along the Kingisepp axis, and Meretskov by conducting a demonstration near Mga and a false concentration near Chudovo.[20] In addition, both fronts had fully integrated partisan operations in the offensive for the first time in the war. In November, the Leningrad Headquarters of the Partisan Movement ordered its partisans to conduct major sabotage and diversionary operations in support of the offensive.

By the time their preparations were complete, both front commanders had created overwhelming superiority over the opposing Germans by concentrating their forces.[21] Govorov's forces outnumbered the Germans three-fold in infantry, four-fold in artillery and six-fold in tanks and self-propelled

guns; Meretskov's by well over three-fold in infantry and artillery and eleven-fold in tanks and self-propelled guns. Their assault forces occupied their final jumping-off positions for the attack two to three nights before the assault, and phased their forces into attack positions the day and night before. Supporting tanks deployed forward during the artillery preparation.

Despite heavy snow, Soviet night bombers pounded German defences on the night of 13/14 January, and at dawn Govorov's artillery rained 104,000 shells on the 9th and 10th Luftwaffe Field Divisions' defences during a 65-minute artillery preparation.[22] At 10:00 hours the massed infantry of the 48th, 90th and 131st Rifle Divisions, leading XXXXIII and CXXII Rifle Corps' assault, lunged forward into the German defensive positions as Fediuninsky and Golikov observed the assault from a command post on Kolokol'nia Hill. The three attacking divisions quickly overcame the Germans' forward defences and, by the day's end, had penetrated 3km (1.87 miles) into the shattered German forward defences along a 10km (6.25-mile) front. Overnight the force advanced another 4km (2.5 miles), while the Forty-Second and Sixty-Seventh Armies fired on enemy defences south and east of Leningrad, confusing the Germans as to when and where the next assault would come.[23] They received their answer at 11:00 hours the next morning, when the Second Shock and Forty-Second Armies struck simultaneously after fresh and intense artillery preparations.

Early on 15 January, Fediuninsky's XXXXIII and CXXII Rifle Corps shattered what remained of the 10th Luftwaffe Division's defences, defeating several III SS Panzer Corps' counterattacks and advancing 6km (3.75 miles) before being halted by heavy German fire west of Ropsha.[24] Less than 20km (12.5 miles) to the east, Maslennikov's Forty-Second Army attacked German defences near Pulkovo at 11:00 hours after its artillery had poured more than 220,000 shells into the enemy's defences. As the artillery barrage shifted into the depths, General Simoniak's XXX Guards Rifle Corps swept forward into the German lines. However, CIX and CX Rifle Corps, on Simoniak's flanks, soon encountered heavy resistance, and the fight degenerated into a slugfest with attacking Soviet infantry gnawing their way through the dense German defences in successive assaults.[25] Simoniak's corps had penetrated up to 4km (2.5 miles) along a 5km (3.12-mile) front by the day's end, but could do no more.[26] Govorov's assaults intensified the next day, when Fediuninsky's lead divisions penetrated the entire depth of the Germans' main defensive belt, and Maslennikov's forces painfully advanced another 4km (2.5 miles), primarily in the sector of Simoniak's corps.

Dissatisfied with his forces' progress, Fediuninsky threw a small mobile group, a reinforced tank brigade, into combat early on 17 January with orders to capture and hold Ropsha.[27] However, German counterattacks halted the assault force when it was only halfway to its objective. Simultaneously, Maslennikov committed his second echelon rifle corps and mobile tank group to exploit Simoniak's success and capture Krasnoe Selo.[28] The mobile group went into action at midday but the Germans, who detected its forward movement, counterattacked and forced it to withdraw to Pulkovo with heavy losses.[29] Despite the setbacks, by the day's end only 18km (11.25 miles) separated the Second Shock and Forty-Second Armies' vanguards. Faced with encirclement, the German 126th Infantry and 9th Luftwaffe Field Divisions clung grimly to a shrinking salient north of Krasnoe Selo and prepared to withdraw their forces to the south.

Despite the threatening situation, Lindemann still exuded confidence on 16 January, informing his army commanders that the Russians had committed all of their forces, and Kuechler that he could win the battle by taking some risks in quiet sectors.[30] The next day, however, Kuechler informed OKH that the situation was deteriorating, and requested Hitler's permission to withdraw forces from the Mga salient back to the Rollbahn line to release two divisions to counter the Soviet assaults southwest of Leningrad.[31] Saying neither yes nor no, Hitler instead suggested that Kuechler abandon the front between Oranienbaum and Leningrad.[32] Lindemann, nevertheless, transferred forces from Mga and Chudovo to reinforce his defences southwest of the city, but to no avail.[33]

While Hitler, Kuechler and Lindemann were debating the Eighteenth Army's fate, Fediuninsky and Maslennikov settled the issue for them by committing their second echelon corps to combat, leaving the Germans no other choice but to withdraw their forces back to Krasnoe Selo. Fediuninsky's entire army surged forward on 18 January and captured Ropsha late the next day. At 21:00 hours, his lead elements linked up with Forty-Second Army forces just south of the town, and the next morning the armies' main forces met all along the front, slamming the door shut on German forces still locked in combat to the north.[34] Farther east, Simoniak's corps captured Krasnoe Selo late on 19 January. During the night the army's mobile tank group attacked westwards from Krasnoe Selo with headlights blazing, demoralizing and defeating the German forces withdrawing south from Petergof, Strel'na and Uritsk, linking up with Second Shock Army forces south of Ropsha, and encircling German forces still defending to the north. However, since the Soviet infantry had fallen well behind the tanks, many German troops were able to successfully infiltrate southwards through the porous Soviet lines on the night of 19/20 January, thereby escaping destruction. Soviet forces liquidated those who had failed to do so on 20 January.

Early on 18 January, Lindemann finally informed Kuechler that his front southwest of Leningrad and near Novgorod was collapsing and, once again, Kuechler sought but was denied permission to withdraw to the Rollbahn line. When Krasnoe Selo fell in the afternoon, on his own volition Kuechler decided to abandon the Mga line and so informed OKH. Hitler approved only after Zeitzler told him that he had already given the order. However, it came too late to save the German defences. In six days of heavy combat, Fediuninsky and Maslennikov's armies had penetrated prepared German defences, advanced 25km (15.6 miles) and linked up at

RIGHT: Another classic Russian Front image. A ski patrol near Novgorod takes up a defensive position. The men blend perfectly into their surroundings, the fur caps under their hoods giving an odd shape to their heads. The man on the left is using his ski-poles to steady his aim.

LEFT: German troops observe a burning Soviet village as they pull back towards the Panther Line in January 1944. As it retreated, the Wehrmacht destroyed anything that could be of use to the advancing Red Army – and forcibly evacuated the civilian population.

Ropsha, restoring a continuous front and communications between the Leningrad Front's disparate forces south and west of the city.[35] In the process, they had destroyed two German divisions and damaged another five, captured more than 1000 prisoners, weakened the Eighteenth Army, and facilitated future operations towards both Krasnogvardeisk and Kingisepp.[36]

While Fediuninsky's and Maslennikov's armies were demolishing German defences southwest of Leningrad, Korovnikov's Fifty-Ninth Army, despite bad weather, unleashed its assaults against the Eighteenth Army's right flank in the Novgorod region. After pulverizing German defences with 133,000 artillery shells, assault detachments from each of his army's first echelon rifle battalions began the ground assault. However, VI Rifle Corps' assault stalled after advancing 1km (.62 miles) into the Germans' first defensive position.[37] Fortunately for Korovnikov, to the south, XIV Rifle Corps' 378th Rifle Division attached prematurely and without orders, exploiting a German withdrawal during the artillery preparation and seizing a portion of the enemy's defences.[38] South of Novgorod, Major-General T. A. Sviklin's Southern Operational Group crossed the ice on Lake Il'men without an artillery preparation, surprised the German defenders and captured a 6 x 4km (3.7 x 2.5-mile) bridgehead on the eastern shore of the lake. Fearing loss of communications between Shimsk and Novgorod, the German XXXVIII Army Corps sent in reinforcements.[39]

Korovnikov also reinforced his advancing forces on 15 January.[40] Once reinforced, VI Rifle Corps advanced 7km (4.3 miles), encircled and defeated the 28th *Jäger* Division, and approached the Chudovo-Novgorod railroad late in the day.[41] The next day the corps brushed aside a regiment of the 24th Infantry Division sent by XXXVIII Army Corps to hold the railroad, and together with XIV Rifle Corps, which had cut the Finev Lug-Novgorod road, tore a gaping 20km (12.5-mile) hole in the Germans' main defence belt. Simultaneously, Meretskov applied increased pressure against the sagging German front by ordering Roginsky's Fifty-Fourth Army to join the assault out of the Volkhov River bridgehead. Although Roginsky's army had advanced only 5km (3.12 miles) by 20 January, his attack prevented XXXVIII Army Corps from sending any forces to the Novgorod region.[42]

South of Novgorod, Korovnikov reinforced his Fifty-Ninth Army's Southern Operational Group with two divisions, which broke out of their bridgehead and cut the Shimsk-Novgorod railroad west of Novgorod.[43] Faced with the possible encirclement of his entire Novgorod force, Lindemann reinforced the force with, initially, four divisions, and later a cavalry regiment and another infantry division.[44] Nevertheless, Korovnikov's army continued its slow but inexorable advance, enveloping German forces in Novgorod from the north and south.[45] On 18 January, Korovnikov committed his army's second echelon to protect his army's right flank and to cooperate with Fifty-Fourth Army forces in the destruction of German forces in the Liuban and Chudovo regions.[46] Lindemann quickly ordered his XXXVIII Army Corps to abandon Novgorod, withdrawing along the only remaining road to the west, to occupy new defences positions at Batetskii protecting Luga from the east.

Bad weather, the swampy and heavily wooded terrain, and a lack of transport slowed the Fifty-Ninth Army's advance.[47] Assisted by sappers, the army's VI Rifle Corps struggled through the frozen swamps, finally cutting the Novgorod-Batetskii railroad late on 19 January. Further south, the Southern Group had cut the Shimsk-Novgorod railroad the previous day, but XIV Rifle Corps made little progress in its attack on Novgorod from the north. While the latter was preparing to storm Novgorod the next morning, the Germans began evacuating the city without interference.[48] At 09:30 hours on 20 January Soviet forces captured Novgorod without a fight, after the last Germans out had destroyed the bridge over the Volkhov River.[49] The loss of Novgorod was not, however, bloodless for the Germans, since VI Rifle Corps and the Southern Group's 372nd Rifle Division encircled and later destroyed some German forces west of the city.[50]

Wasteland at Novgorod

After midnight on 19 January, Kuechler sought Hitler's permission to withdraw what he termed "the five German battalions surrounded by eight Soviet divisions" through the swamps west of Novgorod. Although he still stubbornly claimed that Novgorod was of "extraordinary symbolic significance", Hitler agreed to Kuechler's request, but insisted his forces hold east of the Rollbahn Line. Fifteen minutes later he gave permission for that withdrawal as well, but tried to gain Kuechler's guarantee that he would hold on to the Rollbahn. On 20 January, Kuechler assessed the situation and informed OKW that the tactical setbacks at Novgorod and southwest of Leningrad had resulted from lack of reserves and an overextended front. Since the same conditions still existed, he requested that the withdrawal to the Rollbahn become the first step in a general withdrawal to the Panther Line, as the three divisions released by the withdrawal would soon be consumed in the fighting.

In seven days of combat, Korovnikov's army had penetrated strong enemy defences, liberated Novgorod, and advanced 20km (12.5 miles) westwards, widening its penetration to 50km (31.2 miles). While doing so, it had destroyed or seriously damaged two German divisions, one regiment, four separate battalions and other smaller units, and captured 3000 prisoners.[51] The Germans, however, left Novgorod a virtual wasteland, destroying 2460 out of 2500 homes and most other installations and churches. In addition, only 50 inhabitants remained in the city itself; the remainder had been shipped back to Germany.

The *Stavka*'s Displeasure

Although Govorov's and Meretskov's Fronts had resoundingly smashed both flanks of the Eighteenth Army and threatened it with a general offensive from the Gulf of Finland to Lake Il'men, the *Stavka* was not pleased with their progress. It noted a host of shortcomings in the Second Shock, Forty-Second and Fifty-Ninth Armies' operations and demanded they be corrected.[52] However dissatisfied it was, the *Stavka* took solace in the fact that while the Leningrad and Volkhov Fronts were savaging the Eighteenth Army, Kuechler faced a new crisis on his southern flank. In late December he had ordered Busch's Sixteenth Army, then under attack north of Nevel, to begin withdrawing to new defences west of Novosokol'niki. General Popov's Second Baltic Front pursued, reached the new German defence line on 7 January, and launched a fresh offensive with its Third Shock and Tenth Guards Armies on 12 January, and the Twenty-Second Army two days later. On 18 January, after days of confused and heavy fighting and several regroupings, the Twenty-Second Army captured a narrow sector of the Leningrad-Nevel railroad line before going over to the defence on 20 January.

Although the Second Baltic Front's offensive was not dramatically successful, it did tie down the Sixteenth Army and prevent it from reinforcing the Eighteenth Army. In fact, it forced Kuechler to send two security divisions and the bulk of one infantry division to assist the Sixteenth Army.[53] Worse still, by seizing the Novosokol'niki-Dno rail line, the Twenty-Second Army had severed the Germans' main lateral communications artery, endangering their forces in the Novosokol'niki and Staraia Russa regions. This would become an important factor in Kuechler's decision-making, as he soon faced new crises that threatened to unhinge both his Eighteenth and Sixteenth Armies' defences.

After completing Operation Neva and the Novgorod operations, Govorov and Meretskov, with *Stavka* approval, planned to continue the offensive. This required that the Leningrad Front capture Krasnogvardeisk and Tosno, and the Volkhov Front seize Chudovo to encircle and destroy German forces in the Mga, Tosno and Liuban regions. If successful,

LEFT: Red Army troops warm themselves by a fire on their way west in January 1944. The German roadsign, bearing the old imperial title, about to be engulfed in flames bears the name of the city that the Wehrmacht was never destined to take.

the joint operations would end the Leningrad blockade, defeat the Eighteenth Army, and clear German forces from the northern half of the Leningrad *oblast*. Govorov ordered Maslennikov's Forty-Second Army to capture Krasnogvardeisk, Pushkin, Slutsk and Tosno to cut off German forces south and southeast of Leningrad, and Fediuninsky's Second Shock Army to attack southwards to protect Maslennikov's right flank. Meretskov planned to continue his offensive towards Luga, cut the Pushkin-Dno and Krasnogvardeisk-Luga-Pskov railroads, and encircle and destroy German forces in the Mga, Liuban and Chudovo regions in cooperation with Govorov's forces. He ordered Korovnikov's Fifty-Ninth Army to advance towards Luga and Oredezh, while protecting the Front's left flank. His Fifty-Fourth Army would capture Liuban and envelop the German XXVIII Army Corps from the north, and five partisan regiments would support his offensive and assist in the capture of Oredezh, Batetskii, Utorgosh and Shimsk.

The two Fronts resumed their offensives on 21 January with the Second Shock and Forty-Second Armies attacking towards Krasnogvardeisk, and the Fifty-Ninth Army towards Luga. While the Eighteenth Army's L Army Corps desperately held on to its defences around Krasnogvardeisk, late on 21 January Kuechler flew to the Führer headquarters. Early the next morning he informed Hitler that Krasnogvardeisk would fall unless he allowed him to abandon Pushkin and Slutsk. Hitler categorically rejected Kuechler's pleas, stating: "I am against all withdrawals. We will have crises wherever we are.

There is no guarantee we will not be broken through on the Panther Line. If we go back voluntarily they [the Russians] will get there with only half of his forces. He must bleed himself white on the way. The battle must be fought as far as possible from the German border." Kuechler countered that the army group would not even be able to hold on to the Panther Line if it was too weak to do so when it got there. Hitler, however, was adamant. Blaming the gaps in the front on the egotism of his army group commanders and insisting every square yard of ground be sold at the highest possible price in Russian blood, he demanded that the Rollbahn line be held and sent Kuechler on his way. A resigned Kuechler withdrew his forces to the Rollbahn line, sending part of two divisions to shore up his defences at Krasnogvardeisk.[54] A concerned OKH also sent Kuechler the 12th Panzer Division from Army Group Centre and the 502nd Heavy Tank Battalion from the Sixteenth Army to employ at Krasnogvardeisk.

While Hitler and Kuechler were meeting, Soviet intelligence detected a German withdrawal from Mga and Siniavino and immediately ordered Sviridov's Sixty-Seventh Army to pursue and destroy German forces in the Mga region. Although they failed to catch the withdrawing Germans, Sviridov's forces occupied Mga at 17:00 hours on 21 January.[55] The following day, Govorov ordered Sviridov's army to capture Tosno and clear enemy forces from their Rollbahn line. The next day, Lindemann acknowledged the fact that the Rollbahn line was, in fact, untenable by ordering his troops to begin evacuating Pushkin and Slutsk and reporting to OKH that "it could either accept his decision or send a general to replace him". By the time the Eighteenth Army's forces had completed their withdrawal to the Rollbahn line south of Mga, Soviet forces had already penetrated it in several places.

The German withdrawal from the Rollbahn line forced Govorov and Meretskov to alter their plans significantly for a general offensive and pursuit along the entire front from the Gulf of Finland to Lake Il'men. Since it was no longer necessary for the Forty-Second Army to capture Tosno, Govorov ordered Fediuninsky's Second Shock Army and Maslennikov's Forty-Second Army to attack towards Kingisepp and Bol'shoi Sabsk and reach the Luga River by 30 January. Meanwhile, Sviridov's Sixty-Seventh Army was to attack southwards and westwards to destroy German forces at Pushkin and Tosno, keeping pace with the two armies on its right. If successful, Govorov's offensive would force the Germans to withdraw southwards across the forested and swampy terrain north of Luga, and walk straight into the guns of Meretskov's forces. The *Stavka* approved Govorov's plan on 22 January.

Meretskov's plan complemented Govorov's. He ordered Korovnikov's Fifty-Ninth Army to capture Luga and Starikov's Eighth Army, up to now assigned only secondary missions, to capture Tosno and clear German forces from the remainder of the Rollbahn line. Subsequently, Starikov would transfer his forces to the Fifty-Fourth Army and move with

his headquarters to the Front's left flank to take control of forces attacking Luga. Finally, after capturing Liuban, Roginsky's Fifty-Fourth Army was to help capture Tosno and Ushaki and attack southwestwards in support of the Sixty-Seventh Army and southeastwards towards Oredezh to strike the flank of German forces withdrawing westwards from Chudovo. The *Stavka* approved Meretskov's plan on 22 January, and ordered him to capture Liuban no later than 23–24 January and Luga no later than 29–30 January.

The Second Shock Army began its pursuit on 21 January against skillful German rearguard actions. Because Fediuninsky was unhappy with the pursuit since his subordinate commanders often conducted frontal attacks against German strongpoints and utterly failed to employ manoeuvre, he issued a blistering series of rebukes to correct the errors and spur his forces on.[56] Plagued by the same problems that dogged Fediuninsky, Maslennikov ordered his main force to assault German defences around Krasnogvardeisk at 13:00 hours on 22 January after a 15-minute artillery fire raid.[57] His CXXIII and CXVII Rifle Corps attacked Krasnogvardeisk proper, and CX Rifle Corps advanced southeast to envelop Pushkin and Slutsk. Although by late on 23 January his forces had encircled the German defenders at Pushkin and Slutsk from three sides, they were unable to dislodge German forces from Krasnogvardeisk. Further east, Sviridov's Sixty-Seventh Army captured Mga, but failed to capture Ul'ianovka, Tosno and the Rollbahn line in between. A frustrated Govorov berated his

RIGHT: Soviet sappers search for German mines in newly liberated Petergof, west of Leningrad, in January 1944. The lifting of the siege of Leningrad raised the morale of the whole Soviet people, and was also a great military victory for the Red Army.

army and corps commanders for operating too slowly, exercising poor command and control and using unrealistic linear tactics.

Recriminations also resounded in German ranks as Kuechler accused Lindemann of submitting false estimates of Soviet reserves at the end of December, For his part, Lindemann admitted "mistakes" had been made. Amidst this exchange, grim tidings overwhelmed both commanders as news arrived that Soviet forces were on the outskirts of Krasnogvardeisk and had smashed through the bend of the Luga River southeast of Luga. Though Lindemann tried to patch up his front by throwing in rear-echelon troops, by the day's end on 24 January he grudgingly admitted that his right flank had lost contact with the Sixteenth Army and that Krasnogvardeisk would fall within 24 hours. Kuechler asked for Hitler's permission to withdraw at least to the Luga Line, but that night Zeitzler at OKW told Kuechler that Hitler's orders were to hold the corner posts and make the troops fight to the last. Since there was nothing else to do for the time being, he advised the army group command to be "a little ruthless" for a while.

Fediuninsky's forces continued their advance along the Krasnogvardeisk-Kingisepp railroad on 24 January, but made only modest progress against determined German resistance. On the same day

BELOW: Even with the ground looking less than snow covered, these infantrymen are still wearing their filthy camouflage smocks. Given the envious glances being cast by his comrade, the soldier on the left may be drinking something more potent than water from his mess-tin!

Govorov realigned his forces, reinforcing Maslennikov's army with CVIII Rifle Corps from Fediuninsky's army and transferring Maslennikov's CX Rifle Corps to Sviridov's Sixty-Seventh Army. Over the next two days Fediuninsky's right flank advanced up to 16km (10 miles), and his left flank captured Elizavetino and cut the Krasnogvardeisk-Kingisepp railroad.[58] After reaching the railroad, on 27 January he wheeled his army to the west and began pursuing the German XXVI Army Corps towards Kingisepp. Late that day he transferred his CXXII Rifle Corps to Maslennikov's army.

With his defences crumbling around him, Kuechler attended a National Socialist Leadership Conference at Konigsberg on 27 January. In between Hitler's speeches exhorting faith in the cause as a guarantee of ultimate victory, Kuechler reiterated to the Führer the dire consequences that would follow if he was not allowed to conduct a general withdrawal. Hitler categorically prohibited all voluntary withdrawals and reserved the decision to withdraw for himself. The next day, Kuechler told the attendees that his Eighteenth Army had lost 40,000 casualties and the troops had fought as hard as could be expected. Hitler replied that the statement was "not quite true". He had heard that the army group was not fighting everywhere with as much determination as it might. Kuechler returned to his headquarters a broken man. While knowing he should retreat, all he could talk about was showing more determination and attacking. With what, though, nobody knew.

Given Kuechler's apparent paralysis, Lieutenant-General Eberhard Kinzel, his chief of staff, took matters into his own hands and told Lindemann's chief of staff that the time had come. An order to retreat must be issued, but the army group was forbidden to do that. Therefore, the army would have to act as if the order had been given, issuing its own implementing orders orally rather than in writing. He, Kinzel, would see to it that the army was covered "in the General Staff channel". On 29 January, Kinzel prevailed on Kuechler to at least report to Hitler that the Eighteenth Army was split into three parts and could not hold any kind of a front forward of the Luga River. Lindemann began withdrawing his main forces on the night of 27/28 January, leaving rearguards to protect his movement.[59]

Fediuninsky's forces accelerated their pursuit on 27 January and reached the Luga River on 30 January, seizing small bridgeheads on the river's southern bank. At the same time, Maslennikov's CXXIII and CXVII Rifle Corps pressed German

ABOVE: Marshal of the Soviet Union Leonid Govorov, who commanded the Leningrad Front at the beginning of 1944. A very capable commander, he had led the Fifth Army during Zhukov's 1941 counteroffensive and took part in the defence of Leningrad thereafter.

forces back towards Krasnogvardeisk against dwindling resistance, and his CX Rifle Corps and 79th Fortified Region captured Pushkin and Slutsk. Lindemann then began shifting forces westwards from Krasnogvardeisk to keep open his withdrawal routes to Kingisepp.

The Battle for Krasnogvardeisk proper began early on 25 January when Maslennikov's forces attacked German defences after a 10-minute fire raid.[60] His CVIII Rifle Corps and 220th Tank Brigade had advanced 5km (3.1 miles) by the day's end, cutting the rail line west of the town, but had encountered a German infantry battalion with 15 anti-tank guns and a company of Tiger tanks, which brought the advance to an abrupt halt. After regrouping, the force resumed the attack and fought its way into the town's northwestern section just as CXVII Rifle Corps' 120th Rifle Division penetrated into the town's northeastern section. After an all-night battle, the 120th Rifle Division captured Krasnogvardeisk the following morning. Maslennikov's army pursued,

capturing the important German supply base at Volosovo and reaching the Luga River on 30 January, while Govorov once again shuffled his forces.[61]

While Fediuninsky and Maslennikov's armies were advancing to the Luga River, the Sixty-Seventh Army, on Govorov's left flank, advanced on Pushkin, Slutsk and Tosno against stubborn German opposition. Sviridov's CVIII Rifle Corps captured Ul'ianovka late on 24 January and, after capturing Pushkin and Slutsk, his CX Rifle Corps reached the Izhora River. However, there Sviridov halted his advance temporarily, wasting an excellent opportunity to encircle and destroy the German forces southeast of Slutsk. As the Germans accelerated their withdrawal, the Sixty-Seventh Army continued its advance, capturing Tosno and the western sector of the once formidable Rollbahn line on 25–26 January. Late on 26 January, Govorov once again scolded his army commanders for their slow pursuit, regrouped his forces and issued new orders.[62]

Sviridov's revised orders required his Sixty-Seventh Army to advance towards Siverskii and Luga, protect the Forty-Second Army's right flank, and help the Volkhov Front destroy German forces in the Liuban and Chudovo region to the southeast. Sviridov's army resumed its pursuit on 27 January, but its CXVII Rifle Corps ran into heavy resistance southeast of Krasnogvardeisk, where L Army Corps and the 12th Panzer Division were protecting XXVI and XXVIII Army Corps' withdrawal from the Tosno and Liuban regions.[63] Joined by CX Rifle Corps, the two corps finally overcame the stiff German resistance and captured Siverskii late on 30 January, albeit with considerable difficulty.[64]

While Govorov's armies were advancing towards Kingisepp and Luga, Meretskov's armies advanced on Luga from the east and northeast. Starikov's Eighth Army began its pursuit early on 21 January, linked up with the Sixty-Seventh Army at Mga, and approached the Tosno and Ushaki sector of the Rollbahn line late on 24 January.[65] That night, Starikov turned his forces and sector over to the Fifty-Fourth Army and moved with his headquarters to the front's left wing, where he took control of forces on the Fifty-Ninth Army's left flank on 26 January. On Starikov's left flank, Roginsky's Fifty-Fourth Army advanced 25km (15.6 miles) in five days, but was then halted by heavy German resistance near Liuban along the Rollbahn line.[66] On 25 January Meretskov assigned most of the Eighth Army's forces to the Fifty-Fourth Army, designating them the new CXIX Rifle Corps.

Roginsky's reinforced army resumed its advance during the night of 25/26 January, captured Tosno and Ushaki, and reached the railroad southeast of Liuban.[67] The next day Lindemann withdrew the Spanish Legion from Liuban to Luga and abandoned Liuban. With the capture of Chudovo the same day, Roginsky's forces controlled the entire length of the Oktiabr railroad, the main link between Moscow and Leningrad. Fearing encirclement after their loss of Liuban and Chudovo, XXVIII Army Corps accelerated its withdrawal towards Luga with the Fifty-Fourth Army in pursuit.[68]

Failure Along the Luga Axis

Korovnikov's Fifty-Ninth Army posed the greatest threat to XXVIII and XXXVIII Army Corps, but only if his army could reach Luga and cut off the two corps' withdrawal routes. After capturing Novgorod and regrouping his army, Korovnikov resumed his offensive on 21 January through difficult terrain that required significant engineer support to surmount.[69] Korovnikov's VI Rifle Corps attacked westwards through Batetskii to Luga with CXII Rifle Corps on the right and XIV Rifle Corps attacking southwestwards towards Shimsk on the left. VII Rifle Corps, in second echelon, was to fill the gaps between VI and XIV Rifle Corps and exploit to Peredol'skaia Station on the Leningrad-Dno railroad line southeast of Luga. Meretskov reminded Korovnikov that his forces could cut off and destroy German forces withdrawing from the Tosno, Liuban, Chudovo and Novgorod regions if he advanced decisively. Despite Meretskov's optimism, Korovnikov's advance quickly got bogged down. It did so because Kuechler understood the perils he faced, and quickly reinforced his defences at the junction of his Sixteenth and Eighteenth Armies, with combat groups drawn from other army group sectors.[70]

The advance by Korovnikov's VI Rifle Corps and 59th Tank Brigade faltered badly on 24 January after only minimal gains.[71] Worse still, instead of committing his fresh VII Rifle Corps along the Batetskii axis, Korovnikov ordered it to advance southwards towards Shimsk and Peredol'skaia Station, a decision that overextended his army and ultimately resulted in failure along the Luga axis. Subsequently, the Fifty-Ninth Army's advance turned into a slugfest in difficult terrain, as the troops waded forward in waist-deep water with their supporting tanks and artillery lagging far behind. An increasingly distraught Meretskov demanded that Korovnikov concentrate his forces and capture Luga no later than 29–30 January. However, despite Meretskov's entreaties, VI Rifle Corps made little progress in four days of heavy fighting along the Batetskii-Luga railroad.[72]

Popov's Offensive

While VI Rifle Corps advanced towards Luga at an agonizingly slow pace, Korovnikov's VII and XIV Rifle Corps made deceptively greater progress on the army's left flank. In a rapid dash through the swamps, VII Rifle Corps and accompanying 7th Guards Tank Brigade reached the outskirts of Peredol'skaia Station late on 27 January in cooperation with the 5th Partisan Brigade. VII Rifle Corps also captured Medved from the 8th *Jäger* Division, cutting the Luga-Shimsk road, and XIV Rifle Corps and the 16th Tank Brigade cleared German forces from the western shores of Lake Il'men, reaching the outskirts of Shimsk late on 26 January.[73] Since Meretskov had not anticipated advancing this far south, he ordered the 150th Fortified Region to defend that sector and XIV Rifle Corps to turn northeast and reinforce the attack on Luga. To resolve command and control difficulties, Meretskov ordered Starikov's Eighth Army to take control of forces on the Fifty-Ninth Army's (and his Front's) left flank.[74] Starikov's new army included VII and XIV Rifle Corps, the 7th Guards, 122nd and 16th Tank Brigades, and the 150th Fortified Region. This left Korovnikov's Fifty-Ninth Army with only VI and CXII Rifle Corps and the 29th Tank Brigade with which to capture Batetskii and Luga and Oredezh to the north.

Govorov ordered Korovnikov to continue his advance on Luga, protected by a single rifle division on his right flank.[75] At the same time, Starikov's Eighth Army, on Korovnikov's left, was to capture Peredol'skaia Station, Utorgosh and Pliussa, envelop Luga from the south and southeast, and capture Luga in conjunction with the Fifty-Ninth Army. Although the redeployment of his Eighth Army was designed to shorten the Fifty-Ninth Army's front significantly and ease command and control, it did not do so. When Korovnikov resumed his advance on 27 January, his VI Rifle Corps' attack stalled along the railroad east of Batetskii, while his CXII Rifle Corps fought its way across the Luga River and advanced to within 18km (11.2 miles) of Oredezh on 30 January. However, the weakness of the 2nd Rifle Division on its right flank and Korovnikov's lack of reserves permitted XXVIII Army Corps to escape from the Chudovo region.[76]

ABOVE: To the victors the spoils. Following the fighting and the speech making, these Soviet soldiers prepare to eat and drink from supplies "liberated" from the Germans.

Korovnikov's failure to capture Luga meant that a successful advance on Luga rested in the hands of Starikov's Eighth Army. However, before fulfilling the missions assigned to him by Meretskov, Starikov had to capture Peredol'skaia Station, which was no mean task. Although his VII Rifle Corps and the 5th Partisan Brigade had captured Peredol'skaia Station early on 27 January, thereafter the station changed hands three times in heavy fighting as the Germans committed fresh reserves to the fight, forcing Starikov to commit all of his reserves.[77] Worse still, the Fifty-Ninth Army's VI Rifle Corps lagged far behind, forcing VII Rifle Corps to defend its right flank while weakening its forces attacking towards the west. Although VII Rifle Corps managed to advance several more kilometres westwards by 30 January and cut the Leningrad-Dno railroad, Starikov's army failed to accomplish its mission and Luga remained firmly in German hands. Since the Fifty-Ninth and Eighth Armies' slow advance towards Luga threatened to disrupt its plan to cut off and destroy German forces north and east of Luga, the *Stavka* insisted that Meretskov cut the

road and railroad south of Luga no later than 30–31 January, sending him reinforcements.[78] However, Meretskov's forces failed to do so.[79]

While Govorov's and Meretskov's forces were plodding forward towards Kingisepp and Luga, Popov's Second Baltic Front planned to mount a new offensive against Army Group North's Sixteenth Army to support the offensive to the north. After halting his earlier offensive north and west of Novosokol'niki, Popov regrouped his forces and prepared a new offensive.[80] However, the Sixteenth Army detected the attack preparations, withdrew from Novosokol'niki on 30 January and occupied new defences to the northwest. The Twenty-Second and Tenth Guards Armies pursued, but halted in front of the new German defences. The Second Baltic Front's inactivity and feeble pursuit allowed the Sixteenth Army to dispatch reinforcements to the Eighteenth Army's right flank, which helped stop the Eighth and Fifty-Ninth Armies' advance on Luga.[81]

In more than two weeks of heavy combat, Govorov's and Meretskov's forces had penetrated German defences along the entire front from the Gulf of Finland to Lake Il'men, inflicting a major defeat on the Eighteenth Army. While doing so, their forces drove German forces 100km (62.5 miles) south and southwest of Leningrad and 80km (50

LEFT: As the Red Army pressed forward the German frontline broke. Among the Soviet troops inspecting the German defences can be seen several mounted figures. The Red Army made great use of mounted scouts and did not disband its last cavalry units until the 1950s.

miles) west from Novgorod, and cleared German forces from the main railroad line between Moscow and Leningrad. However, Meretskov's forces had failed to capture Luga by 30 January, and so the Eighteenth Army managed to withdraw its forces relatively intact from Leningrad and the Mga, Chudovo, Liuban and Novgorod regions. While Kuechler succeeded in establishing a new defence line protecting Luga and his vital withdrawal route to Pskov, the Red Army had once and for all raised the blockade of Leningrad and put the entire Eighteenth Army in jeopardy.

Although the Battle for Leningrad did not formally end until 10 August 1944 when Red Army forces drove the last Axis forces from every square metre of the Leningrad region, the battle was really over by 30 January 1944, when the German threat to Leningrad ended. Thereafter, it took until 1 March for the Red Army to expel German forces from the southern portion of the Leningrad region and until 10 August to drive Finnish forces out of the northern Leningrad region.

Govorov's and Meretskov's advance on Narva and Luga was slow and arduous and, despite their best efforts, a badly shaken Eighteenth Army managed to limp back to the Panther Line, where it halted the Red Army's advance. Early in the fighting, Hitler replaced the hapless Kuechler with his favourite fighting general, Field Marshal Walter Model, and the latter attempted in vain to restore the front near Luga by an artful combination of stubborn defence and counterattacks. While the

heavy fighting delayed the Soviet advance and led to complex and heavy fighting, the die was cast and Model's efforts failed. Govorov shifted the bulk of his armies against Model's Eighteenth Army and forced it to abandon Luga. However, by virtue of their strenuous actions, Model's forces managed to hold on to Narva and extract his battered Eighteenth Army safely back to the Panther Line by the end of February, by which time Popov's Second Baltic Front had joined the Soviet westward advance. Having cleared most of the southern Leningrad region of Germans, Soviet forces attempted to penetrate the Panther Line but failed. There the front stabilized until the summer.

Although the Soviet Novgorod-Luga offensive ended the German threat to Leningrad, Finnish forces still occupied positions only 30km (18.7 miles) from the city, which they had seized in the summer of 1941. The Finnish Army remained in those positions for almost three years, to Hitler's annoyance doing little or nothing to contribute to the battle for Leningrad. However, their very presence represented a threat, an embarrassment and a constant reminder of the indignities the Soviet Union had suffered in 1941. Therefore, after the Soviet government failed to drive Finland from the war by diplomatic means in the spring of 1944, in June the Red Army did so militarily. On 10 June 1944, the Leningrad and Karelian Fronts conducted military operations to recapture their lost territories, punish the Finns for allying with Germany, and drive Finland from the war.

On 10 June, Govorov's Leningrad Front began the Vyborg operation to drive Finnish forces from the Karelian Isthmus. The Twenty-First, Twenty-Third and, later, Fifty-Ninth Armies smashed Finnish defences, recaptured the isthmus, and seized Vyborg on 20 June, but were then rebuffed in their attempts to penetrate deeper into Finland between 23 June and 13 July.

Simultaneously, the Karelian Front, commanded by General Meretskov, who was assigned command of the Front after the Volkhov Front was disbanded in February 1944, conducted the Svir-Petrozavodsk offensive operation designed to clear Finnish forces from central Karelia. The operation by the Seventh Separate and Thirty-Second Armies, which lasted until 9 August, developed in two stages, during which Red Army forces liberated the territory between Lakes Onega and Ladoga westwards to the 1939 Finnish-Soviet border. The Battle for Leningrad formally ended on 10 August, the day after the Red Army completed expelling all axis forces from every square metre of the Leningrad region.

The Leningrad, Volkhov and Second Baltic Fronts' Leningrad-Novgorod offensive was immensely significant. First and foremost, by liberating Leningrad it raised the Soviet population's morale, inspired the Soviet Union's allies, and had a crushing effect on German morale. While representing the first stage of the Red Army's winter offensive, it took place simultaneously with and supported major Red Army offensives into Belorussia and the Ukraine. During the course of 45 days, the three fronts smashed deeply echeloned defences the enemy had erected over a period of two years, defeated Army Group North's Eighteenth Army and raised the Leningrad blockade. By the end of February, Red Army forces had liberated all of Leningrad and part of the Kalinin region and entered Soviet Estonia, in the process saving millions of Soviet citizens from German slavery. The offensive opened the Moscow-Leningrad railroad line, gave the Baltic Fleet freedom of action and created prerequisites for driving Finland from the war.

The three Red Army Fronts inflicted severe loses on the German Eighteenth and Sixteenth Armies during the operation, completely destroying three divisions and severely damaging 12 of the Eighteenth Army's divisions and five of the Sixteenth Army's.[82] However, it did so at a considerable cost in Red Army soldiers' lives. Out of a force of 822,000 troops committed to battle, the three Fronts suffered 313,953 casualties, including 76,686 dead, captured or missing.[83]

The Red Army performed several noteworthy feats in the operation. Initially, it secretly transferred the entire Second Shock Army and large amounts of artillery into the Oranienbaum bridgehead. Then it conducted simultaneous offensives 200km (125 miles) apart against the Eighteenth Army's flanks, weakening that army's defences at Leningrad proper. While it failed to destroy the Eighteenth Army, ultimately it drove its forces back to Narva and the Panther Line. The twin offensives spanned a 400km (250-mile) front and reached to a depth of 300km (187.5 miles) in 47 days at an

RIGHT: Killed in action. A Red Army convoy drives past a German graveyard in Ropsha on the outskirts of Leningrad. The small church had been used by the Wehrmacht as a place of worship during the years of the siege.

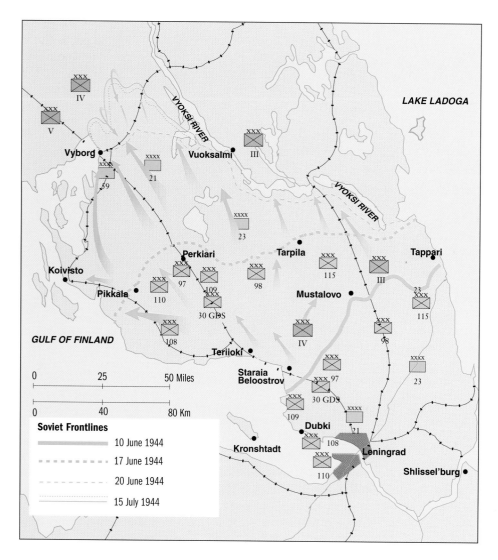

average advance rate of 6.5km (four miles) per day. Govorov and Meretskov employed shock groups which concentrated on 10–12 percent of the front to conduct their penetration operations, and used second echelons, reserves and frequent regroupings to sustain their offensives into the operational depths.

Armies designated to conduct main attacks deployed in two echelons of rifle corps with extensive artillery support. The Second Shock and Forty-Second Armies employed anti-tank reserves, tank reserves and mobile obstacle detachments, while the Forty-Second Army used a strong mobile tank group together with a combined-arms reserve.[84] Within the armies, the rifle corps attacked in one, two or three echelons depending on the situation and, as a rule, rifle divisions formed in single echelon, along with a reserve to

ABOVE: The Soviet Vyborg offensive operation, 10 June–15 July 1944, was the last act in the siege of Leningrad drama. Compared to the fighting in the south against Army Group North, the offensive against the Finns was relatively straightforward and bloodless.

generate the maximum offensive momentum. However, some armies failed to commit their second echelons in timely or effective fashion, thereby weakening the force of the main attack.[85] In addition, army commanders failed to capitalize on their artillery, tank, engineer and aviation support, and neglected to employ manoeuvre when attempting to capture strongpoints and fortified regions. As a result, the infantry advance through the swampy and forested terrain degenerated into progressive gnawing through successive German defence lines.

Throughout the region, it became quite difficult to carry out ammunition and food re-supply and evacuate the wounded. While artillery was immensely valuable when supporting penetrations of strong German defences and reducing strong-points, it proved less useful during operations across difficult terrain because it usually lagged some 20–25km (12.5–15.6 miles) behind the advancing infantry. Bad weather conditions and the shortage of bombers also limited aviation support, even though long-range aviation took up some of the slack.

The Red Army General Staff later identified major deficiencies in the offensives that hindered operations in the difficult terrain. Poor engineer reconnaissance and a shortage of engineer forces made manoeuvre difficult for tank and artillery and, at times, even for infantry. Since it was often easier to manoeuvre from depth than laterally, the value of mobile detachments operating along the few existing roads increased sharply. The swampy and forested roads, even if frozen, also inhibited the establishment of effective communications. Bad terrain and the frequent dispersal of forces along separate axes made wire communications impossible and forced units to rely on radios, which were often in short supply.

Many other deficiencies identified by the General Staff mirrored those apparent in previous operations. For example, intelligence organs failed to reconnoitre the terrain and German defences adequately, and this had an adverse impact of the effectiveness of artillery preparations and supporting barrages. Commanders tended to disperse their forces in an apparent attempt to attack and win everywhere simultaneously, and often neglected to concentrate sufficient forces to achieve decisive penetrations and advances along main attack axes. During operations commanders exercised weak command and control and either neglected entirely or ineffectively conducted night operations. Worse still, both tanks and artillery lagged behind, depriving the infantry of critical artillery and tank support when they most needed it. Finally, when it did occur, supply was either late or inadequate, forcing units to operate without necessary ammunition, fuel or foodstuffs. The foraging that inevitably resulted further reduced the units' combat effectiveness.

All of these problems significantly reduced the rate of advance and prevented the encirclement and destruction of many otherwise vulnerable German forces. Most importantly, staff at the Front, army and corps level lacked experience in the conduct of large-scale offensive operations – and it showed. One notable exception to this rule was the positive role that the partisans played. Partisan brigades, regiments, detachments and small groups conducted reconnaissance and diversionary work during the preparatory period.

Despite these shortcomings, neither the Soviets nor the Germans discounted the Red Army's achievements. The Leningrad-Novgorod offensive was its most successful offensive to date. Its results, the liberation of Leningrad, obviated the need for any more assaults against German forces in the whole of the Leningrad region.

RIGHT: Soviet artillery pounds Army Group North as it retreats through the Baltic states in mid-1944. The Germans managed to fall back to Riga, but by the end of September 1944 Govorov's Leningrad Front had cleared all German forces from Estonia except the Baltic islands.

LENINGRAD.
293.

CHAPTER 10:
CONCLUSIONS

For three long years Leningrad had endured great hardships. Tens of thousands of men, women and children had been killed by enemy bombs and shells and starvation, while hundreds of thousands of Red Army troops had died trying to liberate them. The failure of Army Group North to take the city stands as a lasting testament to the heroism and self-sacrifice of the Russian people.

The Battle for Leningrad justifiably occupies a legendary place in the Red Army's struggle during its Great Patriotic War, if only because the city, acknowledged as the birthplace of the Bolshevik Revolution, represented both a fortress of Socialism and Russian national identity, and a massive example of heroism on an unprecedented scale. While the suffering and fate of Leningraders during the city's three-year siege had tremendous political importance for its military defenders and the Soviet people as a whole, its successful defence and ultimate liberation had an even greater impact on the country's morale.

The Red Army's defence of Leningrad, its numerous and often tragic attempts to raise the siege, and its liberation of the city in early 1944, reflected and affected the Soviet Union's wartime military strategy. During the initial period of war in 1941, the Red Army's Northern (Leningrad) and Northwestern Fronts and Seventh Separate Army were the first Red Army forces to halt the seemingly inexorable German Barbarossa tide. The Red Army conducted a tenacious though costly defence on the approaches to the city, contained German forces in the city's southern suburbs, and, though the city was nearly totally blockaded, thwarted German attempts to complete the city's encirclement from the east. In

November 1941 the Red Army conducted its first successful counteroffensive of the war against the Wehrmacht at Tikhvin and Volkhov. In the process, it exhausted Army Group North, began bleeding it white, and forced the Germans to go on the defence in the entire Leningrad region. This feat challenged enduring German misconceptions about the morale, fighting spirit and staying power of the Red Army and confounded Hitler's Operation Barbarossa.

The Germans' unexpected failure to capture Leningrad in September and October 1941 had far-reaching consequences. First, for the first time in World War II, at Leningrad, the concept of Blitzkrieg failed, reinforcing what had begun to occur in July and August at Smolensk and anticipating what would occur at Moscow in December.

Second, Army Group North's failure to capture Leningrad forced Hitler to alter his Barbarossa strategy. Instead of capturing Leningrad by a swift *coup de main* and then shifting forces to other axes, the desperate Soviet defence of Leningrad between July and December forced the Wehrmacht to reinforce Army Group North with 16 divisions and two brigades, including seven divisions from Army Group Centre. This weakened the main German drive on Moscow, perhaps fatally. During this most critical period of the war, 32 percent of the Wehrmacht's forces operating north of the Pripiat Marshes, including almost two full panzer groups, were tied down in combat along or adjacent to the northwestern axis.

Leningrad figured significantly in the *Stavka's* December 1941 counteroffensive and the Red

LEFT: A Soviet propaganda poster of Stalin in Leningrad. The Soviet dictator, who had made strenuous efforts to save the city during the war, became jealous of its fame and those luminaries of the siege in the years immediately afterwards. It is rumoured that he had a hand in the death of Zhdanov in August 1948.

ABOVE: Like tens of thousands of others, these Red Army troops on patrol near Leningrad were determined that the city would not fall to the Nazis. Their sacrifice was not a consequence of NKVD pressure or other threats; rather, a love of Mother Russia, its people, culture and history.

Army's first strategic offensive in the winter of 1941–42, during which the *Stavka* allocated its new Volkhov Front and four fresh armies, including the Second Shock Army, to combat in the Leningrad region. It used the bulk of these forces to conduct the Liuban offensive, the first large-scale offensive designed to envelop German forces south of Leningrad and raise the blockade by an advance westwards from the Volkhov River. While demonstrating its resolve to raise the blockade, the dramatic but tragic and costly failure educated the *Stavka* on how difficult operations in this region were and would continue to be.

In the summer of 1942, the *Stavka* adopted a "smaller solution" to the problem of raising the Leningrad blockade by attacking to establish a corridor to Leningrad through Siniavino, while distracting the Germans with offensives near Demiansk. Although smaller in scale than the

Liuban offensive, the Volkhov, Northwestern and Leningrad Fronts' offensives at Siniavino and Demiansk in the summer and fall of 1942 demonstrated continued *Stavka* resolve to raise the Leningrad blockade. Although these offensives also failed, they affected the war in other more important theatres by attracting large German forces away from southern Russia and tying down German forces in the Leningrad region. The threat of renewed Red Army offensives and Hitler's fixation on seizing Lenin's city compelled the Wehrmacht to dispatch its Eleventh Army to the region in August and September at the critical moment when the Germans were trying but failing to achieve decisive victory at Stalingrad.

Once again, in early 1943 the *Stavka* demonstrated its concern for Leningrad and capitalized on the German defeat at Stalingrad by mounting Operation Spark to raise the blockade. Although the offensive fell far short of Soviet expectations, it gave the lie to German claims that Leningrad was in their pocket for the taking at any time, and ended all German hopes of starving Leningrad into submission. The partial penetration of the blockade and the establishment of ground communications with the city dramatically improved the Leningrad Front's military capabilities, and paved the way for a series of more powerful and ultimately more successful offensive operations along the northwestern axis. The most ambitious of these offensives was Zhukov's Operation Polar Star, which for the first time sought to implement a "larger solution" to raising the Leningrad siege by enveloping and defeating all of Army Group North. Once it aborted, the operation also symbolized the failure of the *Stavka*'s entire grand design for achieving victory in 1943. In a larger sense, it also signalled the birth of a new, more sober appreciation on the part of the *Stavka* of what would be required to achieve victory in the future.

In the summer and fall of 1943, while momentous events were unfolding at Kursk, Orel, Smolensk, Khar'kov and along the Dnepr River, and, later, in eastern Belorussia and the Ukraine, the *Stavka* returned to a "smaller solution" of the problem of raising the Leningrad blockade. During this period, it relied on a combination of major Soviet offensives elsewhere along the front and limited-objective offensives in the Leningrad region. While the Leningrad and Volkhov Fronts' attempts to envelop and destroy German forces in the Mga,

Siniavino and Tosno regions and significantly widen the Shlissel'burg corridor failed after only limited gains, they did tie down significant German forces and bled Army Group North white. These fierce, costly, but largely ineffective offensives so weakened the German army group that by the fall of 1943 it was clearly no longer capable of withstanding another major Red Army offensive.

Because it understood how weak Army Group North was, and because the raising of the Leningrad blockade was still a high-priority objective, the *Stavka* began its 1944 Winter Campaign in the Leningrad region before expanding it to the entire Soviet-German front. In January, the Leningrad and Volkhov Fronts, joined later by the Second Baltic Front, began large-scale offensive operations that ultimately endured through the summer. From mid-January through February, the Leningrad, Volkhov and Second Baltic Fronts defeated Army Group North, raised the Leningrad blockade, and liberated the

BELOW: The troops of Army Group North fought with tenacity and skill during the three-year siege, but the army group was gradually stripped of units to combat emergencies on other sectors of the front. This meant that it was increasingly unable to tighten the blockade from early 1943 onwards.

southern half of the Leningrad region. By doing so, they paved the way for the liberation of the Baltic region and the defeat of Army Group Centre in Belorussia in the summer of 1944. During the summer campaign, the Leningrad and Karelian Fronts completed liberation of the Leningrad region by defeating Finnish forces on the Karelian Isthmus and in southern Karelia, and forcing Finland to leave the war.

Throughout the war, operations in the Leningrad region tied down between 15 and 20 percent of all Axis forces operating on the German Eastern Front. At the same time, Red Army forces operating along the northwestern axis also suffered roughly 12–15 percent of the army's wartime casualties. Ultimately, the Red Army destroyed or seriously damaged 50 German and Finnish divisions in the region. However, despite the heavy fighting, for a variety of political, geographical and military reasons, the *Stavka* did not consider the northwestern theatre as the most vital strategic axis in the war. That honour belonged to the vital western (Moscow-Minsk-Warsaw-Berlin) and, at times, the southwestern (Kiev-Khar'kov-Stalingrad) strategic axis, where, like the Germans, the *Stavka* well understood that it had to achieve victory if it was to

ABOVE: Horse-drawn transport on the "Road of Life". The ice route across Lake Ladoga, though unable to bring in all that the city required, and in range of German artillery and Luftwaffe aircraft, undoubtedly saved Leningrad from starving in the winter of 1941–42.

prevail in the war. Therefore, both the Wehrmacht and the Red Army consistently concentrated their most important offensive and defensive efforts along these axes. However, this shared appreciation also made it impossible for either side to win along the western axis unless they won elsewhere. In short, the Germans could not capture Moscow in 1941, 1942 or 1943 unless and until they weakened Soviet defences along the Moscow axis by operating successfully along other axes. Conversely, after defeating Army Group Centre at Moscow in 1941 and 1942 and at Rzhev in late 1942, the Red Army appreciated that it could not win along the western axis unless it achieved victory elsewhere.

Within this context, the Red Army's victory at Tikhvin conditioned its victory at Moscow, and its partially successful and failed offensives in 1942 and 1943 contributed marginally to the Red Army's victories along the western and southwestern axes.

Likewise, the Red Army's victory at Leningrad in early 1944 paved the way for Soviet victory in Belorussia and the western Ukraine in the summer of 1944 by weakening the Wehrmacht overall, and by releasing fresh, large reserves for employment along other critical axes. Most importantly, however, throughout the war Leningrad symbolized the Soviet Union's and Red Army's resilience, staying power and will to achieve ultimate victory.

The Defences at Leningrad

The Battle for Leningrad made significant contributions, both positive and negative, to the evolution of what the Soviets and Russians term military art, which encompasses the realms of military strategy, operational art and tactics. Despite defeats of catastrophic proportions, severe shortages of human and material resources, and appalling terrain and weather conditions, the *Stavka*, Red Army fronts and the Leningraders themselves organized the successful defence of the city in the summer, fall and winter of 1941. While conducting a stubborn, costly and often desperate defence along the approaches to Leningrad, the *Stavka* also incorporated a degree of "offensiveness" in its defence that most historians have since overlooked.

The short, but exceedingly violent Red Army counterstrokes organized by Vatutin and Zhukov at Sol'tsy in July, at Staraia Russa in August, and at Krasnoe Selo and Mga in August and September 1941 played an enormous role in the successful defence. These counterstrokes and other counterattacks surprised the Germans, seriously disrupted their offensive plans, and forced them to disperse their forces, weaken their shock groups and significantly alter their attack axes, slowing their advance and winning the time necessary to erect stronger defences along key operational axes. As a result, the closer the Germans advanced towards Leningrad, the fiercer the resistance became. Although German forces succeeded in reaching Lake Ladoga and in blockading the city from the land, they could not capture it. Given time to mobilize, Leningrad's defenders thwarted every German attempt to capture the city.

Leningrad's defences set new standards of sophistication for the defence of a modern major city. Operating skillfully under the most trying of circumstances, the Northern and Leningrad Fronts erected complex and deeply echeloned defences along the most critical southern and southwestern approaches to the city that incorporated the entire depth of the blockaded region and the city itself. For the first time during the war, the defences consisted of multiple fortified defensive lines, incorporating continuous trench lines, defensive regions, positions and lines, and fortified regions, which while durable, also permitted forces to manoeuvre. The defence incorporated trenches, fortifications (pillboxes and bunkers), extensive obstacles, overhead cover for troops, and anti-artillery, anti-tank and anti-aircraft defences in the city itself. Most importantly, for the first time in the twentieth century, the defence of the city worked. Subsequently, the successful defence of Leningrad generated practical experiences that contributed to the defence of other cities, such as Stalingrad, and the contents of numerous Red Army directives, regulations and instructions on the defence of cities and defence in general. These techniques also proved valuable to the Red Army when it conquered German-occupied cities such as Poznan, Breslau, Budapest and Berlin.

For the first time in recent military history, the Leningrad and Volkhov Fronts solved the problem of defeating a large blockading force and raising a siege by operations from inside and outside the besieged city. Despite the privations wrought by the siege and the often harsh weather conditions, the Leningrad Front organized its own attacks from within the city and successfully broke out, defeating a strong enemy grouping in the process. It accomplished this feat, however, only after repeated failures and with the vital assistance of the Volkhov Front attacking from the outside. This required close coordination between the two fronts attacking from within and from without, which they did not achieve until January 1943.

Examples of Deep Echeloning

The Leningrad Front's Operation Spark in January 1943, which it conducted across the ice of the Neva River against well-prepared enemy defences in winter conditions, was also unique because it required skillful employment and coordination of artillery and engineers to cross the river successfully. Likewise, the Leningrad Front's Operation Neva (the Ropsha-Krasnoe Selo offensive operation) in January 1944 was also unique in that the two forces conducting the initial operation were only 10–15km (6.25–9.3 miles) apart. This required deep echeloning to penetrate German defences and deal with enemy tactical and operational reserves. The offensive skillfully employed artillery support and tailored assault groups to overcome enemy strongpoints.

However, these successful operations were punctuated by a host of major and minor offensive defeats, all characterized by similar mistakes and appallingly high Red Army losses. The Liuban disaster and the destruction of the Second Shock Army in July 1942 headed this undistinguished list of defeats, followed closely by the Siniavino defeat of September 1942, when the new Second Shock Army once again perished. These and other defeats at Siniavino, Krasnyi Bor, Mga and Tosno in 1943 underscored how difficult it was for the Red Army to educate itself in the conduct of modern war. In these defeats, and even in other successful military operations, Red Army commanders often displayed ineptitude in reconnaissance, command and control, combined-arms coordination and support, and the intricacies of sound logistical support. When they overcame these deficiencies they did so by a curiously Soviet combination of sheer force of will, callousness and cold brutality.

The Effect of Terrain

Admittedly, both the Leningrad and Volkhov Fronts conducted their operations in difficult terrain and equally difficult weather conditions. As the German Army learned in 1941, even during the summer, the forested, swampy and lake- and river-infested terrain severely inhibited military operations. In winter, when the temperature often plummeted to -10 degrees Fahrenheit and periodic thaws punctuated periods of extreme frost, operations of any sort, and particularly offensive operations, became exceedingly difficult to conduct. This was particularly true when inexperienced commanders and forces operated without communications and adequate artillery and armour support against well-prepared and deep defences manned by the world's best-trained and most experienced soldiers. Even when adequately supported, the Red Army's offensive operations against strong German defences required artillery, infantry and tanks to manoeuvre constantly in often heavily restrictive terrain and conduct river crossings over numerous major and minor rivers and streams.

Unlike in other theatres of war, the harsh terrain and weather conditions in the Leningrad region inhibited manoeuvres by tanks and artillery and the movement of supporting forces and supplies of any sort, particularly on the offense. This meant that Red Army infantry had to perform the bulk of the defensive and offensive fighting, often in terrain that required them to operate in small groups separated from one another. In these conditions, artillery support was critical to

defensive and offensive success. Thus, the Leningrad Front used artillery to help defeat the German September assault on the city by firing its artillery and employing aviation counter-preparation. Despite severe shortages of weaponry and ammunition, the artillery fire disorganized and weakened the German attack sufficiently for infantry and tanks to hold out. Later, Red Army artillery played a vital role in penetrating the heavy German defences by softening up enemy defences prior to infantry and tank assaults, in a direct fire mode to destroy specific German strongpoints, and in a counter-battery role to counter German artillery.

Unlike other sectors of the front, where large tank forces proved decisive in achieving victory, at Leningrad the Red Army had to operate and ultimately achieve victory without large-scale armour support because the poor terrain, harsh weather conditions and limited road network restricted the employment of tracked vehicles. Those small tank forces that operated in the region did so at considerable cost. The two Fronts employed separate tank brigades, regiments and battalions primarily in small groups to provide infantry support during penetration operations, or to support specific groups, such as advanced guards or forward detachments during exploitation operations. In a few isolated instances, tank forces formed the nucleus of mobile tank groups designated to complete penetrations or lead exploitations. Additionally, for the first time in the war, amphibious tanks participated in river-crossing operations, for example, across the Neva River in January 1943.

The Question of Logistics

Given the restrictive terrain, the absence of trafficable roads and the strong German defences, engineer and sapper forces played a vital role both in preparing defences and supporting offensive operations. On the offensive, engineers prepared roads and jumping-off positions, cleared mines and obstacles prior to and during penetration operations, supported river crossings, helped overcome strong German defences, and supported forces moving across difficult terrain. Often engineers were integrated into rifle regiments and divisions and special-purpose task forces such as mobile tank groups and forward detachments.

The defence of Leningrad was the first instance when naval forces (Baltic Fleet and Ladoga Flotilla), aviation and air defence (PVO) forces were operationally subordinate to Front control. This permitted

ABOVE: To celebrate the end of the three-year siege, Leningraders decorated their city as best they could. These women office workers are putting up Soviet flags at the entrance to their building.

the Front commander to concentrate his forces more effectively on the most important defensive and offensive missions. For example, the *Stavka* formed a special operational aviation group subordinate to the Northwestern Direction Command on 14 August 1941 and, two months later, a similar group under the Leningrad Front. These groups, which centralized air forces under the Front commander and permitted him to employ them more effectively, served as models for Red Army air armies formed in 1942. Aviation in general, and long-range aviation in particular, played an equally vital role in both defensive and offensive operations, even in times when aircraft were in short supply.

Finally, as is the case in any offensive or defensive military operation in any war, logistics proved to be the single most important constraint on achieving success in the defence and on the offensive. This was particularly true of the Leningrad Front, whose forces remained besieged and deprived of routine supplies in virtually every operation up to January

1944. To a lesser extent, the Volkhov Front faced the same problem given its over-extended and often convoluted supply lines to Vologda, Moscow and the Soviet rear area. Rear-service forces also had to cope with the poor road network and severe weather and terrain conditions. The most impressive logistical feat during the Leningrad blockade was the construction and maintenance of the various ice roads across Lake Ladoga and between Leningrad, Kronshtadt and the Oranienbaum bridgehead. At the same time, hundreds of logistical organizations at every level of command struggled to supply forces with the ammunition, fuel and food necessary to sustain military operations. This was the case even after the blockade was lifted, since Red Army forces were advancing great distances across regions totally laid to waste by the Germans.

Since the war's end, historians have tended to treat military operations around Leningrad as a sideshow to more momentous operations elsewhere along the Soviet-German front. They have focused primarily on the symbolic significance of the Leningrad defence and its population's brave and stoic resistance. While these factors were important, so too were the military operations that took place in the region, even if many failed and they lacked

LEFT: A.A. Zhdanov, head of the Leningrad Party Committee, flanked by Party and military officials, is seen here congratulating the 45th Order of Lenin Rifle Division on receiving its Guards status. Such ceremonies were performed with increasing pomp as the war drew on and Russian patriotism was encouraged.

the drama associated with more famous battles in other front sectors.

As was the case with the Soviet Union as a whole, the Communist Party ruled supreme in all matters during the Leningrad blockade. Party leaders such as Zhdanov and Kuznetsov, and Party executive committees at the regional, district and city level, played a vital role in mobilizing the city's population and resources for defence, organizing the defence itself, and enforcing discipline, order and morale in the city and its defending forces. They did so while closely coordinating with, and in some instances dominating, military authorities. It is no coincidence that the militarily incompetent Voroshilov presided over so many operations in the region and Stalin's caustic henchman, Mekhlis, attended Meretskov during the failed Liuban offensive.

In a sense, strict and, at times, ruthless political control was necessary both to organize the city's defences so that it could survive and to counter natural panic, defeatism and even instances of sabotage that characterized Leningrad's existence during the days when it was most imperiled. Militarily, it was also required to steel the backbone of Leningrad's defenders when they faced Germans at the city's gates from late 1941 through 1942. The crude and callous ruthlessness of Zhukov in September, so incomprehensible to Western observers in peace or in war, takes on far greater meaning when considering the results of his actions. The cold hard fact is that Leningrad was saved in part by his actions, at a time when few, even Stalin, retained any hopes for

its salvation. On the other hand, there was far less excuse for applying the same ruthless methods in 1942, 1943 and 1944 that had saved the city during the initial year of war. While the Liuban and Siniavino disasters in 1942 could be attributed to inexperience, the failures of the summer of 1943 could not. Ultimately, Govorov, Meretskov and many of their army commanders learned how to operate effectively on the offense. Interestingly enough, however, they did not do so in the summer until their offensive against the Finns in June 1944.

As many authors have vividly pointed out, Leningrad's population paid the greatest price for the city's successful defence. They did so by defending the city as soldiers, air defenders or auxiliaries, by manning the city's factories, and by simply surviving the rigours of the worst siege in recent history.

Although Leningraders died by the hundreds of thousands, those that remained continued at their posts until liberation was assured. By virtue of their work, Leningrad's industry continued to produce and support the city's defence throughout the blockade. Their intensive work in industry and the supply effort created the reserves necessary to conduct the January 1943 offensive and the subsequent offensive that finally liberated the city in 1944. After the blockade was raised, industrial production increased sharply.

However, in human terms the price of victory was appalling. Although it will probably never be determined accurately, the cost in civilian dead probably reached one million. While the

Extraordinary Commission for the Investigating of Nazi War Crimes, which presented its findings at the Nuremberg War Crimes trials after the war's end, estimated that the blockade produced 642,000 civilian dead, this figure represents the low end of this gruesome spectrum. Recent estimates place civilian losses at between 800,000 and one million. The 800,000 figure juxtaposes Leningrad's prewar population of 2.5 million with its December 1943 population of 600,000, and takes into account the one million evacuees and 100,000 Red Army conscripts. The figure of one million includes the roughly 642,000 souls who died during the siege and another 400,000 who perished or otherwise disappeared during the evacuations.

The military casualties were nearly as staggering. During the two months of its existence, the Northern Front lost 85,459 killed, captured or missing and 62,905 wounded or sick for a total of 148,364 soldiers. It successor, the Leningrad Front, lost 467,525 killed, captured or missing and 1,287,373 wounded or sick for a total of 1,755,898 throughout four years of war. Two-thirds of these casualties occurred during the Battle for Leningrad. The Volkhov Front lost 298,623 killed, captured or missing, and 667,234 wounded or sick for a total of

965,857 casualties during its existence. Finally, in almost four years of war, the Karelian Front suffered 110,435 killed, captured or missing and 309,825 wounded for 420,260 total casualties. Finally, the Fourth, Fifty-Second and Seventh Separate Armies lost roughly 56,000 killed, captured or missing and 91,000 wounded or sick for a total of 147,000 casualties over the course of their existence. By the war's end, by conservative official count, the fighting in the Leningrad region had cost the Red Army 1,017,881 killed, captured or missing, and 2,418,185 wounded or sick, for a total loss of 3,437,066 soldiers. This figure represented just over 10 percent of the Red Army's 10 million wartime killed, captured or missing, more than 13 percent of its 18.2 million wounded or sick, and 12 percent of its 28.2 million total casualties.

Considering the northwestern strategic axis as a whole, one must also add the Northwestern, Baltic and Second Baltic Fronts' casualties. The

BELOW: Throughout the siege good relations between the armed forces and the civilian population had been encouraged. To this end, visiting the wounded was regarded by many as a serious duty. In this case a young girl, dressed in her finest and looking very healthy, is delivering the post to a hospital ward.

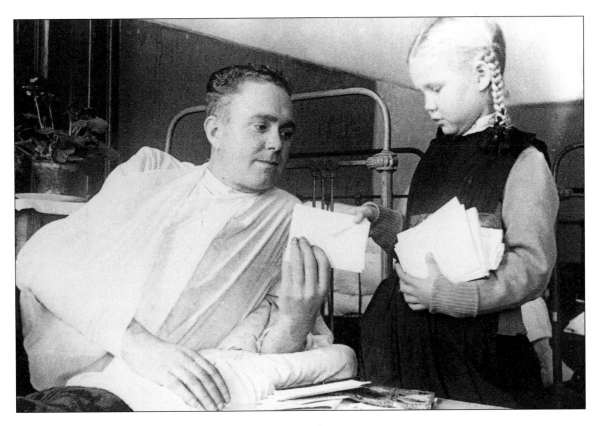

Northwestern Front lost 88,798 killed, captured or missing, 246,653 wounded or sick, for a total of 335,451 casualties between 1941 and 1943. In addition, from its formation in late 1943 to 1945, the Baltic Front and its successor, the Second Baltic Front, lost 39,579 killed, captured or missing and 152,097 wounded or sick for a total of 525,127 casualties. When added to the losses in the Battle for Leningrad, this results in 1,146,258 killed, captured or missing and 2,816,925 wounded or sick, for a total of 3,964,193 casualties suffered in fighting along the northwestern strategic axis. The total represents 11.4 percent of the Red Army's total wartime killed, captured or missing, 15.4 percent of its total wounded and sick, and 14 percent of its total wartime casualties. These percentages reflect the relative importance of the northwestern axis with respect to the western, southwestern and southern axes.

Thus, the number of soldiers and civilians who perished during the Battle for Leningrad amounted to the awesome total of between 1.6 and two million souls. These figures associated with the defence of a single city are six times greater than the United States' total death toll during the entirety of World War II.

In the broadest sense, the course and outcome of the Battle for Leningrad represented the entire Great

ABOVE: A child being evacuated from Leningrad during the siege. Hitler had commented that the Slavs were "a rabbit family who would never proceed beyond the family association if not forced to do so by a ruling class." But those at Leningrad successfully defied his so-called "master race" for three years.

Patriotic War in microcosm. The fierce defence in mid-1941, the dramatic rebuff to the Germans in late 1941, the abortive attempts to penetrate the blockade in 1942, the cracking of the blockade in 1943, and the unambiguous victories of 1944 parallel the Red Army's feats elsewhere along the Soviet-German front. However, while the turning point in the Red Army's fortunes on the Soviet-German front as a whole occurred between Stalingrad in November 1942 and Kursk in July 1943, that turn in the north did not occur until January 1944. This was so because by 1943 both sides understood that the war would be won or lost along the western and southwestern axes.

Although the Battle for Leningrad played a significant role in the war's ultimate outcome, its role was not militarily decisive . In terms of drama, symbolism and sheer human suffering, however, the Battle for Leningrad has no peer either in the Great Patriotic War or in any other modern war.

CHAPTER 1 NOTES

1 Once fully developed, the city encompassed an area of 570 square kilometres (369 square miles), bordered on the north by the Pargolovo highlands, on the south by the Pulkova, Duderhof and Ligovo highlands, and on the east by the Koltushi highlands. Its coastal climate, characterized by mild winters and frequent thaws, contrasts sharply with that of the remainder of Russia. The city's average temperature is 7.9 degrees (C) in January and 17.7 degrees in July. The adjacent Neva River is generally frozen for four months each year.

2 The construction required wooden piles be driven into the earth to provide a firm foundation.

3 St. Petersburg remained the Russian Empire's capital from 1712, when Peter the Great moved his court to the city, to 1728, when Catherine the Great's son and successor, Peter II, who disliked the city, moved the imperial court back to Moscow. After Peter II's death at age 15, his successor, Anne, moved the capital back to St. Petersburg in 1732.

4 Although St. Petersburg often eclipsed Moscow, the latter, whose population reached 306,000 in 1830 and 1,092,000 in 1905, gradually became Russia's main centre of manufacturing and trade, particularly for the textile industry, and of intellectual life, through Moscow University.

5 These included V. G. Belinsky, N. G. Chernyshevsky, N. A. Dobroliubov and D. I. Pisarev.

6 While the old Tsarist Army was demobilizing in February 1918 and the Red Guard was being transformed into a new Red Army, the Germans advanced on Petrograd, Belorussia, the Ukraine and Odessa. The Red Guards' and Red Army's failure to halt the Germans forced the new Bolshevik government to negotiate the Treaty of Brest-Litovsk, which established the Soviet Union's border along the western border of Petrograd region.

7 A total of 170,000 Leningraders served in the Red Army during the Civil War. As a result, a 5 December 1919 decree of the 7th All-Russian Congress of Soviets awarded the Leningrad proletariat with the Order of the Red Banner.

8 Introduced at the 10th Party Congress, the New Economic Policy (NEP) permitted some private property to exist in the agricultural and industrial arenas.

9 Stalin blamed Kirov's 1 December 1934 murder on a Trotskyite student and, by extension, on Trotsky.

10 The Leningrad Military District's commanders included A. I. Egorov (April–September 1921), V. M. Gittlis (September 1921–October 1925), B. M. Shaposhnikov (October 1925–May 1927 and September 1935–June 1937), A. I. Kork (May 1927–June 1931), M. N. Tukhachevsky (May 1928–June 1931), I. P. Belov (June 1931–September 1935), P. E. Dybenko (June 1937–April 1938), M. S. Khozin (April 1938–January 1939), K. A. Meretskov (January 1939–January 1940), S. K. Timoshenko

(January–June 1940), M. P. Kirponis (June 1940–January 1941), and M. M. Popov (January–June 1941). Many of these fell victim to the purges.

11 The LMD headquarters directed operations during the war's first phase from 30 November 1939 through 9 February 1940, but suffered embarrassing defeats in all sectors. The Northwestern Front, created on 7 January 1940 on the base of the LMD, directed operations in the second phase from 10 February until the war's end in March 1940. The Northwestern Front was dissolved on 26 March 1940, when its forces returned to LMD control.

12 The 1336 aircraft included 394 bombers, 902 fighters and 40 reconnaissance aircraft.

13 Subsequently, the NKO reorganized the LMD's headquarters into the Northern Front on 24 June 1941, and, in turn, subdivided the Northern Front into the Karelian and Leningrad Fronts on 23 August 1941. The Northern and Leningrad Fronts continued to fulfill the responsibilities of the district military headquarters. The NKO reformed the Leningrad Military District on 15 July 1941 as the Northern Front's rear service organ, and the General Staff subordinated the new military district to the Northern Front on 25 July 1941. The NKO finally disbanded the LMD on 21 August 1941 to fill out the Leningrad Front's headquarters.

14 Subsequently, the NKO reorganized the 2nd PVO Corps into the Leningrad PVO Corps Region in November 1942 to improve command and control. Later, it supplemented the Leningrad Corps Region with the Ladoga PVO Brigade Region and transformed it into the Leningrad PVO Army, commanded by Major-General of the Coastal Service G. S. Zashikhin, in January 1942.

15 The Kronshtadt base was founded as the Petrograd Naval Base in March 1919, but was abolished after the Civil War. On 6 November 1939, a Soviet Naval Fleet (*Voenny Morskoi Flot* – VMF) order re-established the base because of the deteriorating international situation and used it as a base for the Baltic Fleet during the Soviet-Finnish War. After the war's end the VMF deactivated the base on 5 July 1940, but reactivated in once again in October 1941 as the Baltic Fleet's primary base for the defence of Leningrad.

16 The naval base's existence dated back to 1809–1917, when the Russian Empire controlled Hango. The base reverted to Finland in 1917. In turn, the Finns turned the port over to the Soviet Union in March 1940 on the basis of a 30-year lease and the Soviet Union turned it into a fortified naval base.

17 The flotilla's commanders were Captain 2d Rank S. V. Zemlianichenko (June–July 1941), Vice-Admiral P. A. Trainin (July 1941), Captain 1st Rank V. P. Bogolepov (July–August 1941), Captain 1st Rank (Vice Admiral on 16 September) B. V. Khoroshkhin (August–October 1941), and Captain 1st Rank (Vice Admiral from January 1944) V. S. Cherikov (October 1941–November 1944).

CHAPTER 2 NOTES

1 The directive's final objective was "the establishment of a defensive barrier against Asiatic Russia along the general line of the Volga and Arkhangel'sk." Based upon its previous military performance and the presumed state of the opposing Red Army, German military planners assumed the Wehrmacht could accomplish this task within eight to 10 weeks. So confident was Hitler of victory, that on 11 June 1941 he issued yet another directive (No 32) ordering 60 divisions be left on security duty in occupied Russia so that the bulk of the Wehrmacht could be deployed elsewhere.

2 The force totalled 20 infantry, three panzer and three motorized divisions.

3 The two motorized corps consisted of the 1st and 6th Panzer and 36th Motorized Divisions and the 8th Panzer and 3rd Motorized Divisions, respectively.

4 The Eighteenth Army consisted of XXVI, XXXVIII and I Army Corps and the Sixteenth Army contained X, XXVIII and II Army Corps.

5 Kuznetsov's military district fielded 269,702 men, 7019 guns and mortars, 1549 tanks (1274 operational), and 1262 combat aircraft (1078 operational) on 22 June 1941.

6 Once at Daugavpils on the Dvina, Hitler ordered Hoepner's Fourth Panzer Group to advance on Ostrov, but von Leeb ordered a 12-hour delay to permit the Sixteenth Army to catch up with his advancing panzers.

7 The *Stavka* gave Kuznetsov three rifle corps from *Stavka* reserve with which to do so.

8 North of Leningrad, the Northern Front's Seventh Army (three rifle divisions) defended the border north of Lake Ladoga, and the Twenty-Third Army, consisting of XIX and L Rifle Corps with four rifle divisions, and the 198th Motorized Division, defended from the Gulf of Finland to west of Lake Ladoga.

9 To the north, the Finnish Army was to assault Leningrad from the northwest between Lakes Onega and Ladoga and assist Army Group North in capturing Leningrad.

10 The Luga Defence Line was intended to be a 10–15km (6.25–9.3–mile) -deep defence of barriers, minefields and anti-tank guns behind the Luga River, 100km (62 miles) south of Leningrad. At the same time, Popov had to defend the city's northern approaches with his Twenty-Third Army and the approaches into central Karelia and Murmansk in the far north with his Seventh and Fourteenth Armies.

11 The LOG consisted initially of the 70th, 171st, 177th and 191st Rifle Divisions, the 1st, 2nd and 3rd People's Militia Divisions (DNO), the 1st Separate Mountain Rifle Brigade, and supporting artillery.

12 When the first of the LOG's divisions, the 177th Rifle, arrived south of Luga on 4 July, the line was so incomplete that an additional 25,000 labourers were mobilized to accelerate its construction. Thereafter, additional forces occupied the defences, while the front inched perilously northwards towards it. The 191st Rifle Division occupied the Kingisepp sector, the 111th Rifle Division, which had been shattered in fighting east of Pskov, withdrew to back up the 177th south of Luga, and the remaining forces filtered into position between 10 and 14 July. As of 14 July, the LOG consisted of the 177th and 191st Rifle Divisions, XXXXI Rifle Corps' 90th, 111th, 118th and 235th Rifle Divisions, the 1st Mountain Rifle Brigade, the 1st, 2nd and 4th DNOs, and the Leningrad "S. M. Kirov" infantry and rifle-machine gun school.

13 The Rear Line Construction Directorate (USTOR) was headed by Major-General P. A. Zaitsev, Popov's Deputy Commander for Fortified Regions, and employed construction forces and 30,000 civilians to work round-the-clock on the new defences.

14 Stalin established the State Defence Committee (GKO), a virtual war cabinet, on 30 June to control the State's management of the war more effectively. On 10 July Stalin reorganized the *Stavka* (headquarters) of the Main Command (SHK), which had been organized on 24 June to centralize the control of military operations, into the *Stavka* of the High Command (SVK) with himself as its chairman. Later, on 8 August, Stalin assumed the title of Supreme High Commander, and thereafter the organ was known as the *Stavka* of the Supreme High Command (SVGK).

15 On 10 July, the LOG consisted of the 191st and 177th Rifle Divisions, the 1st and 2nd DNOs, the 1st Sep. Mountain Rifle Brigade, and XXXXI Rifle Corps (111th, 90th, 235th and 118th Rifle Divisions), the latter refitting east of Luga.

16 Vatutin's plan called for the Northwestern Front's Eleventh Army to counterattack along the Sol'tsy-Dno axis with two shock groups. The northern group's 21st Tank Division of I Mechanized Corps and the 70th and 237th Rifle Divisions of XVI Rifle Corps were to attack the 8th Panzer Division's exposed positions around Sol'tsy from the north. Other LOG's forces to the west and the 1st DNO and 1st Mountain Rifle Brigade defending along the Novgorod axis were to support and reinforce the northern group's assault. The southern group, which consisted of XXII Rifle Corps' 180th, 182nd and 183rd Rifle Divisions, was to attack Sol'tsy from the east with the 183rd Rifle Division; the other two divisions were to strike the 8th Panzer Division's communications routes to the southwest.

17 While the bulk of Leeb's army group was attacking towards Leningrad, Eighteenth Army elements were clearing Soviet forces from the army group's left flank in Estonia and along the Baltic coast to deprive the Soviets of vital naval and air facilities in the region. Between 11 July and 28 August, the Eighteenth Army's XXVI and XXXXII Army Corps defeated the Soviet Eighth Army and occupied Tartu, Parnu and Tallin. The *Stavka* ordered Tallin evacuated on 26 August. At a cost of heavy losses, including roughly 20,000 prisoners, the Soviet defence of Estonia tied down four German divisions and marginally weakened the German Luga and Novgorod groupings. Thereafter, in September and October, German forces seized the Moon Islands off the Estonian coast while Finnish forces eliminated the Soviet naval base at Hango.

18 The LOG's 1st DNO and 1st Separate Mountain Rifle Brigade defended the Shimsk-Novgorod axis.

19 The command transferred the 272nd Rifle Division to the Seventh Army at Petrozavodsk, the 265th Rifle Division to the Twenty-Third Army on the Karelian Isthmus, the 268th Rifle Division to the Eighth Army in Estonia, and the 281st Rifle Division to the Kingisepp defensive sector.

20 *Stavka* Letter No 1, dated 15 July, to the Northern Front abolished the rifle corps link within armies and created smaller armies, consisting of five to six divisions each for ease of control.

21 The Kingisepp Sector, made up of Baltic Fleet coastal units, the 90th and 191st Rifle Divisions, the 2nd DNO and 4th Light DNO, the Leningrad Infantry School, the 14th Anti-Tank Brigade, Armoured Train No 60, and the 519th RVK Howitzer Artillery Regiment, was responsible for defending the Kingisepp axis. The Luga Sector had the mission of protecting the Luga highway axis with the 111th, 177th and 235th Rifle Divisions, the 2nd Tank Division, the 1st Rifle Regiment, 3rd DNO, the 260th and 262nd Machine gun-Artillery Battalions, and the Leningrad Artillery School's Rifle-machine Gun School and Battalion. Finally, the Eastern Sector, consisting of the 1st DNO, 1st Separate Mountain Rifle Brigade, and the 261st and 263rd Machine gun-Artillery Battalions, was to protect the Novgorod axis. Major-General V. V. Semashko commanded the Kingisepp Sector and Major-Generals A. N. Astanin and F. N. Starikov commanded the Luga and Eastern Sectors, respectively. Presumably, General Piadyshev was arrested for dereliction of duty.

22 The *Stavka* had already dispatched nine rifle and two cavalry divisions to the Northwestern Front by early August.

23 Commanded by Lieutenant-General S. D. Akimov, the Forty-Eighth Army consisted of the 1st DNO, the 70th, 128th and 237th Rifle Divisions, the 1st Separate Mountain Rifle Brigade, and the 21st Tank Division.

24 Fuehrer Directive No 34 of 30 July provided even more precise instructions regarding the capture of Leningrad.

25 The Eighteenth Army's XXXXII Army Corps was to join the advance after it had captured Tallin and completed operations in Estonia.

26 The 58th Infantry Division protected the Northern Group's left flank.

27 The Sixteenth Army comprised X, II, L and XXIII Army Corps deployed from north to south.

28 Soviet critiques credit the failure to the difficult terrain, poor command and control, lack of adequate anti-aircraft support, and the quick reaction of Army Group North.

29 See Luttichau manuscript.

30 Erickson, 189.

31 This force included the remnants of the Eighth Army's 48th, 125th, 191st, 268th, 11th and 118th Rifle Divisions and the 1st Naval Infantry Brigade, and the Kingisepp Defensive Sector's 2nd DNO, 1st Guards DNO, and the1st Tank and 281st Rifle Divisions.

32 See Luttichau manuscript.

33 Erickson, 187.

34 The Fifty-Fourth Army was formed in late August and early September under Marshal G. I. Kulik. Under *Stavka* control, it was formed on the base of XXXXIV Rifle Corps and consisted of the 285th, 286th, 310th and 314th Rifle Divisions, 27th Cavalry Division, 122nd Tank Brigade, and 119th Separate Tank Battalion. Its mission was to defend along the Volkhov River. The Fourth Army, commanded by Lieutenant-General V. F. Iakovlev, formed in late September under *Stavka* control. It consisted of the 285th, 292nd and 311th Rifle Divisions and the 27th Cavalry Division (the 285th Rifle and 27th Cavalry Divisions from the Fifty-Fourth Army). It deployed along the Volkhov River in early October. The Fifty-Second Army, commanded by Lieutenant-General N. K. Klykov, formed in August 1941 on the base of XXV Rifle Corps as a separate army under *Stavka* control. It consisted of the 276th, 285th, 288th, 292nd, 312th, 314th and 316th Rifle Divisions and occupied defences along the Volkhov River at the end of August.

35 XXXIX Motorized Corps consisted of the 12th and 18th Panzer and 20th Motorized Divisions.

36 This thrust was to be supported by the First Air Fleet and VII Air Corps.

37 The NAG consisted of the remnants of XVI Rifle Corps' 237th Rifle Division, the 1st Mountain Rifle Brigade, and the fresh 305th Rifle Division.

38 The Fifty-Fifth Army, under Major-General I. G. Lazarev, was to defend the western portion of the sector with the 168th, 70th, 90th and 237th Rifle Divisions, the 4th DNO, and the Slutsk-Kolpino Fortified Region. The Forty-Second Army, under Lieutenant-General F. S. Ivanov, was to defend the eastern sector and Krasnogvardeisk proper with the 2nd and 3rd DNOs, the 291st Rifle Division, and the Krasnogvardeisk Fortified Region.

39 Popov ordered the Forty-Eighth Army to employ the refitted 311th and 128th Rifle Divisions and 1st Separate Mountain Rifle Brigade in the larger counterattack.

40 The 122nd Infantry Division attempted to cross the Izhora River at Ivanovskoe.

41 The encircled forces included the 111th, 177th, 90th, 70th, 235th, 237th Rifle Divisions, the 1st and 3rd DNO, and the 24th Tank Division.

42 The directive went on to state: "First and foremost, however, it is necessary to strive to encircle Leningrad completely, at least from the east, and, if weather conditions permit, conduct a large-scale air offensive on Leningrad. It is especially important to destroy the water supply stations. As soon as possible, Army Group North's force must begin an offensive northwards in the Neva River sector to help the Finns overcome the fortifications

along the old Soviet-Finnish border, and also to shorten the frontlines and deprive the enemy of the ability to use the air bases. In cooperation with the Finns, prevent enemy naval forces from exiting Kronstadt into the Baltic Sea (Hango and the Moonzund Islands) by using mine obstacles and artillery fire.

"Also, isolate the region of combat operations at Leningrad from the sector along the lower reaches of the Volkhov as soon as forces necessary to perform this mission become available. Link up with the Karelian Army on the Svir River only when enemy forces have been destroyed in the Leningrad region."

43 XXXXI Motorized Corps consisted of the 1st, 6th and 8th Panzer and 36th Motorized Divisions, and XXXIX Motorized Corps the 12th Panzer, and 18th and 20th Motorized Divisions. Eighteenth Army consisted of XXVI, XXXVIII, L and XXVIII Army Corps.

44 XXXVIII Army Corps consisted of the 1st, 58th, 291st and later 254th Infantry Divisions, and L Army Corps the SS Police and 269th Infantry Divisions.

45 XXVIII Army Corps consisted of the 121st, 96th and 122nd Infantry Divisions.

46 The Forty-Second Army consisted of the 2nd and 3rd Guards DNOs, and the Krasnogvardeisk Fortified Region.

47 The Fifty-Fifth Army consisted of the 90th, 70th, 168th Rifle Divisions, the 1st and 4th DNOs, the Slutsk-Kolpino Fortified Region, and the 84th and 86th Tank Battalions.

48 The Eighth Army's 191st, 118th, 11th and 281st Rifle Divisions defending opposite XXXVIII Army Corps.

49 In addition, the 155th Rifle and 1st NKVD Rifle Divisions defended the Neva River front east of Leningrad.

50 The Forty-Eighth Army was disbanded on 14 September, and its forces were transferred to the Fifty-Fourth Army.

51 These included the 500th Rifle Regiment on 10 September, the 1st Naval Infantry Brigade on 12 September, and the newly formed 5th DNO on the same day.

52 The 2nd DNO and 500th Rifle Regiment defended Dutergov, the 3rd DNO and 1st Naval Infantry Brigade Krasnoe Selo, and the 5th DNO Pulkovo.

53 The 168th Rifle Division defended the Fedorovskoe sector east of Slutsk.

54 See Luttichau manuscript.

55 The reported presence of the 27th Cavalry Division on Schmidt's flank was incorrect.

56 When the 8th Panzer arrived at XXXIX Corps three days later, it was no longer needed.

57 Indicative of his mood, Stalin had sent a letter to Churchill on 3 September describing the deteriorating situation in the Ukraine and at Leningrad, lamenting the absence of a second front and large-scale material aid, and describing the effects on Britain of Soviet defeat. In the letter, Stalin suggested that Churchill send up to 30 divisions to Arkhangel'sk or via Iran to help the Red Army. Churchill noted the letter's "utter unreality" in a remark of 15 September. See Luttichau draft.

58 The Military Council was enlarged on 17 September by the addition of Admiral I. S. Isakov, Chief of the Main Naval Staff and *Stavka* representative.

59 The 3rd Guards DNO's and 1st Naval Infantry Brigade defended north of Krasnoe Selo; the villages of Sosnovka and Finskoe Koirovo changed hands several times during the fighting.

60 Uritsk was defended by the Forty-Second Army's 10th and 11th Rifle Divisions.

61 The new defence line extended from Ligovo through Miasokombinat to Rybatskoe.

62 Erickson, 192.

63 Shcherbakov was to make his attack with the 191st and 281st Rifle Divisions, reinforced by the 10th and 11th Rifle Divisions, and the remnants of the Forty-Second Army's 3rd DNO. While doing so, he was to protect his extended right flank by withdrawing the 5th Naval Infantry Brigade to new defences along the Kovashi River and retain the 125th and 286th Rifle Divisions in reserve.

64 The Eighth Army's front finally stabilized along the Novyi Petergof, Tomuzi and Petrovskaia line.

65 Soviet accounts claim that intelligence forewarned the Leningrad Front and its army commands of the impending attack, permitting them to deal effectively with it.

66 Pulkovo Heights were defended by the 5th DNO, the 500th Rifle Regiment and the 5th Separate Machine-gun Artillery Battalion.

67 The NOG had been organized on 2 September from the 46th and 115th Rifle Divisions and the 4th Armoured Car Regiment. Kulik's Fifty-Fourth Army consisted of the 128th and 310th Rifle Divisions, the 21st Tank Division, and the 1st Mountain Rifle Brigade from the former Forty-Eighth Army, reinforced in late September by the 3rd and 4th Guards and

286th and 294th Rifle Divisions, and the 16th and 122nd Tank Brigades. Its strength was 85,000 men.

68 Although court-martialed for his failure and reduced to the rank of major-general, later the politically loyal Kulik would return to army command with predictably poor results.

69 The Germans transferred two parachute regiments of the 7th Parachute Division from Germany, one infantry regiment from Army Group Centre, the Spanish 250th "Blue" Division, and the 72nd Infantry Division from Western Europe to the Leningrad region. In addition, it forced Leeb to transfer the 8th Panzer Division and part of the 96th Infantry Division from south of Leningrad to the Siniavino sector.

70 Soviet sources claim that Leeb's forces fighting for the coastal bridgehead and the Krasnogvardeisk and Slutsk-Kolpino Fortified Regions suffered 40-50 percent losses (killed or wounded).

71 XXXIX Motorized Corps took with it the 1st, 6th, 8th Panzer and 36th Motorized Divisions. To compensate for this loss, the OKH began transferring the 227th and 212th Infantry Divisions from France to Army Group North.

72 The 6th Panzer Division departed late on 15 September, the 1st Panzer Division on 19 September, the 36th Motorized Division on 20 September, and the corps headquarters on 20 September.

73 Erickson, 195.

74 The front north of Leningrad also stabilized on the Karelian Isthmus and along the Svir River.

CHAPTER 3 NOTES

1 The Twenty-Third Army fielded the 43rd, 123rd, 142nd, 198th, 265th and 291st Rifle Divisions, a special NKVD Rifle Brigade, the 22nd Fortified Region, and the 48th and 106th Separate Tank Battalions. The Eighth Army consisted of XVI Rifle Corps' 10th, 11th and 85th Rifle Divisions, the 48th, 80th, 191st and 281st Rifle Divisions, the 2nd Naval Infantry Brigade, the 76th Separate Latvian Rifle Regiment, the 2nd Separate Tank Regiment, and an armoured car battalion.

2 The Forty-Second Army defended the 17km (10.6-mile) sector from Ligovo to Pulkovo with two rifle divisions in first echelon and three rifle divisions and one naval infantry and one rifle brigade in second echelon, supported by the Baltic Fleet. The army consisted of the 13th, 44th, 56th, 189th and 21st NKVD Rifle Divisions, the 6th and 7th Naval Infantry Brigades, the 268th, 282nd and 291st Separate Machine gun-Artillery Battalions, and the 51st Separate Tank Battalion, and supporting artillery and engineers. The Fifty-Fifth Army defended the 30km (18.75-mile) sector from east of Pulkovo to the Neva River at Putrolovo with five rifle divisions in first echelon and one in second echelon, with a fortified region (seven separate artillery-machine gun battalions) occupying cut-off positions to the rear. The Fifty-Fifth Army fielded the 70th, 86th, 90th, 125th, 168th and 268th Rifle Divisions, the 17th Rifle Division's 55th Rifle Regiment, the Slutsk-Kolpino Fortified Region, and the 84th and 86th Separate Tank Battalions. The Neva Operational Group defended northwards along the Neva to Lake Ladoga with the 115th and NKVD Rifle Divisions, the 4th Naval Infantry Brigade, and the 1st, 4th and 5th Destroyer and 107th Separate Tank Battalions.

3 The ESOG consisted of the 265th, 86th, 20th, 191st and 177th Rifle Divisions, the 123rd and 124th Tank Brigades, the 107th Separate Tank Battalion, and supporting artillery.

4 Khozin's shock group consisted of the 3rd and 4th Guards and 310th Rifle Divisions, 16th and 122nd Tank Brigades, and two artillery regiments. Khozin's 286th and 294th Rifle Divisions supported the attack on the shock group's flanks, and the 128th Rifle Division, 1st Mountain Rifle Brigade and 21st Tank Division either conducted local attacks or defended the remainder of the army's sector.

5 On the *Stavka's* orders, Khozin resumed the Siniavino offensive on 2 November, this time with even stronger forces, but the offensive failed after several days of heavy fighting.

6 The Fourth Army included the 285th, 311th and 292nd Rifle Divisions, the 27th Cavalry Division, and the 119th Separate Tank Battalion. One rifle regiment was in reserve.

7 The Fifty-Second Army included the 288th and 267th Rifle Divisions, whose 6000 men each defended sectors of 46 and 34km (28.75 and 21.25 miles) respectively.

8 The NAG consisted of the 305th and 180th Rifle and 43rd Tank Divisions.

9 In accordance with *Stavka* instructions, the Fifty-Fourth Army transferred its 310th and 4th Guards Rifle Divisions to the Fourth Army on 23 October. At the same time, the *Stavka* moved the Leningrad Front's 191st Rifle Division to Sitomlia, 40km (25 miles) southwest of Tikhvin, and the 44th Rifle Division to Tikhvin by air to occupy defences along the Sias' River, 20km (12.5 miles) to the 191st Rifle Division's rear. In addition, the *Stavka* sent the 92nd Rifle and 60th Tank Divisions to the Tikhvin region from its reserves on 30 October. Meanwhile, on 20 October, the Northwestern Front reinforced the Fifty-Second Army with its 259th Rifle Division and a Katiusha battalion.

10 The Fifty-Second Army now consisted of the 288th, 267th and 259th Rifle Divisions.

11 The Germans captured Kalinin on 17 October and seemed capable of attacking northwest along the Moscow-Leningrad railroad line. However, the *Stavka* mounted a major counterstroke, planned and led by Vatutin, against German forces defending Kalinin. The counterstroke, which was the first serious reverse suffered by German forces in Operation Typhoon, almost recaptured the city and certainly ended Wehrmacht hopes of advancing northwestwards to support Leeb at Tikhvin.

12 The two Fourth Army shock groups consisted of the 191st Rifle Division and one regiment each from the 44th Rifle and 60th Tank Divisions in the Sitomlia region, and the 4th Guards Rifle Division and two regiments of the 60th Tank Division 25km (15.6 miles) to the south.

13 This counterattack was timed to coincide with the Leningrad Front's failed attempt to revive its offensive at Siniavino.

14 The Fourth Army's headquarters abandoned its records and all of its vehicles in its haste to escape Tikhvin.

15 The Fourth Army defended the Volkhov axis with its 285th, 311th and 310th Rifle Divisions, and part of the 292nd Rifle Division.

16 The 310th Rifle Division counterattacked near Zelenets Station.

17 Meretskov, who had served as Chief of the Red Army General Staff before January 1941, was imprisoned on groundless charges of treason.

18 These were the 285th, 310th, 311th and 292nd Rifle Divisions and the 6th Naval Infantry Brigade.

19 On 1 December Meretskov's Fourth Army consisted of the 4th Guards, 44th, 65th, 92nd and 191st Rifle Divisions, the 1st Grenadier Rifle Brigade, the 27th Cavalry Division, the 60th Tank Division, the 46th Tank Brigade, and the 119th, 120th and 128th Separate Tank Battalions.

20 The Northern Group consisted of two regiments of the 44th Rifle Division, the 167th Rifle Regiment, the 46th Tank Brigade, and the 159th Pontoon Battalion. The Eastern Group contained one regiment of the 44th Rifle Division, the 191st and 27th Cavalry Divisions, the 60th Tank Division's 120th Regiment, and the 128th Separate Tank Battalion.

21 The Southern Group consisted of the 92nd and 4th Guards Rifle Divisions and one regiment of the 292nd Rifle Division.

22 On 1 December Fediuninsky's Fifty-Fourth Army consisted of the 3rd Guards, 80th, 128th, 285th, 286th, 294th, 310th and 311th Rifle Divisions, the 1st Mountain Rifle and 6th Naval Infantry Brigades, the 21st Tank Division (with no tanks), the 16th and 122nd Tank Brigades, and the 1st and 2nd Ski Battalions.

23 On 1 December Krykov's Fifty-Second Army consisted of the 111th, 259th, 267th and 288th Rifle Divisions. The Novgorod Army Group's 180th and 305th Rifle Divisions joined the Fifty-Second Army's attack, leaving the 3rd Tank Division, which lacked tanks and was being converted into the 25th Rifle Division, to defend the rest of its sector.

24 Klykov's attacked with his four divisions deployed across a 48km (30-mile) front and assaulted the strongpoint at Malaia Vishera with only two-regiments of the 259th Rifle Division.

25 The withdrawing Germans halted at an intermediate "swamp" position in mid-December, but fell back to the Volkhov River by the month's end.

26 The shock group consisted of the 3rd Guards, 310th and 311th Rifle Divisions and the 16th Naval Infantry Brigade.

27 The first shock group, formed on 1 December, consisted of the 80th, 311th and 285th Rifle Divisions, the 6th Naval Infantry Brigade, and the 122nd Tank Brigade.

28 According to official accounts, the Fifty-Fourth, Fourth and Fifty-Second Armies suffered 40,589 casualties, including 22,743 killed, captured or missing, in their Tikhvin defence out of 135,700 troops engaged. The Tikhvin counteroffensive cost the Red Army another 48,901 casualties, including 17,924 killed, captured or missing, out of 192,950 engaged. In addition, the Fifty-Fourth Army and Neva Operational Group lost 54,979 men, including 22,211 killed, captured or missing, out of 71,270 involved in the sideshow at Siniavino.

29 See Luttichau draft.

CHAPTER 4 NOTES

1 Zhdanov was, simultaneously, Secretary of the Leningrad Regional and City Party Committees, Communist Party Politburo member, *Stavka* advisor, Member of the Soviet Fleet's Main Military Council, and personal friend of Stalin.

2 The order read: "In accordance with the 22 June 1941 order of the Presidium of the USSR's Supreme Soviet, 'Concerning the Military Situation', and on the basis of the orders of the military authorities, the Executive Committee of the Leningrad City Council of Workers' Deputies has decided:

1. To enlist the services of able civilians of both sexes between the ages of 16 and 50 for men and between the ages of 16 and 45 for women, excluding workers working in defence industries, in (defensive) work…

5. To establish the following work routine for the fulfillment of work obligations:
a) Non-working work-capable civilians of both sexes — eight hours per day.
b) Office workers and workers — three hours per day after work.
c) Students of functioning educational institutions — three hours per day after class.

3 Ultimately, the population helped build the Pskov and Ostrov Fortified Regions, the Luga Defence Line and associated cut-off positions at Kingisepp, Luga, Batetskaia, Chudovo and Kirishi, and defensive regions and lines closer to Leningrad at Krasnogvardeisk, Uritsk, Pulkovo, Kolpino, and along the right bank of the Neva River.

4 For example, between 22 June and 13 September, Trusts Nos. 16, 53 and 55, Factory No. 5, and the Barricady, Kirov, Ordzhonikidze and Izhorsk Factories prepared 378 armoured and reinforced concrete gun-firing points, 678 machine-gun firing points, and 24,046 reinforced concrete anti-tank pyramids in the Luga, Kingisepp, Krasnogvardeisk and Slutsk-Kolpino Fortified Regions and the city of Leningrad. The official count stated that the population built 592km (370 miles) of open anti-tank ditches, 459km (286 miles) of escarpments and counter-escarpments, 48km (30 miles) of anti-tank obstacles, 134km (84 miles) of blockades, 24km (15 miles) of barricades, 667 anti-tank hedgehogs and *chevaux-de-frise*, 329km (206 miles) of barbed wire entanglements, 11,500 squad foxholes, 772km (482 miles) of communications trenches, 1527 shelters, 2072 command, observation and medical points, and about 4500 pillboxes and small and large bunkers between 22 June and 31 December 1941.

5 These included the Kirov, Moscow and Volodarsk sectors (districts) in the north and the Primorskii (coastal), Vyborg and Krasnogvardeisk sectors in the south.

6 The Forty-Second Army's anti-tank regions fielded 342 anti-tank guns, including 17 guns per kilometre of front. It deployed 50 percent of its anti-tank guns in its main defensive belt, 20 percent in the second belt and 30 percent on the city's outskirts.

7 Initially, the VOG consisted of a rifle brigade, ski detachment, two machine-gun companies, eight 45mm gun batteries, 18 sail (ice) boats, and four reserve companies.

8 The three divisions' total strength of 30,917 men fell 2–3000 men short of stated requirements.

9 The 2nd DNO was actually 653 men above its required strength. The 4th Guards DNO was renamed the 5th DNO on 11 September.

10 By 30 September, 96,776 Leningraders had volunteered for the People's Militia Army, including 20,647 Communist Party and 13,457 Komsomol members, and 32,000 women for auxiliary services.

11 A DNO consisted of three rifle regiments, one artillery regiment, a reconnaissance detachment, a communications company, a sapper battalion or company, a medical battalion, and an auto-transport company.

12 These were the 13th (5th DNO), 44th (3rd Gds. DNO), 56th (7th DNO), 80th (1st Gds. DNO), 85th (2nd DNO), 86th (7th DNO), and 189th (6th DNO) Rifle Divisions.

13 In addition to mobilizing militia, workers' detachments and women, military and Party organs provided the population with minimal military training to increase the combat readiness of workers' formations. On 3 March 1942, the city Party Bureau ordered factory directors and party secretaries to help regional military commissariats improve universal military training and strengthen Leningrad's defences. While Party organizations were responsible for meeting the minimal needs of DNOs and workers' and destruction detachments, factories provided weapons, equipment, uniforms and supplies to mobilizing units from their own internal resources above and beyond the requirements of normal production plans.

14 The GKO issued instruction on the employment of women on 23 March and 13 April 1942.

15 All lights were prohibited on the streets and in buildings, and protective covers masked necessary road and rail signals.

16 For example, the population of Oktiabrskii district dug more than 4000m (13,123ft) of slit trenches, prepared 214 basement bomb shelters, painted about one million square meters (3.28 million square feet) of attic covers with super-phosphates, and performed hundreds of other tasks within the first 45 days of war.

17 During this period, 280 German aircraft dropped 528 explosive and 135 incendiary bombs during six separate air raids on 19 September, and more than 200 explosive bombs in three separate raids on 27 September.

18 Production from 22 June to 31 December 1941 included thousands of mortars and submachine guns, three million shells and mines, 40,000 multiple rocket launcher rounds, more than 42,000 aerial bombs, great quantities of rifle ammunition, 491 tanks, and 317 artillery pieces.

19 Production during the first nine months of 1942 totalled 1935 mortars, 1975 heavy machine guns, 22,000 submachine guns, 187 tanks (repaired) and 360 guns (repaired). During the entire year, ammunition production totalled 1,700,000 shells and mines, 22,000 bombs, and 1,260,000 hand grenades.

20 During the first winter, special departments supplied 17,000 soldiers' families with fuel, more than 9000 families with daily monetary payments, more than 20,000 persons with shoes and clothing, and more than 10,000 families with living quarters. In addition, Komsomol social brigades and the Red Cross provided medical and food assistance to many families.

21 Specifically, the norms decreased on 2 and 7 September, 1 October, and 13 and 20 November. In decreasing order, the norms applied to five categories of people, including frontline soldiers, rear area troops, priority workers, engineers and technical personnel, and employees, dependents and children.

22 For example, the inhabitants of the region's southeastern district smuggled 305 tonnes (300 tons) of foodstuffs into the city from 28–30 January, and Leningraders received more than 509 tonnes (500 tons) of bread, meat and other products from occupied regions in May 1942. This was possible because rivers, lakes and swamps, impenetrable most of the year, froze and could be traversed in winter.

23 The Leningrad Front appointed Engineer 1st Rank V. G. Monakhov, the Deputy Chief of the front's Automobile-road Department, as the 101st BAD's commander. The situation was extremely precarious because the railroad connecting Kobona with Vologda and the Soviet interior was the last available rail route to the rear, and it ran through Volkhov, then threatened by German forces, and Tikhvin, which German forces had already captured. This forced the Leningrad Front to build and employ the much longer 102nd BAD, which bypassed Tikhvin until Soviet forces could recapture the town. The 102nd BAD, which was commanded by Major-General of the Quartermaster Service A. M. Shilov, absorbed the 101st BAD on 7 December after the Red Army recaptured Tikhvin. LMD history, 267.

24 Major A. S. Mozhaev's road exploitation regiment began reconnoitring and marking primary and alternative routes across the ice once Shlissel'burg Bay began freezing over in mid-November. The first reconnaissance group, consisting of the 88th Separate Bridge Construction Battalion, under Military-Technician 1st Rank V. Sokolov, marked the first route on 17 and 18 November, and the second group under Major Mozhaev himself reached Kobona the same day. However, the groups determined that the 100mm (3.93in) of ice was not sufficiently thick to support heavy transport, which required a minimum of 200mm (7.87in); therefore, most of the supply transports had to wait for the ice to thicken. During the delay, light carts transported the first cargoes of flour across the lake from Kobona on 19 November, with each cart carrying a modest load of two to four sacks of flour. The next day, Major-General of the Quartermaster Service F. N. Lagunov, the Chief of the Leningrad Front's rear services, twice travelled across the lake's ice from Kokkorevo to Kobona by light vehicle to test the ice's load-carrying capacity. The first substantial vehicular column (60 cargo trucks with 33.5 tonnes [33 tons] of flour) crossed the lake on 22 November despite a heavy snowstorm. Travelling in column formation along tracks prepared by horse transport, the trucks reached Leningrad on 23 November. A second column carrying 19.3 tonnes (19 tons) reached Leningrad the next day.

25 This required clearing and re-clearing ice hummocks and snowdrifts from more than 33,000 square metres (two square miles) of roadway. During this process, the front's road service levelled 824km (515 miles) of ice and snow walls, cleared snow from 2200km (1375 miles) of road surface, and built 260km (162 miles) of detours around intersections and dangerous sectors.

26 The communications network alone extended 168km (105 miles).

27 For example, the road supplied 71 tonnes (70 tons) on 25 November, 156.7 tonnes (154 tons) on the 26th, 128 tonnes (126 tons) on the 27th, 200 tonnes (196 tons) on the 28th, and 130 tonnes (128 tons) on the 29th, which was insignificant compared with needs.

28 This amounted to 998 tonnes (980 tons) of flour, 2.9 tons of barley, 830 tonnes (815 tons) of soybeans, 11 tonnes (11 tons) of malt, 435 tonnes (427.7 tons) of slab fat, and 1.1 tonnes (1.1 tons) of bran. The 1700 wagon loads of fuel was equivalent to 36 trainloads of fuel or 120 trainloads of wood.

29 By 20 January the Leningrad Front had amassed 10-11 days' worth of flour, five days' of grain, 9-10 days' of butter, four days' of fat, and 8 days' of sugar in city warehouses, at Ladoga Station on the lake's western bank, and en route across the ice. A like quantity amount was stored on the lake's eastern bank and at Voibokalo and Zhikharevo on the railroad line to Volkhov.

30 By this time, engineers and technical workers were receiving 400 grams (14 ounces) per day, employees 300 grams (10.5 ounces), dependents and children 250 grams (8.8 ounces), workers in priority shops 575 grams (20.3 ounces) (up from 500), frontline forces 600 grams (21.1 ounces) (up from 500), and rear service troops 400 grams (14.1 ounces).

31 The road carried 367,608 tonnes (361,109 tons) of cargo during the winter, including 267,142 tonnes (262,419 tons) of food, 8507 tonnes (8357 tons) of forage, 32,484 tonnes (31,910 tons) of ammunition, 35,342 tonnes (34,717 tons) of fuel and lubricants, 22,414 tonnes (22,818 tons) of coal, and 904 tonnes (888 tons) of other cargo. In addition, 2036 tonnes (2000 tons) of health-enhancing high calorie products such as chocolate and eggs made it into Leningrad across the ice road.

32 Among the first partisan forces formed were 13 partisan detachments made up of students and faculty of the Lesgaft Institute of Physical Culture.

33 For example, the Glovsk district fielded three partisan detachments, six diversionary groups, and several underground Party groups and the Luga district – a total of 17 partisan detachments and diversionary groups. By the end of 1941, 88 regional and district secretaries, 29 chiefs of district and city committees, and hundreds of other local officials directed the underground effort.

34 For example, the Lesgaft Institute student partisan detachment blew up the railroad bend on the Luga-Siversk railroad in July. In late July and August, the 5th Leningrad Partisan Regiment destroyed 40 trucks and light vehicles on the Pskov-Luga road, blew up the Pskov-Porkhov railroad line, damaged Lokot' Station, and conducted numerous small ambushes. Also in July, the Leningrad University and Art Institute Student Detachment destroyed the railroad bridge across the Igol'nyi River on the Shapki-Tosno road and damaged several trains. To the south, six detachments in the Luga district destroyed several German tanks and aircraft, 24 ammunition trucks, four motorcycles, 36 bicycles, and seven bridges, and destroyed the German garrison at Voloshovo.

35 A *krai* was an administrative subdivision under a *raion* (district).

36 Soviet sources claim that, during this period, the partisans killed 11,493 German soldiers and officers, captured five guns, 30 machine guns, 98 tanks and armoured cars, 1632 vehicles, 316 motorcycles, 71 aircraft, 66 locomotives, 807 wagons, platforms and railroad cars, eight warehouses, 320 bridges, and eight garrisons and headquarters, and captured many prisoners. It is likely that these figures remain apocryphal.

CHAPTER 5 NOTES

1 However, the aircraft remained under army control, since the front's air staff, which had been created in December 1941, lacked the means to control the aircraft.

2 The 345 aircraft included 82 bombers, half of which were older models, five assault planes and 258 fighters. The Leningrad Front allocated 67 fighters to protect its communications and 25 to protect Leningrad proper. The remaining 166 fighters, half of which were in disrepair, were to support the ground forces.

3 Soviet after-action critiques noted dryly that the attacks failed both because of the fierce German resistance and the front's congenital penchant for dissipating its strength in fruitless and repetitive assaults on German strongpoints.

4 Sokolov, a former NKVD officer and close associate of Lavrenti Beria, the head of the Soviet NKVD, lacked military experience and was woefully unfit to plan, coordinate or participate in such a complex operation.

5 General Staff critiques cited poor command, control and coordination and force dispersal as the major reasons the offensive failed.

6 The General Staff attributed the failures to weak cooperation, ineffective employment of tanks and artillery, and undue reliance on costly frontal attacks.

7 Kuechler assigned these responsibilities on 22 January, and forces reinforced their positions on the flanks of the penetration in early February.

8 Group Haenecke consisted of small combat groups from the 215th and 61st Infantry Divisions.

9 By this time, Kurochkin's Northwestern Front had reached the eastern outskirts of Staraia Russa and had encircled the German II Army Corps in the Demiansk region. In addition, on 23 February Kuechler had assigned the entire region north and south of the Soviet penetration to the Eighteenth Army. The new boundary between the Eighteenth and Sixteenth armies ran due west from Lake Il'men.

10 During the January offensive, the Kalinin Front's forces encircled the German II Army Corps' right flank in Kholm. Kuechler then sent XXXIX Motorized Corps to the region to mount a relief operation in March.

11 Soviet sources claim that the Germans lost three divisions: 12,000 dead, 185 guns, 135 mortars, 29 tanks, 340 machine guns, 4150 submachine guns and rifles, 320 motorcycles, 560 bicycles, and 125 supply wagons during the encirclement battle.

12 The *Stavka* also reinforced its forces with five artillery and three mortar regiments in early March and an aviation shock group in mid-March.

13 Soviet critiques credited the failure to weak air and artillery support and poor command, control and communications. Kurochkin prepared the offensive too quickly, in part because intelligence reported that the Germans were about to mount an effort to relieve their Demiansk garrison

14 Soviet critiques blamed the Demiansk failure on inexperience in destroying large encircled forces, poor command, control and coordination, congenital underestimation of German capabilities and intentions, and a failure to fortify the junctions between cooperating forces.

CHAPTER 6 NOTES

1 Along the northwestern axis, the Leningrad Front's Second Shock and Fifty-Fourth Armies were deep in the Eighteenth Army's rear, but were themselves enveloped from three sides by German forces. The Northwestern Front forces threatened the flanks and rear of Sixteenth Army forces occupying the Demiansk salient and Ramushevo corridor. Along the western (Moscow) axis, Soviet forces in a deep salient jutting westwards from Ostashkov towards Velikie Luki threatened Army Group Centre's forces in the Rzhev and Viaz'ma areas with encirclement, but were themselves threatened with encirclement. In the south, the Southwestern and Southern Fronts' forces in the Barvenkovo salient south of Kharkov threatened German Army Group South's defences at Kharkov. In the Donbas and on the Crimean peninsula, the North Caucasus Front threatened to relieve Sevastopol from its bridgehead on the Kerch peninsula.

2 The *Stavka* had reinforced Khozin's front with 25 artillery-machine gun battalions, six anti-tank regiments, 500 heavy and 1000 light machine guns, 5000 submachine guns, and two tank brigade with 50 tanks each by 1 June.

3 XXXVIII Army Corps' losses were 30 percent. Forces participating in the operation included I Army Corps' 254th, 61st, 121st and SS Police Infantry Divisions, and XXXVIII Army Corps' 58th Infantry Division, the 2nd SS Infantry Brigade and the 20th Motorized Division.

4 Army General A. M. Vasilevsky, the Deputy Chief of the General Staff, was sent to assist Meretskov in the capacity of *Stavka* representative.

5 Kuechler also proposed two operations in the south. Operation *Brueckenschlag* involved a joint attack with Army Group Centre against the Soviet salient in the German rear southwest of Ostashkov, and Operation *Schlingpflanze* (Vine) an assault to widen the north flank of the Ramushevo corridor to Demiansk.

6 Directive No 45 ordered Army Group South, now split into Army Groups A and B, to conduct Operation *Braunschweig* to liquidate Red Army forces in the great bend of the Don River.

7 Operation *Nordlicht* was codenamed Operation *Georg* within the Eighteenth Army.

8 Ultimately, the OKH cancelled Operation *Moorbrand* later in the summer because by then the situation had changed substantially. However, Hitler insisted that *Nordlicht* go ahead as scheduled.

9 These included the 121st and 61st Infantry, 5th Mountain Division, and part of 12th Panzer Division. During the same period the Northwestern Front conducted near constant offensive operations against German forces at Demiansk and Staraia Russa, both to eliminate the German salient and reduce the chances of a German offensive at Leningrad. These operations, which took place from 3–20 May, 17–24 July, 10–21 August and 15–16 September, failed to make any progress, but tied down the Sixteenth Army and prevented it from taking any action to support the Eighteenth Army at Leningrad.

10 The Eighteenth Army consisted of 21 infantry divisions, one panzer division (the 12th) and one infantry brigade.

11 Naval infantry and boats from the Baltic Fleet were to secure crossing sites over the Neva.

12 The Eighth Army's shock group consisted of VI Guards Rifle Corps with the 3rd, 19th and 24th Guards Rifle Divisions and the 265th Rifle Division.

13 Major-General N. A. Gagen's IV Guards Rifle Corps also reinforced Klykov's new army.

14 The deeply echeloned formation was designed both to overcome the heavy German defences quickly and to sustain the attack into the depths.

15 This support included two tank brigades, five separate tank battalions, 12 artillery and nine mortar regiments, four separate mortar battalions, three M-13 Katiusha regiments and seven M-30 Katiusha battalions.

16 The 128th Rifle Division was to screen the shock group's right flank from Workers' Settlement No 7 to Moskovskaia Dubrovka, and the 11th and 286th Rifle Divisions the right flank from Turyshkino to Krasnyi Bor.

17 The regrouping effort involved the movement of 479 trains and 253 supply convoys between 7 August and 17 September. The delays were due to the limited capacity of railroad lines into concentration areas, poor command and control, and the slow regrouping itself, when units had to be moved to the rear to refill before going back to the front.

18 The tactical density of the Volkhov Front's attacking forces was up to five rifle battalions, more than 100 guns and mortars and nine tanks per kilometre of front.

19 The initial attacking force was the 268th Rifle Division, and it was later reinforced by elements of the 43rd, 70th and 136th Rifle Divisions. Soviet critiques indicate that this and other Fifty-Fifth Army attacks failed primarily because of poor command and control and inadequate artillery and engineer support.

20 The 128th Rifle Division was on the shock group's right flank, and the 11th and 286th Rifle Divisions were on its left.

21 IV Guards Rifle Corps consisted of the 259th Rifle Division and the 22nd, 23rd, 32nd, 33rd, 53rd, 137th and 140th Rifle and 98th and 122nd Tank Brigades.

22 During the withdrawal the forces abandoned all of their equipment. Soviet critiques credit the failure to poor command and control and inadequate fire support.

23 Govorov's assault across the Neva River forced Manstein to move the 28th Jäger Division from Siniavino to the Neva Front.

24 Soviet sources optimistically estimated that the Germans lost 60,000 men, 200 tanks, 200 guns, 400 mortars and 730 machine guns.

25 The Germans estimated that Soviet losses included 36,000 dead, 12,370 prisoners and 244 destroyed or captured tanks.

26 Candid Soviet after-action critiques attributed the failure of the second Siniavino offensive to a variety of causes. Despite Meretskov's careful preparations, command and control, reconnaissance, concentration and cooperation among attacking forces continued to be poor. Meretskov and his subordinate army commanders committed their second echelons and reserves to combat in piecemeal fashion and often too late to make a difference. The critiques credited these failures to inexperienced command cadres and staffs, particularly at the platoon and company level, and poor staff procedures. On the other hand, the critiques noted the offensive's positive effect of forcing the Germans to cancel their planned offensive to capture the city and divert forces from the south. The offensive also seriously eroded German strength, weakened their defences, and paved the way for a more successful offensive in the future by imparting necessary experience to the Soviet command cadres and staffs.

27 OKH Operations Order No 1.

CHAPTER 7 NOTES

1 The General Staff collected and analyzed the experiences from the defence of Odessa, Sevastopol and Stalingrad and provided it to the Leningrad Front.

2 These defences included 150km (93.75 miles) of anti-tank ditches, escarpments and counter-escarpments, 202km (126 miles) of barbed wire entanglements, 7178 rifle squad trenches, 627km (392 miles) of communications trenches, 140 pre-fabricated iron and reinforced concrete works, 487 armoured firing points, 176 encasements for tanks and tank turrets, 1500 anti-tank obstacles (pyramids), 1395 earth and timber bunkers, 809 firing points in buildings, and 1089 command and observation posts or blindages.

3 For example, by October the Forty-Second and Fifty-Fifth Armies' defensive sectors south of Leningrad were equipped with 656 artillery and 2094 machine-gun bunkers, 536 mortar firing positions, 800 anti-tank rifle firing positions, 2000 blindages and bunkers, 600km (375 miles) of anti-tank and anti-infantry obstacles, and 350km (219 miles) of communications trenches.

4 The daily shipment targets were 2456 tonnes (2500 tons) of food, 305 tonnes (300 tons) of ammunition, 102 tonnes (100 tons) of military equipment, 102 tonnes (100 tons) of coal and fuel oil, and 305 tonnes (300 tons) of lubricants to the city and 1018 tonnes (1000 tons) of cargo and 3000 people daily from the city to the Soviet rear.

5 Shipbuilders constructed 14 metal barges, 31 towed wooden boats and 118 small capacity self-propelled boats for use on the lake, and fisherman provided 17 self-propelled boats and four towed boats.

6 The largest of these ships carried 32,576 tonnes (32,000 tons) of cargo. In addition to the foodstuffs, 15.4 percent of the cargo was coal, 16.7 percent lubricants and 17.9 percent weaponry and other military cargo. Also included were 4186 sheep and goats, 7723 small cattle, 4388 horses, wood and medical supplies.

7 For example, about 100 German aircraft struck the port of Kobona on 28 May, but anti-aircraft gunners shot down an estimated 19 enemy aircraft.

8 This force consisted of four Italian torpedo boats, four German cutters, seven self-propelled amphibious assault boats, 12 self-propelled landing barges, and one headquarters, one medical and four transport ships.

9 According to Soviet accounts, the Finns formed an amphibious force of 23 boats and seven cutters armed with 88mm and 37mm guns and 22mm automatic guns on 9 October, and prepared to land the force on the island. However, Soviet aircraft discovered and heavily damaged the flotilla on 13 October and forced the postponement of the operation. The Finns began a new landing attempt from Sortavala on 22 October, concealed by a storm on the lake. Once again, two Soviet patrol cutters discovered the force in time and the Soviet garrison repelled the attack, sinking 17 Finnish boats, shooting down 14 enemy aircraft and capturing 61 prisoners. This small victory ended all enemy attempts to operate on the lake.

10 Engineers ceased work on the ice railroad on 19 January.

11 The two truck columns consisted of 300 GAZ-AA trucks, each one carrying a load of 1000kg (2200lb), and 143 ZIS-5s trucks.

12 The total tonnage in the winter of 1942–43 included 113,825 tonnes (111,813 tons) of food, 55,333 tonnes (54,355 tons) of ammunition and 18,938 tonnes (18,603 tons) of coal. In addition, 12,368 horses, 1431 vehicles, and 133,144 personnel reinforcements entered the city via the road, with 88,932 evacuees from the city.

13 The Germans conducted 140 air raids and dropped more than 280 bombs during the winter.

14 The Ladoga water routes took over the transport tasks while the railroad was being repaired.

15 At first, all rail transport along the two railroads took place at night on the basis of special plans (graphics) for one-way and two-way movement. By the end of June, however, all rail traffic was running two ways almost constantly.

16 The Germans employed as many as 100 bombers and 40 fighters a time against the bridges. Although they succeeded in destroying one bridge on 1 June, construction troops and engineers replaced the destroyed bridge with a wooden bridge within five days and a metal bridge by 19 June. German aircraft destroyed the wooden bridge again on 19 June and the metal bridge on the 21st. However, these bridges were again rebuilt on 23 June and 2 July respectively.

17 The total volume of supplies amounted to 524,779 tonnes (515,500 tons), over half of which was wood. Shipments during the spring and summer included 79,515 tonnes (78,109 tons) of wood, 53,838 tonnes (52,886 tons) of food, 4516 tonnes (4436 tons) of fuel, and 12,757 tonnes (12,532 tons) of coal sent into Leningrad, and 42,032 tonnes (41,300 tons) of cargo shipped out of Leningrad.

18 The water routes reverted to control of the Northwestern River Ferry Service.

19 The Leningrad Operational Group consisted of partisan detachments in the Tosno and Liuban regions organized into two battalions commanded by E. F. Tuvalovich and K. I. Volovich. The Valdai Operational Group consisted of partisan detachments in the Staraia Russa, Polovsk, Zaluch'e and Molvotitsy regions in the southwestern and southern reaches of Leningrad region, and the third operational group operated in the Volkhov Front's sector.

20 In March, for example, it combined the Leningrad and Volkhov Operational Groups under A. A. Guzeev's command to improve command and control. The following month, it reorganized the Valdai Operational Group's detachments into the 3rd Partisan Brigade, commanded by A. V. German, and the 4th Partisan Brigade, commanded by A. P. Luchin.

21 For example, the Tosno and Liuban detachments operated against German communications lines, but with only limited effectiveness, during the Volkhov Front's Liuban offensive. Farther south, in January and February the partisans around Gdov supported the Northwestern Front's Demiansk offensive by disrupting German communications between Pskov and Gdov and Gdov and Kingisepp. In addition, partisans near Ostrov, Dno, Porkhov, Soshikhin and Belebelkov supported the Northwestern Front's operations around Demiansk and Kholm. These partisans achieved much success when they assisted Red Army forces in the seizure of Kholm on 18 January and the capture of Iasski on 5 February and Dedovichi on 22 February. However, in each case German relief attacks forced the partisans and Red Army forces to abandon the towns.

22 For example, the Party sent 25 special partisan groups of 7–9 men each to Gdov, Pskov, Luga, Oredezh, Pliuss, Strugokrasnensk, Kingisepp and other regions. Throughout this period Soviet records indicate that partisan actions inflicted 15,000 losses on German troops and destroyed 114 rail and road bridges, 26 warehouses, 69 tanks, 500 vehicles and 13 aircraft.

23 The 2nd Partisan Brigade operated southeast of Dno and the 3rd Partisan Brigade south of Poochka Station. Detachments commanded by A. I. Iakumov, M. I. Shchurov, L. P. Durygin, D. A. Shakhrinsky and F. S. Makarov and tens of diversionary groups operated in the forests east of Pskov. Detachments led by B. M. Prokhorov, T. Ia. Pechatnikov, S. A. Sergeev, G. F. Bol'shov, A. A. Zabelina, G. I. Bogdanov, the 1st Partisan Brigade and tens of other detachments operated northeast of Gdov. Finally, the 4th Partisan Brigade operated in the southern part of the *oblast*.

24 The German punitive expedition, consisting of 6000 troops from the 218th Infantry Division, the 4th Blocking Regiment, security units and punitive detachments, conducted the pacification operation in fighting that lasted until 10 September. During this period, German forces captured villages in the Belebelkovskii, Dedovichi and Poddorsk regions, destroyed houses, farms and other buildings and persecuted the local inhabitants.

25 The 2nd and 3rd Brigades moved to Ostrov, Slavkovichi and Novorzhesnk, the 1st and 4th Brigades moved to Gdov and Slantsy, and remaining detachments moved to Novgorod, Sol'tsy, Utorgosh' and Luga regions.

26 The regional centres were at Ostrov, Pskov, Dno, Strugkrasnensk, Dedovichi, Gdov, Kingisepp, Luga, Oredezh, Novgorod and Porkhov.

27 The 5th Partisan Brigade, headed by K. D. Karitsky, had formed in the Slavkovichi region in the winter of 1942–43 from the Staraia Russa and Dedovichi detachments. A. D. Kondrat'ev's 4th Partisan Brigade was formed from the 5th Brigade in mid-1943 to conduct operations in the southern part of Leningrad region. The 11th Partisan Brigade, first commanded by A. P. Luchin and, later, by N. A. Brednikov, combined the Oredezh, Novgorod, Bataisk and other detachments operating at the junction of the Leningrad and Volkhov Fronts. The 3rd "A. V. German" Partisan Brigade continued to operate in the Ostrov and Soshikhin regions, and the 2nd "N. G. Vasil'ev" Partisan Brigade, commanded successively by M. I. Timokhin, A. N. Rachkov and N. I. Sinel'nikov, redeployed from the Novgorod to the Pskov region in summer 1943. In addition, several separate partisan regiments and detachments operated throughout the region.

28 The 6th Partisan Brigade, under V. P. Ob'edkov, formed in September from the 2nd

Brigade and the 7th and 8th Partisan Brigades, under A. V. Alekseev and L. B. Tsinchenko, formed in the regions administered by the Pskov, Ostrov, and Porkhov Party District Committees. The 9th Partisan Brigade, commanded by N. G. Svetlov, formed during the fall in the Gdov, Slantsev, Liady, Os'mian and Luga regions. T. A. Novikov's 10th Partisan Brigade formed in the Dno and Struga regions, and A. A. Inginen's 12th Partisan Brigade formed from detachments in the Kingisepp region also in late fall. Finally, the 13th Partisan Brigade, under A. V. Iurtsev, which was the last to form, organized on 11 January 1944 in the southern portion of Dedovichi region.

29 For example, in the Leningrad region, the 3rd Partisan Brigade conducted multiple attacks on the Pskov-Porkhov railroad line on 21 August that put the railroad out of action for eight days. In September several partisan brigades conducted Operation *Bol'shoi Koncert* (Large Concert) against the Luga-Pskov railroad line. Soviet sources claim that partisans killed an estimated 17,000 German troops from 1 January through 1 September 1943 and destroyed or damaged a considerable amount of German equipment, including156 trains, 133 locomotives, and 2452 rail cars, platforms and water towers, 19 rail and 151 road bridges, 72,020 telephone and telegraph lines, 12 tanks and 26 guns, 50 warehouses, and 37 small garrisons or security posts.

30 For example, the 2nd Partisan Brigade raided Pliussa Station on the Leningrad-Pskov railroad line, blowing up a bridge, destroying a train and freeing Soviet prisoners-of-war, and killing a reported 136 Germans. In fact, in September the 775 partisan fighters of the 5th Partisan Brigade fomented popular uprisings in many villages, converting the movement into a full revolt in its operational region. In October the brigade captured the town of Pliussa and the southern portion of the Luga and Bataisk regions, preventing German occupying authorities from either gathering the harvest or removing much of the population to forced labour camps in Germany or German-occupied territory. The 9th Partisan Brigade created similar conditions in the Gdov, Slantsev, Liady, Os'min and Kingisepp regions in early October by organizing uprisings in Utorgosh, Pliussa, Luga, Gdov, Slantsev, Os'min, Liady, Volosovo and elsewhere in cooperation with the 12th Brigade. Soon the uprising spread to the Pekovets region, where the 2nd and 3rd Partisan Brigades were operating.

CHAPTER 8 NOTES

1 The frontlines were a mere 4km (2.5 miles) south of the city and only 30km (18.75 miles) to the northwest and southeast.

2 The Twenty-Third Army consisted of five rifle divisions, one rifle brigade, two fortified regions and one tank brigade; the Coastal Operational Group fielded two rifle divisions, two rifle brigades, two naval infantry brigades, two separate machine gun-artillery battalions and one separate tank battalion.

3 The Forty-Second Army fielded five rifle divisions, one fortified region, one tank brigade, and one separate tank regiment; the Fifty-Fifth Army consisted of four rifle divisions, one fortified region and one tank brigade.

4 The Sixty-Seventh Army consisted of three rifle divisions, two rifle brigades, one ski brigade, one fortified region, two separate tank battalions and supporting artillery. The army's 46th Rifle Division defended Porogi-Vyborgskaia Dubrovka sector and a small bridgehead across the Neva River near Moskovskaia Dubrovka, and the 11th Rifle Brigade was deployed from Vyborgskaia Dubrovka to the Gannibalovka River, 4km (2.5 miles) south of Shlissel'burg. The army's 16th Fortified Region defended the western shores of Lake Ladoga, the 55th Rifle Brigade defended the ice road along with the Ladoga Flotilla, and a small garrison manned Oreshek Fortress at the mouth of the Neva opposite Shlissel'burg. Dukhanov retained the 45th Guards and 86th Rifle Divisions and the 35th Ski Brigade in army reserve. The Sixty-Seventh Army's divisions ranged in strength from

7–10,000 men each and the brigades from 3–5800 men each, and the army as a whole fielded 850 guns and mortars, 400 M-30 multiple rocket launchers, and slightly more than 50 tanks. The army's operational density was 12km (7.5 miles) per defending division.

5 The 136th and 268th Rifle Divisions, the 61st and 122nd Rifle Brigade, the 34th Ski Brigade, the 13th Fortified Region, and the 61st and 122nd Tank Brigades constituted Govorov's reserve.

6 Leningrad Front air forces included the 275th Fighter, 276th Bomber and 277th Assault Aviation Divisions, the 196th and 286th Fighter, 23rd Guards and 897th Bomber, and 13th Reconnaissance Aviation Regiments, and the 12th Mixed Aviation Regiment, which was still forming.

7 The Leningrad PVO Army included VII Fighter Aviation Corps with 80 aircraft operationally subordinate to the Thirteenth Air Army, six medium and one small-calibre anti-aircraft artillery regiments, and one heavy machine-gun anti-aircraft artillery regiment.

8 The Baltic Fleet performed multiple missions. First, it prevented German forces from seizing Kotlin Island and other islands in the Gulf of Finland by an attack across the ice and protected the sea approaches to Leningrad in cooperation with the Twenty-Third Army, the Coastal Group and the Internal Defences of the City. In addition, it protected the ice roads across the Gulf of Finland, helped defend Lake Ladoga's western shore and the ice roads across the lake with coastal artillery and the Ladoga Military Flotilla's ships, and defended Novaia Ladoga on the lake's eastern shore.

9 The Eighth Army consisted of eight rifle divisions, one rifle brigade, one tank regiment and two separate tank battalions; the Second Shock Army fielded two rifle divisions, two rifle brigades, one naval infantry brigade, two tank brigades, four separate tank battalions and supporting artillery.

10 The operational density in the Volkhov Front's Eighth and Second Shock Armies' sectors was one division per 4km (2.5 miles) of front. The Eighth Army's divisions numbered from 3800–9500 men (5400 on average), and the Second Shock Army 6500–7000 men. The two armies fielded 1700 guns and mortars, 130 Katiushas, and over 100 tanks.

11 Meretskov's reserve included the 71st Rifle Division and the 37th and 39th Ski Brigades.

12 The 96th Infantry and 5th Mountain Divisions were in army group reserve.

13 The First Air Army conducted 4700 bombing sorties against Leningrad with flights of three to six aircraft each between 1 October and 31 December.

14 L Army Corps consisted of the 225th and 215th Infantry, 9th Luftwaffe Field and 2nd SS Divisions; LIV Army Corps contained the 250th Spanish "Blue", SS Police and 5th Mountain Divisions.

15 XXVI Army Corps' 170th Infantry Division and one regiment of the 227th Infantry Division defended along the Neva River facing west, and the remainder of the 227th,1st and 223rd Infantry Divisions were deployed from Shlissel'burg past Voronovo facing north and east. I Army Corps consisted of the 69th, 132nd, 61st, 11th, 217th and 21st Infantry Divisions.

16 XXVII Army Corps consisted of the 24th and 121st Infantry and 28th *Jäger* Divisions, and XXXVIII Army Corps the 254th and 212th Infantry and 1st Luftwaffe Field Divisions.

17 The salient was defended by XXVI Army Corps' 1st, 227th and 170th Infantry Divisions, LIV Army Corps' SS Police Division and part of the 5th Mountain Division, and the Eighteenth Army's reserve 96th Infantry Division.

18 The Germans constructed defensive regions at Workers' Settlements Nos 1 and 2, Shlissel'burg and Siniavino. Five centres of resistance located at Shlissel'burg, Gorodok 1 and 2, Arbuzovo and Annenskoe faced the Sixty-Seventh Army, and another at Lobanovo protected the railroad line to Mga Station. In addition, six additional centres of resistance at Lipka, Workers Settlement No 8, Gontovaia Lipka, Tortolovo, Mishino and Porech'e faced the Eighth Army. Finally, the Germans formed deep defensive positions anchored on Workers' Settlements Nos 1 and 5 and Siniavino in the depths, and numerous additional rear defence lines.

19 If successful, the Uritsk offensive would halt the German artillery bombardment of Leningrad, restore freedom of manoeuvre between Leningrad and Kronshtadt to the Baltic Fleet's ships, and significantly widen the southern sector of the Leningrad defences.

20 The Sixty-Seventh Army was to penetrate German defences between Gorodok 2 and Shlissel'burg and simultaneously along the shores of Lake Ladoga. The Second Shock and Eighth Armies were to penetrate German defences between Lake Ladoga and Mishino. The two shock groups were to link up near Siniavino.

21 Although the front staffs planned both operations in detail, the ultimate attack date depended on ice conditions on the Neva River and Lake Ladoga.

22 Govorov recommended that each shock group consist of seven to eight rifle divisions, with four divisions in first echelon, three in second echelon and one in reserve, and be supported by substantial tank, artillery and engineer forces.

23 The *Stavka* reinforced Govorov's front with the 224th Rifle Division, the 102nd, 123rd, 138th, 250th and 142nd Rifle Brigades, the 7th Anti-aircraft Artillery Division and three aerosleigh battalions. It sent Meretskov's front the 18th, 147th, 239th, 364th and 379th Rifle Divisions and the 53rd Engineer-Sapper Brigade from Moscow, the 11th, 12th and 13th Ski Brigades from Arkhangel'sk, and four aerosleigh battalions. The NKO also provided the two fronts with new equipment necessary to form sizeable new artillery and armoured forces. These included four artillery divisions, 10 mortar regiments, two anti-aircraft artillery regiments and one tank regiment in the Volkhov Front and one artillery division, one artillery brigade, three artillery regiments, five guards mortar battalions, three mortar regiments, one tank regiment and four separate tank battalions in the Leningrad Front. These reinforcements increased the Volkhov Front's personnel strength by 22 percent, guns by 20 percent and mortars by 30 percent, and the Leningrad Front's personnel strength by 10 percent.

24 The precise second stage mission was to clear the Kirov railroad and reach the Voronovo, Voskresenskoe, Sigalovo and Voitolovo line by the month's end.

25 Dukhanov's shock group was to attack along the Mar'ino-Siniavino axis to destroy German strongpoints on the left bank of the Neva River, and capture Arbuzovo, Workers' Settlement No 2 and Shlissel'burg. Subsequently, Dukhanov was to commit his second-echelon forces and overcome the German centres of resistance at Annenskoe, Mustolovo, Workers' Settlement No 6, Siniavino and Workers' Settlements Nos 5 and 1.

26 The Sixty-Seventh Army was supported by 22 artillery and mortar regiments, 15 engineer-sapper and pontoon battalions, and other specialized units.

27 Romanovsky's immediate mission was to destroy German forces in the Lipka, "Kruglaia" grove and Gaitolovo regions with his strong left flank and capture the German strongpoints at Workers' Settlements Nos 1 and 5, and the centre of resistance at Siniavino to disorganize the entire German defence.

28 Two engineer-sapper brigades, 37 artillery and mortar regiments and other specialized units supported the Second Shock Army.

29 The completed plan for cooperation was far more detailed then previous plans, instructing the two shock groups on every aspect of the operation and establishing guidelines for every aspect of staff planning.

30 The Sixty-Seventh Army's 46th Rifle Division, 55th Rifle and 35th Ski Brigades, and 16th Fortified Region defended the western bank of the Neva River and the ice road across Lake Ladoga. The Baltic Fleet reinforced the Sixty-Seventh Army with 23 batteries of fixed and railroad artillery. These included 88 long-range 130–356mm guns from the Fleet training grounds, four minesweeper squadrons and three cannon ships positioned on the Neva River.

31 The Second Shock Army's 22nd Rifle Brigade was to protect the southern shore of Lake Ladoga east of Lipka during the offensive.

32 The fact that the shock groups were attacking towards one another against objectives only 13–15km (8.1–9.3 miles) apart made coordination both essential and difficult.

33 Govorov concentrated 144 guns and mortars per kilometre of front in the Sixty-Seventh Army's sector and reinforced this fire with three guards mortar regiments and 12 battalions in the penetration sector to increase the preparation's effectiveness. In addition, he formed long-range action and special designation groups to destroy enemy artillery and engage important targets in the depth, and a guards mortar group to support the second echelon during its commitment into the penetration. Finally, to improve infantry support, Govorov formed counter-mortar groups in each attacking division to supplement the fire of infantry support groups. Govorov initially employed simultaneous barrage fire to a depth of 1km (.62 miles). When the barrages ended, artillery fired successive fire concentrations and laid down a dense zone of final protective fires 250m (820ft) from the Neva River's bank to protect the advancing infantry. Before and during the infantry assault, massed direct fire by 22 guns per kilometre of front would prevent the Germans from destroying the ice cover over the Neva River. The front allocated three full combat loads of artillery to the Sixty-Seventh Army and retained 1.5–5 loads at front and army depots, and planned to employ 3.3–5 combat loads during the penetration to a depth of 5km (3.1 miles). This far exceeded the quantities of ammunition allocated to previous offensives.

34 Meretskov concentrated 180 guns and mortars per kilometre of front, not including the two heavy brigades and four guards mortar brigades, and allocated 2206 guns and mortars to support the Second Shock Army. His artillery preparation also relied on heavy direct fire along the forward edge involving 18 guns per kilometre of front. The front supplied the Second Shock Army with between 2–2.5 to five combat loads of ammunition, and ordered all regimental and divisional artillery to be mounted on skis or sleighs and heavy machine guns on skis or snow carts to improve their mobility.

35 The Thirteenth Air Army's 414 aircraft included 52 bombers, 85 assault planes, 242 fighters and 35 reconnaissance and other type aircraft.

36 In addition, the fighters concentrated on attaining air superiority and providing air cover for the troops.

37 The 395 aircraft included 35 bombers, 174 assault aircraft, 163 fighters and 23 reconnaissance aircraft.

38 The 152nd, 220th and 61st Light Tank Brigades and the 189th and 119th Separate Tank Battalions supported the Sixty-Seventh Army.

39 The 16th, 98th, 122nd, and 185th Tank Brigades, the 32nd Guards Tank Penetration Regiment, and the 50th, 501st, 503rd, and 507th Separate Tank and 32nd and 44th Aerosleigh Battalions supported the Second Shock Army. The 25th Separate Tank Regiment and 107th and 502nd Tank Battalions supported the Eighth Army. The Sixty-Seventh Army employed the bulk of its tanks on the shock group's left flank to assist in the rapid capture of the Siniavino centre of resistance. The 372nd, 256th and 191st Rifle Divisions, which were attacking in the centre, had no armour support.

40 Leningrad Front engineers had to assist in the crossing on the Neva River, prepare movement routes in the roadless terrain, and organize jumping-off and assault positions. Prior to the offensive they widened and deepened existing trenches and constructed an elaborate system of ditches 4–600m (1312–1968ft) from the river to protect the movement of troops from the railroad to the jumping-off positions along the river. They also built an extensive system of command and observation points, numerous covered gun firing positions, particularly for direct fire over the river, and heating and rest bunkers and cabins covered with waterproof canvas for entire platoons. While the army regrouped, they constructed up to 50km (31.2 miles) of winter roads (two routes per division) and cut paths through the minefields using specially prepared overhead explosives. During the attack, and under enemy fire, they built wooden crossings over the Neva with a capacity of up to 61 tonnes (60 tons) so that medium and heavy tanks could cross the river. Their most important combat contribution was the employment of assault and destruction groups especially tailored to destroy specific German strongpoints, and engineer obstacle battalions and miner battalions to fortify occupied lines and protect the flanks.

41 The Leningrad Front still lacked an adequate depot system and was short of vehicular transport, fuel and medical supplies.

42 Operation Mars was the third Rzhev-Sychevka operation. The first operation had taken place in February–March 1942 as part of the Red Army's Winter offensive, and the second operation, which was a dress rehearsal for Operation Mars, occurred in August and September 1942. All three operations sought to defeat Army Group Centre, and all three failed.

43 Along the southern axis, the Don Front was destroying the German Sixth Army encircled at Stalingrad, the Voronezh and Southwestern Fronts were driving German forces westwards from the Don River, and the Southern Front was advancing on Rostov. Along the southwestern axis, the Briansk Front was preparing to strike the German Second Army at Voronezh, and along the western axis the Kalinin Front was battling with German forces near Velikie Luki. All of these operations were occurring simultaneously.

44 Heavy snowfall began at midday, limiting air support to just over 100 sorties on the first day of the attack.

45 Soviet critiques noted that the 128th Rifle Division failed to manoeuvre properly, exploit its heavy weaponry, concentrate its direct fires, or cooperate properly with its supporting tanks.

46 Ovchinnikov's mission was to bypass Workers' Settlement No 8 from the south, attack towards Workers' Settlement No 5, and link up with the Sixty-Seventh Army.

47 The Fourteenth Air Army flew 550 air sorties on 12 January but none on the 13th.

48 Colonel A. P. Ivanov's 123rd Rifle Division, Colonel P. I. Pinchuk's 152nd Tank Brigade, and Lieutenant-Colonel F. F. Shishov's 123rd Rifle Brigade supported the 136th Rifle Division. Colonel V. P. Iakutovich's 13th Rifle Division, Lieutenant-Colonel A. V. Batluk's 102nd Rifle Brigade, and Lieutenant-Colonel Koshchienko's 142nd Naval Rifle Brigade reinforced the 268th Rifle Division at Gorodok Nos 1 and 2.

49 Lieutenant-Colonel Ia. F. Potekhin's 34th Ski Brigade.

50 The 123rd Rifle Brigade captured Workers' Settlement No 3, but the 268th Rifle Division failed to capture Settlement Nos 1 and 2. After four days of combat, the 123rd Rifle Division and 102nd Rifle Brigade captured the woods east of Gorodok No 2, but could accomplish nothing more. The Thirteenth Air Army flew 919 air sorties on 14 and 15 January as the weather improved markedly.

51 On Meretskov's orders, Romanovsky committed General Ovchinnikov's 18th and Colonel V. N. Fedorov's 71st Rifle Divisions, supported by the 98th Tank Brigade, into combat on 13 January. Colonel P. A. Popapov's 191st Rifle Division went into combat against German defences north of "Kruglaia" grove on 14 January. Finally, Major-General P. N. Chernyshev's 239th and Colonel I. B. Gribov's 11th Rifle Divisions, the 12th and 13th Ski Brigades, and the 122nd Tank Brigade went into action over the next three days.

52 Group Huhner, defending from Shlissel'burg to north of Siniavino, consisted of the remnants of the 227th, 61st and 5th Mountain Infantry Divisions.

53 The 136th Rifle Division's 269th Rifle Regiment linked up with the 18th Rifle Division's 424th Rifle Regiment at 11:45 hours south of Workers' Settlement No 5.

54 Dukhanov's 142nd Naval Infantry and 138th Rifle Brigades attacked towards Siniavino, and his 102nd Rifle and 220th Tank Brigades and 123rd Rifle Division struck Gorodok No 1.

55 During the offensive Soviet forces captured German strongpoints at Shlissel'burg, Mar'ino, Lipka, Workers' Settlements Nos 1, 2, 3, 4, 5, 6, 7 and 8, and Podgornyi Station.

56 For their contributions to the victory, the GKO awarded the designations of 63rd and 64th Guards to General Simoniak's 136th and Colonel Poliakov's 327th Rifle Divisions, and 30th Guards to Lieutenant-Colonel Khrustitsky's 61st Tank Brigade.

57 The Soviets claim to have killed and wounded 19,000 German soldiers, captured 1275 prisoners, and destroyed 272 guns, 1200 machine guns and more than 300 mortars during Operation Spark.

58 Harrison E. Salisbury, *The 900 Days: The Siege of Leningrad* (New York: Harper & Row, 1969), 548.

59 For example, on 31 January 1943 only two regiments of the Spanish 250th Infantry Division defended the sector from Pushkin to Ivanovskoe south of Leningrad opposite the Leningrad Front's Fifty-Fifth Army. At the same time, just the 69th, 132nd and 81st Infantry Divisions defended the 100km- (62-mile-) wide sector opposite the Volkhov Front's Fifty-Fourth Army.

60 The *Stavka* expanded the offensive because it recognized the difficulties involved in mounting an offensive in the immediate Leningrad region.

61 Special Group Khozin, whose forces and commanders were handpicked by the *Stavka*, consisted of Lieutenant-General M. E. Katukov's newly formed First Tank Army and Lieutenant-General F. I. Tolbukhin's new Sixty-Eighth Army.

62 In addition, part of the Fifty-Fourth Army was to attack Liuban to both distract the Eighteenth Army and tie down its forces.

63 The Fifty-Fifth Army consisted of the 45th and 63rd Guards, 43rd, 46th, 56th, 72nd, 131st and 268th Rifle Divisions, the 56th and 250th Rifle, 34th and 35th Ski, and the 222nd Tank Brigades, and the 31st Tank Regiment.

64 Sviridov deployed the 45th and 63rd Guards and 43rd Rifle Divisions, 34th Ski Brigade, and 31st Tank Regiment in first echelon.

65 The mobile group, commanded by Major-General I. M. Liuboitsev, consisted of the 35th Ski and 122nd Tank Brigades.

66 The Fifty-Fourth Army comprised the 115th, 166th, 177th, 198th, 281st, 285th, 294th, 311th, 374th and 378th Rifle Divisions, the 14th and 140th Rifle Brigades, the 6th Naval Rifle Brigade, and the 122nd and 124th Tank Brigades.

67 On 1 February 1943 the Second Shock Army comprised the 64th Guards, 11th, 18th, 71st, 128th, 147th, 314th, 364th, 376th and 379th Rifle Divisions, the 72nd Rifle and 73rd Naval Rifle, and 16th and 98th Tank Brigades, the 32nd Guards Tank Regiment, and the 501st, 503rd and 507th Separate Tank Battalions. The Sixty-Seventh Army comprised the 13th, 46th, 90th, 142nd, 189th and 224th Rifle Divisions, the 11th, 55th, 56th, 102nd, 123rd, 138th, 142nd and 250th Rifle and 1st, 61st, 152nd and 220th Tank Brigades, the 31st and 46th Guards Tank Regiments, the 86th and Separate Tank Battalions, and the 16th Fortified Region.

68 Reinforcements included the 24th Infantry Division, portions of the 2nd SS Motorized Infantry Brigade, the Flanders Legion, and remnants of the 11th, 21st and 227th Divisions, which had been severally damaged in the fighting at Siniavino.

69 The 250th Division's Fusilier Battalion lost almost 90 percent of its strength.

70 The 166th, 198th, 311th and 378th Rifle Divisions, the 14th and 140th Rifle Brigades, the 6th Naval Rifle Brigade, and the 124th Tank Brigade.

71 Soviet critiques credited the defeat to the strongly fortified enemy defences, faulty reconnaissance, poor Soviet command and control at all levels of command, clumsy employment of tanks (which invariably became separated from the infantry), and ineffective artillery support.

72 The beginning of the German withdrawal from the Demiansk salient, codenamed Operation *Tsitin*, began on 19 February and totally disrupted Zhukov's plans for Operation Polar Star.

73 By this time German forces had abandoned most of the Demiansk salient.

74 The *Stavka*'s decision was based on intelligence information that the German Eighteenth Army was concentrating strong forces near Siniavino, with the intention of conducting both a flank attack against the Fifty-Fifth Army from positions at Pushkin and against the Sixty-Seventh and Second Shock Army to restore the blockade.

75 Voroshilov supervised operations in the Leningrad region, which were supposed to achieve their objectives by 25 March.

76 The *Stavka* was reacting to the counteroffensive by Manstein's Army Group South against Soviet forces in the Donbas, Khar'kov and Belgorod areas.

77 The Northwestern Front's Twenty-Seventh Army assaulted German defences east of Staraia Russa, and the Eleventh, Thirty-Fourth and Fifty-Third Armies attacked German defences south of Ramushevo. The latter group advanced to the Red'ia River before the attack failed.

78 The Fifty-Second Army comprised the 65th, 225th, 229th and 310th Rifle Divisions, the 38th Ski Brigade, the 34th and 53rd Aerosleigh Battalions, and the 16th Fortified Region, but no tanks. Meretskov reinforced the army with the 229th and 310th Rifle Divisions just prior to the attack.

79 The SS Police Division was subordinate to LIV Army Corps. It was reinforced by the Flanders Legion and supported on the right by the 24th Infantry Division and on the left by the 250th Spanish Division.

80 The 502nd Heavy Tank battalion was equipped with 88mm flak guns and several Tiger tanks.

81 For example, the Flanders Legion counted only 45 survivors out of its initial strength of 500 men.

82 Starikov concentrated his 286th, 256th, 378th, 374th and 265th Rifle Divisions in first echelon, supported by the 35th, 25th, 33rd and 50th Tank Regiments. The 239th, 64th Guards and 364th Rifle Divisions, and the 122nd and 185th Tank Brigades, were in second echelon, and the 372nd Rifle Division and 58th Rifle Brigade were in reserve. General Meretskov supported Starikov's army with most of his front's artillery.

83 The mobile group, which consisted of the 64th Guards Rifle Division's 191st Guards Rifle Regiment and a battalion of the 122nd Tank Brigade, cut the railroad east of Turyshkino Station. The bad weather prevented the Fourteenth Air Army from providing it with air support.

84 Hitler harboured some hopes of conducting new offensives in the Leningrad region, but only if the Wehrmacht achieved victory at Kursk. The German defeat at Kursk ended any such hope.

85 Once the Red Army defeated the German offensive, which the *Stavka* correctly assumed would be at Kursk, it planned to launch multiple offensives of its own, beginning against the flanks of German forces in the Kursk region and then expanding to encompass the entire front.

86 Govorov withdrew the Sixty-Seventh Army's nine rifle divisions, one tank brigade and two tank regiments into reserve for rest and refitting, and Meretskov withdrew four rifle divisions, three tank brigades and one tank regiment into front reserve and ordered its component armies to form reserves of one or two divisions each.

87 According to Foreign Armies East (*Fremde Heere Ost*) estimates, on 20 July Army Group North numbered 760,000 men organized into 43 infantry divisions and was opposed by 734,000 Soviet troops, backed up by 491,000 reservists. The same report indicated that Army Group North had 49 tanks and 407 guns and mortars facing an estimated 209 Soviet tanks and 2793 guns and mortars, backed up by 843 tanks and 1800 guns and mortars in reserve.

88 Simoniak's corps consisted of the 45th, 63rd and 65th Guards Rifle Divisions, supported by the 30th Guards and 220th Tank Brigades and the 31st and 29th Guards Tank Regiments.

89 The 90th, 268th, 43rd and 123rd Rifle Divisions, deployed from west to east, were to attack east of Siniavino.

90 The Eighth Army's immediate mission was to penetrate German defences and reach the Tortolovo-Karbusel' line. Subsequently, it was to exploit the offensive to link up with the Sixty-Seventh Army's forces at Mga, while detaching at least two rifle divisions and one tank brigade to strike Siniavino from the south.

91 The first shock group consisted of the 18th and 378th Rifle Division in first echelon and the 379th and 239th Rifle Divisions in second, and the southern shock group comprised the 256th and 364th Rifle Divisions in first echelon and the 165th and 374th Rifle Divisions in second. Starikov reinforced each first-echelon division with a tank regiment and assigned his 16th and 122nd Tank Brigades to the second echelon with orders to exploit the offensive. The Eighth Army included the 32nd, 33rd, 35th and 50th Guards and 25th and 185th Separate Tank Regiments, but their precise subordination during the attack remains obscure.

92 The 372nd Rifle Division defended the army's right flank, and the 265th and 382nd Rifle Divisions and 1st and 22nd Rifle Brigades conducted the supporting attack on the left. The 286th Rifle Division and 58th Rifle Brigade were in reserve.

93 In his main attack sector, Starikov's force of at least 50,000 men and over 150 tanks outnumbered the German defenders by a factor of almost five to one and far more in armour, but the ratio was considerably less favourable in the secondary attack sector.

94 The Thirteenth Air Army flew 540 air support sorties on the first day of the operation.

95 Over the course of several days, the Germans committed, first, the 58th and then the 28th Jäger and 126th Infantry Divisions with supporting tanks into combat near Siniavino.

96 Worse still, many of Starikov's supporting tanks got bogged down in the marshy terrain or were blown up by enemy mines and anti-tank guns.

97 The 379th and 165th Rifle Divisions reinforced and the 18th and 256th Rifle Divisions withdrew.

98 The 256th and 374th Rifle Divisions and 35th and 30th Guards Tank Regiments reinforced the 378th, 364th and 165th Rifle Divisions already fighting in the region.

99 The 311th Rifle Division and the 503rd Separate Tank Battalion.

100 It remains unclear who ordered Govorov to launch the September assault.

101 The 45th, 63rd and 64th Guards Rifle Divisions attacked Siniavino with the 120th, 124th and 196th Rifle Divisions on the left, and the 123rd and, later, the 11th and 268th Rifle Divisions on the right.

102 XXVIII Army Corps' 12th Luftwaffe Field Division and 81st, 132nd and 96th Infantry Divisions occupied the salient, which jutted out to the northeast along the Volkhov River north of Chudovo.

103 The Fourth Army was commanded by Lieutenant-General N. I. Gusev.

104 In its October Nevel offensive, the Soviet Kalinin Front drove a wedge between Kuechler's Sixteenth Army and adjacent Army Group Centre.

105 The northern half of the line was anchored on natural obstacles such as the Narva River and Lakes Chud and Pskov. The southern half jutted eastwards to protect the major road and rail centres at Pskov and Ostrov, and tied in with Army Group Centre's portion of the line south of Nevel. When occupied the line would shorten Army Group North's front by 25 percent.

106 Southwestwards from the frontlines, the most important intermediate positions were the Mga, Kussinka, Rollbahn (railroad), 2nd Wolchow, Oredesh, Ingermannland and Luga positions.

107 The most important strongpoints were at Gattschina (Krasnogvardeisk), Tschudowo (Chudovo), Nowgorod (Novgorod), Luga, Jamburg (Kingisepp) and Narwa (Narva). A 50,000-man construction force, including thousands of people levied from the civilian population, improved communications back to Riga and Dvinsk, built 6000 bunkers, 800 of which were concrete, laid 200km (125 miles) of barbed wire, and dug 40km (25 miles) of trenches and anti-tank traps. Construction materials rolled in at a rate of 100 railcar loads per day during November and December.

108 The Leningrad Front suffered 390,794 casualties, including 88,745 killed, captured or missing; the Volkhov Front 321,404 casualties, including 77,904 dead, captured or missing; and the Northwestern Front 335,451 casualties, including 88,798 killed, captured or missing.

109 For example, the Spanish 250th Division lost 3200 men, or about 30 percent of its strength, in the February fighting and other divisions suffered equally heavy losses.

CHAPTER 9 NOTES

1 According to Soviet estimates, on 1 January 1944 the German Armed Forces numbered 10,680,000 men, of which seven million were in the field forces and the remainder in the reserves. At this time, the German ground forces numbered 4,399,000, of which 2,740,000 (63 percent) were deployed on the Eastern Front, organized into 198 divisions and six brigades. German records indicate that the German Army fielded 2,498,000 men on the Eastern Front on 14 October 1943, organized into 151 infantry and 26 panzer divisions. In addition, the Finns, Hungarians and Romanians fielded another 500,000 men, bringing the Axis total to 3,068,000 men. These forces faced 6,165,000 Soviet troops.

2 The Second Shock Army replaced the Coastal Operation Group in November 1943 and the Fifty-Fifth Army was absorbed into the Sixty-Seventh Army in late December 1943. Admiral Tributs' Baltic Fleet (Admiral V. F. Tributs), still subordinate to the Leningrad Front, was based at Leningrad and Kronshtadt and was defending sea communications between Leningrad and the Oranienbaum bridgehead.

3 The Fourth Army had been disbanded in November to improve front command and control.

4 When formed on the base of the former Briansk Front, the Baltic Front occupied the sector between the Northwestern and First Baltic (former Kalinin) Fronts. On 26 November the *Stavka* disbanded the Northwestern Front and assigned its sector and the First Shock Army's sector to the Second Baltic Front.

5 As of 14 January, the Leningrad Front's strength was 417,600 men, the Volkhov Front 260,000, and the Second Baltic Front's First Shock Army 54,900 men, which, with the Baltic Fleet's 89,600 men, totalled 822,000 men available to participate in the forthcoming operation. In addition, about 35,000 partisans organized into 13 partisan brigades were operating in Army Group North's rear area.

6 South of Leningrad, Colonel-General Lindemann's Eighteenth Army manned defences from the Gulf of Finland to Lake Il'men opposite the Leningrad and Volkhov Fronts. After losing seven infantry divisions to other sectors from September through December, the Eighteenth Army received one division (SS Panzergrenadier Division *Nordland*) and two brigades (SS Panzergrenadier Brigade *Nederland* and the 1000-man Spanish Legion). On 1 January, by Soviet estimates, the army had 14 infantry, five Luftwaffe field and one panzergrenadier divisions, one divisional combat group, and three infantry and one panzergrenadier brigade. In addition, the Eighteenth Army formed two artillery groups, the first north of Krasnoe Selo to bombard Leningrad and the second north of Mga to bombard Soviet communications routes into Leningrad. By Soviet estimates, the Eighteenth Army still fielded 4950 guns and mortars, 200 tanks and assault guns and 200 aircraft of the First Air Fleet. South of Lake Il'men, Colonel-General Busch's Sixteenth Army, consisting of 18 infantry divisions, one Luftwaffe field division, one infantry brigade and composite Group *Eicholm* (17 battalions) faced the Second Baltic Front. According to German records, on 14 October Army Group North's 44 divisions (including forces in Northern Finland) with a strength of 601,000 men, 146 tanks and 2389 guns and mortars faced an estimated 959,000 Soviet troops, 650 tanks and 3680 guns and mortars. Discounting the forces in northern Finland, the Eighteenth and Sixteenth Armies fielded roughly 500,000 men from the Gulf of Finland to north of Nevel against about 800,000 Soviet troops.

7 Army Group North defended in single echelon, with three security divisions and one training division in reserve, though occupied against the partisans. In addition, the Eighteenth Army had one infantry division in reserve, and Sixteenth Army had three infantry divisions in reserve.

8 German defences at Oranienbaum consisted of a single defensive belt with two positions and few fortified strongpoints, manned by one regiment of the SS Police Division, SS Panzergrenadier Division *Nordland* and the 10th and 9th Luftwaffe Field Divisions. The strongest German defences were opposite the Leningrad Front's Forty-Second Army and the Volkhov Front's Fifty-Ninth Army, where the fortified main defensive belt was 4–6km (2.5–3.7 miles) deep and was backed up by a second belt 8–12km (5–7.5 miles) to the rear.

9 The strongest centres of resistance were at Uritsk, Staro-Panovo, Novo-Panovo, Bol'shoi Bittolovo, Aleksandrovka, Pushkin, Krasnoe Selo, Hill 172.3 (Voron'ia Hill), Mga, Podberez'ia, Khutini, Kirillovskoe Monastery and Novgorod.

10 Initially, in late 1943, Kuechler concluded that the Red Army was planning a large-scale offensive around Leningrad and Novgorod to encircle the Eighteenth Army, and decided to forestall the offensive and shorten the front by conducting a planned withdrawal to the Panther Line. However, by early January the threat of a major offensive seemed to have diminished somewhat. While disturbed by the obvious Soviet build-up in the Oranienbaum bridgehead, Army Group North assessed that the Leningrad Front was relying on replacements from Leningrad's population, and the Red Army offensives at Vitebsk and farther south seemed to be drawing off reserves. Accordingly, from 29 December to 4 January, the OKH transferred three divisions from the Eighteenth to the Sixteenth Army.

11 Since the *Stavka* was conducting simultaneous offensives in the Leningrad and Novgorod regions and in Belorussia and the Ukraine, additional reinforcements were scarce. Nevertheless, it assigned the Volkhov Front additional long-range aviation forces and one self-propelled artillery regiment, and the Leningrad Front four self-propelled artillery regiments, tank reserves and one assault engineer-sapper brigade.

12 There were two operational variants: "Neva 1" in the event of an enemy withdrawal and "Neva 2" in the event a fully fledged penetration was necessary. The front began planning for "Neva 2" in November, after transferring the Second Shock Army into the Oranienbaum bridgehead.

13 The Thirteenth Air Army, II Guards Fighter Aviation Corps (PVO) and part of the Baltic Fleet's Air Forces were to provide artillery and material support.

14 If the Forty-Second Army's assault failed, the Second Shock Army's CVIII Rifle Corps and 152nd Tank Brigade were to attack towards Krasnoe Selo and Dudergof from second echelon. If the army linked up successfully with the Forty-Second Army, its second echelon was to advance southwards in pursuit and capture key German withdrawal routes southwest of Leningrad. Initially, Fediuninsky's army was to advance 17–21km (10.6–13.1 miles) in a period of 5–6 days.

15 Govorov transferred his Second Shock Army from Leningrad to the Oranienbaum bridgehead using the Baltic Fleet to transport the army via the ice roads over the Gulf of Finland. The entire process took from 5 November to 21 January and was still under way when the offensive began. By that time, the front had moved the Second Shock Army headquarters, five rifle divisions (the 11th, 43rd, 90th, 131st and 196th), 13 RVGK artillery regiments, two tank and one self-propelled artillery regiments, one tank brigade, and 700 wagons with ammunition and other cargoes into the bridgehead. During the same period, the front regrouped most of its artillery from the Mga-Siniavino sector to the Oranienbaum bridgehead and the Forty-Second Army's sector.

16 Maslennikov retained two rifle divisions in reserve. His plan required the Forty-Second Army's forces to advance 20–25km (12.5–15.6 miles), but set no time limits on its advance. Govorov allocated 80 percent of his front's artillery, the Baltic Fleet's naval guns and the bulk of its supporting aviation to support the Forty-Second and Second Shock Armies' assault. While planning a 100-minute preparation to precede the attack, for deceptive purposes he also ordered the Sixty-Seventh Army to conduct an artillery preparation. A total of 653 aircraft from the Thirteenth Air Army provided air support against an estimated 140 German aircraft. As had been the case in earlier operations, largely due to the heavy German defences, difficult terrain and problems associated with moving large armoured forces into the Leningrad region, armoured operations were limited primarily to infantry support. His armour strength was 550 tanks and self-propelled guns. Govorov's front also relied heavily on engineers to overcome the powerful German defences, the swampy forested terrain and the severe winter weather conditions.

17 If German forces began to withdraw from the Tosno and Chudovo regions, the two armies were clear enemy forces from the railroad from Tosno to Chudovo and attack towards Luga to assist both the Leningrad Front and the Fifty-Ninth Army in the destruction of the Eighteenth Army. Meretskov assigned specific missions to his armies between mid-October and 31 December.

18 The Southern Operational Group consisted of the 58th Rifle Brigade, 299th Rifle Regiment, a 225th Rifle Division ski battalion and the 34th and 44th Aerosleigh Battalions.

19 Korovnikov's army to advance 30km (18.75 miles) in 3–5 days and liberate Novgorod, while the depth of the front's entire operation was 110–120km (68.75–75 miles). Meretskov also assigned 80 percent of his artillery and most of his air assets to support the Fifty-Ninth Army and planned to precede his ground assault with a 110-minute artillery preparation. He supported his assault with 257 aircraft from the Thirteenth Air Army and 330 additional night bombers from four long-range aviation corps provided by the *Stavka*, against the roughly 103 German aircraft that could operate in his sector. Meretskov's armour, which totalled 231 tanks and 25 self-propelled guns, performed the same infantry support function. While performing the same tasks as the Leningrad Front's engineers, those in the Volkhov Front had to prepare numerous crossings over the Volkhov and other rivers, and Lake Il'men. For this reason, Meretskov assigned additional engineer forces to the Fifty-Ninth Army.

20 The Germans responded to the deception by transferring the Panzergrenadier Brigade *Nederland* to the region from Yugoslavia. So effective was the deception that even Red Army personnel believed the assault would occur in that region. The Germans also regrouped their forces prior to the offensive. The OKH transferred the 96th and 254th Infantry Divisions from the Eighteenth Army to Army Group South. The Eighteenth Army shifted the 61st Infantry Division from the Mga region to just north of Krasnogvardeisk beginning on 10 January, and the SS Panzergrenadier Brigade *Nederland* to positions opposite the Second Shock Army's right flank in response to the Soviet deception plan. To the south, the Sixteenth Army moved its reserve, the 290th Infantry Division, to the Shimsk, Utorgosh and Sol'tsy region, to back up German defences at the junction of the Sixteenth and Eighteenth Armies.

21 Govorov concentrated 72 percent of his infantry, 68 percent of his artillery and all of his tanks and self-propelled guns in the Second Shock and Forty-Second Armies' sector, and Meretskov concentrated 48 percent of his infantry, 55 percent of his artillery, almost all of his Katiushas, and 80 percent of his armour in the Fifty-Ninth Army's sector. Tactical concentration increased this superiority by a factor of two to three.

22 The 9th and 10th Luftwaffe Divisions belonged to III SS Panzer Corps.

23 The 12th Tank Brigade and the 22nd and 204th Tank Regiments supported Fediuninsky's attacking corps.

24 Three construction battalions and a battalion from SS Panzergrenadier Division *Nordland* conducted the counterattacks.

25 The Forty-Second Army faced L Army Corps' 126th, 170th and 215th Infantry Divisions.

26 Soviet critiques claim that the limited progress by both armies was due to poor reconnaissance and command and control, particularly in the Second Shock Army, the inability of heavy weapons to keep up with the infantry, and an effective counter-barrage by L Army Corps' artillery that blunted the Forty-Second Army's ground assault. Thus, the Second Shock Army's 204th Tank Regiment lost 19 tanks in enemy minefields, five in enemy trenches and four tanks while crossing the Chernaia River. The Forty-Second Army's 260th Tank Regiment got bogged down in an anti-tank ditch and subsequently lost six KVs to German mines.

27 The mobile group consisted of the 152nd Tank Brigade with a self-propelled artillery regiment, a truck-mounted rifle battalion, a light artillery battalion and three sapper battalions on trucks.

28 Maslennikov committed his CXXIII Rifle Corps on XXX Guards Rifle Corps' right flank. The mobile tank group, formed around a nucleus of the 1st Red Banner and 220th Tank Brigades, was to envelop Krasnoe Selo from the west.

29 The mobile tank group consisted of the two tank brigades reinforced by two self-propelled artillery regiments, an anti-aircraft artillery regiment, an anti-tank artillery battery and two sapper companies,

30 Lindemann committed his last reserve, the 61st Infantry Division, in support of the shattered 10th Luftwaffe Division on 14 and 15 January in an attempt to slow the Second Shock Army's advance.

31 The Rollbahn Line was forward and parallel to the railroad and road from Leningrad to Chudovo.

32 Kuechler protested that to do so would permit the Soviets to unite their forces for an even stronger assault.

33 Lindemann reinforced his defences north of Krasnoe Selo with portions of his 225th and 21st Infantry Divisions from Mga and Chudovo, and the SS *Nordland* and 11th Infantry Divisions.

34 The Second Shock Army's CVIII Rifle Corps went into action early on 18 January, and CXXII Rifle Corps captured Ropsha the next day. The forward elements of the 168th Rifle Division (CVIII Rifle Corps) linked up with the 54th Engineer Battalion of the Forty-Second Army's mobile group just south of Ropsha late on 19 January.

35 The victory also improved front command and control, logistical support and manoeuvre capabilities.

36 The Leningrad Front also reported destroying or capturing 265 guns (85 heavy), 159 mortars, 30 tanks and 18 warehouses with ammunition.

37 The attack stalled because the infantry support tanks arrived late and many fell victim to craters and swamps due to poor reconnaissance and engineer work. Nevertheless, during the night sappers built a bridge over the Volkhov River capable of carrying tanks.

38 The neighbouring 1254th Regiment joined the attack, and the force overcame the first two German trenches and seized a small bridgehead over the Pit'ba River at Malovodskoe.

39 The corps sent the 290th Infantry Division's 503rd Infantry Regiment and the Cavalry Regiment *Nord* to block the Soviet advance south of Novgorod, and the 24th Infantry Division (from Mga) north of Novgorod.

40 The reinforcements included one rifle division from second echelon and an armoured car battalion from his reserve to develop success south of Novgorod. To the north, he committed, first, the 16th Tank Brigade and a self-propelled artillery regiment in VI Rifle Corps' sector, and then the 65th Rifle Division and 29th Tank Brigade from his second-echelon CXII Rifle Corps.

41 The 6th and 29th Tank Brigades and VI Rifle Corps' 239th Rifle Division reached the road.

42 Roginsky's mission was to capture Liuban, prevent the Germans from reinforcing their defences at Novgorod, and assist the Fifty-Ninth Army in the destruction of the German XXVIII and XXXVIII Army Corps. Initially, Roginsky attacked with his 80th Rifle Division and CXV Rifle Corps (the 281st and 285th Rifle Divisions), but subsequently his 44th Rifle Division joined the assault early on 17 January by attacking south of the Tigoda River.

43 The 225th and 372nd Rifle Divisions reinforced the Southern Operational Group.

44 The initial reinforcements included elements of the 24th and 21st Infantry Divisions from Mga, the 250th Infantry Division from Sol'tsy and the 8th Jäger Division. Later, the SS Cavalry Regiment *Nord* went into action south of Novgorod on 16 January and the 121st Infantry Division from Tosno north of Novgorod on 17 January.

45 According to Soviet critiques, poor army and corps command and control, heavy German fortifications, the poor terrain and a thaw hindered the Fifty-Ninth Army's advance and permitted the Germans to bring up fresh reserves.

46 The committed forces included CXII Rifle Corps and 122nd Tank Brigade.

47 The front's 52nd Separate Auto Regiment lacked 48 percent of its required trucks and the 11th Regiment 82.3 percent. The two regiments were short of 666 vehicles in all.

48 Soviet critiques faulted the XIV Rifle Corps' commander for poor reconnaissance.

49 XIV Rifle Corps' 191st and 225th Rifle Divisions and VII Rifle Corps' 382nd Rifle Division captured Novgorod.

50 These included elements of the 28th Jäger and 1st Luftwaffe Field Divisions, two separate battalions, and elements of the SS Cavalry Regiment *Nord*.

51 Soviet sources reported destroying or capturing 182 guns, 120 mortars, 263 vehicles, 21 tractors and 28 warehouses filled with supplies.

52 Among the most serious of these deficiencies were poor exploitation of manoeuvre to bypass or envelop enemy strongpoints, lack of night combat, inadequate reconnaissance of German defences, and ineffective command and control, particularly at army and corps levels.

53 The 290th Infantry Division.

54 The 227th and part of the 225th Infantry Divisions.

55 Soviet critiques faulted Sviridov's CXVIII Rifle Corps for its slow reaction, stating that its forward detachment operated "slowly and indecisively".

56 A 29 January barb read: "You have not fulfilled your mission of the day on 23. 1. 44. In spite of my orders, the army's formations continue to mark time in place before the severely damaged enemy forces, neither suffering casualties nor having absolute success. As before, the corps commanders are displaying slowness, are directing combat weakly, and not directing the corps to employ manoeuvre and decisive movement forward. Exploiting our slowness, the enemy, who is covering in small groups, is withdrawing his main forces south and southwest from Krasnogvardeisk and Elizavetino."

57 The German L Army Corps defended Krasnogvardeisk with its 11th and 170th Infantry Divisions and remnants of the 126th, 61st, 215th and 225th Infantry Divisions, and Pushkin and Slutsk with the 215th and part of the 24th Infantry Divisions. Heavy artillery was positioned southeast of Krasnogvardeisk and the 12th Panzer Division and 502nd Panzer Battalion were beginning to concentrate south and southwest of the town.

58 XXXXIII and CIX Rifle Corps were on Fediuninsky's right flank, and CXXII and CVIII Rifle Corps were on his left flank.

59 Regiments and battalions left behind battalion- and company sized rearguards reinforced by artillery and tanks to conduct delaying actions in villages and along roads. The Germans destroyed or mined bridges and roads. The heaviest resistance was along the railroad line towards Kingisepp on the army's left flank.

60 Combat groups from the 126th, 225th, 9th Luftwaffe Field, 11th and 215th Infantry Divisions defended the approaches to Krasnogvardeisk.

61 At 16:00 hours on 26 January, Govorov transferred CXXII Rifle Corps from the Second Shock Army to the Forty-Second Army and the Forty-Second Army's CXVII Rifle Corps to the Sixty-Seventh Army.

62 Soviet critiques note that Sviridov's army "failed to fulfil the front commander's demand to destroy the German forces in the Pushkin, Slutsk, Ul'ianovka and Tosno regions and reach the Vyritsa-Lisino-Korpus line by 26 January because of weak command and control." Govorov then transferred CXVII Rifle Corps from the Forty-Second to the Sixty-Seventh Army and withdrew the Sixty-Seventh Army's CXVI Rifle Corps and 13th Rifle Division into the front reserve.

63 Sviridov's CX and CXVIII Rifle Corps captured their designated objectives on 28 January and, after being relieved by the 14th Fortified Region on 29 January, reverted to front reserve in Pushkin.

64 Since CX and CXVII Rifle Corps had only recently been assigned to the army, command and control was poor. The experienced 12th Panzer Division and remnants of the 212th, 126th and 11th Infantry Divisions defended from southeast of Krasnogvardeisk to Siverskii. It took three days of heavy fighting to expel them from the town.

65 A single German division delayed the army's main forces for several hours along the Mga River. Unknown to the Eighth Army, the experienced 227th Infantry Division, which had been defending along the Mga River, had been transferred to Krasnogvardeisk, leaving only the 212th Infantry Division with 7750 men to defend the entire sector. Starikov's two rifle divisions and single rifle brigade, numbering 13,167 men, were unable to overcome the German forces in so formidable a defence.

66 The Fifty-Fourth Army faced the German XXVIII Army Corps' 121st and 21st Infantry Divisions, the Spanish Legion, and combat groups from the SS Police and 12th and 13th Luftwaffe Field Divisions. The corps began withdrawing its left flank on the night of 20/21, sending the SS Police Division southwards to oppose the Fifty-Ninth Army, while the 21st Infantry and 13th Luftwaffe Divisions continued defending along the Volkhov River near Chudovo opposite the Fifty-Fourth Army's left flank

67 The 121st Infantry Division abandoned the town late on 29 January after being enveloped from three sides.

68 A successful link-up by the Fifty-Fourth and Fifty-Ninth Armies would have encircled both XXVIII and XXXVIII Army Corps northeast of Luga.

69 The Fifty-Ninth Army's mission was to penetrate the Germans' second defensive belt before enemy reinforcements arrived, capture Batetskii, and advance to Luga from the east. Korovnikov provided significant engineer support to his VI, VII and CXII Rifle Corps so that they could cross the roadless and heavily forested swampland spanning the entire region east of Luga.

70 For example, by the day's end on 21 January Combat Group *Schuldt* (2nd SS Brigade, 28th Jäger Division, 24th, 121st and 21st Infantry Divisions) defended from Spasskaia Polist' to Tatino Station and covered the Finev Lug axis, along which XXVIII Army Corps was withdrawing from the Liuban-Chudovo region. Group *Speth* (1st Luftwaffe Division and elements of Cavalry Regiment *Nord*) defended the defile between the swamps from Zapol'e to Vashkovo. The 8th Jäger Division defended from Izori to Lent'evo, and Group *Feurguth* (290th Infantry Division and Cavalry Brigade *Nord*'s main body) defended along the railroad from Novgorod to Shimsk.

71 Soviet after-action-reports noted that VI Rifle Corps was exhausted and woefully under-strength from its earlier fighting, its accompanying 29th Tank Brigade had only eight operational tanks, and was required to penetrate a prepared defence in thaw conditions.

72 Meretskov criticized Korovnikov for his army's slow advance, noting, in particular, CXII and VI Rifle Corps' failure to employ manoeuvre and their ski battalions, and their poor reconnaissance and frequent resort to frontal attacks. VI Rifle Corps was able to penetrate the Germans' second defensive line and reach the Luga River late on 26 January only by committing its second echelon.

73 By this time, VII Rifle Corps had penetrated the German second defensive belt and had advanced up to 35km (21.8 miles) to the west and southwest in five days, threatening the Leningrad-Dno railroad in the Peredol'skaia region.

74 Command and control was difficult since the entire Volkhov Front had only four cable companies.

75 The 2nd Rifle Division was on the Fifty-Ninth Army's right flank.

76 It was still possible, however, for CXII Rifle Corps to block the German withdrawal, but only if the corps could capture Oredezh in timely fashion. XXVIII Army Corps had to use the Oredezh-Luga road since partisans had blown up the railroad.

77 The Germans first committed the 285th Security Division and later part of the 12th Panzer Division to the fighting at Peredol'skaia Station.

78 One *Stavka* message read: "Do not engage in battle for Shimsk and Sol'tsy. It is not the main effort. Cover along that axis. The main thing is to capture Luga as quickly as possible. Upon capturing Luga deploy for an advance on Pskov along two axes." It then reinforced his front with 15,000 replacements and 130 tanks.

79 Soviet General Staff critiques attributed the failure to the front's lack of concentration, poor terrain and weather conditions, extended supply lines, lack of effective air support due to bad weather, the inability of artillery to keep up with the infantry, and excessive tank

losses. Meretskov's four supporting tank brigades and self-propelled regiments had only 19 tanks and four guns on 2 February, and the separate tank regiments and battalions were in the same state.

80 Popov shifted his Tenth Guards Army to new positions southwest of Novosokol'niki, and prepared to attack with his Sixth and Tenth Guards Armies and part of the Twenty-Second Army.

81 These transfers included the 8th Jäger Division, part of the 21st Luftwaffe Field Division, two battalions of the 32nd and 132nd Infantry Divisions, the 303rd Assault Gun Battalion, and the 58th Infantry Division from the Sixteenth Army's right flank.

82 During the period from 14 January to 14 February, the Leningrad and Volkhov Fronts reported capturing 180 tanks, 1800 guns, 4660 machine guns, 22,000 rifles or submachine guns, 1,810,000 shells, 17 million cartridges, 2648 vehicles, 615 railroad wagons, 353 warehouses, and 7200 German soldiers.

83 During their summer operations in Karelia, the Karelian and Leningrad Fronts suffered 96,375 casualties, including 23,674 dead, captured or missing, out of 451,500 troops committed to combat.

84 The employment of this reserve permitted XXX Guard Rifle Corps to attack in single echelon.

85 For example, the Second Shock Army committed its second-echelon CVIII Rifle Corps over a period of two days (the 196th Rifle Division on 18–19 January and the 168th Rifle Division on 19 January). In another instance, the Forty-Second Army committed its combined-arms reserve into combat one regiment at a time, and command and control failed. This error, combined with poor reconnaissance, inadequate artillery and engineer support, and weak command and control, negated the effectiveness of the mobile tank group. Finally, the Volkhov Front's Fifty-Ninth Army committed its second-echelon CXII Rifle Corps on a secondary axis, dissipating the army's effectiveness and slowing its advance.

86 The Leningrad Headquarters of the Partisan Movement reported that 22,000 partisans in Leningrad *oblast* killed 21,556 Germans and destroyed 58,563 rails, 51 railroad and 247 road bridges, 136 trains, 509km (318 miles) of telegraph lines, 1620 vehicles, 811 carts, 28 warehouses, 33 tanks, and four aircraft between 14 January and 1 March 1944.

APPENDIX 1

Red Army Order of Battle in the Leningrad Region

22 JUNE 1941
NORTHERN FRONT

SEVENTH ARMY
54th Rifle Division
71st Rifle Division
168th Rifle Division
237th Rifle Division

26th Fortified Region (Sortavalo)
208th Separate Anti-aircraft Artillery
 Battalion
55th Mixed Aviation Division
184th Separate Sapper Battalion

FOURTEENTH ARMY
XXXXII Rifle Corps
 104th Rifle Division
 122nd Rifle Division
14th Rifle Division
52nd Rifle Division
23rd Fortified Region (Murmansk)

104th High Command Reserve Gun
 Artillery Regiment
1st Tank Division (I Mechanized
 Corps)
1st Mixed Aviation Division
42nd Corrective-Aviation Squadron
31st Separate Sapper Battalion

TWENTY-THIRD ARMY
XIX Rifle Corps
 115th Rifle Division
 122nd Rifle Division
L Rifle Corps
 43rd Rifle Division
 70th Rifle Division
 123rd Rifle Division
27th Fortified Region (Keksholm)
28th Fortified Region (Vyborg)
24th Corps Artillery Regiment
28th Corps Artillery Regiment
43rd Corps Artillery Regiment
573rd Gun Artillery Regiment
101st Howitzer Artillery Regiment
108th High-power Howitzer Artillery
 Regiment (RGK)

519th High-power Howitzer Artillery
 Regiment (RGK)
20th Separate Mortar Battalion
27th Separate Anti-aircraft Artillery
 Battalion
241st Separate Anti-aircraft Artillery
 Battalion
X Mechanized Corps
 21st Tank Division
 24th Tank Division
 198th Motorized Division
 7th Motorcycle Regiment
5th Mixed Aviation Division
41st Bomber Aviation Division
15th Corrective-Aviation Squadron
19th Corrective Aviation Squadron
109th Motorized Engineer Battalion
153rd Separate Engineer Battalion

FRONT SUBORDINATE
177th Rifle Division
191st Rifle Division
8th Rifle Brigade
21st Fortified Region
22d Fortified Region (Karelian)
25th Fortified Region (Pskov)
29th Fortified Region
541st Howitzer Artillery Regiment
 (RGK)
577th Howitzer Artillery Regiment
 (RGK)
II Corps PVO
 115th Anti-aircraft Artillery
 Regiment
 169th Anti-aircraft Artillery
 Regiment
 189th Anti-aircraft Artillery
 Regiment
 192nd Anti-aircraft Artillery
 Regiment
 194th Anti-aircraft Artillery
 Regiment

351st Anti-aircraft Artillery
 Regiment
Vyborg Brigade PVO Region
Murmansk Brigade PVO Region
Pskov Brigade PVO Region
Luga Brigade PVO Region
Petrozavodsk Brigade PVO Region
I Mechanized Corps
 3rd Tank Division
 163rd Motorized Division
 5th Motorcycle Regiment
2nd Mixed Aviation Division
39th Fighter Aviation Division
3rd Fighter Aviation Division PVO
54th Fighter Aviation Division PVO
311th Reconnaissance Aviation
 Regiment
103rd Corrective-Aviation Squadron
12th Engineer Regiment
29th Engineer Regiment
6th Pontoon-Bridge Regiment

1 AUGUST 1941
NORTHERN FRONT

SEVENTH ARMY
54th Rifle Division
71st Rifle Division
3rd DNO
3rd Naval Infantry Brigade
9th Motorized Rifle Regiment
24th Motorized Rifle Regiment
452nd Motorized Rifle Regiment

108th High-power Howitzer Artillery
  Regiment (RGK)
47th Separate Mortar Battalion
Petrozavodsk Brigade PVO Region
2nd Tank Regiment
7th Motorcycle Regiment
55th Mixed Aviation Division
18th Separate Engineer Battalion

EIGHTH ARMY
X Rifle Corps
  10th Rifle Division
  11th Rifle Division
XI Rifle Corps
  16th Rifle Division
  48th Rifle Division
  125th Rifle Division
  118th Rifle Division
  268th Rifle Division

22nd NKVD Rifle Division
47th Corps Artillery Regiment
51st Corps Artillery Regiment
73rd Corps Artillery Regiment
39th Separate Anti-aircraft Artillery
  Battalion
103rd Separate Anti-aircraft Artillery
  Battalion
29th Separate Sapper Battalion
80th Separate Sapper Battalion

FOURTEENTH ARMY
XXXXII Rifle Corps
  104th Rifle Division
  122nd Rifle Division
14th Rifle Division
52nd Rifle Division
23rd Fortified Region
1st Motorized Rifle Regiment (1st
  Tank Division)

104th Howitzer Artillery Regiment
  (RGK)
208th Separate Anti-aircraft Artillery
  Battalion
Murmansk Brigade PVO Region
Separate tank battalion
1st Mixed Aviation Division
31st Separate Sapper Battalion

TWENTY-THIRD ARMY
XIX Rifle Corps
  115th Rifle Division
  142nd Rifle Division
  168th Rifle Division
43rd Rifle Division
123rd Rifle Division
367th Rifle Regiment (71st Rifle
  Division)
27th Fortified Region
28th Fortified Region
24th Corps Artillery Regiment
28th Corps Artillery Regiment
101st Howitzer Artillery Regiment
  (RGK)
577th Howitzer Artillery Regiment
  (RGK)

20th Separate Mortar Battalion
27th Separate Anti-aircraft Artillery
  Battalion
241st Separate Anti-aircraft Artillery
  Battalion
485th Separate Anti-aircraft Artillery
  Battalion
198th Motorized Division
5th Mixed Aviation Division
53rd Separate Engineer Battalion
54th Separate Engineer Battalion
40th Pontoon-Bridge Battalion
41st Pontoon-Bridge Battalion
234th Separate Sapper Battalion

LUGA OPERATIONAL GROUP
XXXXI Rifle Corps
  111th Rifle Division
  177th Rifle Division
  235th Rifle Division
1st Rifle Regiment (3rd DNO)
260th Separate Machine-gun Artillery
  Battalion

262nd Separate Machine-gun
  Artillery Battalion
541st Howitzer Artillery Regiment
  (RGK)
Luga Brigade PVO Region
24th Tank Division
259th Separate Sapper Battalion

Kingisepp Defence Sector
90th Rifle Division
191st Rifle Division
2nd DNO
4th DNO

Leningrad Kirov Infantry School
21st Fortified Region
1st Tank Division
60th Separate Armoured Train

FRONT SUBORDINATE
265th Rifle Division
272nd Rifle Division
281st Rifle Division
1st GDNO
2nd GDNO
3rd GDNO
4th GDNO
8th Rifle Brigade
22nd Fortified Region

29th Fortified Region
Krasnogvardeisk Fortified Region
II PVO Corps
Svir Brigade PVO Region
Vyborg Brigade PVO Region
7th Fighter Aviation Division PVO
39th Fighter Aviation Division
2nd Bomber Aviation Division
1st Mixed Aviation Brigade

1 SEPTEMBER 1941
LENINGRAD FRONT

EIGHTH ARMY
11th Rifle Division
48th Rifle Division
118th Rifle Division
125th Rifle Division
191st Rifle Division
268th Rifle Division
76th Latvian Rifle Regiment

266th Separate Machine-gun Artillery
  Battalion
47th Corps Artillery Regiment
73rd Corps Artillery Regiment
1st/24th Corps Artillery Regiment
39th Separate Anti-aircraft Artillery
  Battalion
103rd Separate Anti-aircraft Artillery
  Battalion

FORTY-SECOND ARMY
2nd GDNO
3rd GDNO
Krasnogvardeisk Fortified Region
51st Corps Artillery Regiment
690th Anti-tank Artillery Regiment

Mixed Artillery Regiment
704th Artillery Regiment (198th
  Motorized Division)
42nd Pontoon-Bridge Battalion
106th Motorized Engineer Battalion

FIFTY-FIFTH ARMY
70th Rifle Division
90th Rifle Division
168th Rifle Division
237th Rifle Division
1st DNO
4th DNO

2nd Rifle Regiment (3rd GDNO)
Slutsk-Kolpino Fortified Region
14th Anti-tank Artillery Brigade
24th Corps Artillery Regiment
47th Separate Mortar Battalion
84th Separate Tank Battalion
86th Separate Tank Battalion

SOUTHERN OPERATIONAL GROUP
XXXXI Rifle Corps
  111th Rifle Division
  177th Rifle Division
  235th Rifle Division
1st Rifle Regiment (3rd DNO)
260th Separate Machine-gun Artillery
  Battalion
262nd Separate Machine-gun
  Artillery Battalion

274th Separate Machine-gun Artillery
  Battalion
Anti-tank Artillery Regiment (Major
  Bogdanov)
Luga Brigade PVO Region
24th Tank Division
24th Pontoon-Bridge Battalion
259th Separate Sapper Battalion

FIFTY-SECOND SEPARATE ARMY (STAVKA)
267th Rifle Division
285th Rifle Division
288th Rifle Division
292nd Rifle Division

312th Rifle Division
314th Rifle Division
316th Rifle Division
442nd Corps Artillery Regiment
881st Anti-tank Artillery Regiment

TWENTY-THIRD ARMY
XIX Rifle Corps
  142nd Rifle Division
  265th Rifle Division
43rd Rifle Division
123rd Rifle Division
291st Rifle Division
708th Rifle Regiment (115th Rifle
  Division)
577th Howitzer Artillery Regiment
  (RVGK)
28th Corps Artillery Regiment

241st Separate Anti-aircraft Artillery
  Battalion
485th Separate Anti-aircraft Artillery
  Battalion
Vyborg Brigade PVO Region
198th Motorized Division (less
  artillery regiment)
7th Fighter Aviation Regiment
153rd Fighter Aviation Regiment
235th Assault Aviation Regiment
41st Pontoon-Brigade Battalion
234th Separate Sapper Battalion

FORTY-EIGHTH ARMY
138th Rifle Division
311th Rifle Division
1st Mountain Rifle Brigade
170th Separate Cavalry Regiment

541st Howitzer Artillery Regiment
  (RVGK)
21st Tank Division
109th Motorized Engineer Battalion
12th Separate Sapper Battalion

KOPOR OPERATIONAL GROUP
1st GDNO
2nd DNO
522nd Rifle Regiment (191st Rifle
  Division)

519th Howitzer Regiment (RVGK)
2nd Tank Regiment (1st Tank
  Division)
295th Separate Sapper Battalion

FRONT SUBORDINATE
10th Rifle Division
16th Rifle Division
115th Rifle Division
281st Rifle Division
4th Guards DNO
1st Rifle Division NKVD
8th Rifle Brigade
3rd Rifle Regiment (1st DNO)
22nd Fortified Region
29th Fortified Region
101st Howitzer Artillery Regiment
108th High-power Howitzer Artillery
  Regiment
  (RVGK)
16th Separate Mortar Battalion

20th Separate Mortar Battalion
27th Separate Anti-aircraft Artillery
  Battalion
II PVO Corps
Svir Brigade PVO Region
1st Tank Division (less 2nd Tank
  Regiment)
48th Separate Tank Battalion
VII Fighter Aviation Corps PVO
8th Fighter Aviation Division
39th Fighter Aviation Division
2nd Mixed Aviation Division
53rd Separate Engineer Battalion
54th Separate Engineer Battalion
21st Pontoon-Bridge Battalion

1 JANUARY 1942
LENINGRAD FRONT

Eighth Army

10th Rifle Division
86th Rifle Division
1st Rifle Division NKVD
11th Rifle Brigade
4th Naval Infantry Brigade
101st Howitzer Artillery Regiment
6th Anti-tank Artillery Regiment
7th Anti-tank Artillery Regiment

20th Separate Mortar Battalion
486th Separate Anti-aircraft Artillery
 Battalion
28th Separate Armoured Train
Separate armoured car battalion
439th Fighter Aviation Regiment
2nd Separate Sapper Battalion
112th Separate Sapper Battalion

Twenty-Third Army

123rd Rifle Division
142nd Rifle Division
291st Rifle Division
22nd Fortified Region
260th Howitzer Artillery Regiment
577th Howitzer Artillery Regiment
27th Separate Anti-aircraft Artillery
 Battalion

241st Separate Anti-aircraft Artillery
 Battalion
48th Separate Tank Battalion
106th Separate Tank Battalion
30th Separate Armoured Train
5th Mixed Aviation Regiment
117th Reconnaissance Aviation
 Squadron
234th Separate Sapper Battalion

Forty-Second Army

13th Rifle Division
189th Rifle Division
21st Rifle Division NKVD
247th Separate Machine-gun Artillery
 Battalion
291st Separate Machine-gun Artillery
 Battalion
292nd Separate Machine-gun
 Artillery Battalion
14th Artillery Brigade PVO
47th Artillery Regiment
73rd Artillery Regiment
541st Howitzer Artillery Regiment

1st Anti-tank Artillery Regiment
2nd Anti-tank Artillery Regiment
3rd Anti-tank Artillery Regiment
4th Anti-tank Artillery Regiment
5th Anti-tank Artillery Regiment
3rd Special-power Artillery Battalion
72nd Separate Anti-aircraft Artillery
 Battalion
89th Separate Anti-aircraft Artillery
 Battalion
51st Separate Tank Battalion
29th Separate Engineer Battalion
54th Separate Engineer Battalion
106th Separate Engineer Battalion

Fifty-Fifth Army

11th Rifle Division
43rd Rifle Division
56th Rifle Division
70th Rifle Division
72nd Rifle Division
85th Rifle Division
90th Rifle Division
125th Rifle Division
177th Rifle Division
268th Rifle Division
261st Separate Machine-gun Artillery
 Battalion
267th Separate Machine-gun Artillery
 Battalion
283rd Separate Machine-gun Artillery
 Battalion
289th Separate Machine-gun Artillery
 Battalion

290th Separate Machine-gun Artillery
 Battalion
24th Corps Artillery Regiment
28th Corps Artillery Regiment
690th Anti-tank Artillery Regiment
2nd Special-power Artillery Battalion
47th Separate Mortar Battalion
198th Separate Anti-aircraft Artillery
 Battalion
84th Separate Tank Battalion
86th "People's Avenger" Separate
 Armoured Train
2nd Separate Engineer Battalion
53rd Separate Engineer Battalion
325th Separate Sapper Battalion
367th Separate Sapper Battalion

Fifty-Fourth Army

3rd Guards Rifle Division
80th Rifle Division
115th Rifle Division
128th Rifle Division
198th Rifle Division
281st Rifle Division
285th Rifle Division
286th Rifle Division
294th Rifle Division
311th Rifle Division
1st Mountain Rifle Brigade
6th Naval Infantry Brigade
2nd Separate Ski Regiment
4th Separate Ski Battalion
5th Separate Ski Battalion
882nd Artillery Regiment
883rd Artillery Regiment

"Akkuks" Howitzer Artillery Regiment
2d/5th Guards-mortar Regiment
4th/4th Guards-mortar Regiment
21st Tank Division
16th Tank Brigade
122nd Tank Brigade
60th Separate Armoured Train
18th Bomber Aviation Regiment
46th Fighter Aviation Regiment
563rd Fighter Aviation Regiment
116th Reconnaissance Aviation
 Squadron
5th Separate Engineer Battalion
109th Separate Engineer Battalion
135th Separate Engineer Battalion
136th Separate Engineer Battalion
262nd Separate Engineer Battalion
12th Separate Sapper Battalion

Coastal Operational Group

48th Rifle Division
2nd Naval Infantry Brigade
5th Naval Infantry Brigade
3rd Separate Rifle Regiment Baltic
 Fleet

50th Separate Naval Infantry
 Battalion Baltic Fleet
519th Howitzer Artillery Regiment
Separate mortar battalion
286th Separate Tank Battalion
295th Separate Sapper Battalion

FRONT SUBORDINATE

168th Rifle Division
265th Rifle Division
8th Rifle Brigade
9th Rifle Brigade
20th Rifle Division NKVD
13th Motorized Rifle Regiment NKVD
1st Separate Ski Battalion
Separate guards-mortar battalion
123d Tank Brigade
124th Tank Brigade
Battalion, separate tank brigade
107th Separate Tank Battalion
"Baltietz" Separate Armoured Train
"For the Fatherland" Separate
  Armoured Train

26th Separate Armoured Train
2nd Mixed Aviation Division
39th Fighter Aviation Division
92nd Fighter Aviation Division
127th Fighter Aviation Regiment
286th Fighter Aviation Regiment
Headquarters, 90 Mixed Aviation
  Division
Headquarters, 91st Mixed Aviation
  Division
21st Pontoon-bridge Battalion
41st Pontoon-bridge Battalion
42nd Pontoon-bridge Battalion

VOLKHOV FRONT

SECOND SHOCK ARMY

327th Rifle Division
22nd Rifle Brigade
23rd Rifle Brigade
24th Rifle Brigade
25th Rifle Brigade
53rd Rifle Brigade
57th Rifle Brigade
58th Rifle Brigade
59th Rifle Brigade
39th Separate Ski Battalion
40th Separate Ski Battalion
41st Separate Ski Battalion

42nd Separate Ski Battalion
43rd Separate Ski Battalion
44th Separate Ski Battalion
18th Artillery Regiment
839th Howitzer Artillery Regiment
160th Separate Tank Battalion
162nd Separate Tank Battalion
121st Bomber Aviation Regiment
522nd Fighter Aviation Regiment
704th Light Bomber Aviation
  Regiment
1741st Separate Sapper Battalion
1746th Separate Sapper Battalion

FOURTH ARMY

4th Guards Rifle Division
44th Rifle Division
65th Rifle Division
92nd Rifle Division
191st Rifle Division
310th Rifle Division
377th Rifle Division
1st Grenadier Rifle Brigade
27th Cavalry Division
80th Cavalry Division
84th Separate Ski Battalion
85th Separate Ski Battalion
86th Separate Ski Battalion
88th Separate Ski Battalion
89th Separate Ski Battalion
90th Separate Ski Battalion

881st Artillery Regiment
6th Guards-mortar Battalion
9th Guards-mortar Battalion
46th Tank Brigade
119th Separate Tank Battalion
120th Separate Tank Battalion
128th Separate Tank Battalion
3rd Reserve Aviation Group
  160th Fighter Aviation Regiment
  185th Fighter Aviation Regiment
  239th Fighter Aviation Regiment
  218th Assault Aviation Regiment
  225th Bomber Aviation Regiment
159th Pontoon-bridge Battalion
248th Separate Sapper Battalion

FIFTY-SECOND ARMY

46th Rifle Division
111th Rifle Division
225th Rifle Division
259th Rifle Division
267th Rifle Division
288th Rifle Division
305th Rifle Division
25th Cavalry Division
442nd Artillery Regiment
448th Artillery Regiment
561st Artillery Regiment

884th Anti-tank Artillery Regiment
44th Guards-mortar Battalion
2nd Guards Fighter Aviation Regiment
513th Fighter Aviation Regiment
313th Assault Aviation Regiment
673rd Light Bomber Aviation
  Regiment
3rd Separate Engineer Battalion
4th Separate Engineer Battalion
770th Separate Engineer Battalion
771st Separate Sapper Battalion
55th Pontoon-bridge Battalion

FIFTY-NINTH ARMY

366th Rifle Division
372nd Rifle Division
374th Rifle Division
376th Rifle Division
378th Rifle Division
382nd Rifle Division
45th Separate Ski Battalion
46th Separate Ski Battalion
47th Separate Ski Battalion
48th Separate Ski Battalion

49th Separate Ski Battalion
50th Separate Ski Battalion
104th Separate Guards-mortar
  Battalion
105th Separate Guards-mortar
  Battalion
203rd Separate Guards-mortar
  Battalion
163rd Separate Tank Battalion
166th Separate Tank Battalion

FRONT SUBORDINATE

87th Cavalry Division
137th High-power Howitzer Artillery
   Regiment
430th High-power Howitzer Artillery
   Regiment
216th Separate Anti-aircraft Artillery
   Battalion
2nd Reserve Aviation Group
   138th Bomber Aviation Regiment

283rd Fighter Aviation Regiment
434th Fighter Aviation Regiment
515th Fighter Aviation Regiment
504th Assault Aviation Regiment
520th Fighter Aviation Regiment
539th Separate Motorized Engineer-
   Sapper Battalion

1 JANUARY 1943
LENINGRAD FRONT

TWENTY-THIRD ARMY

10th Rifle Division
92nd Rifle Division
142nd Rifle Division
291st Rifle Division
27th Rifle Brigade
17th Fortified Region
22nd Fortified Region
260th Army Artillery Regiment
336th Gun Artillery Regiment
91st Anti-tank Artillery Regiment

883rd Anti-tank Artillery Regiment
104th Army Mortar Regiment
532nd Mortar Regiment
73rd Separate Anti-aircraft Artillery
   Battalion
618th Separate Anti-aircraft Artillery
   Battalion
152nd Tank Brigade
30th Separate Armoured Train
915th Mixed Aviation Regiment
234th Separate Engineer Battalion

FORTY-SECOND ARMY

85th Rifle Division
109th Rifle Division
125th Rifle Division
189th Rifle Division
79th Fortified Region
14th Guards Army Artillery Regiment
73rd Army Artillery Regiment
289th Anti-tank Artillery Regiment
304th Anti-tank Artillery Regiment
384th Anti-tank Artillery Regiment
509th Anti-tank Artillery Regiment
705th Anti-tank Artillery Regiment

760th Anti-tank Artillery Regiment
533rd Mortar Regiment
631st Anti-aircraft Artillery Regiment
72nd Separate Anti-aircraft Artillery
   Battalion
1st Tank Brigade
31st Guards Tank Regiment
1st Separate Armoured Car Battalion
2nd Separate Armoured Car Battalion
914th Mixed Aviation Regiment
54th Separate Engineer Battalion
585th Separate Engineer Battalion

FIFTY-FIFTH ARMY

43rd Rifle Division
56th Rifle Division
72nd Rifle Division
90th Rifle Division
14th Fortified Region
12th Guards Army Artillery Regiment
126th Gun Artillery Regiment
690th Anti-tank Artillery Regiment

531st Mortar Regiment
474th Anti-aircraft Artillery Regiment
71st Separate Anti-aircraft Artillery
   Battalion
220th Tank Brigade
71st Separate Armoured Train
987th Mixed Aviation Regiment
325th Separate Engineer Battalion
367th Separate Engineer Battalion

SIXTY-SEVENTH ARMY

45th Guards Rifle Division
46th Rifle Division
86th Rifle Division
11th Rifle Brigade
55th Rifle Brigade
123rd Rifle Brigade
138th Rifle Brigade
142nd Naval Rifle Brigade
35th Ski Brigade
16th Fortified Region
Artillery Division
   380th Light Artillery Regiment
   596th Light Artillery Regiment
   871st Light Artillery Regiment
   311th Gun Artillery Regiment
   1155th Gun Artillery Regiment
   56th Howitzer Artillery Regiment
   511th Howitzer Artillery Regiment
   577th Howitzer Artillery Regiment
28th Light Artillery Regiment
1106th Gun Artillery Regiment
High-power artillery battalion
882nd Anti-tank Artillery Regiment

127th Mortar Regiment
134th Mortar Regiment
144th Mortar Regiment
174th Mortar Regiment
175th Mortar Regiment
5th Guards-mortar Brigade
523rd Separate Guards-mortar
   Battalion
524th Separate Guards-mortar
   Battalion
525th Separate Guards-mortar
   Battalion
465th Anti-aircraft Artillery Regiment
632nd Anti-aircraft Artillery Regiment
89th Separate Anti-aircraft Artillery
   Battalion
108th Separate Anti-aircraft Artillery
   Battalion
613th Separate Anti-aircraft Artillery
   Battalion
86th Separate Tank Battalion
118th Separate Tank Battalion
3rd Separate Armoured Car Battalion
407th Mixed Aviation Regiment
53rd Separate Engineer Battalion

COASTAL OPERATIONAL GROUP

48th Rifle Division
168th Rifle Division
50th Rifle Brigade
56th Rifle Brigade
48th Naval Rifle Brigade
71st Naval Rifle Brigade

338th Separate Machine-gun Artillery
  Battalion
519th Howitzer Artillery Regiment
184th Mortar Regiment
287th Separate Tank Battalion
295th Separate Engineer Battalion

FRONT SUBORDINATE

13th Rifle Division
123nd Rifle Division
136th Rifle Division
224th Rifle Division
268th Rifle Division
102nd Rifle Brigade
162nd Rifle Brigade
250th Rifle Brigade
34th Ski Brigade
13th Fortified Region
Internal Defence of Leningrad
  122nd Separate Machine-gun
  Artillery Battalion
  123rd Separate Machine-gun
  Artillery Battalion
  124th Separate Machine-gun
  Artillery Battalion
  125th Separate Machine-gun
  Artillery Battalion
  130th Separate Machine-gun
  Artillery Battalion
  131st Separate Machine-gun
  Artillery Battalion
38th Guards-mortar Regiment
320th Guards-mortar Regiment
321st Guards-mortar Regiment
7th Anti-aircraft Artillery Division
  785th Anti-aircraft Artillery
  Regiment

803rd Anti-aircraft Artillery
  Regiment
970th Anti-aircraft Artillery
  Regiment
988th Anti-aircraft Artillery
  Regiment
92nd Separate Anti-aircraft Artillery
  Battalion
116th Separate Anti-aircraft Artillery
  Battalion
61st Tank Brigade
222nd Tank Brigade
Bn/Separate tank regiment
5th Separate Aerosleigh Battalion
17th Separate Aerosleigh Battalion
42nd Separate Aerosleigh Battalion
72nd Separate Armoured Train
2nd Special Designation (Spetsnaz)
  Engineer Brigade
52nd Engineer-Sapper Brigade
7th Guards Battalion of Miners
8th Pontoon-Bridge Battalion
12th Pontoon-Bridge Battalion
14th Pontoon-Bridge Battalion
18th Pontoon-Bridge Battalion
21st Pontoon-Bridge Battalion
41st Pontoon-Bridge Battalion
42nd Pontoon-Bridge Battalion
106th Separate Engineer Battalion
267th Separate Engineer Battalion
447th Separate Sapper Battalion

THIRTEENTH AIR ARMY

273rd Fighter Aviation Division
275th Fighter Aviation Division
276th Bomber Aviation Division
277th Assault Aviation Division

5th Long-range Reconnaissance
  Aviation Squadron
10th Fighter Aviation Squadron
12th Corrective Aviation Squadron

Second Shock Army

11th Rifle Division
18th Rifle Division
71st Rifle Division
128th Rifle Division
147th Rifle Division
191st Rifle Division
256th Rifle Division
314th Rifle Division
327th Rifle Division
372nd Rifle Division
376th Rifle Division
22nd Rifle Brigade
561st Army Artillery Regiment
168th High-power Howitzer Artillery
 Regiment
5th Mortar Brigade (2nd Artillery
 Division)
122nd Army Mortar Regiment
191st Army Mortar Regiment
192nd Army Mortar Regiment
193rd Army Mortar Regiment
194th Army Mortar Regiment
499th Army Mortar Regiment
502nd Army Mortar Regiment
503rd Army Mortar Regiment
504th Army Mortar Regiment
165th Mortar Regiment
20th Guards-Mortar Regiment (less
 211th Battalion)
29th Guards-Mortar Regiment
43rd Anti-aircraft Artillery Division
 464th Anti-aircraft Artillery
 Regiment

635th Anti-aircraft Artillery
 Regiment
1463rd Anti-aircraft Artillery
 Regiment
1464th Anti-aircraft Artillery
 Regiment
45th Anti-aircraft Artillery Division
 1st Anti-aircraft Artillery Regiment
 2nd Anti-aircraft Artillery Regiment
 737th Anti-aircraft Artillery
 Regiment
15th Separate Anti-aircraft Artillery
 Battalion
213th Separate Anti-aircraft Artillery
 Battalion
16th Tank Brigade
98th Tank Brigade
122nd Tank Brigade
185th Tank Brigade
32rd Guards Tank Regiment
500th Separate Tank Battalion
501st Separate Tank Battalion
503rd Separate Tank Battalion
507th Separate Tank Battalion
32nd Separate Aerosleigh Battalion
44th Separate Aerosleigh Battalion
22nd Separate Anti-aircraft Armoured
 Train
696th Mixed Aviation Regiment
136th Separate Engineer Battalion
770th Separate Engineer Battalion

Fourth Army

44th Rifle Division
288th Rifle Division
310th Rifle Division
24th Rifle Brigade
58th Rifle Brigade
39th Ski Brigade
206th Separate Machine-gun Artillery
 Battalion

8th Guards Army Artillery Regiment
211th Guards-Mortar Battalion (20th
 GMD)
7th Guards Tank Brigade
32nd Separate Armoured Train
689th Mixed Aviation Regiment
365th Separate Engineer Battalion

EIGHTH ARMY

80th Rifle Division
265th Rifle Division
286th Rifle Division
364th Rifle Division
1st Rifle Brigade
53rd Rifle Brigade
73rd Naval Rifle Brigade
71st Guards Army Artillery Regiment
70th Army Artillery Regiment
884th Anti-tank Artillery Regiment
145th Mortar Regiment (5th Mortar Brigade)
146th Army Mortar Regiment
500th Army Mortar Regiment
501st Army Mortar Regiment
30th Guards-Mortar Regiment
318th Guards-Mortar Regiment
509th Separate Heavy Guards-Mortar Regiment
512th Separate Heavy Guards-Mortar Regiment
41st Anti-aircraft Artillery Division
  244th Anti-aircraft Artillery Regiment

245th Anti-aircraft Artillery Regiment
463rd Anti-aircraft Artillery Regiment
634th Anti-aircraft Artillery Regiment
177th Separate Anti-aircraft Artillery Battalion
25th Separate Tank Regiment
107th Separate Tank Battalion
502nd Separate Tank Battalion
47th Separate Armoured Car Battalion
49th Separate Armoured Car Battalion
50th Separate Armoured Train Battalion
4th Separate Anti-aircraft Armoured Train
123rd Separate Anti-aircraft Armoured Train
935th Mixed Aviation Regiment
112th Separate Engineer Battalion

FIFTY-SECOND ARMY

65th Rifle Division
165th Rifle Division
225th Rifle Division
38th Ski Brigade
150th Fortified Region
448th Army Artillery Regiment
506th Army Mortar Regiment

231st Guards-Mortar Battalion (28th GMR)
34th Separate Aerosleigh Battalion
53rd Separate Aerosleigh Battalion
662nd Mixed Aviation Regiment
109th Separate Engineer Battalion
366th Separate Engineer Battalion

FIFTY-FOURTH ARMY

115th Rifle Division
177th Rifle Division
198th Rifle Division
281st Rifle Division
285th Rifle Division
291st Rifle Division
311th Rifle Division
140th Rifle Brigade

6th Naval Infantry Brigade
319th Guards-Mortar Regiment
461st Separate Anti-aircraft Artillery Battalion
124th Tank Brigade
48th Separate Armoured Car Battalion
691st Mixed Aviation Regiment
364th Separate Engineer Battalion

FIFTY-NINTH ARMY

2nd Rifle Division
377th Rifle Division
378th Rifle Division
382nd Rifle Division
37th Ski Brigade
42nd Separate Machine-gun Artillery Battalion
47th Separate Machine-gun Artillery Battalion
215th Separate Machine-gun Artillery Battalion

367th Army Artillery Regiment
505th Army Mortar Regiment
28th Guards-Mortar Regiment (less 231st GMBn)
29th Tank Brigade
48th Separate Armoured Train
660th Mixed Aviation Regiment
539th Separate Motorized Engineer-Sapper Battalion
771st Separate Engineer Battalion

FOURTEENTH AIR ARMY

II Fighter Aviation Corps
   209th Fighter Aviation Division
   215th Fighter Aviation Division
279th Fighter Aviation Division
280th Bomber Aviation Division
281st Assault Aviation Division
844th Transport Aviation Regiment
8th Long-range Reconnaissance
   Aviation Squadron
28th Corrective Aviation Squadron

FRONT SUBORDINATE

239th Rifle Division
379th Rifle Division
11th Ski Brigade
12th Ski Brigade
13th Ski Brigade
2nd Artillery Division
   20th Light Artillery Brigade
   7th Gun Artillery Brigade
   4th Howitzer Artillery Brigade
13th Guards Army Artillery Regiment
21st Army Artillery Regiment
24th Army Artillery Regiment
430th High-power Howitzer Artillery
   Regiment
46th Anti-aircraft Artillery Division
   21st Anti-aircraft Artillery Regiment
   22nd Anti-aircraft Artillery
   Regiment
   23rd Anti-aircraft Artillery Regiment
   24th Anti-aircraft Artillery Regiment

707th Anti-aircraft Artillery Regiment
   (45th AAD)
168th Separate Anti-aircraft Artillery
   Battalion
216th Separate Anti-aircraft Artillery
   Battalion
23rd Separate Armoured Train
1st Engineer-Miner Brigade
39th Special Designation Engineer
   Brigade
   (Spetsnaz)
53rd Engineer-Sapper Brigade
8th Guards Battalion of Miners
734th Separate Miner-Sapper
   Battalion
32nd Pontoon-Bridge Battalion
34th Pontoon-Bridge Battalion
36th Pontoon-Bridge Battalion
38th Pontoon-Bridge Battalion
55th Pontoon-Bridge Battalion
40th Separate Engineer Battalion
135th Separate Engineer Battalion

1 JANUARY 1944
LENINGRAD FRONT

SECOND SHOCK ARMY

XXXXIII Rifle Corps
   48th Rifle Division
   90th Rifle Division
   98th Rifle Division
CXXII Rifle Corps
   11th Rifle Division
   131st Rifle Division
   168th Rifle Division
43rd Rifle Division
50th Rifle Brigade
48th Naval Rifle Brigade
71st Naval Rifle Brigade
16th Fortified Region
116th Corps Artillery Regiment
154th Corps Artillery Regiment
533rd Separate Heavy Gun Artillery
   Battalion
535th Separate Heavy Gun Artillery
   Battalion
760th Anti-tank Artillery Regiment
230th Guards Mortar Regiment

144th Mortar Regiment
184th Mortar Regiment
281st Mortar Regiment
30th Guards-Mortar Regiment
318th Guards-Mortar Regiment
322nd Guards-Mortar Regiment
803rd Anti-aircraft Artillery Regiment
92nd Separate Anti-aircraft Artillery
   Battalion
116th Separate Anti-aircraft Artillery
   Battalion
152nd Tank Brigade
98th Separate Tank Regiment
204th Separate Tank Regiment
222nd Separate Tank Regiment
17th Separate Aerosleigh Battalion
42nd Separate Aerosleigh Battalion
4th Separate Armoured Car Battalion
295th Separate Engineer Battalion
447th Separate Engineer Battalion
734th Separate Engineer Battalion

TWENTY-THIRD ARMY

10th Rifle Division
92nd Rifle Division
142nd Rifle Division
17th Fortified Region
22nd Fortified Region
8th Corps Artillery Regiment
336th Gun Artillery Regiment

94th Anti-tank Artillery Regiment
883rd Anti-tank Artillery Regiment
276th Mortar Regiment
618th Separate Anti-aircraft Artillery
   Battalion
5th Aerosleigh Battalion
1st Separate Armoured Car Battalion

FORTY-SECOND ARMY

XXX Guards Rifle Corps
  45th Guards Rifle Division
  63rd Guards Rifle Division
  64th Guards Rifle Division
CIX Rifle Corps
  72nd Rifle Division
  109th Rifle Division
  125th Rifle Division
CX Rifle Corps
  56th Rifle Division
  85th Rifle Division
  86th Rifle Division
189th Rifle Division
79th Fortified Region
18th Artillery Penetration Division
  65th Light Artillery Brigade
  58th Howitzer Artillery Brigade
  3rd Heavy Howitzer Artillery
  Brigade
  80th Heavy Howitzer Artillery
  Brigade
  120th High-power Howitzer
  Artillery Brigade
  42nd Mortar Brigade
23rd Artillery Penetration Division
  79th Light Artillery Brigade
  38th Howitzer Artillery Brigade
  2nd Heavy Howitzer Artillery
  Brigade
  96th Heavy Howitzer Artillery
  Brigade
  21st Guards High-power Howitzer
  Artillery
  Brigade
  28th Mortar Brigade
1157th Corps Artillery Regiment
1106th Gun Artillery Regiment
1486th Gun Artillery Regiment
52nd Guards Separate Heavy Gun
  Artillery Battalion
304th Anti-tank Artillery Regiment
384th Anti-tank Artillery Regiment
509th Anti-tank Artillery Regiment
705th Anti-tank Artillery Regiment
1973rd Anti-tank Artillery Regiment
104th Mortar Regiment

174th Mortar Regiment
533rd Mortar Regiment
534th Mortar Regiment
20th Guards-Mortar Regiment (less
  211th GMBn)
38th Guards-Mortar Regiment
320th Guards-Mortar Regiment
321st Guards-Mortar Regiment
7th Anti-aircraft Artillery Division
  465th Anti-aircraft Artillery
  Regiment
  474th Anti-aircraft Artillery
  Regiment
  602nd Anti-aircraft Artillery
  Regiment
  632rd Anti-aircraft Artillery Regiment
32nd Anti-aircraft Artillery Division
  1377th Anti-aircraft Artillery
  Regiment
  1387th Anti-aircraft Artillery
  Regiment
  1393rd Anti-aircraft Artillery
  Regiment
  1413rd Anti-aircraft Artillery
  Regiment
631st Anti-aircraft Artillery Regiment
72nd Separate Anti-aircraft Artillery
  Battalion
1st Tank Brigade
220th Tank Brigade
31st Guards Separate Tank Regiment
46th Guards Separate Tank Regiment
49th Guards Separate Tank Regiment
205th Separate Tank Regiment
260th Separate Tank Regiment
1439th Self-propelled Artillery
  Regiment
1902nd Self-propelled Artillery
  Regiment
2nd Separate Armoured Car Battalion
71st Separate Armoured Train
  Battalion
72nd Separate Armoured Train
  Battalion
54th Separate Engineer Battalion
585th Separate Engineer Battalion

SIXTY-SEVENTH ARMY

CXVI Rifle Corps
  13th Rifle Division
  46th Rifle Division
  376th Rifle Division
CXVIII Rifle Corps
  124th Rifle Division
  128th Rifle Division
  268th Rifle Division
291st Rifle Division
14th Fortified Region
81st Gun Artillery Brigade
267th Guards Gun Artillery Regiment
21st Gun Artillery Regiment
260th Gun Artillery Regiment
564th Gun Artillery Regiment
599th Howitzer Artillery Regiment
532nd Separate Heavy Gun Artillery
  Battalion
289th Anti-tank Artillery Regiment
690th Anti-tank Artillery Regiment
882nd Anti-tank Artillery Regiment
884th Anti-tank Artillery Regiment
122nd Mortar Regiment

127th Mortar Regiment
134th Mortar Regiment
175th Mortar Regiment
193rd Mortar Regiment
504th Mortar Regiment
567th Mortar Regiment
970th Anti-aircraft Artillery Regiment
988th Anti-aircraft Artillery Regiment
71st Separate Anti-aircraft Artillery
  Battalion
73rd Separate Anti-aircraft Artillery
  Battalion
108th Separate Anti-aircraft Artillery
  Battalion
613th Separate Anti-aircraft Artillery
  Battalion
14th Separate Armoured Train
  Battalion
53rd Separate Engineer Battalion
234th Separate Engineer Battalion
325th Separate Engineer Battalion
367th Separate Engineer Battalion
8th Separate Flame-thrower Battalion

THIRTEENTH AIR ARMY

276th Bomber Aviation Division
277th Assault Aviation Division
275th Fighter Aviation Division
283rd Fighter Aviation Regiment

13th Reconnaissance Aviation
  Regiment
12th Corrective Aviation Squadron
49th Corrective Aviation Squadron
52nd Corrective Aviation Squadron

FRONT SUBORDINATE

CVIII Rifle Corps
  196th Rifle Division
  224th Rifle Division
  314th Rifle Division
CXVII Rifle Corps
  120th Rifle Division
  123rd Rifle Division
  201st Rifle Division
CXXIII Rifle Corps (Headquarters)
III Artillery Corps (Headquarters)
51st Gun Artillery Brigade
12th Guards Gun Artillery Regiment
14th Guards Gun Artillery Regiment
73rd Gun Artillery Regiment
126th Gun Artillery Regiment
129th Gun Artillery Regiment
409th Separate Heavy Gun Artillery
  Battalion
4th Guards-Mortar Division
  2nd Guards-Mortar Brigade
  5th Guards-Mortar Brigade
  6th Guards-Mortar Brigade
536th Separate Anti-tank Artillery
  Battalion
1st Separate Aerostatic Balloon
  Artillery
  Observation Battalion
8th Separate Aerostatic Balloon
  Artillery
  Observation Battalion

43rd Anti-aircraft Artillery Division
  464th Anti-aircraft Artillery
  Regiment
  635th Anti-aircraft Artillery
  Regiment
  1463rd Anti-aircraft Artillery
  Regiment
  1464th Anti-aircraft Artillery
  Regiment
785th Anti-aircraft Artillery Regiment
758th Separate Anti-aircraft Artillery
  Battalion
30th Guards Tank Brigade
17th Guards Tank Regiment
261st Separate Tank Regiment
1344th Self-propelled Artillery
  Regiment
3rd Separate Armoured Car Battalion
2nd Special Designation Engineer
  Brigade (Spetsnaz)
52nd Engineer-Sapper Brigade
5th Heavy Pontoon-Bridge Regiment
7th Guards Battalion of Miners
34th Separate Engineer Battalion
106th Separate Engineer Battalion
1st Guards Pontoon-Bridge Battalion
21st Pontoon-Bridge Battalion
42nd Pontoon-Bridge Battalion
175th Separate Back-pack Flame-
  thrower Company

VOLKHOV FRONT

EIGHTH ARMY

CXIX Rifle Corps
  286th Rifle Division
  374th Rifle Division
18th Rifle Division
364th Rifle Division
1st Rifle Brigade
22nd Rifle Brigade
258th Light Artillery Regiment (20th
  LAB)
8th Guards Gun Artillery Regiment
71st Guards Gun Artillery Regiment
223rd Guards Gun Artillery Regiment
500th Mortar Regiment
18th Guard-Mortar Regiment
41st Antiaircraft Artillery Division

245th Anti-aircraft Artillery
  Regiment
634th Anti-aircraft Artillery
  Regiment
1468th Anti-aircraft Artillery
  Regiment
177th Separate Anti-aircraft Artillery
  Battalion
33rd Guards Tank Regiment
185th Tank Regiment
32nd Separate Aerosleigh Battalion
49th Separate Armoured Car
  Battalion
50th Separate Armoured Train
  Battalion
4th Separate Armoured Train
112th Separate Engineer Battalion

FIFTY-FOURTH ARMY

CXI Rifle Corps
  44th Rifle Division
  288th Rifle Division
CXV Rifle Corps
  281st Rifle Division
  285th Rifle Division
  14th Rifle Brigade
  53rd Rifle Brigade
80th Rifle Division
177th Rifle Division
198th Rifle Division
2nd Fortified Region
1097th Gun Artillery Regiment
194th Mortar Regiment
499th Mortar Regiment
29th Guards-Mortar Regiment
244th Anti-aircraft Artillery Regiment
  (41st AAD)
463rd Anti-aircraft Artillery Regiment
  (41st AAD)

1467th Anti-aircraft Artillery Regiment
1469th Anti-aircraft Artillery Regiment
15th Separate Anti-aircraft Artillery
  Battalion
124th Separate Tank Regiment
107th Separate Tank Battalion
501st Separate Tank Battalion
48th Separate Armoured Car
  Battalion
32nd Separate Armoured Train
  Battalion
48th Separate Armoured Train
  Battalion
22nd Separate Anti-aircraft Armored
  Train
2nd Guards Special Designation
  Engineer Brigade
  (Spetsnaz)
9th Assault Engineer-Sapper Brigade
8th Guards Battalion of Miners
364th Separate Engineer Battalion
539th Separate Engineer Battalion

FIFTY-NINTH ARMY
VI Rifle Corps
  65th Rifle Division
  239th Rifle Division
  310th Rifle Division
XIV Rifle Corps
  191st Rifle Division
  225th Rifle Division
  378th Rifle Division
CXII Rifle Corps
  2nd Rifle Division
  372nd Rifle Division
  377th Rifle Division
  24th Rifle Brigade
150th Fortified Region
2nd Artillery Division
  20th Light Artillery Brigade
  7th Gun Artillery Brigade
  10th Guards Howitzer Artillery
  Brigade
121st High-power Howitzer Artillery
  Brigade
13 Guards Gun Artillery Regiment
70th Gun Artillery Regiment
367th Gun Artillery Regiment
448th Gun Artillery Regiment
1096th Gun Artillery Regiment
5th Mortar Brigade
30th Mortar Brigade
192nd Mortar Regiment
505th Mortar Regiment
506th Mortar Regiment
10th Guards-Mortar Brigade
12th Guards-Mortar Brigade
28th Guards-Mortar Regiment
319th Guards-Mortar Regiment
211th Guards-Mortar Battalion (20th
  GMR)
3rd Separate Aerostatic Balloon
  Artillery Observation Battalion
45th Anti-aircraft Artillery Division
  707th Anti-aircraft Artillery

Regiment
  737th Anti-aircraft Artillery Regiment
  1465th Anti-aircraft Artillery
  Regiment
  1466th Anti-aircraft Artillery
  Regiment
  1470th Anti-aircraft Artillery
  Regiment
  213th Separate Anti-aircraft Artillery
  Battalion
  461st Separate Anti-aircraft Artillery
  Battalion
16th Tank Brigade
29th Tank Brigade
122nd Tank Brigade
32nd Guards Separate Tank Regiment
35th Guards Separate Tank Regiment
50th Guards Separate Tank Regiment
25th Separate Tank Regiment
1433rd Self-propelled Artillery
  Regiment
1434th Self-propelled Artillery
  Regiment
500th Separate Tank Battalion
502nd Separate Tank Battalion
503rd Separate Tank Battalion
34th Separate Aerosleigh Battalion
44th Separate Aerosleigh Battalion
47th Separate Armoured Car Battalion
1st Engineer-Sapper Brigade
2nd Guards Separate Engineer
  Battalion
35th Separate Engineer Battalion
40th Separate Engineer Battalion
109th Separate Engineer Battalion
135th Separate Engineer Battalion
365th Separate Engineer Battalion
34th Pontoon-Bridge Battalion
36th Pontoon-Bridge Battalion
55th Pontoon-Bridge Battalion
9th Separate Flame-thrower Battalion

FRONT SUBORDINATE
VII Rifle Corps
  256th Rifle Division
  382nd Rifle Division
58th Rifle Brigade
11th Guards Separate Antiaircraft
  Artillery Battalion

168th Separate Antiaircraft Artillery
  Battalion
7th Guards Tank Brigade
123rd Separate Armoured Train
12th Engineer-Sapper Brigade
38th Pontoon-Bridge Battalion

FOURTEENTH AIR ARMY
280th Bomber Aviation Division
281st Assault Aviation Division
269th Fighter Aviation Division
386th Fighter-Bomber Aviation
  Regiment
742nd Reconnaissance Aviation
  Regiment
844th Transport Aviation Regiment

4th Aviation Regiment Civil Aviation
  Fleet
44th Corrective Aviation Squadron
59th Corrective Aviation Squadron

APPENDIX 2

German Order of Battle in the Leningrad Region

22 JUNE 1941
ARMY GROUP NORTH

EIGHTEENTH ARMY

XXVI Army Corps
  291st Infantry Division
  61st Infantry Division
  217th Infantry Division
XXXVIII Army Corps

58th Infantry Division
I Army Corps
  11th Infantry Division
  1st Infantry Division
  21st Infantry Division

SIXTEENTH ARMY

X Army Corps
  30th Infantry Division
  126th Infantry Division
XXVIII Army Corps
  122nd Infantry Division
  123rd Infantry Division

II Army Corps
  121st Infantry Division
  12th Infantry Division
  32nd Infantry Division
  253rd Infantry Division

Fourth Panzer Group

XXXXI Motorized Corps
  1st Panzer Division
  269th Infantry Division
  6th Panzer Division
  36th Motorized Division

LVI Motorized Corps
  290th Infantry Division
  8th Panzer Division
  3rd Motorized Division
  SS *Totenkopf* Motorized Division

ARMY GROUP & OKH RESERVES

XXIII Army Corps (Army group)
  254th Infantry Division
  251st Infantry Division
  206th Infantry Division
L Army Corps (OKH)

86th Infantry Division
SS Police Infantry Division
207th Security Division
285th Security Division
281st Security Division

1 AUGUST 1941
ARMY GROUP NORTH

EIGHTEENTH ARMY

XXXXII Army Corps
  291st Infantry Division
  217th Infantry Division

XXVI Army Corps
  254th Infantry Division
  61st Infantry Division
  93rd Infantry Division

FOURTH PANZER GROUP

XXXVIII Army Corps
  58th Infantry Division
XXXXI Motorized Corps
  1st Infantry Division
  1st Panzer Division
  36th Motorized Division

LVI Motorized Corps
  269th Infantry Division
  8th Panzer Division
  SS Police Infantry Division
  3rd Motorized Division

SIXTEENTH ARMY

XXVIII Army Corps
  122nd Infantry Division
  121st Infantry Division
  SS *Totenkopf* Motorized Division
I Army Corps
  11th Infantry Division
  21st Infantry Division
X Army Corps
  126th Infantry Division

30th Infantry Division
290th Infantry Division
II Army Corps
  123rd Infantry Division
  32nd Infantry Division
  12th Infantry Division
L Army Corps (Ninth Army control)
  251st Infantry Division
  253rd Infantry Division

1 SEPTEMBER 1941
ARMY GROUP NORTH

EIGHTEENTH ARMY

XXXXII Army Corps
  61st Infantry Division

217th Infantry Division
254th Infantry Division

FOURTH PANZER GROUP

XXVI Army Corps
  93rd Infantry Division
XXXVIII Army Corps
  1st Infantry Division
  291st Infantry Division
XXXXI Motorized Corps
  6th Panzer Division
  36th Motorized Division
  1st Panzer Division

L Army Corps
  269th Infantry Division
  SS Police Infantry Division
  8th Panzer Division

SIXTEENTH ARMY

XXXIX Motorized Corps
  12th Panzer Division
  20th Motorized Division
  18th Motorized Division
XXVIII Army Corps
  96th Infantry Division
  121st Infantry Division
I Army Corps
  21st Infantry Division
  11th Infantry Division
  122nd Infantry Division

126th Infantry Division
X Army Corps
  290th Infantry Division
  30th Infantry Division
LVI Motorized Corps
  SS *Totenkopf* Motorized Division
  3rd Motorized Division
II Army Corps
  123rd Infantry Division
  32nd Infantry Division
  12th Infantry Division

1 JANUARY 1942
ARMY GROUP NORTH

EIGHTEENTH ARMY

XXVI Army Corps
  217th Infantry Division
  93rd Infantry Division
  212th Infantry Division
L Army Corps
  58th Infantry Division
  SS Police Infantry Division
  121st Infantry Division
  122nd Infantry Division
XXVIII Army Corps
  96th Infantry Division
  1st Infantry Division

227th Infantry Division
223rd Infantry Division
269th Infantry Division
IR, 291st Infantry Division
Part, 12th Panzer Division
I Army Corps
  11th Infantry Division
  21st Infantry Division
  291st Infantry Division
XXXIX Motorized Corps
  12th Panzer Division
  20th Motorized Division

SIXTEENTH ARMY

XXXVIII Army Corps
  61st Infantry Division
  215th Infantry Division
  126th Infantry Division
  250th Spanish Infantry Division
X Army Corps
  290th Infantry Division
  30th Infantry Division
  SS *Totenkopf* Motorized Division

18th Motorized Division
II Army Corps
  12th Infantry Division
  32nd Infantry Division
  123rd Infantry Division

Army group reserves
8th Panzer Division
81st Infantry Division

1 JANUARY 1943
ARMY GROUP NORTH

EIGHTEENTH ARMY

L Army Corps
  225th Infantry Division
  9th Luftwaffe Field Division
  215th Infantry Division
  2nd SS Infantry Division
LIV Army Corps
  250th Spanish Infantry Division
  2 SS Police Infantry Brigade
  5th Mountain Division
XXVI Army Corps
  170th Infantry Division
  227th Infantry Division
  1st Infantry Division
  223rd Infantry Division
I Army Corps
  69th Infantry Division

132nd Infantry Division
61st Infantry Division
11th Infantry Division
217th Infantry Division
21st Infantry Division
XXVIII Army Corps
  24th Infantry Division
  121st Infantry Division
  28th Jäger Division
XXXVIII Army Corps
  254th Infantry Division
  212th Infantry Division
  1st Luftwaffe Field Division
  10th Luftwaffe Field Division
  96th Infantry Division
  285th Security Division

SIXTEENTH ARMY

X Army Corps
  18th Motorized Division
  5th Jäger Division
  21st Luftwaffe Field Division
Group Hohne
  8th Jäger Division
  290th Infantry Division
  225th Infantry Division
  126th Infantry Division

II Army Corps
  122nd Infantry Division
  30th Infantry Division
  329th Infantry Division
  32nd Infantry Division
  12th Infantry Division
  123rd Infantry Division
Group Tiemann
  218th Infantry Division
  93rd Infantry Division

1 JANUARY 1944
ARMY GROUP NORTH

EIGHTEENTH ARMY

III SS Panzer Corps
  IR, SS Police Infantry Division
  SS *Nordland* Panzergrenadier
  Division
  10th Luftwaffe Field Division
  9th Luftwaffe Field Division
L Army Corps
  126th Infantry Division
  170th Infantry Division
  215th Infantry Division
LIV Army Corps
  11th Infantry Division
  24th Infantry Division
  225th Infantry Division

XXVI Army Corps
  61st Infantry Division
  227th Infantry Division
  254th Infantry Division
  212th Infantry Division
XXVIII Army Corps
  Spanish Legion
  121st Infantry Division
  2nd Luftwaffe Field Division
  96th Infantry Division
  21st Infantry Division
  13th Luftwaffe Field Division
XXXVIII Army Corps
  2nd Latvian SS Brigade
  28th Jäger Division
  1st Luftwaffe Field Division

SIXTEENTH ARMY

X Army Corps
  30th Infantry Division
  8th Jäger Division
  21st Luftwaffe Field Division
II Army Corps
  218th Infantry Division
  93rd Infantry Division
  331st Infantry Division
XXXXIII and VI SS Army Corps
  205th Infantry Division
  15th Latvian SS Brigade
  83rd Infantry Division

263rd Infantry Division
69th Infantry Division
I Army Corps
  58th Infantry Division
  122nd Infantry Division
  290th Infantry Division
  23rd Infantry Division
VIII Army Corps
  329th Infantry Division
  81st Infantry Division
  Group Jackeln
  Group Wagner (132nd ID)

APPENDIX 3

A Rough Comparison of Red Army and Wehrmacht Forces

RED ARMY

FRONT

1941: (June) 4–6 armies, 1–3 mechanized/cavalry corps

1941: (December 1941) 4–6 armies, one cavalry corps

1942: 3–6 armies, 1 tank army, 1–2 tank, mechanized, or cavalry corps

1943: 3-6 armies, 1–2 tank armies, one air army, 3–5 tank, mechanized or cavalry corps, 1–2 artillery divisions

1944–45: 6–7 armies, 1–3 tank armies, one air army, 1–3 tank, mechanized, or cavalry corps, one artillery penetration division

ARMIES

1941: (June) Rifle Army

...   2–3 rifle corps (6–15 rifle

...   divisions), one mechanized or cavalry corps

...   (60–80,000 men, 400–700 tanks)

1941: (December) Rifle Army

...   5–6 rifle divisions or brigades, 1–2 cavalry divisions, 1–2 tank

...   brigades or battalions

...   (70,000 men, 20–90 tanks)

1942: Rifle Army

...   6–10 rifle divisions or brigades,

...   2–4 tank brigades, 1–2 tank corps

...   (80–100,000 men, 250–450 tanks)

...   Tank Army

...   2–3 tank corps, one cavalry corps,

...   1–3 rifle or cavalry divisions, one tank brigade

...   (35,000 men, 350–500 tanks)

...   Air Army

...   4–12 fighter, bomber, assault, or mixed aviation divisions

1943: Rifle Army

...   rifle corps (7–12 rifle divisions),

...   3–4 tank or self-propelled artillery brigades,

...   1–2 tank, mechanized or cavalry corps

...   (80–130,000 men, 250–450 tanks)

...   Tank Army

...   two tank corps, one mechanized corps

...   (46,000 men, 450–560 tanks)

...   Air Army

...   2–3 fighter aviation divisions,

...   1–2 bomber aviation divisions, 1 assault

...   aviation division (700–1000 aircraft)

1944–45: Rifle Army

...   three rifle corps (7–12 rifle divisions),

...   1–3 artillery brigades, 2–3 tank or

...   self-propelled artillery regiments, one tank,

...   mechanized or cavalry corps

...   (80–120,000 men, 300–460 tanks)

...   Tank Army

...   two tank corps, one mechanized corps

...   (48–50,000 men, 450–700 tanks)

...   Air Army

...   1–5 fighter, bomber, or assault

...   aviation corps or 2–5 aviation divisions

Wehrmacht

ARMY GROUP

1941: 2–3 armies, 1–3 panzer groups

1942: 2–3 armies, 1–2 panzer armies

1943: 2–3 armies, 1–2 panzer armies

1944–45: 2–3 armies, 1–2 panzer armies

ARMIES (PANZER GROUPS)

1941: Field Army

...   2–4 army corps

...   Panzer Group

...   2–3 motorized corps, 1–2 army corps

1942: Field Army

...   3–4 army corps,

...   1–2 motorized corps

...   Panzer Army

...   2–3 motorized corps,

...   1–2 army corps

1943: Field Army

...   3–6 army or panzer corps (corps groups)

...   Panzer Army

...   3–5 panzer or army corps

1944–45: Field Army

...   4–6 army or panzer corps (corps groups)

...   Panzer Army

...   3–6 panzer or army corps (corps groups)

RED ARMY CORPS

1941: (June) <u>Rifle Corps</u>
... two rifle divisions (50,000 men)
... <u>Mechanized Corps</u>
... two tank and one motorized division
... (36,080 men, 1,031 tanks)
... <u>Cavalry Corps</u>
... two cavalry divisions
... (19,430 men, 128 tanks)
1941: (December): <u>Rifle Corps</u> (none)
... <u>Mechanized Corps</u> (none)
... <u>Cavalry Corps</u>
... two cavalry divisions, one light
... cavalry division (12,000 men)
1942: <u>Rifle Corps</u>
... 2–3 rifle divisions (25–37,000 men)
... <u>Tank Corps</u>
... three tank brigades, one motorized rifle brigade
... (7800 men, 168 tanks)
... <u>Cavalry Corps</u>
... three cavalry divisions (14,000 men)
1943: <u>Rifle Corps</u>
... three rifle divisions (37,000 men)
... <u>Tank Corps</u>
... three tank brigades, one motorized rifle brigade,
... one self-propelled artillery regiment
... (10,977 men, 220 tanks)
... <u>Mechanized Corps</u>
... three mechanized brigades,
... one tank brigade, one self-propelled artillery regiment
... (15,018 men, 229 tanks)
... <u>Cavalry Corps</u>
... three cavalry divisions,
... one self-propelled artillery regiment
... (21,000 men, 129 tanks)
1944–45: <u>Rifle Corps</u>
... three rifle divisions, one artillery brigade
... brigade, one self-propelled artillery regiment
... (20–30,000 men, 21 tanks)
... <u>Tank Corps</u>
... three tank brigades, 1 motorized rifle brigade,
... three self-propelled artillery regiments
... (12,010 men, 270 tanks)
... <u>Mechanized Corps</u>
... three mechanized brigades, one tank brigade,
... three self-propelled artillery regiments
... (16,442 men, 246 tanks)
... <u>Cavalry Corps</u>
... three cavalry divisions,
... 1–2 self-propelled artillery regiments
... (22,000 men, 150 tanks)

WEHRMACHT CORPS

1941: <u>Army Corps</u>
... 1–5 infantry divisions
... <u>Motorized Corps</u>
... two panzer divisions, one motorized
... division, 1–2 infantry divisions

1942: <u>Army Corps</u>
... 3–5 infantry divisions, one panzer or
... motorized division
... <u>Motorized Corps</u>
... 1–2 panzer divisions,
... 1–2 motorized divisions,
... 1–2 infantry divisions
1943: <u>Army Corps</u>
... 3–5 infantry divisions, one panzer or
... panzergrenadier division
... <u>Panzer Corps</u>
... 2–3 panzer or panzergrenadier
... divisions, 1–2 infantry divisions

1944–45: <u>Army Corps</u>
... 3–6 infantry, panzer or
... panzergrenadier divisions
... <u>Panzer Corps</u>
... 3–6 panzer, panzergrenadier or
... infantry divisions

RED ARMY DIVISIONS

1941: (June) <u>Rifle Division</u>
... three rifle regiments, two artillery regiments,
... one tank battalion
... (14,483 men, 16 tanks)
... <u>Tank Division</u>
... two tank regiments, one motorized rifle regiment
... (10,940 men, 375 tanks)
... <u>Motorized Division</u>
... three motorized rifle regiments
... (10,000 men)
... <u>Cavalry Division</u>
... four cavalry regiments, one tank regiment
... (9,240 men, 64 tanks)
1941: (December) <u>Rifle Division</u>
... three rifle regiments,
... one artillery regiment
... (11,626 men)
... <u>Cavalry Division</u>
... three cavalry regiments (light or regular)
... (3447–4200 men)
1942: <u>Rifle Division</u>
... three rifle regiments, one artillery regiment
... (10,386 men)
... <u>Cavalry Division</u>
... three cavalry regiments
... (4619 men)
... <u>Destroyer Division</u>
... two destroyer brigades
... (4000 men)
... <u>Fortified Region</u>
... 4–6 machine-gun artillery battalions
... (4100 men)
1943: <u>Rifle Division</u>
... three rifle regiments, one artillery regiment
... (9380 men)
... <u>Cavalry Division</u>
... three cavalry regiments, 1 tank regiment
... (6000 men, 39 tanks)
... <u>Destroyer Division</u>
... two destroyer brigades
... (4000 men)
... <u>Fortified Region</u>
... 4–6 machine-gun artillery battalions
... (4100 men)

1944–45: <u>Rifle Division</u>
... three rifle regiments, one artillery regiment
... (9380 men)
... <u>Cavalry Division</u>
... three cavalry regiments, 1 tank regiment
... (6000 men, 39 tanks)
... <u>Fortified Region</u>
... 4–6 machine-gun artillery battalions
... (4100 men)

WEHRMACHT DIVISIONS

1941: <u>Infantry Division</u> three infantry regiments (nine infantry battalions)
... (17,000 men)
... <u>Mountain Division</u> three infantry regiments
... (13,000 men)
... <u>Jäger Division</u> two infantry regiments (13,000 men)
... <u>Panzer Division</u>
... one panzer regiment (2–3 panzer battalions),
... two motorized infantry regiments (five motorized infantry battalions,
... four truck- and one motorcycle-mounted)
... (14,000 men, 150–202 tanks)
... <u>Motorized Division</u>
... two motorized infantry regiments (six motorized infantry battalions),
... one panzer battalion (16,000 men, 30–50 tanks)
... <u>Waffen-SS Infantry Division</u>
... three infantry regiments (six infantry battalions) (14,000 men)
... <u>Security Division</u>
... two security regiments (10,000 men)
1942: <u>Infantry Division</u> three infantry regiments (6-9 infantry battalions)
... (15,500–17,000 men)
... <u>Jäger Division</u> two infantry regiments (13,000 men)
... <u>Panzer Division</u> 1 panzer regiment (2–3 panzer battalions),
... two motorized infantry regiments (five motorized infantry battalions,
... four truck- and one motorcycle-mounted)
... (14,000 men, 150–202 tanks)
... <u>Motorized Division</u>
... two motorized infantry regiments
... (six motorized infantry battalions), one panzer battalion
... (16,000 men, 30–50 tanks)
... <u>Waffen-SS Infantry Division</u> three infantry regiments (six infantry battalions)
... (14,000 men)
... <u>Waffen-SS Motorized</u> (same as motorized division)
... (15,000)
... <u>Luftwaffe Field Division</u>
... 2–3 infantry regiments (4–6 battalions)
... (10–12,500 men)
... <u>Security Division</u> two security regiments (10,000 men)
1943–45: <u>Infantry Division</u> 2–3 infantry regiments (six infantry battalions)
... (10-12,500 men)
... <u>Jäger Division</u> two infantry regiments (13,000 men)
... <u>Panzer Division</u>
... one panzer regiment (2–3 panzer battalions), two motorized infantry
... regiments (five motorized infantry battalions, four truck- and one
... motorcycle-mounted)
... (13–17,000 men, 100–130 tanks)
... <u>Panzergrenadier Division</u>
... two motorized infantry regiments (six motorized infantry battalions),
... one panzer battalion
... (16,000 men, 3–50 tanks)
... <u>Waffen-SS Panzer Division</u> (same as panzer division)
... (17,000 men, 200-250 tanks)
... <u>Luftwaffe Field Division</u> 2–3 infantry regiments (4–6 battalions)
... (10–12,500 men)
... <u>Security Division</u> two security regiments (10,000 men)

RED ARMY BRIGADES

1941: (June) <u>Rifle Brigade</u> three rifle battalions (4500 men)

1941: (December) <u>Rifle Brigade</u> three rifle battalions (4480 men

... <u>Naval Rifle Brigade</u> three battalions (4334 men)

... <u>Naval Infantry Brigade</u> 4–6 infantry battalions (4480–6000 men)

... <u>Tank Brigade</u> two tank battalions, one motorized rifle battalion (1471 men, 46 tanks)

... <u>Ski Brigade</u> three ski battalions (3800 men)

1942: <u>Rifle Brigade</u> four rifle battalions (5125 men)

... <u>Naval Rifle Brigade</u> (Infantry): four rifle battalions (5125 men)

... <u>Tank Brigade</u> two tank battalions, one motorized rifle battalion (1038 men, 53 tanks)

... <u>Motorized Rifle Brigade</u> three motorized rifle battalions (3151 men)

... <u>Ski Brigade</u> three ski battalions (3800 men)

... <u>Destroyer Brigade</u> one artillery antitank regiment, two antitank rifle battalions, one

... mortar battalion one engineer-mine battalion, one tank battalion

... (1791 men, 32 tanks)

1943: <u>Rifle Brigade</u> four rifle battalions (5125 men)

... <u>Naval Rifle Brigade</u> four rifle battalions (5125 men)

... <u>Tank Brigade</u> three tank battalions, one motorized rifle battalion (1354 men, 65 tanks)

... <u>Mechanized Brigade</u> three motorized rifle battalions, one tank regiment (3558 men, 39 tanks)

... <u>Motorized Rifle Brigade</u> three motorized rifle battalions (3500 men)

... <u>Ski Brigade</u> three ski battalions (3800 men)

1944–45: <u>Rifle Brigade</u> four rifle battalions (5125 men)

... <u>Tank Brigade</u> three tank battalions, one motorized rifle battalion (1354 men, 65 tanks)

... <u>Mechanized Brigade</u> three motorized rifle battalions, one tank regiment (3354 men, 39 tanks)

... <u>Motorized Rifle Brigade</u> three motorized rifle battalions (3500 men)

RED ARMY SEPARATE REGIMENTS AND BATTALIONS

1941–45: <u>Aerosleigh Battalion</u> three aerosleigh companies (100 men, 45 aerosleighs)

... <u>Tank Battalion</u> four tank companies (189 men, 36 tanks)

... <u>Tank Regiment</u> four tank companies (572 men, 39 tanks)

... <u>Tank Penetration Regiment (Heavy)</u> four tank companies (215 men, 21 tanks)

... <u>Tank Engineer Regiment</u> four tank companies (374 men, 21 tanks)

... <u>Machine-gun Artillery Battalion</u> four machine-gun companies (667 men in 1942,

... 669 men in 1943)

... <u>Armoured Train Battalion</u> one armoured train

NKVD FORCES

1941–45: <u>NKVD Rifle (Motorized Rifle) Division</u>

... 3–5 regiments, 1–2 battalions (8–14,000 men)

... <u>NKVD Rifle Brigade</u> 4–8 rifle battalion (4500 men)

... <u>NKVD Regiment</u> three rifle battalions (1651 men)

APPENDIX 4

Soviet Military and Civilian Casualties in the Battle for Leningrad

MILITARY

FORCES	INITIAL STRENGTH	LOSSES KIA, MIA, CAPTURED	WIA SICK	TOTAL
LENINGRAD STRATEGIC DEFENSIVE OPERATION *(10 July–30 September 1941)*				
Northern Front (10.7–23.8.41)	153,000	40,391	15,044	55,535
Northwestern Front (10.7–30.9.41)	272,000	96,953	47,835	144,788
Leningrad Front (23.8–30.9.41)	–	65,529	50,787	116,316
Fifty-Second Separate Army (1.9–30.9.41)	–	1721	2389	4110
Baltic Fleet (entire period)	92,000	9384	14,793	24,177
Total	517,000	214,078	130,848	344,926
...				
STARAIA RUSSA OFFENSIVE OPERATION *(12–23 August 1941)*				
Northern Front (Forty-Eighth Army)	ca 100,000	–	–	ca 33,000
Northwestern Front (Eleventh, Twenty-Seventh, Thirty-Fourth Armies)	327,099	–	–	128,550
Total	427,099	–	–	158,550
SINIAVINO OFFENSIVE OPERATION *(10 September–28 October 1941)*				
Fifty-Fourth Army (Leningrad Front, 26.9), Neva Operational Group	71,270	22,211	32,768	54,979
TIKHVIN DEFENSIVE OPERATION *(16 October–18 November 1941)*				
Fifty-Fourth Army (Leningrad Front), Fourth & Fifty-Second Separate Armies	135,700	22,743	17,846	40,589
TIKHVIN STRATEGIC OFFENSIVE OPERATION *(10 November–30 December 1941)*				
Fifty-Fourth Army (Leningrad Front)	55,600	6,065	11,486	17,551
Fourth Separate Army	62,700	8,916	16,018	24,934
Fifty-Second Separate Army	42,660	871	1769	2,640
Novgorod Operational Group	31,900	2072	1704	3,776
Total	192,950	17,924	30,977	48,901
...				
LIUBAN' OFFENSIVE OPERATION *(7 January–30 April 1942)*				
Volkhov Front, Fifty-Fourth Army (Leningrad Front)	325,700	95,064	213,303	308,367
2D SHOCK ARMY ESCAPE FROM ENCIRCLEMENT *(13 May–10 July 1942)*				
Second Shock, Fifty-Second, Fifty-Ninth Armies	231,900	54,774	39,977	94,751
SINIAVINO OFFENSIVE OPERATION *(19 August–20 October 1942)*				
Leningrad Front (Neva Operational Group, Sixty-Seventh Army, Thirteenth Air Army), Volkhov Front (Second Shock, Eighth Army, Fourteenth Air Army), Baltic Fleet, Ladoga Flotilla	190,000	40,085	73,589	113,674

OPERATION TO PENETRATE THE LENINGRAD BLOCKADE ("ISKRA")
(12–30 January 1943)

Leningrad Front (Sixty-Seventh Army, Thirteenth Air Army)	133,300	12,320	28,944	41,264
Volkhov Front (Second Shock Army, Eighth Army, Fourteenth Air Army)	169,500	21,620	52,198	73,818
Total	**302,800**	**33,940**	**81,142**	**115,082**

DEMIANSK OFFENSIVE OPERATION ("POLAR STAR")
(15–28 February 1943)

Northwestern Front	327,600	10,016	23,647	33,663

STARAIA RUSSA OFFENSIVE OPERATION
(4–19 February 1943)

Northwestern Front	401,190	31,789	71,319	103,108

MGA-SINIAVINO OFFENSIVE OPERATION
(22 June–22 August 1943)

Leningrad Front (Sixty-Seventh Army, Thirteenth Air Army), Volkhov Front (Eighth Army, Fourteenth Air Army) ...	253,300	20,890	59,047	79,937

LENINGRAD-NOVGOROD STRATEGIC OFFENSIVE OPERATION
(14 January–1 March 1944)

Leningrad Front (minus Twenty-Third Army)	417,600	56,564	170,876	227,440
Volkhov Front	260,000	12,011	38,289	50,300
First Shock Army (Second Baltic Front) (14.1–10.2.44)	54,900	1283	3759	5042
Second Baltic Front (10.2–1.3.44)	–	6659	23,051	29,710
Baltic Fleet	86,600	169	1292	1461
Total	**822,100**	**76,686**	**237,267**	**313,953**

VYBORG-PETROZAVODSK STRATEGIC OFFENSIVE OPERATION
(10 June–9 August 1944)

Karelian Front (Seventh, Thirty-Second Armies, Seventh Air Army) (21.6–9.8.44)	202,300	16,924	46,679	63,603
Leningrad Front (Twenty-First, Twenty-Third Armies, Thirteenth Air Army)	188,800	46,679	24,011	30,029
Baltic Fleet, Ladoga and Onega Flotillas	60,400	732	2011	2743
Total	**451,500**	**23,674**	**72,701**	**96,375**

NARVA OFFENSIVE OPERATION
(24–30 July 1944)

Leningrad Front (Second Shock, Eighth Armies, Thirteenth Air Army	136,830	4685	18,602	23,287

SUMMARY OF MILITARY PERSONNEL LOSSES

NORTHERN FRONT (64 days)		LENINGRAD FRONT (1353 days)	
Dead	22,334	Dead	332,059
Missing and captured	61,537	Missing and captured	111,142
Non-combat dead	1138	Non-combat dead	24,324
Total Irrevocable	**85,459**	**Total Irrevocable**	**467,525**
Wounded	60,271	Wounded	949,761
Sick	2634	Sick	333,326
Frostbitten	–	Frostbitten	4286
Total medical	62,905	Total medical	1,287,373
Grand total	**148,364**	**Grand total**	**1,755,898**

SUMMARY OF CIVILIAN PERSONNEL LOSSES IN THE SIEGE OF LENINGRAD

Summer 1943 estimate (Extraordinary Commission to Investigate Nazi Crimes)	642,000
1945 estimate (Nurnberg Trials)	642,000
1952 estimate	632,253
1965 estimate	greater than 800,000

(V. M. Koval'chuk and G. P. Sobolev, Leningradskii rekviem [Leningrad requiem], Voprosy istorii, No 12, December 1965. Based on pre-war population of 2.5 million and December 1943 population of 600,000 with one million evacuees and 100,000 conscripted into the Red Army)

2000 estimate	**641,000 (in the siege proper)**
	1,000,000 (in the siege and during the evacuation)

(Russian Military Encyclopedia)

BIBLIOGRAPHY

Babin, A. I., ed. *Na volkhovskom fronte 1941–1944 gg.* (At the Volkhov Front 1941–1944). Moscow: "Nauka," 1982.

Burdick, Charles and Jacobsen, Hans-Adolf. *The Halder War Diary, 1939–1942.* Novato, CA: Presidio, 1988.

Carell, Paul. *Hitler Moves East 1941–1943.* Boston: Little, Brown and Company, 1963.

Carell, Paul. *Scorched Earth: The Russian-German War, 1943–1944.* Boston: Little, Brown and Company, 1966.

Fediuninsky, I. I. *Podniatye po trevoge* (Raising the alarm). Moscow: Voenizdat, 1964.

Fedoruk, A. G., ed. *Na beregakh Volkhova* (On the banks of the Volkhov). Leningrad: Lenizdat, 1967.

Glantz, David M. *Forgotten Battles of the German-Soviet War (1941–1945), volume I: The Summer-Fall Campaign (22 June–4–December 1941).* Carlisle, PA: Self-published, 1999.

Glantz, David M. *Forgotten Battles of the German-Soviet War (1941–1945), volume II: The Winter Campaign (5 December 1941–April 1942).* Carlisle, PA: Self-published, 1999.

Glantz, David M. *Forgotten Battles of the German-Soviet War (1941–45), volume III: The Summer Campaign (12 May–18 November 1942).* Carlisle, PA: Self-published, 1999.

Glantz, David M. *Forgotten Battles of the German-Soviet War (1941–1945), volume IV: The Winter Campaign (19 November 1942–21 March 1943).* Carlisle, PA: Self-published, 1999.

Glantz, David M. *Forgotten Battles of the German-Soviet War (1941–1945), volume V, parts 1 and 2: The Summer–Fall Campaign (1 July–31–December 1943).* Carlisle, PA: Self-published, 2000.

Goure, Leon. *The Siege of Leningrad.* Stanford: Stanford University Press, 1962.

Grechko, A. A., ed. *Istoriia Vtoroi Mirovoi voiny 1939–1945 v dvenadtsati tomakh* (A history of the Second World War 1939–1945 in 12 volumes). Moscow: Voenizdat, 1973–1982.

Grechko, A. A., ed. *Sovetskaia voennaia entsiklopediia v bos'mi tomakh* (Soviet military encyclopaedia in eight volumes). Moscow: Voenizdat, 1976–1980.

Gribkov, A. I. Ed. *Istoriia Ordena Lenina Leningradskogo voennogo okruga* (A history of the Order of Lenin Leningrad Military District). Moscow: Voenizdat, 1974.

Heinrici, Gotthard. *The Campaign in Russia.* Unpublished manuscript in the National Archives, Washington, D. C. Iarukhov, V. M. *Cherez Nevu* (67-ia armiia v boiakh po proryvu blokady Leningrada)

(Across the Neva: The 67th Army in the penetration of the Leningrad Blockade). Moscow: Voenizdat, 1960.

Karasev, A. V. *Leningradtsy v gody blokady 1941–1943* (Leningraders in the years of the blockade 1941–1943). Moscow: Akademii Nauk SSSR, 1959.

Kasatonov, V. A. ed., *Sniatie blokady Leningrada i osvobozhdenie Pribaltiki 1944–1944 gg., kniga pervaia i vtoraia* (The raising of the Leningrad blockade and the liberation of the Baltic 1941–1944). Moscow: "Nauka," 1991.

Kazakov, K. P. *Ognevoi val nastupleniia* (offensive barrages). Moscow: Voenizdat, 1986.

Kirsanov, N. A. *Po zovu Rodiny: Dobrovol'cheskie formirovaniia Krasnoi Armii v period Velikoi Otechestvennoi voiny* (At the call of the Homeland: Volunteer formations of the Red Army in the Great Patriotic War). Moscow: "Mysl'," 1974.

Kolesnik, A. D. *Narodnoe opolchanie gorodov-geroev* (The people's militia of hero cities). Moscow: "Nauka," 1974.

Kolesnik, A. D. *Opolchenskie formirovaniia Rossiiskoi Federatsii v gody Velikoi Otechestvennoi voiny* (Militia formations of the Russian Federation in the Great Patriotic War). Moscow: "Nauka," 1988.

Korovnikov, I. T. *Novgorodsko-luzhskaia operatsiia: Nastuplenie voisk 59-i armii (ianvar'–feval' 1944 g)* (The Novgorod-Luga operation: The 59th Army's offensive January–February 1944). Moscow: Voenizdat, 1960.

Korovnikov, I. T., Lebedev, N. S., Poliakov, Ia. G. *Na trekh frontakh: Boevoi put' 59-i Armii* (On three fronts: The combat path of the 59th Army). Moscow: Voenizdat, 1974.

Kuznetsov, V. A, ed. *Vtoraia udarnaia v bitve za Leningrad* (The 2d Shock in the Battle for Leningrad). Leningrad: Lenizdat, 1983.

Luttichau, Charles V. P. von. *The Road to Moscow: The Campaign in Russia 1941.* Washington, D. C.: Office of the Chief of Military History, 1985. Unpublished Center for Military History Project 26-P.

Manstein, Erich von. *Lost Victories.* Chicago: Henry Regnery, 1958.

Meretskov, K. A. *Na sluzhbe narodu* (Serving the people). Moscow: Politizdat, 1988.

Oborona Leningrada 1941–1944: Vospominaniia i dnevniki uchastnikov (The defense of Leningrad: Recollections and diaries of participants). Leningrad: "Nauka," 1968.

Pavlov, D. V. *Leningrad v blockade* (Leningrad in the blockade). Moscow: Voenizdat, 1958.

Pavlov, Dmitri V. *Leningrad 1941: The Blockade.* Chicago: The University of Chicago Press, 1965.

Platonov, S. P. Ed. *Bitva za Leningrada 1941–1944* (The Battle for Leningrad 1941–1944). Moscow: Voenizdat, 1964.

Pospelov, P. N., ed. *Istoriia Velikoi Otechestvennoi voiny Sovetskogo Soiuza 1941–1945 v shesti tomakh* (A history of the Great Patriotic War of the Soviet Union 1941–1945 in six volumes). Moscow: Voenizdat, 1960–1965.

Rodionov, I. N. ed. *Voennaia entsiklopediia v vos'mi tomakh* (A military encyclopaedia in 8 volumes). Moscow: Voenizdat, 1997–1999.

Salisbury, Harrison E. *The 900 Days: The Siege of Leningrad.* New York: Harper & Row, 1969.

Samsonov, A. M., ed. *Krasnoznamennyi baltiiskii flot v Velikoi Otechestvennoi voine 1941–1945* (The Red Banner Baltic Fleet in the Great Patriotic War 1941–1945). Moscow: "Nauka," 1981.

Sbornik materialov po izucheniiu opyta voiny No 3 (noiabr'–dekabr' 1942 g.) (A collection of materials for the study of war experiences No 3 (November–December 1942)). Moscow: Voenizdat, 1943.

Sbornik materialov po izucheniiu opyta voiny No 9 (noiabr'–dekabr' 1943 g.) (A collection of materials for the study of war experiences No 9 (November–December 1943)). Moscow: Voenizdat, 1944.

Sbornik materialov po izucheniiu opyta voiny No 12 (mai-iiun' 1944 g.) (A collection of materials for the study of war experiences No 12 (May- June 1944)). Moscow: Voenizdat, 1944.

Sbornik materialov po izucheniiu opyta voiny No 16 (ianvar'–feval' 1945 g.) (A collection of materials for the study of war experiences No 16 (January–February 1945)). Moscow: Voenizdat, 1945.

Seaton, Albert. *The Russo-German War 1941–1945.* New York: Praeger Publishers, 1970.

Stupnikov, N. A., ed. *Dvazhdy krasnoznamennyi baltiiskii flot* (The twice Red Banner Baltic Fleet). Moscow: Voenizdat, 1990.

Sviridov, V. P., Iakutovich, V. P., Vasilenko, V. E. *Bitva za Leningrad 1941–1944* (The Battle for Leningrad 1941–1944). Moscow: Lenizdat, 1962.

Werth, Alexander. *Leningrad.* London: Hamish Hamilton, 1944.

Wykes, Alan. *The Siege of Leningrad: Epic of a Survival.* New York: Ballantine Books, 1968.

Zhilin, P. A. Ed. *Na severo-zapadnom fronte 1941–1943* (On the Northwestern Front 1941–1944). Moscow: "Nauka," 1969. Zhukov, G. *Reminiscences and Recollections,* Volume 1. Moscow: Progress, 1974.

Ziemke, Earl F. *Stalingrad to Berlin: The German Defeat in the East.* Washington, D. C.: Office of the Chief of Military History United States Army, 1968.

Ziemke, Earl F., Bauer, Magna E. *Moscow to Stalingrad: Decision in the East.* Washington, D. C.: Office of the Chief of Military History United States Army, 1987.

Zolotarev, V. A. Ed. "General'nyi shtab v gody Velikoi Otechestvennoi voiny: Dokumenty i materialy 1941 god" (The General Staff in the Great Patriotic War: Documents and materials from 1941) in *Russkii arkhiv: Velikaia Otechestvennaia, 23 12 (1)* (The Russian archives: The Great Patriotic War, Vol 23, No 12 (1)). Moscow: "TERRA," 1997.

Zolotarev, V. A. Ed. "General'nyi shtab v gody Velikoi Otechestvennoi voiny: Dokumenty i materialy 1942 god" (The General Staff in the Great Patriotic War: Documents and materials from 1942) in *Russkii arkhiv: Velikaia Otechestvennaia, 23 12 (2)* (The Russian archives: The Great Patriotic War, Vol 23, No 12 (2)). Moscow: "TERRA," 1999.

Zolotarev, V. A. Ed. "General'nyi shtab v gody Velikoi Otechestvennoi voiny: Dokumenty i materialy 1943 god" (The General Staff in the Great Patriotic War: Documents and materials from 1943) in *Russkii arkhiv: Velikaia Otechestvennaia, 23 12 (3)* (The Russian archives: The Great Patriotic War, Vol 23, No 12 (3)). Moscow: "TERRA," 1999.

Zolotarev, V. A. Ed. "Stavka VGK: Dokumenty i materialy 1941 god" (The Stavka VGK: Documents and materials of 1941) in *Russkii arkhiv: Velikaia Otechestvennaia, 16 5 (1)* (The Russian archives: The Great Patriotic War, Vol 16, No 5 (1)). Moscow: "TERRA," 1996.

Zolotarev, V. A. Ed. "Stavka VGK: Dokumenty i materialy 1942" (The Stavka VGK: Documents and materials of 1942) in *Russkii arkhiv: Velikaia Otechestvennaia, 16 5 (2)* (The Russian archives: The Great Patriotic War, Vol 16, No 5 (2)). Moscow: "TERRA," 1996.

Zolotarev, V. A. Ed. "Stavka Verkhovnogo Glavnokomandovaniia: Dokumenty i materialy 1943 god" (The Stavka VGK: Documents and materials of 1943) in *Russkii arkhiv: Velikaia Otechestvennaia, 16 5 (3)* (The Russian archives: The Great Patriotic War, Vol 16, No 5 (3)). Moscow: "TERRA," 1999.

Zolotarev, V. A. Ed. "Stavka VGK: Dokumenty i materialy 1944–1945" (The Stavka VGK: Documents and materials of 1944) in *Russkii arkhiv: Velikaia Otechestvennaia, 16 5 (4)* (The Russian archives: The Great Patriotic War, Vol. 16, No 5 (4)). Moscow: "TERRA," 1999.

Zolotarev, V. A., ed. *Velikaia Otechestvannaia voina 1941–1945: Voenno-istoricheskie ocherki v chetyrekh tomakh* (The Great Patriotic War 1941–1945: Military-historical essays in four volumes). Moscow: "Nauka," 1998–1999.

Zubakov, V. E. *Nevskaia tverdynia: Bitva za Leningrad v gody Velikoi Otechestvennoi voiny (1941–1944)* (The Neva stronghold: The Battle for Leningrad in the Great Patriotic War (1941–1944)). Moscow: Voenizdat, 1960.

INDEX